OF T

The Modern Period
1830–1999

Isle of Man, after R. Creighton, from Samuel Lewis, Topographical Dictionary of England, c. 1845

A New History of the Isle of Man
VOLUME 5

The Modern Period
1830–1999

Edited by
JOHN BELCHEM

LIVERPOOL UNIVERSITY PRESS

First published 2000 by
LIVERPOOL UNIVERSITY PRESS
Liverpool L69 7ZU

© 2000 Liverpool University Press

British Library Cataloguing-in-Publication Data
A British Library CIP record is available

ISBN 0-85323-716-6 (hardback)
ISBN 0-85323-726-3 (paperback)

Design and production: Janet Allan

Typeset in 11/12.5pt Monotype Sabon
by Wilmaset Ltd, Birkenhead
Printed by Henry Ling Ltd, Dorchester

Contents

List of Illustrations

Acknowledgements

There is not space to thank all those who have helped with the production of this collective enterprise. Special mention should be accorded to Roger Sims and his ever helpful staff at the Manx National Heritage Library; to Shirley O'Hea and Muriel McVaney for their keyboard and other skills; to a range of experts for their advice and encouragement, including Vivien Allen, Peter Clamp, Frank Cowin, Peter Edge, Peter Farrant, John Sharpe and Sir David Wilson. Thanks are due to many other people and organisations for their invaluable assistance in this Centre for Manx Studies project. Particular thanks should be extended to the Isle of Man Government for generous financial help including funding for replacement teaching during 1997–98, which enabled the editor to concentrate on research and writing this volume. Manx National Heritage and the Manx Heritage Foundation also gave significant financial support, and Manx Airlines and the Sefton Hotel, Douglas, helped by reducing travel and accommodation costs. Finally, two of the contributors deserve special thanks: Ann Harrison, the first (and definitive) point of reference on many issues, and Fenella Bazin, the illustrations editor and main point of contact with the Centre for Manx Studies.

Notes on Contributors

Dr Fenella Bazin has published widely on music of the Isle of Man. A classically trained musician from a Manx family with a long tradition of music-making, her current research interests include West Gallery anthems, popular social music and the continuing Manx enthusiasm for hymn-writing.

John Beckerson, an economic and social historian with research interests in the history of government-sponsored tourist promotion, is currently compiling an oral and documentary history of the Manx boarding-house trade.

Professor John Belchem is Head of the School of History at the University of Liverpool. He has published extensively on popular politics and radicalism; research interests now focus on Liverpool, Celtic identities and the Irish Sea region.

Ulla Corkill graduated from Stockholm University and has lived on the Isle of Man since 1972. Her specialised interest in nineteenth-century Manx literature developed out of extensive research on Hall Caine, the 'Manx novelist'.

Yvonne Cresswell has been Curator of Social History at Manx National Heritage since 1987, and is currently researching for a thesis on Manx folklore.

Martin Faragher trained as a primary school teacher and eventually became a lecturer in Education Studies. During a long absence from his native Isle of Man he developed an active interest in its history and culture, and continues it on his return there.

Robert Fyson, former Senior Lecturer in History at Staffordshire University, now researches, writes and occasionally lectures on Manx and Staffordshire history.

Ann Harrison was formerly the Archivist in charge of Manx National Archives and subsequently the first Public Records Officer for her native Isle of Man.

Stephen Harrison is the Director of Manx National Heritage, the award-winning multi-disciplinary statutory agency responsible for heritage preservation and interpretation in the Isle of Man. He is an Honorary Fellow of the University of Liverpool, and a Fellow of the Museums Association of Great Britain, and of the Society of Antiquaries of London and Scotland.

Robert Kelly was a journalist for 36 years, during which time he was editor of the *Isle of Man Examiner*, *Isle of Man Times*, *Manx Star* and numerous other Manx publications. He now writes on diverse aspects of Manx history and heritage.

Professor David Kermode is Professor Emeritus in Political Studies in the School of Social Science, Liverpool John Moores University. He is currently working on a book on Manx constitutional and political development in the twentieth century.

Dr Jennifer Kewley Draskau is 'ethnic Manx' and is currently researching Manx English. Having taught for twenty years at the Universities of Copenhagen and Aarhus, she is an Honorary Senior Research Fellow in the Department of English Language and Literature, University of Liverpool.

Susan Moroney, a former secretary and RAF officer, is now undertaking postgraduate research at the University of Liverpool on twentieth-century Manx art.

Alistair Ramsay worked as a political and business journalist for Manx newspapers from 1980 to 1997.

Robert Thomson retired to the Isle of Man from the post of Reader in Celtic at the University of Leeds. A student of the Manx language for the best part of sixty years, he has lectured and written about it whenever opportunity has arisen.

Derek Winterbottom was Head of History at Clifton College before moving to the Isle of Man in 1994. His specialist works include a biography of the Manx poet T.E. Brown and a study of the Island's Governors since 1765.

Abbreviations

CCD	Chief Constable's Diaries
Examiner	*Isle of Man Examiner*
HO	Home Office
JMM	*Journal of the Manx Museum*
MNHL	Manx National Heritage Library
PP	Parliamentary Proceedings
PRO	Public Record Office
Proceedings	*Proceedings of the Isle of Man Natural History and Archaeological Society*
SRO	Scottish Record Office
WU Record	*Workers' Union Record*

A.W. Moore (1853–1898) *Arthur Moore was descended from two long-established and eminent Manx families, the Moores of Cronkbourne and the Christians of Milntown. After Rugby and Trinity College, Cambridge, he returned to the Island to work in the family linen factory, combining this with his passion for Manx history. As well as the two-volume* History of the Isle of Man, *he published at his own expense a number of important, scholarly books on subjects ranging from Manx Gaelic, folklore and music. At the time of his death, he was co-editing the book on Anglo-Manx Dialect. He also took an active part in Manx business and politics, becoming a successful Speaker of the House of Keys.*

Introduction

JOHN BELCHEM

It is a singular fact, that, in the present age of active inquiry, there should be in the midst of the British European dominions an isolated spot retaining its primitive constitution, the peculiar characters of which are scarcely known beyond the narrow space over which their influence extends. That such a country, and such a constitution do actually exist, is pretty generally known, yet few or none have deemed any investigation of the peculiarities of either worthy of notice ... The Isle of Man presents to us the singular phenomenon alluded to.[1]

Such lack of interest in the Isle of Man, a cause of bewilderment in 1811, has continued to prevail. Resident antiquarians, full of Victorian fervour, endeavoured to secure the 'light of catholic publicity', vaunting the significance of 'local peculiarities of the most interesting and important nature':

Inhabited by an aboriginal tribe of the great Celtic family, with language, institutions, and laws peculiar to itself ... to this day a separate realm, independent of the Imperial Parliament, and under its native and aboriginal Legislature ... The Central Isle of the British Group, connected with Scotland geographically and geologically, with Ireland ethnologically, with England politically, and with the three kingdoms ecclesiastically, merits more attention from the United Kingdom than it has ever received.[2]

These pretensions notwithstanding, historians have yet to display academic interest. Recent developments in historiographical theory and practice offer some encouragement. Feminist historians have noted that the Isle of Man was the first to extend the parliamentary franchise to female property owners. However, after this pioneer exercise in 1881,

1] J. Johnson, *A View of the Jurisprudence of the Isle of Man* (Edinburgh, 1811), iii–iv.
2] See the 'Prospectus' inserted in the MNHL copy of *Publications of the Manx Society*, I (Douglas, 1859).

the Island was to be notoriously backward in its gender politics.[3] Post-modern perspectives offer more promise as historical fashion favours small-scale reconstruction of the marginal, liminal and idiosyncratic. Historians, however, have still to discover the little Manx nation, surely an ideal case-study. With devolution on the political agenda, British history has given way to 'four nations' history, but the Isle of Man, a Crown dependency constitutionally outside the United Kingdom, is excluded still[4] – Irish historical 'revisionism' has challenged the myths surrounding the Act of Union, but no such reassessment has been undertaken of Manx revestment in the British Crown in 1765.[5] In the changing balance between core and periphery, the Isle of Man has yet to find a place, despite its geographical position: a tiny speck within the eastern Atlantic archipelago, it lies at the very centre of the British Isles.[6] Adrift in the Irish Sea, the juxtaposition of Britishness and Celticism was particulary acute in this 'land of home rule'. Here, indeed, is a prime example of the complexity of historical 'identities'. Slightly other than English, the Manx have displayed what Sir Frank Kermode has described as 'mild alienation' and 'qualified foreignness', characteristics which await historical deconstruction.[7]

Historians have left investigation of the Island and its 'peculiarities' to archaeologists, geologists, geographers, ethnographers and other field work disciplines.[8] These intellectual boundaries, a consequence of academic professionalisation, lacked salience and authority a century

3] A.M. Butler and J. Templeton, *The Isle of Man and the first votes for women* (Occasional Paper, Department of Political Studies, Sheffield City Polytechnic, 1980).
4] R. Samuel, 'British dimensions: "four nations history" ', *History Workshop Journal*, 40 (1995), iii–xxii.
5] L. Kennedy and D.S. Johnson, 'The Union of Ireland and Britain, 1801–1921' in D.G. Boyce and A. O'Day (eds), *The Making of Modern Irish History: revisionism and the Revisionist Controversy* (London, 1996), 34–70. Janet Austin, a postgraduate at the University of Liverpool, has recently begun research on revestment.
6] Although the nation remains the 'major narrative principle' of this volume, it is to be hoped it will find favour with post modernist historians for whom 'writing from the periphery is coming to be much more interesting than writing from the centre' see Patrick Joyce, 'The return of history: postmodernism and the politics of academic history in Britain', *Past and Present*, 158 (1998), 225-7.
7] Frank Kermode, *Not Entitled* (London, 1996), 19. See also his article 'Faces of Man' in *Observer Magazine*, 1 July 1979.
8] Manx historiography has been shaped by historical and economic geographers. See: R.H. Kinvig, *A History of the Isle of Man* (Liverpool, 1944); J.W. Birch, *The Isle of Man: A Study in Economic Geography* (Cambridge, 1964) and V. Robinson and D. McCarroll (eds), *The Isle of Man: Celebrating a Sense of Place* (Liverpool, 1990). Political scientists have come to recognise the Island as 'a fascinating area of study': see

ago when A.W. Moore wrote his records-based *History of the Isle of Man*. A gifted polymath, Moore was an avid scholar of anything and everything Manx, the Celtic culture of Ellan Vannin under threat from 'the summer flood of Saxon trippers'. An indefatigable antiquarian, he produced a remarkable range of monographs, the foundation texts of Manx studies.[9] The leading figure in the late-nineteenth-century Manx 'renaissance', Moore helped to construct the traditions necessary to safeguard Manx cultural distinctiveness and its devolved political status. Through assertion of Celticism, a project which tended to downgrade Norse contributions to the Island's hybrid 'Scandio-Celtic' past, the little Manx nation girded itself against cultural anglicisation yet remained unquestionably loyal to the British Empire.[10] It is these issues of image, identity and representation which dominate Volume 5 of the *New History of the Isle of Man*. The purpose is not simply to update Moore's *History* in historiographical approach and chronological cover, but to examine the ways and means by which Moore and other culture brokers constructed a sense of Manxness.

Following a successful 'rebranding' exercise at the end of the Napoleonic Wars, the Isle of Man offered itself as 'one of the few places in Europe where moderate people may be moderately happy at moderate expense'.[11] Having shed its associations with smugglers, runaway debtors and other unwanted and unsavoury 'transports', the Island promoted itself as tax and retirement haven – free from direct taxation, poor rates, serious crime or party political turmoil – for British subjects of 'small incomes and pinched circumstances'.[12] Throughout its modern history the Isle of Man has had to depend on the economic presence of such 'stranger-residents': from half-pay officers and other lesser beneficiaries of the Hanoverian fiscal-military state (whose numbers were to diminish with Victorian retrenchment

---

Jeff Richards, 'Electoral change in a small community: the Isle of Man revisited', *Parliamentary Affairs*, 40 (1987), 388–408.

9] See the biographical sketch of Moore, 'one of the *Manninee dooie* of modern times', in William Cubbon, *Island Heritage* (Manchester, 1952), 321–3; and his obituary in *Celtic Review*, VI (1909–10), 283–6.

10] For further discussion of Moore and these themes see John Belchem, 'The Little Manx Nation: antiquarianism, ethnic identity and home rule politics in the Isle of Man, 1880–1918', *Journal of British Studies*, 39 (2000), 217–40.

11] Hannah Ann Bullock, *History of the Isle of Man, with a Comparative View of the Past and Present State of Society and Manners* (London, 1816), xii.

12] See my chapter, 'The Onset of Modernity, 1830–80', below.

and reform of 'Old Corruption') to more recent post colonial arrivals, the 'When I's', (so named for their propensity to perorate on 'When I was in Rhodesia' and so on). To attract such 'come-overs', the Manx needed to retain favourable fiscal, duty and other differentials, no mean achievement as successive British governments, driven by administrative convenience and ideological imperative, displayed decreasing tolerance for anomalies and deviations from fiscal, constitutional and other norms. This determination to preserve residual post-revestment privileges, rights and independence – the political project of mainstream Manx nationalism – cut across the ethnic essentialism cherished by cultural nationalists.[13] Not without irony, independence from Westminster – Manx 'home rule' – was symbolised (and upheld) by differentials principally for the benefit of new residents attracted to the Island from 'across'.

As the political and economic sections of this volume attest, much of the narrative of Manx history was driven by fiscal and constitutional relations with the United Kingdom.[14] Despite steady upward pressure on duty levels in the mid nineteenth century, the Manx managed to resist full-scale assimilation. For a brief period, indeed, genteel pensioners and rentiers were joined by 'strangers' of a different kind – Chartists, trade unionists, pioneer communists, feminists, vegetarians, teetotallers and assorted faddists – attracted to the Island by fiscal and postal privileges which enabled them to publish cheaply, free from British 'taxes on knowledge'.[15] Matters took a different turn, however, with the advent of Gladstonian finance and its promise of the 'free breakfast table'. Henceforth, British duties on basic goods were steadily reduced, down to (irreducible) levels prevailing in the Island. Financial relations were put on a new footing by the much-applauded Isle of Man Customs, Harbours and Public Purposes Act 1866, drawn up by Governor Loch, a landmark reform (accompanied by the introduction of the representative principle in the House of Keys) which separated Manx finances from those of the United Kingdom, and gave the Island limited access to the surplus revenue (the annual and accumulated funds 'appropriated' by the Treasury) to finance much-needed public

---

13] For the flavour of Manx ethnic essentialism, the life-long passion of Mona Douglas for race, blood and tradition, see her novel *Rallying Song* (Douglas, 1981).

14] See in particular the contributions by David Kermode and Alistair Ramsay. Kermode is currently preparing an updated version of his indispensable analysis of *Devolution at Work: A Case Study of the Isle of Man* (Farnborough, 1979).

15] John Belchem, 'The neglected "unstamped": the Manx pauper press of the 1840s', *Albion*, 24 (1992), 605–16.

works and harbour improvements. However, the cost was considerable: the loss of 'cheap living' and the consequent demise of the 'half-pay paradise'.

Economic adaptation, a recurrent feature of modern Manx history (as Derek Winterbottom's contribution attests), was quickly effected. As fiscal differentials were eroded by 'common purse' arrangements, gentlemanly rentiers were squeezed out, to be replaced by summer 'trippers', holiday-making 'cotton-balls' from the adjacent industrial north of England. In the past the Island had welcomed a higher class of tourist, the intrepid explorer attracted by the scenery, folklore and myth which placed the Isle of Man on the adventurous Romanticist agenda (as noted by Ulla Corkill and other contributors). Infrastructural development initiated by Loch, followed by heavy investment by Anglo-Manx business syndicates, transformed the Island into 'one large playground for the operatives of Lancashire and Yorkshire'.[16] Where previously Mona had offered domestic repose for the gentlemanly bon viveur, it now had to control the public saturnalian excesses of the working-class holiday-maker, lewd behaviour which, critics averred, placed summertime Douglas on a par with 'guilty Sodom'.[17] For all its economic benefits – and these lasted only for a brief ten-week season – mass tourism aggravated cultural, social and geographical tensions on the Island. The issue of Sunday opening of public houses, a question which divided commercial urban tourist interests from religious and rural opinion, caused perpetual friction. The 'permit' election of 1897 – so-called because it hinged upon the issue of private licences, or permits, for the sale of beer, stout and perry in boarding-houses from 1 May to 30 September – revealed deep divisions in Manx politics, no longer concealed beneath its traditional non-partisan veneer.[18] The origins of the Manx National Reform League and of the Manx Labour Party can both be traced to rural, Nonconformist, temperance opposition to the urban-based, drink-supported lobby allied to the Insular establishment.[19] No less important, however, was the cultural

---

16] John Belchem, '"The playground of Northern England": the Isle of Man, Manxness and the northern working class' in N. Kirk (ed), *Northern Identities* (Aldershot, 2000), 71–86. Passenger arrivals reached a peak of 634,512 in 1913. See also C.P. Cooper and S. Jackson, 'Tourism in the Isle of Man: historical perspectives and contemporary problems', *Manchester Geographer*, new series, III, 2 (1982), 18–30.

17] Rev. Thomas Rippon, *The Morals of Douglas* (Douglas, 1894).

18] Samuel Norris, *Manx Memories and Movements* (3rd ed, 1941, Douglas, 1994), ch 5.

19] Jeffrey Vaukins, *The Manx Struggle for Reform*, unpublished M Phil thesis, University of Lancaster, 1984.

interaction facilitated by tourist provision, temporary release from the 'everyday background of Lenten morbidity'.[20] Those who mingled with trippers in pleasure palaces and dance halls, among the biggest in Europe, came into contact with the very latest styles and fashions of commercial popular culture.

'The Isle of Man is not now what it was even five-and-twenty years ago', the Manx novelist Hall Caine lamented in 1891:

> It has become too English of late. The change has been sudden ...
> God forbid that I should grudge the factory hand his breath of the
> sea and glimpse of gorse-bushes; but I know what price we are
> paying that we may entertain him.[21]

Much as he regretted such 'anglicization', Hall Caine appreciated the economic indispensability of the holiday traffic and did everything in his power to promote the Island: at the height of his world wide success, he found time to write a small guide for the Isle of Man Steam Packet Company. Cultural nationalists displayed similar ambivalence. Indeed, the antiquarianism of Moore and his contemporaries can be seen as a retrieval exercise in Celtic 'heritage' – a form of niche-marketing, perhaps – which would reshape, not reject, the crucial tourist industry.[22] While confirming the Manx in their identity as something more than mere 'West Britons', the elaboration of Celticism, with its stress on antiquity, difference and mystery, would also attract 'the better class of visitor'.[23] Ethnicity was to the fore, but class factors seem to have carried weight with Manx culture-brokers.

The high point of mass tourism coincided with the 'Manx renaissance' (a major theme of the cultural history section of this volume co-ordinated by Fenella Bazin and Martin Faragher), the Insular inflexion of the wider 'Gaelic revival'. In this critical conjuncture old attitudes were to be called into question, even stood on their head. Back in the seventeenth century northern England had set the standard for the local Manx elite. In language and culture, wealthier inhabitants imitated the Lancashire gentry, while the Manx Gaelic-speaking common folk followed what were dismissively considered as Irish patterns. By the late nineteenth century, as Robert Thomson's contribution attests, matters had become inverted. The Manx gentry, disdainful of the northern working-class tripper, immersed themselves in ethno centric

20] Kermode, *Not Entitled*, 15–21.
21] Sir Thomas Henry Hall Caine, *The Little Manx Nation* (London, 1891), 155–6.
22] Belchem, ' "Playground of Northern England" '.
23] 'A protest', *Mannin*, 8 (Nov 1916), 483.

antiquarianism. True to their new found Celtic credentials, they endeavoured to retrieve the dying Manx Gaelic language through the establishment in 1899 of the Manx Language Society, soon renamed (with due political correctness) Yn Cheshaght Ghailckagh (YCG). The bulk of the population, wise to economic opportunity, had long since abandoned the language (and its stigma of poverty and ignorance) in favour of an Anglo-Manx dialect, increasingly influenced (as Jennifer Kewley-Draskau observes) by popular northern idioms.[24] YCG could not reverse the process: at best, it may have slowed the rate of decline, protracting the process of language death among existing speakers. Efforts to extend the language base into new areas – including educated Celtic enthusiasts faced with the daunting task of learning Gaelic *ab initio* – were less encouraging. Lacking Moore's gifts, other leading figures in Manx cultural nationalism struggled to acquire the language. Hence, protection of the Anglo-Manx dialect, or rather the Insular vernacular immortalised by T.E. Brown, soon became the decisive linguistic issue, the voice of resistance to incorporation into England. As far as pan-Celticists were concerned, however, Ellan Vannin appeared a lost cause for a greater Gaelic Union. Manxland was no more than 'a piece of Lancashire which had gone adrift'.[25]

As the little Manx nation acquired the symbolic and cultural trappings of nationhood, fissures and fractures became apparent, divisions which acquired an unwonted political dimension during the stormy years of Raglan's governorship, 1902–18.[26] Although apostrophised in the new national anthem,[27] Manx 'home rule' was something of a misnomer, if not a myth, dependent (among other restraints) on the pivotal role of the British-appointed Lieutenant-Governor, the Island's sole executive and Chancellor of the Exchequer. Under Raglan 'home rule' political consensus fractured along socio-economic lines. The Legislative Council, the upper chamber of Tynwald, composed of unaccountable 'colonial' officials appointed from within the Anglican, landed and legal ranks of the resident 'establishment', were unwavering in support of Raglan's autocratic and reactionary stance. An

---

24] George Broderick, *Language Death in the Isle of Man*, Habilitationsschrift, University of Mannheim, 1997.
25] Iolar Finn, 'Language and nationality in the Isle of Man', *Irish Freedom*, Jan 1914, reprinted in *Celtic History Review*, 2 (1996), 10–11.
26] Nicola Pattinson, a postgraduate student at the University of Liverpool, is currently researching the Raglan years.
27] For a fascinating analysis of the anthem see Fenella Bazin's paper ' "Mylecharaine": a forgotten call to nationhood', presented to the conference on Folksong Tradition and Revival, July 1998.

The Laxey strike, 1907 *The number of strikes during the latter part of the nineteenth century reflected the serious unrest felt by many Manx workers, and led to the foundation of the Manx branch of the Independent Labour Party in 1908. (MNHL)*

Edwardian 'die-hard', Raglan deployed his powers to veto 'new Liberal' reform: the Manx were denied the welfare and other benefits gained by British workers and citizens. Under pressure from without, the House of Keys stood forward for constitutional and other reforms, but (with characteristic diffidence) stopped short of the demand for responsible government.[28] The onset of war accentuated the divisions, bringing unprecedented prosperity to some (in particular those who supplied the internment camps), while many endured abject misery as the visiting industry collapsed.[29] In the absence of the social policy, direct taxation and other redistributive measures which applied 'across', the Island became 'a paradise for the rich but a purgatory for the poor'.[30] Freedom from income tax, the tangible symbol of Manx independence (and a boon to the wealthy), placed workers and

28] (Deemster) T.W. Cain, 'Constitutional reform in the twentieth century', *Proceedings of the Isle of Man Natural History and Antiquarian Society*, X (1993–5), 201–24.
29] B.E. Sargeaunt, *The Isle of Man and the Great War* (Douglas, nd).
30] Christopher Shimmin, *Outlines from Manx History* (Peel, 1916), 26.

their families at comparative disadvantage. To the dismay of Manx nationalists, an annexation movement gained ground among the Manx working class, attracted by welfare and fiscal arrangements in the United Kingdom. *Mannin*, the journal of Celtic cultural nationalism – and a fervent supporter of the British war effort – argued against any political change, whether incorporation into the United Kingdom as an English county (the 'Manxshire' option favoured by some reformers in the nineteenth century) or complete 'national' independence (a proposal which was to find increasing support in the twentieth century among advocates of a federation of the Celtic nations).[31] This was a critical time for those who wished to safeguard the Island's distinctive cultural heritage and political status. As he concluded his *Outlines from Manx History* in 1916, Christopher Shimmin recognised the need to move beyond antiquarianism and the myth of home rule into progressive social and economic reform for the benefit of the Manx working class. In 1918, as Robert Fyson shows, the Manx labour movement displayed its power in a successful general strike. Raglan was humiliated, and fiscal reform secured: income tax was introduced along with a promise of no further increases in indirect taxation. Once the war had ended, and Raglan departed, further reforms were implemented (in belated and partial fulfilment of the recommendations of the MacDonnell Commission, 1911).

As David Kermode affirms, it was not until 1958 that the formality of 'regional self-government' was secured, paving the way for the MacDermott Commission and further advance (along lines advocated since the Raglan years by Samuel Norris) towards 'competent representative government'.[32] Their special status assured, the Manx were able to re-establish significant fiscal differentials, this time in levels of direct taxation. The Island was in need of economic rejuvenation. In recent decades it had enjoyed relative prosperity: tourism remained buoyant during the inter war years (boosted by the popularity of the TT races, as featured in the hit George Formby film *No Limit*);[33] and unlike the previous experience, there was widespread participation in the economic benefits of internment and military training during the

---

31] G. Fred Clucas, 'Should our national legislature be abolished?', and H. Derwent Simpson, 'A Protest', *Mannin*, 8 (Nov 1916), 475–80, and 481–5; 'Notes', *Mannin*, 9 (May 1917), 564–5.
32] Cain, 'Constitutional Reform', 221–2. Samuel Norris, *This Manx Democracy!* (Douglas, 1945).
33] The screenplay was written by Walter Greenwood, author of *Love on the Dole* (1933), which includes a holiday idyll in the Isle of Man.

Celebrating the relief of Mafeking in Douglas, 1900 *Loyalty to Crown and country has been a powerful element in the Manx psyche, even at the height of the call for Home Rule. During wartime Manx men and women rallied to arms and even today the Island has consistently been a leader in fund-raising for the British Legion's Poppy Appeal. (MNHL)*

Second World War. By the late 1950s, however, the Island was stagnating in an adverse economic conjuncture – decline in the visiting industry, recession in fishing, reduction in population. Using its new powers, the Manx government looked to low rates of income tax (and no surtax) to attract wealthy new residents to inject some vitality into the ailing economy. The requisite 'fat cats', however, chose other locations: 'Man watched with rising envy, as the cream of the millionaire crop settled on Jersey and Guernsey.' Pensioners from the north were the main arrivals, accompanied by bricklayers, transient labour to construct brash bungalows and Spanish-style seaside residences, heedless of Manx culture and tradition.[34] Manx Celticism – which had long since passed from antiquarians into the guardianship of a new generation of enthusiastic folk performers, inspired by Mona Douglas and the frugal traditionalism of her 'Rallying Song for Aeglagh Vannin' ('youth of Man') – had managed to withstand the northern 'tripper'.[35] Confronted by the materialism of the new (and permanent) alien influx, cultural nationalism acquired a political dimension.[36] Mec Vannin, established in 1961 as a 'resistance movement', developed into an electoral political party (an ironic outcome, against the grain of Manx non-partisan political culture);[37] Fo Halloo, true to its name, followed an 'underground' path in the early 1970s, making arson attacks on the new bungalows of 'migrant tax exiles', justified in the name of the Celtic 'not-rich' against the English 'rich';[38] Irree Magh (Insurrection) called (quite unavailingly) for 'open rebellion in order to

34] 'The Manx scratch for more fat cats', cutting from *Wall Street Journal*, 1989, in MNHL: F65/1/2x.

35] MNHL has pamphlets and other holdings for Aeglagh Vannin, *c*.1936–45; and Ellynyn ny Gael ('Arts of the Gael'), *c*.1956–74. Its holdings on Caarjyn Vannin ('Friends of Mannin') – for which Mona Douglas also supplied the 'Rallying Song' – relate only to the 1970s. Mona Douglas's papers in the MNHL are currently being catalogued. Aeglagh Vannin followed in the path of Ny Maninee Aegey ('The Young Manx'), established by Sophia Morrison at the turn of the century: see Bernard Moffat, 'Ripples in a Celtic tide: evolution of Manx nationalism', *Celtic History Review*, I, 2 (1995), 18–20.

36] D.G. Nixon, *Dissent in a Celtic Community: Class and Ethnicity in the Isle of Man*', unpublished MA thesis, University of Massachusetts, 1983. The first nationalist group was a shadowy organisation, Ny Manninee Dooie ('The True Manx'), founded during the Second World War to advocate neutrality: it lacked support, being regarded as pro-German: see P.B. Ellis, *The Celtic Revolution* (Talybont, 1985), 158.

37] Mec Vannin material is available in MNHL at L3f. See also *Celtic News*, 6 (1964–5), 4-5; and, for its development as a party, Richards, 'Electoral change', 398–404.

38] MNHL holds 18 poorly cyclostyled news-sheets produced by Fo Halloo, 1973–6. See also 'The ungovernable Isle of Man', *International Times*, IV, 4 (1978).

preserve our nation, heritage and country (or what's left of it)'.[39] Cultural critics from 'across' condemned the architectural vandalism and philistinism of bungalow-builders and developers whose blots on the landscape lacked the aesthetic good taste implanted by the gentlemanly stranger-residents of the early nineteenth century.[40] For the ordinary Manx citizen, however, the point of concern was the rapid inflation in property prices: rich come-overs were pricing local residents out of the housing market. Given the number of retired people among the new residents, there were popular fears of an undue burden on Manx health and welfare services. Census statistics, however, displayed a favourable demographic profile, and underlined the steady success of the new residents policy.[41]

Much the same applied to the development of the financial sector, facilitated by the rescheduling of the sterling area in 1972 and the removal of exchange controls in 1979. Here too the Channel Islands were the preferred location, but exponential growth in the sector ensured that the Isle of Man was soon 'cashing in' as the 'Isle of Money'.[42] A new pressure group, Pobblaght Soshiallagh Vannin, issued a Manx Republican Socialist Charter: Celtic nationalism was henceforth to be secured through nationalisation of finance, insurance and all key industries.[43] For clarity of message, FSFO abandoned Gaelic for English (the last two letters being an abbreviated Anglo-Saxon injunction to the financial sector), but continued (albeit with minimal impact) the direct action tradition of arson and daubing attacks.[44] Cultural critics again condemned crass development, the 'rash of new commercial building whose mediocrity would be worthy of comment even in the dullest of Britain's industrial cities'.[45] Manx workers remained preoccupied with practical issues, concerned by the divisive aspects of unprecedented economic growth. 'The finance sector now tends to pay at the levels of south-east England, rather than the English north-west as previously', the *Financial Times* observed in a special

---

39] See the handbill in MNHL at L3f.

40] Gavin Stamp, 'The future of Man', *Spectator*, 28 Sept 1985.

41] P.H. Craine, *Population Growth in the Isle of Man: The Combined Economic and Population Policy of a Low Tax Area* (Discussion Paper Series, Dept of Geography, University of Liverpool, 1979).

42] 'The Isle of Money', *Sunday Times*, 8 Feb 1987; 'The Isle of Man Cashes in', *Observer*, 25 Feb 1990.

43] See the news-sheets at MNHL L3/MR; and Diarmuid O'Breaslain, 'The development of Manx nationalism, part 2', *Celtic History Review*, II, 4 (1997), 22–3.

44] 'What put the snarl on the Manx cat's face', *Sunday Times*, 26 Mar 1989.

45] Gavin Stamp, 'Greed's threat to the future of Man', *Independent*, 21 Oct 1989.

Celtic Congress *In 1921 the Celtic Congress met in the Island. Members visited 'Cummal Beg', Cregneash, the summer home of the Reverend William Cooke, described by William Cubbon as 'a good Manx scholar'. Back row from left: Dr G. Prys Williams, Mona Douglas, Mrs H.P. Kelly, Professor Agnes O'Farrelly, Mrs Johnson, William Cubbon (at back), Reverend William Cooke, Sir Fred Clucas SHK, Sir John McLeod. Middle row from left: Mrs Hemmings Hurst, A.P. Graves MA, Reverend Lauchlin Maclean Watt, Earl Cassiliss, Ernest Rhys. Standing left: Mrs Kennedy Fraser.*

survey of the Island: 'The gap between earnings in the finance sector and the rest of the economy is therefore increasing social and political tension.'[46] Although the Island experienced its own 'winter of discontent', pressures were held in check by welfare and other redistributive provisions, essential aspects of the 'prosperous and caring society' made possible, as Alistair Ramsay shows, by flush government revenue and enhanced political autonomy. In the new ministerial (but still not party-based) system the Manx government aspired to assert its independence, to show itself 'wise enough to follow what is good in the United Kingdom and elsewhere but bold enough to opt for differences where they are needed to suit the Island'. Retention and extension of the welfare state, at a time of Thatcherite reverse elsewhere, came to symbolise Manx independence (previously some-what stigmatised by association with birching and sexual repression).

Although some tensions remain, the Island seems to have adjusted well to the finance sector, offering a role model of 'post-industrial' development.[47] Future success, however, depends on the continuation of off shore advantage and on acceptable standards of probity and accountability, factors by no means entirely in Manx control. There is no obvious alternative. Manx tourism is long past its 'product life-cycle'.[48] Recent efforts at revival have proved unavailing, hindered not just by the climate (and package-holiday competition) but also by ambiguous marketing messages, a reprise of earlier divisions over the requisite 'class' of visitor. Some advertising campaigns, directed at northerners ill-disposed to 'foreign' travel, have stressed nostalgia and tradition, values defined in quintessentially British terms, a no-nonsense return to the good old days of seaside summer holidays, lovingly preserved on the 'time-warp' Island.[49] With such visitors in mind, the Department of Tourism and Transport has advocated caution in the revived use of Manx Gaelic on signposts and place-names. Other forms of 'heritage' promotion, however, deliberately emphasise ethno cultural difference, building upon the initial Manx renaissance to attract the 'New Age' Celtic niche market, the metropolitan post modernist cultural tourist in search of 'real' or 'authentic' experience at the

---

46] *Financial Times*, 24 May 1989.

47] Robinson and McCarroll, *The Isle of Man*, 268–70.

48] C. Cooper and S. Jackson, 'Destination life cycle: the Isle of Man case study', *Annals of Tourism Research*, 16 (1989), 377–98.

49] For a considerably earlier example of this approach, see *Christian Miscellany and Family Visiter*, 2nd series, XV (1869), 336–9, which recommended the Isle of Man to the tourist with 'a horror of Continental cookery, pervasive smells, passports, and Popery'.

periphery. The various heritage centres of the award-winning 'Story of Mann', located throughout the Island, offer convenient access to a ready-packaged, Gaelic theme-park past (with some Norse – briefly accorded prominence in the Tynwald Millennium Year, 1979 – thrown in for good measure).[50]

The growth of the finance sector has brought significant demo-graphic change: native-born Manx are now (just) in the minority. At this point Manx Gaelic has become politically correct and socially desirable, available even at nursery school, a fashion which seemingly unites natives and new arrivals.[51] Now all but indistinguishable in its daily speech patterns from the north of England, the Isle of Man, enmeshed in multinational finance, is seeking a symbolic public language to secure its distinct identity. It is this complex and symbiotic cultural context which has also stimulated interest in Manx studies and led to this *New History*.

The purpose of this volume is to encourage further research in modern Manx history. A report on progress, it does not purport to be comprehensive or definitive. Given the pressure on space, it was decided to avoid undue replication. Hence the relative lack of attention to certain areas. These include: demography and emigration, in which authoritative studies by historical geographers are already available – some new census-based material, however, is analysed by John Beckerson in the statistical appendix;[52] and legal history, an important area for the proverbially litigious Manx, now the subject of extensive research and publication.[53] As an interim attempt at overview and

---

50] Richard Prentice, *Tourism as Experience: Tourists as Consumers* (Edinburgh, 1996, inaugural lecture, Queen Margaret College).

51] Richard Prentice, 'The "Manxness of Mann": renewed immigration to the Isle of Man and the nationalist response', *Scottish Geographical Magazine*, 106 (1990). Stephen Miller, 'Mending up the rags: the return of Manx Gaelic', *Planet: The Welsh Internationalist*, 101 (1993), 83–7. The Manx branch of the Celtic League, a pan-Celtic organisation, had long campaigned for a Manx Studies adviser to the Board of Education: see *Celtic League and Anti-Militarist Alliance News*, 15 (nd, 1981?) in MNHL L6C7f.

52] See Vaughan Robinson's authoritative chapter on 'Social Demography' in Robinson and McCarroll, *The Isle of Man*, 133–58.

53] Peter Edge is the leading expert in the field. His publications have highlighted four major themes: professionalisation of the Manx bar and judiciary, see 'Lawyers' Empires: the anglicisation of the Manx Bar and Judiciary', *Journal of the Legal Profession*, 19 (1994–5); increased use of English case law, see 'Doctrinal effects of smallness: the authority of English decisions on the common law in Manx courts', *Northern Ireland Law Quarterly*, 46 (1995); an increasingly complicated relationship

conspectus, the volume may disappoint readers in search of specialised detail (or personal anecdote) relating to a particular location, industry, denomination, means of transport, sport, cultural pursuit, or other specificity.[54] They should consult the rich array of heritage publications which chronicle (and celebrate) particular aspects of the modern Manx past. Volume 5, however, is not the preserve of stuffy academic historians. Contributors come from a refreshing variety of backgrounds: styles may differ, but there is a common commitment to both scholarship and accessibility. Extending beyond 'heritage' (and its tourist potential), our intention is to stimulate and engage the wide audience which modern Manx history deserves.

One final point by way of introduction. Starting dates are always arbitrary and flexible, but a number of factors can be listed in justification of the choice of 1830. The last vestiges of feudalism were extinguished in 1829 when the British Crown acquired (at considerable expense) the Atholls' manorial rights and privileges. The origins of the Isle of Man Steam Packet Company, the Island's lifeline, can be traced to 1830 (a regular steamship service between Douglas and Liverpool had begun a year earlier in 1829). Fishing and mining entered a period of expansion – the first modern mining company, the Isle of Man Mining Company, commenced operations in 1828. Farming enjoyed a run of good harvests in the 1830s, prompting optimism, investment and the establishment of the Isle of Man Agricultural Society in 1840. The foundation stone of King William's College, embodiment of the educational and clerical establishment, was laid in 1830 – the 'Preface' to Cregeen's *Dictionary of the Manks Language*, published in 1835, trusted that the college would endow a professorship in the vernacular tongue, a venerable ancient language, still essential for the pastoral edification of the peasantry (and for certain legal matters), but

---

between the legislative powers and practices of Tynwald and those of Parliament, see 'David, Goliath and supremacy: the Isle of Man and the sovereignty of the United Kingdom Parliament', *Anglo-American Law Review*, 24 (1995); and major changes in Manx law and procedure, often reflecting similar changes in English law and procedure, see *Manx Public Law* (Preston, 1997).

54] Here it should be noted that both Canon John Gelling's *History of the Manx Church* (Douglas, 1998) and Derek Winterbottom's prosopographic study of *Governors of the Isle of Man since 1765* (Douglas, 1999) were published after this volume went to press. Important new research projects are about to begin, including a two-year M Phil studentship, sponsored by Heron & Brearley, on the brewing industry.

otherwise despised, neglected and in decay.[55] In associational culture, the focus of Ann Harrison's research, the first temperance society and the first local lodge of the Oddfellows were both established in 1830. Manx journalism (and reform politics) took a major leap forward with the appearance of *Mona's Herald* in 1833. Methodism, a powerful influence on the Island, broke from the Manx Church in 1836. Such separation was less pronounced than in England, but within a few years controversy over civil registration and the solemnisation of marriage united Wesleyan and Primitive Methodists along with Presbyterians, Independents and Roman Catholics against the Anglican establishment. Manx of all creeds, however, rallied to defend the bishopric of Sodor and Man, under threat of annexation to Carlisle in the 1830s. Although settled by high political compromise – the see was allowed to retain its independence in return for final settlement of the commutation of tithes in 1839 – the successful outcome was regarded as a triumph for a new force in the Island, public opinion. Thenceforth, the Manx were strengthened in their resolve to resist the British mania for 'assimilation, annexation and amalgamation'.[56]

55] A. Cregeen, *A Dictionary of the Manks Language* (Douglas, 1835: rpt, 1910).
56] *Mona's Herald*, 17 Apr 1844.

The Onset of Modernity, 1830–80

JOHN BELCHEM

According to A.W. Moore the Isle of Man underwent epochal change in 1866. Governor Loch's reforms marked 'the termination of what might be called the medieval history of Man'.[1] Technically, the last vestiges of 'feudalism' were extinguished when the British Crown acquired the Atholls' manorial rights and privileges in 1829 (at a cost of £417,114), but the onset of 'modernity' has always been identified with Loch's reforming regime.[2] Little interest has been shown in the preceding decades, either as a coda to feudalism or the prelude to reform.[3] In remedying this neglect this chapter aims to explore the complex processes of stasis and change in early and mid-nineteenth-century Man, the historical perspective within which Loch's achievement should be assessed.

Mona, the Paradise of the Half-pay

By the early nineteenth century the Isle of Man had at last adjusted to the revestment of 1765, capitalising on its unique position, geographically at the centre of the British Isles but politically distinct from the United Kingdom, to offer cheap and convenient domicile for British subjects of 'small incomes and pinched circumstances'.[4] Previously the Island was notorious as sanctuary and asylum for smugglers, runaway debtors (who, until a change in Manx law in 1814, could not be sued on the Island for debts contracted elsewhere) and other unwanted and

1] A.W. Moore, *A History of the Isle of Man* (2 vols, London, 1900), ii, 685.
2] 'The year 1866 was a crucial turning point in Manx history and may well be regarded as the one that ushered in the modern phase of the nation's development, both politically and economically', R.H. Kinvig, *A History of the Isle of Man* (2nd ed, Liverpool, 1950), 147.
3] For example, D.G. Kermode's (otherwise) authoritative *Devolution at Work: A Case Study of the Isle of Man* (Farnborough, 1979) takes no account of the 1829-66 period.
4] Bowring's speech at Castletown, 27 Sept, reported in *Mona's Herald*, 9 Oct 1844.

unsavoury 'transports', a 'notable Cave of Adullam' the Reverend Hugh Stowell Brown fulminated, for 'men of broken fortune and questionable character'.[5] By the end of the Napoleonic Wars a more favourable image had been established, thanks in part to a number of travel journals and guide books which sought to disabuse mistaken opinions 'both as to the natural character of the Island, and the moral character of its inhabitants'.[6] Henceforth the Island took advantage of its cheap commodities and fiscal privileges to promote itself as a safe and comfortable haven (without direct taxation, poor rates, serious crime or political turmoil) for the lesser beneficiaries, superannuated and otherwise, of Hanoverian governmental and financial growth – 'one of the few places in Europe where moderate people, may be moderately happy at a moderate expense'.[7] A convenient arrangement for the British and Manx alike, the system was to persist (despite steady erosion of differentials) until Loch's reforms, after which nostalgia developed for ' "the good old times" of no taxes and cheap living'.[8]

An outpost of the 'fiscal-military' state, blessed with the benefits of British liberty but without the attendant debt and tax burden, the Island steadily acquired a polite society composed of the 'younger sons of noble families, of the gentleman of good old lineage but impoverished fortune, of numerous retired military and naval officers, and of the dilettante in search of literary and artistic quiet'.[9] 'The boon may be considered an act of grace', James McCrone, the Island agent for the Commissioners of Woods and Forests, opined as he extolled

> the sound policy of selecting such a locality within Her Majesty's dominions where half pay officers, many of them worn out in the service of their country, and widows and annuitants may enjoy the necessaries of life, such as sugar and tea, and some of its luxuries at such prices as induces them to spend their limited incomes at home,

---

5] Hugh Stowell Brown, *His Autobiography* (London, 1887), 3.

6] 'The former is supposed by many persons to be, as I have frequently heard it described, an uninteresting spot, half-rock and half rabbit-warren; and the latter to be composed of fishermen, smugglers and individuals in embarrassed circumstances, availing themselves of the mild laws of the Island, which do not allow of personal arrests for the recovery of debts contracted out of it', N. Jefferys, *A Descriptive and Historical Account of the Isle of Man* (Newcastle-upon-Tyne, 1809), xi–xii.

7] H.A. Bullock, *History of the Isle of Man* (London, 1816), xii.

8] *Brown's Isle of Man Directory 1882* (Douglas, 1881), 64. *Gentleman's Magazine*, Aug 1825, calculated that 'a person may live as well on the Isle of Man with £200 a year, as he could with £300 in England'.

9] Katherine A. Forrest, *Manx Recollections: Memorials of Eleanor Elliott* (London and Douglas, 1894), 10.

in place of driving them away to spend the same in France or elsewhere abroad.[10]

Tynwald calculated that, if Customs privileges were removed by assimilation, the half-pay officers and their like would be compelled 'to retire to foreign countries, and thus totally withdraw from the United Kingdom an annual income which in the aggregate is estimated at £100,000'.[11]

A retirement haven for those who wished 'to be exempted from the pressure of taxation, and to support themselves on a respectable, yet economical plan',[12] Mona became 'the Paradise of the half-pay': ' "The puny Ensign, puffed with punch and beer / Who struts and starves on forty pounds a year" / elsewhere, becomes ennobled when he touches this fair isle – talks of his old port, and invites you to imbibe his Chateau Margaux.'[13] The new stranger-residents enjoyed an urban and genteel life (and language) apart from the 'spuds and herring' subsistence of the rural native majority, the 'genuine Manx people', whose main articles of sustenance, Richard Townley observed, were 'as far removed from luxuries as almost any people upon the face of the globe'.[14] Many in-comers were attracted to Douglas, the most 'English' of the Island's towns, which duly enjoyed considerable prosperity and growth. Beneath the surface etiquette of 'convivial societies, assemblies and card-parties', however, there were signs of cultural tension. Mutual suspicion, previously implanted by the 'extravagance' of fugitive debtors, was to persist:

> The harmony of society in Douglas is sometimes marred by mutual prejudices. In many of the natives, notwithstanding a show of politeness and hospitality, there is secret aversion to strangers; and in several of the English an unreasonable contempt of the Manks. The one is deemed too shrewd and selfish; and the other too prodigal . . .

10] McCrone to Normanby, 20 Jan 1840 (PRO, Kew: HO98/82). McCrone had earlier served as chief tithe agent of proctor for the Duke of Atholl; see David Craine, *Manannan's Isle* (Douglas, 1955), 201–2.

11] Council and Keys to Ready, nd, (MNHL: 9191/11/4, Letterbook iv, f 257).

12] Samuel Haining, *A Historical Sketch and Descriptive View of the Isle of Man* (Douglas, 1822), 55–6.

13] Undated cutting from *Morning Herald* (MNHL: Excerpts from Journals, i, f 36).

14] Richard Townley, *A Journal Kept in the Isle of Man* (2 vols, Whitehaven, 1791), i, 42. For further details of the diet ('butter-milk, potatoes, barley-cakes, stir-about and herrings'), living conditions and character of the Manx peasantry, see George Woods, *An Account of the Past and Present State of the Isle of Man* (London, 1811), 43–5, and 90–3, and Bullock, *History*, 350–7.

the English gentlemen, resident here, are more acquainted with convivial enjoyments, than with the pleasure of retirement. They are more Bon Vivants, than Penserosos ... But the prodigality of the English, frequently exceeding their income, becomes highly culpable. It injures the natives; it affects the credit of other strangers; and often precipitates themselves into deepest distress.[15]

Having welcomed the gentlemanly stranger-residents as an addition to their society, the leading Manx families were unable (or unwilling) to match such conspicuous consumption. Habitual economy, Hannah Bullock noted approvingly, was a principal character trait of the Manx, for whom 'no sacrifice is exacted to ostentation'. Among the insular establishment, the old Castletown 'clique', there was a marked retreat into social (and political) conservatism, expressed in increasing criticism (or barely concealed envy) of Douglas and its commercialised 'leisure' economy.[16] (It is surely significant that Henry Bloom Noble, the most successful 'rags to riches' entrepreneur of the century, began in the wine and spirits trade in Douglas, an in-comer servicing the needs of gentlemanly stranger-residents, before diversifying his interests and acquiring great wealth but never holding public office.)[17]

The cultural and social tensions provoked by the arrival of these early 'new residents' should not be overdrawn. The balance of trade being against the Island, the 'sums brought in by strangers ... increased the circulation and gave the necessary stimulus to commerce and agriculture'.[18] As gentlemanly (if over-indulgent) rentiers, the in-comers provided the means both to resource the insular economy and to reinforce its non-industrial and anti-entrepreneurial character, a matter of pride for the local establishment who held 'chevaliers d'industrie' in particular contempt.[19] However, gentlemanly stranger-residents were to be kept socially and politically in their place. Even Sir William Hillary, the most distinguished and cultured of their number and an

15] David Robertson, *A Tour through the Isle of Man: To Which is Subjoined a Review of the Manks History* (London, 1784: rpt, Newcastle-upon-Tyne, 1970), 24–5. See also Jefferys, *Descriptive and Historical Account*, 63–6.
16] Bullock, *History*, 328. Castletown, Bullock (220) observed, was 'not so flourishing in its trade, or so gay from the influx of strangers as its rival Douglas, yet it affords in the opinion of many a much pleasanter retreat to persons unconnected with trade, or those who prefer a quiet social intercourse to a mixed society'.
17] I am grateful to J. Sharpe for allowing me to consult his manuscript biography of Noble.
18] Bullock, *History*, 327–8.
19] *Manx Sun*, 8 Mar 1848.

aspirant for the post of Lieutenant-Governor on Colonel Smelt's death,[20] failed to gain full acceptance:

> He was an Englishman by birth, education and connexion, and an Englishman he should ever remain. But he ever had felt a deep interest in the prosperity of the Isle of Man, his adopted country … their scenery, their associations, their institutions, all were dear to him; he had married among them. Yet for all this the law declared him to be a stranger; it accounted him for all this an alien, and refused to recognise him as a Manxman … Manxmen when they set foot on English ground, were entitled to every privilege of Englishmen. The army, the navy, the bench, the church, all the departments of state were open to him; yet an Englishman was not privileged as a Manxman here. These were inconveniences which he felt could not long be endured.[21]

Quite as much as the fiscal privileges enjoyed by in-comer and native alike, such 'inconveniences' were the very stuff of Manx independence and autonomy. While the Manx language went into rapid decline, other aspects and inflexions of Manxness – constitutional, legal, political and fiscal distinctiveness – were jealously guarded by the insular legislature and the Castletown clique.

The Manx Establishment
Although a dependency of the British Crown, the Isle of Man took pride in its continuing privileges and autonomy. Constitutional arrangements allowed the fiction of Manx independence to persist. In the absence of the extensive machinery of Crown colonial administration to which Loch aspired, 'colonial' government at Castletown operated through limited amounts of patronage and continuing respect for traditional institutions. Taken together, these secured the support of the leading landed, legal and Anglican families, producing a 'Government Party', loyal to the British Governor but fiercely opposed to 'every attempt to modify the peculiar laws and civil institutions of the country, formed in a remote and feudal age, to the progressive condition of the times'.[22]

20] Hillary to Melbourne, 16 Aug 1832 (PRO: HO98/77). For biographical sketches (mainly concerned with his lifeboat connections), see Constance Mona Douglas, *This is Ellan Vannin: A Miscellany of Manx Life and Lore* (Douglas, 1965), 38–41; and Samuel Norris, *Manx Memories and Movements* (1938: rpt Douglas, 1994), 45–58.
21] Hillary's speech at Peel reported in *Mona's Herald*, 1 Oct 1844.
22] A Stranger (John Welch), *A Six Days' Tour through the Isle of Man; or, A Passing View of its Present Natural, Social and Political Aspect* (Douglas, 1836), 72.

Hallowed by history, Tynwald Court was the joint assembly of the
two chambers (or estates) of the Manx legislature, the Council and the
Keys, convened under the presidency, pleasure and veto of the
Lieutenant-Governor (who also sat ex-officio as Chancellor and
Judge of the superior judicial courts). Emanating from the Lord's
Council of the fifteenth century, the Council, or upper house, with a
maximum membership of eleven (the Governor included), served both
as Legislative Council and as a Privy or Executive Council: the
Attorney-General, the Clerk of the Rolls, the two Deemsters (judges),
the Water Bailiff (the Admiral or Judge of the Court of Admiralty) and
the Receiver-General were appointed by the Crown, as were the Bishop
and the Archdeacon; the remaining members, the two Vicars-General,
were in the patronage of the Bishop. The method and honour of
appointment, the highest aspiration of the Manx elite, ensured
invariable support for the Lieutenant-Governor, although Loch was
later to seek an absolute assurance to this effect from Council members
who enjoyed Crown patronage.[23] Taken together with lesser functionaries servicing or outside the Council, there were some twelve or
thirteen paid public offices, a legal establishment whose disproportionate size, cost and influence came under increasing criticism.[24] In a
report to Whitehall on 'the Institutions of the Island, which are so
extraordinary, and so unlike any thing in existence on the face of the
earth, and withal so expensive', McCrone calculated that savings of at
least £2,000 a year could be afforded 'while every end of Justice might
be more purely administered'; but he refrained from particulars on 'this
delicate subject' lest he be placed 'under the ban of every Member of
the Judicial functionaries, from the Lieut. Gov. [*sic*] downwards'.[25]
   The House of Keys, the lower chamber of the legislature, was
composed of twenty-four 'principal landowners', the 'Gentry of the
Island both in talent and property'.[26] It had long been self-elected.

23] See the correspondence on the constitution between Loch and Attorney-General
Gell, Apr 1881 (MNHL: Printed Confidential Documents, Sir Henry B. Loch, 1873–
1882). For useful earlier descriptions, see J. Johnson, *A View of the Jurisprudence of
the Isle of Man* (Edinburgh, 1811); and James Clarke, *A View of the Principal Courts in
the Isle of Man* (Liverpool, 1817).
24] See the extract from the *Isle of Man Times*, 20 Mar 1847, and other critical material
collected by Bowring in *Papers Relative to the Political Condition of the Isle of Man*
(PRO: HO45/943). See also the 'Return showing the several Ecclesiastical and Civil
Official Situations, judicial and otherwise, held by persons who have been admitted
Members of the Manx Bar', PP 1847 (48) LIX.
25] McCrone to Phillipps, 24 Mar 1837 (PRO: HO98/79).
26] Drinkwater to Loch, 2 Feb 1863 (SRO: Loch Papers, GD268/116).

Membership was for life: when a vacancy occurred by death or resignation, the House nominated two names, one of whom was 'elected' by the Governor. In-comers were not debarred from sitting in the Keys, but social closure was clearly evident. The 'natives', Joseph Train observed, had come to regard membership 'as highly honourable as that of knight of the shire is in Great Britain'.[27] Extensive landed property and 'an accurate knowledge of insular laws and customs' were considered essential prerequisites for the discharge of legislative and judicial functions.[28] 'Non-natives have occasionally been elected Members', a reform petition acknowledged, 'but through a dominant faction with which they have generally been connected by family ties.'[29] By membership and function – a number of lawyers (no fewer than seven in 1846) sat in the House, which also served as court of appeal from verdicts of juries in civil cases – the Keys cemented the alliance between the leading landed and legal families. Reformers were later to protest against such closely knit 'thraldom': 'The whole of the Legislative Council and Legislative Assembly, are so mingled, twisted, and interwoven through each other, that the same individuals confront you in some guise or other, from the lowest to the Highest Court in the land.'[30] On this solid basis of influence and power, G.W. Dumbell, lawyer, landowner, Member and Secretary of the House of Keys, was to develop substantial banking, commercial and mining interests, following a more 'privileged' (and protected) route to fortune than that ventured by Henry Noble.[31]

After 1833 the behaviour of the establishment came under critical public scrutiny in the columns of *Mona's Herald*, a liberal paper published by Fargher and Walls. As advocates of reform and improvement, they held the Castletown clique responsible for the persistence of otherwise discredited traditions and practices. According to their account, the extensive looting of the *John Fairfield*, wrecked on the Island in November 1834 en route from Liverpool to Havana, was prolonged (if not facilitated) by dereliction of duty on the part of George Quirk, the Water Bailiff, and other officials.[32] Investigation into

---

27] J. Train, *An Historical and Statistical Account of the Isle of Man* (2 vols, Douglas, 1845), ii, 198.

28] House of Keys, 27 Jan 1845 in PP 1845 (106) XLV, Memorials to HM Govt from the Isle of Man on Reform of the House of Keys.

29] Memorial from Douglas in PP 1846 (88) XXXIII, Correspondence on Reform of the House of Keys.

30] *Manx Liberal*, 17 Apr 1847.

31] C. Chappell, *The Dumbell Affair* (Prescot, 1981), ch 4.

32] Memorial of W. Walls and R. Fargher, nd (PRO: HO98/77).

these 'scenes of outrageous and unparalleled plunder' (a matter of serious concern in Whitehall) exonerated Quirk from complicity in nefarious plundering, but it exposed the worst aspects of the Insular establishment: nepotism, pluralism, absenteeism and intolerance of criticism. Ready, a soldier-diplomat (previously Governor of Prince Edward Island) who had been sworn in as Lieutenant-Governor in December 1832, was strenuous in defence of Quirk, having recently appointed him to the vacant (but no longer remunerated) post of Receiver-General. A reliable supporter in the Council and Ready's personal secretary, Quirk derived his income from fees and from the salaries of his other offices as Water Bailiff (£300 a year), and Clerk of the Council (£100 a year). Quirk's brother, James, also held a number of offices: Keeper of the Manorial Rolls, High Bailiff of Douglas and Acting Attorney-General, at a combined annual income of £275 (plus fees).[33] The non-residence of James Clarke, the Attorney-General, who lived in Lancashire where he had other responsibilities as Recorder of Liverpool, had previously caused little concern. (The practice of non-residence was to be continued by his successors, also members of the English Bar, but only for limited periods and on terms approved and regulated by the Home Office.)[34] 'I have been led to think from all my friends in the Island', Clarke quipped to Russell, 'that my non-residence, as it kept me out of party feuds, was of considerable service to the Island.'[35] In his absence James Quirk filed an ex-officio information against Fargher and Walls for defamation of his brother in their newspaper. This was a draconian over reaction, the use of a measure intended 'only to meet instances where danger to the state or government can be apprehended'. The merchants and shipowners of Liverpool (whose insurance agents had confirmed Fargher's and Walls's version of events) protested in the strongest terms to the Home Office where there was a growing conviction that continued critical comments in *Mona's Herald* were 'to a certain degree true, though expressed with improper asperity'.[36] Clarke was ordered across the water to undertake a full investigation. Ready defused further criticism by instituting a wide-ranging programme, drawn up with Clarke's legal assistance, to

33] See the correspondence between Ready and the HO, Apr–June 1835, in MNHL: Letterbook iv, f 108–29, and in PRO: HO98/77–8.
34] Ready to Maule, 13 Nov 1838 in MNHL: Letterbook iv, f 338–42. See also Graham to Ogden (Clarke's successor), 10 Feb 1844 (PRO: HO99/19 f 16–18); and Hope to Waddington, 20 Aug 1857 (MNHL: Letterbook viii, f 189–93).
35] Clarke to Russell, 30 Oct 1835 (PRO: HO98/78).
36] Russell to Clarke, 25 May 1835 (PRO: HO99/18 f 128-35). Clarke's report, 18 May 1835 (PRO: HO98/78).

Col. John Ready *championed law and order when the Island was subject to serious unrest. He made known to the Home Office his support of the Manx system of government. He had become Governor of the Island in 1832 after serving in a similar role during a period of rapid growth in the economy of Prince Edward Island. His departure from Prince Edward Island in 1831 was 'deeply regretted by the people'. His death on the Isle of Man is believed to have been due to accidental poisoning.*

improve law and order on the Island: new acts were drafted for the suppression of riots and the punishment of plunderers of wrecked vessels; a new 'higher class' of magistrates were appointed under the chairmanship of Lieutenant-General Goldie; and, after much haggling over the cost, there was a major expansion of the police force, unchanged since 1777.[37]

Once the thirty-odd constabulary force was in place, the government decided to reduce the size (and hence cost) of the military establishment.[38] Ready considered the decision most unwise. Public order was at risk from a number of factors: hostility to Irish immigrant labourers;[39] rivalry between Manx, Cornish and Irish fishing crews at Peel (fierce clashes later to be refought in Kinsale);[40] and direct action by hungry urban crowds to stop the export of potatoes and other produce (rioting was so serious in late 1838 that Tynwald instituted an embargo on potato exports).[41] Confronted by such recurrent points of tension as the 'spud and herring' economy became increasingly commercialised and urban (and English in speech), Ready and his successors (Hope and Pigott) called repeatedly (but unavailingly) for more funds for the police and a larger military presence. Given the low rates of remuneration – at £20 a year constables' wages barely exceeded the pay of a common labourer[42] – there were serious problems of staff recruitment and retention. Refusing to recognise the Island as a special case, the Treasury insisted that extra funding should be provided the English way, through local rates.[43] As paymaster, it subjected Manx police budgets to rigorous scrutiny: tenders for uniforms (even, on occasion, samples of cloth) were sent to the Commissioners of Metropolitan Police to check against extra-

37] See correspondence between Ready and HO, June 1835–Apr 1836 in MNHL: Letterbook iv, f 149–219, and in PRO: HO98/78 and 99/18.

38] Ready to Maule, 13 Nov 1838, 29 Mar, 25 Apr, 2 July and 18 Sept 1839 (MNHL: Letterbook iv, f 338–69).

39] Ready to Russell, 9 June 1835 (MNHL: Letterbook iv, f 139–40). Catholic churches were occasionally the target of crowd action; see Hope to Waddington, 27 Jan 1859 (MNHL: Letterbook viii, f 474–9).

40] Ready to Maule, 29 Mar and 18 Sept 1839 (MNHL: Letterbook iv, f 351–2 and 367–9). Larcom (Dublin Castle) to Fitzroy, 30 Nov 1853 (MNHL: Letterbook vii, f 4).

41] Ready to Maule, 18 Sept 1839 (MNHL: Letterbook iv, f 367–9. See also the entries for 19 Jan 1837 and from Oct 1838 to Apr 1839 in Council Book ii (MNHL: 9191/4/2), f 159–60, and 251–9.

42] Hope to Somerville, 5 May 1847 (MNHL: Letterbook v, f 352–4).

43] Waddington to Hope, 20 Nov, and Hope to Bouverie, 1 Dec 1851 (MNHL: Letterbook vi, f 283–92).

vagance.[44] The refusal to enlarge the military presence, further depleted during the Crimean War, led both Hope and Pigott to express considerable anxiety about the maintenance of order in the mountain districts where 'disafforestation' (or enclosure) was set to remove grazing, turbary (digging for turf and peat) and other rights, the 'moral economy' traditionally enjoyed by smallholders, labourers, miners and other 'commoners'.[45]

In law and order, as in other areas, significant advance was not forthcoming until Loch took office. As he saw it, efficient reorganisation of the police, a major Island-wide overhaul to dispense with the old order under the High Bailiffs (unelected officials with duties similar to the English Borough Reeves of yore) was the necessary first step before the public would approve the introduction of a rate-finance scheme. Furthermore, urgent action was required to deal with new problems (an indication of the development of the Manx economy): the rowdyism of mass tourism; and the dangerous concentration of miners, 'a somewhat turbulent and difficult class to manage', in isolated communities. Since the holiday-makers were British and the English-owned mines contributed substantially, via royalties, to the surplus revenue of the Island paid into the Consolidated Fund, he was able to persuade the Treasury to assist with the costs of the initial reorganisation. It was a pity, however, that the first Chief Constable, Captain Thompson, had to be dismissed within weeks of appointment, on account of insobriety.[46]

Lieutenant-Governors had to negotiate hard with the British government on a number of fronts: to preserve the fiscal differentials (preferential duties) necessary for the service economy of the gentlemanly stranger-residents; to secure adequate resources to keep order amongst the native Manx who worked with 'spade and net'; and to ensure that Whitehall defrayed the full expenses (beyond the salaries of the Castletown establishment) of Insular government. After much negotiation, final settlement of the commutation of tithes in 1839 – a concomitant of the decision to overturn the recommendation of the Ecclesiastical Commissioners and allow the see of Sodor and Man to

44] As well as voluminous correspondence in the Letterbooks, see the file on police uniforms in PRO: HO45/6198.

45] Pigott to Clive, 18 Apr, and 7 Nov; to Waddington, 27 Apr 1861 (MNHL: Letterbook ix, f 256, 268, and 335–7).

46] Loch to HO, 2 May 1863 (MNHL: Letterbook ix, f 589–95); to Capt Thompson, 23 Aug, and to Howard, 20 Oct 1863 (SRO: Loch Letterbook, GD268/942, f 25–6, and 44–8). For HO approval see Waddington to Loch, 4 July 1863 (PRO: HO99/19, f 493).

retain its independence after Bishop Ward's death – was put in jeopardy when the Treasury refused payment of the expenses of the valuers, who had gone over budget.[47] Considerable energies were expended in seeking to extract the smallest sums from Whitehall where, it seemed, parsimony was compounded by ignorance of the particular circumstances of the Island. In the absence of consultation with the Lieutenant-Governor, Bills were passed at Westminster which extended to the Isle of Man without, as Deemster Drinkwater protested, 'a proper machinery for working them here and are therefore, as far as this Island is concerned, a dead letter'.[48] Loch wrote to the Home Office to insist on the omission of the Island from Shaftesbury's Ecclesiastical Courts Bill:

> The Manx Ecclesiastical Courts are so interwoven with the Jurisdiction and procedure of the temporal Courts within the Island, that merely extending a measure calculated to meet certain requirements in the English Ecclesiastical Courts, would only lead to serious embarrassment.

He then persuaded the Treasury to make funds available for a Manx 'parliamentary agent', similar in function to the Scottish agent, to keep an eye on English Bills which extended to the Island and, if necessary, insert clauses 'to ensure the proper working of the Measure in the Manx Courts'.[49]

In the course of relentless and often unavailing negotiation with the British government, Loch's predecessors were prone to 'go native': dismayed by Whitehall, they moved closer to the Castletown clique in defence of the gamut of Manx rights, privileges and anomalies. 'Perhaps a better form of Government could not be framed for meeting the wants of a small community' Ready enthused as he instructed the Home Office on the history and development of the Manx constitution. The Crown derived considerable benefits from revestment arrangements – control of the revenue, choice of members and sanction of the laws – and should thus respect residual Manx rights and privileges.[50]

47] There is much correspondence on this complex issue in: Council Book ii (see in particular the Bishop to G. Quirk, 12 Jan 1838, f 201–3, and details of the final valuation and expenses at f 309–10 and 369); Letterbook iv (see in particular Phillipps to Ready, 20 Feb 1838, Ready to Maule 26 Sept 1839, and to Manners Sutton, 21 Aug 1842, f 318–19, 370–1 and 486–7); and PRO: HO98/81.
48] Drinkwater to Pigott, 2 Mar 1861 (PRO: HO45/7115).
49] Loch to HO, 20 Mar and 5 Apr 1869 (PRO: HO45/7115).
50] Ready to Manners Sutton, 14 Feb 1845 (PRO: HO45/943, and MNHL: Letterbook iv, f 536–42).

Whitehall was less enthusiastic. Driven by administrative convenience and ideological imperative, successive British governments displayed decreasing tolerance for anomalies, deviations and 'inconsistencies' from fiscal, constitutional and other norms. On occasion, as with the lottery scheme proposed in 1839, swift and decisive action was necessary to prevent the Manx from exploiting legal loopholes.[51]

In an age of retrenchment and 'responsible' government, Westminster was adamant that the Isle of Man, like all British possessions, should attain financial self-sufficiency and solvency. The priority, enjoined upon successive Lieutenant-Governors, was to ensure against any drain on the British Treasury. Duties had to be set at a level which, while covering the cost of government, would prevent any injury to the British revenue through a reversion to the smuggling trade, and secure a profitable return (for the United Kingdom Consolidated Fund) on the price paid for revestment and subsequent purchase of manorial rights. In this last respect the Isle of Man was a case apart, different from the Channel Islands (otherwise the nearest equivalent):

> The revenues of the Channel Islands are in some measure the property of those islands, at the disposal of the Royal Courts, with the consent of Her Majesty in Council, and are at present applicable to island purposes. The revenues of the Isle of Man belong to the public, upon whose behalf they were purchased of the Duke of Atholl, and after the current expenditure of the island is defrayed, under the sanction of the Lords Commissioners of Her Majesty's Treasury, the surplus is available for the general purposes of the country.[52]

As applied in practice, these policy considerations combined to circumscribe the functions (and hence cost) of government on the Island, preventing the kind of public improvements (and policing) which developed with such municipal pride in Victorian England, while at the same time ensuring a substantial surplus revenue for the Treasury in Whitehall. 'We are not only the poorest dependency of England', Fargher protested, 'but in proportion to our extent, the most profitable dependency of the British crown.'[53]

Political tensions between the Island and Britain extended beyond mere fiscal matters – the retention of differentials in the face of pressure for Customs assimilation – to the more contentious question of the surplus revenue. The Manx sought to preserve their cherished

51] Baring to Phillipps, 4 May 1839 (PRO: HO98/81).
52] Manners Sutton to Hope, 12 Nov 1845 in PP 1846 (88) XXXIII.
53] *Mona's Herald*, 17 Apr 1844.

exemption from rates and taxes by gaining access to the annual and accumulated surplus revenue, funds which would facilitate harbour and other improvements. Here they encountered resolute British opposition. Imperial assertion was underwritten by powerful ideological rhetoric. Having based their case on tradition, privilege and exceptionalism, the Manx were lectured on the universal benefits of free trade and rate-funded, representative local self-government. Such progressive prescriptions were anathema to the Insular establishment, for whom the 'whole circumstances of the Island are in direct disproof of the eligibility of both the political and economic dogmas of Whig or Liberal legislation and government'.[54] As ideology intruded into the independence debate, Manx reformers (with recent come-overs to the fore) came to appreciate that their struggle was as much against the established 'clique' in control of the Island as against the imperial Parliament.

The Anti-assimilation Campaigns of the 1830s

Confronted by the zeal of the newly reformed Parliament in the 1830s – the Whig mania for 'assimilation, annexation and amalgamation' – the Manx were unanimous in defence of traditional rights and privileges, united in fear that 'the whole fabric of our Constitution will be undermined, and the inevitable result will be Taxation'.[55] The proposed merger of the bishopric of Sodor and Man with that of Carlisle, followed by various parliamentary pronouncements on Customs reform pointed ominously towards outright incorporation (via political attachment to the county of Cumberland) into the United Kingdom.[56] Resistance was organised through formal and other channels in a carefully orchestrated display of Manx feeling, extending beyond the Council and the Keys in Tynwald Court to embrace 'public opinion'. In its 'constitutional' conduct and rhetoric Manx 'extra-parliamentary' politics bore a striking resemblance to the platform agitations of early-Victorian Britain. First deployed to save the bishopric, the mechanisms of 'pressure from without' – open public meetings, house-by-house canvassing for petitions and the appointment of delegates ready to defend Manx interests at the bar of the House of Commons – were put into more extensive operation in July 1836 when the government announced proposals for Customs assimilation. As it

---

54] *Manx Sun*, 9 Aug 1848.
55] *Mona's Herald*, 30 Oct 1844. T.W. Corlett to W. Sayle, 6 June 1836 (MNHL: 5429/4A).
56] Murray, McHutchin and Drinkwater to Ready, 9 Mar 1835 (MNHL: Letterbook iv, f 90–1).

happened, lack of time compelled the government to withdraw the measure, but the committee of delegates wisely remained on stand-by.[57] On 3 January 1837 the Privy Council for Trade, having again considered the 'inconveniences that arise from the present relative positions of the United Kingdom and the Isle of Man', announced that there were to be 'certain alterations in the existing Laws of Customs and Navigation, which will tend to place the trade of that Island as nearly, and as early as practicable, upon the same footing as that of this country'. Lord John Russell was instructed to sound out the opinion of the local authorities.[58]

'It is not saying too much that the greatest alarm is felt by all Classes in this Island on the proposed assimilation of duties', Governor Ready reported. He enclosed (and endorsed) a joint response from the Council and the Keys, warning that

> the Island may relapse into the state in which it was after passing the Revesting Act in 1765, when the trading towns became almost deserted, the rents and lands fell to one third of their former value, and very many of the Inhabitants although affectionately attached to their native land, were obliged to forsake it, and seek their bread in foreign lands.[59]

Joseph Train, temporarily resident in the Island to complete his historical research, observed how 'every class of the community seemed to indulge in the most gloomy forebodings of the disasters which would inevitably result from such a radical change in their fiscal regulations'.[60] A mass petitioning campaign began with a public meeting in Douglas, chaired by Sir William Hillary: the High Bailiffs of the other towns and the Captains of the parishes were instructed to convene public meetings to elect delegates to attend 'general' meetings in Douglas; and a deputation was appointed to wait upon the Lieutenant-Governor and Tynwald to co-ordinate a joint approach to London through a tripartite delegation representing the Council, the Keys and the 'mercantile, agricultural and trading interests'.[61]

57] *Manx Sun*, 15 July 1836. *Mona's Herald*, 17 Jan 1837. For details of the public campaign to save the bishopric see Hillary to Ready, 30 June (MNHL: Letterbook iv, f 232) and Ready to Maule, 4 July 1836 (PRO: H98/79).
58] Maule to Ready, 6 Jan 1837 (PRO: HO99/18, f 225–6).
59] Ready to Maule, 20 Jan 1837 (MNHL: Letterbook iv, f 255–61).
60] Train, *Historical and Statistical Account*, ii, 321.
61] *Mona's Herald*, 17 Jan 1837. *Manks Advertiser*, 31 Jan 1837, cutting in the Bluett Papers (MNHL), a large box of documents (not catalogued until after this chapter was written) on the anti-assimilation campaign, originally deposited in the Samuel Harris

The main petition, signed by 3,783 inhabitants, stressed the dire consequences of assimilation as the inevitable departure of the half-pay officers and 'numerous worthy, yet reduced families' would reduce the Isle of Man to 'a depressed, forsaken speck in the empire'. This gloomy prognosis was underlined in supporting petitions from those whose livelihoods depended upon servicing the 'stranger-residents': the 'working joiners, house carpenters, cabinet makers, masons, stone cutters, plasterers, painters and glaziers and others employed in house building in the town and neighbourhood of Douglas', and the 'Isle of Man Building Society and Proprietors of Houses':

> If our few remaining privileges are taken from us – the very name of which has been of essential service to us – there will be little to induce our present sojournirs [*sic*] to stay amongst us ... Multitudes of mechanics and labourers now enjoying the blessing of abundant work and comfortable support for their families, will be entirely thrown out of employ.[62]

As well as co-ordinating the petitions, the lawyer J.C. Bluett (previously a member of the 1836 committee) drafted a lengthy two-pronged briefing document for the proposed London delegation. These 'economic observations' showed how they should first contest the existence of 'inconveniences' or abuses in the existing arrangements (timber duties and shipbuilding apart), and then refute the possibility of any benefit to the Island from free trade and commerce, given its lack of raw materials, capital, manufacturing knowledge, skilled labour and proper transport facilities.[63] It was on this second point, Bluett came to realise, that the Manx and the British were the further apart:

> It is considered at the Board of Trade that the Island is perfectly blind to her own interests, and that keeping her eyes steadfastly fixed upon the trifling advantage of cheap luxuries they lose sight of the incalculably great benefits they might derive from their local situation. Almost equidistant from England, Ireland and Scotland she ought to be but one vast warehouse for each.

To put matters straight, he asked Hillary to issue a pamphlet 'to shew our absolute unfitness for the benefits of Trade and Commerce'.[64]

Papers. Not all this material was available for consultation at the time of R.E.C. Forster's study of 'The deputation to London in 1837', *JMM*, VI (1964), 197–9.

62] All petitions are in both draft and final printed form in the Bluett Papers.

63] 'Observations upon the plan by his Majesty's Government 1837' (MNHL: Bluett Papers).

64] See the five letters from Bluett to Hillary, March–May 1837 (MNHL: Bluett Papers).

Hillary struck the requisite pessimistic tone (although he also took the opportunity to rehearse the argument for his pet project, a publicly funded central refuge harbour for the Irish Sea at Douglas):

> Without sea ports, how can foreign commerce be induced to fix her abode in this Isle? and where are such ports to be found? The Isle of Man does not possess a single harbour which is not too often open to the extreme of peril: every port dry at low water; all surrounded with formidable rocks and a dangerous coast ... Without coal, without water-power sufficient in summer to keep the commonest corn-mill going three days in a week, with a scanty population, principally employed in agriculture and the fisheries, whence can the hope of introducing manufactures arise? ... With an ungrateful soil and a stormy climate, with a long winter, and a short summer, how can the Isle of Man compete with the commerce of the surrounding shores. Yet for these chimerical hopes are they told to expel the officer on half pay, the reduced gentleman on scanty means, the strange who, uniting economy with recreation, visits the Isle, and to trust for compensation to these remote, improbable contingencies.[65]

Having set up base in London, Bluett was dismayed by the misconceptions, factionalism and jealousies which delayed the arrival of the rest of the delegation. From his preliminary lobbying (for which he was to be criticised for exceeding his duties) he discovered that time was not on their side: both political parties were committed to the principle and policy of assimilation; no hope could be placed in a change of ministry; but negotiation, if conducted promptly and firmly, was likely to secure significant concession and compromise on points of detail.[66] Various controversies, however, delayed the selection of fellow members of the people's delegation: the tergiversation of T.A. Corlett, and the questionable reputation of John James Moore. 'Notwithstanding his second election, there exists in the minds of all respectable persons a strong prejudice against him', Craigie reported, 'subscriptions are even refused for his support':

> We are tumbling into a faction as fast as possible, and a strong feeling is getting abroad the Keys and the Council are working

65] Sir William Hillary, Observations on the Proposed Changes in the Fiscal and Navigation Laws of the Isle of Man: Addressed to the Delegates from that Island to His Majesty's Government (Douglas, 1837), 12–13.
66] Bluett's letters to Hillary, and to Ready, 15 Jan–29 Mar 1837 (MNHL: Bluett Papers).

against the interests of the people. So much for the unity of doctrines promulgated by empty heads and politicians.

Although isolated in London, the hapless Bluett was not immune from carping criticism:

> The thing you must expect that many of the factious and discontented will cry out against your paid services. I hope there is a clear understanding about your pay ... You are considered as a freeman acting from the influence of a strong *patriotic and disinterested motives* [*sic*]. Wise asses to expect that you would leave your business and family for six weeks *from l'amour patrie.*[67]

Hillary was sympathetic to Bluett's plight, but even here there was some misunderstanding: in return for payment, Hillary expected Bluett to provide public reports on what were private and confidential discussions with politicians and Treasury officials.[68] Eventually, at the beginning of May, the London delegation assembled, a mere five in number, without any representatives from Council, even though the Home Office had raised no objection to the selection of Deemster Christian and McHutchin, the Clerk of the Rolls.[69] Dr Garrett and John Moore, representatives from the Keys, joined the people's delegates, Corlett, J.J. Moore and Bluett.

Their first task, the presentation of a dire economic prognosis to C.P. Thompson, President of the Board of Trade, was soon accomplished, after which the delegation concentrated on the 'constitutional case' against assimilation.[70] In a lengthy letter to Lord John Russell, the Home Secretary, they remonstrated against the imposition of proposals in contravention of both the Manx constitution and the British constitution:

> If then the claim in question rests on the constitution of the Isle of Man, it will be found that no tax, duty, or custom could or can at any time be imposed, without the joint assent of the Lord of the Island, of the Council, and of the House of Keys, which is the House of Assembly of the representatives of the people of the island.
>
> If it depend on the constitution of Great Britain, we have only to remind your Lordship that it is a vital part of its constitution, that no tax can be imposed without the consent of the tax-payers. The Isle of

67] Craigie's letters to Bluett, 17 Mar–21 May 1837 (MNHL: Bluett Papers).
68] Hillary's letters to Bluett, 20 Mar–5 May 1837 (MNHL: Bluett Papers).
69] Maule to Hillary, 22 Feb 1837 (PRO: HO99/18, f 259–60).
70] Bluett Papers contain draft and amended final versions of the letters presented to Thompson on 17 May and to Russell on 8 June 1837.

Man, however, forms no part of the United Kingdom, and hence its consent can only be obtained by its local Legislature.

Reference to a poignant historical parallel enabled the delegation to underline the Island's unique constitutional position and make claim to the surplus revenue:

> If the Isle of Man stood to England in the relation of a colony to its mother country, we apprehend that our right to the control and disposal of any surplus revenue, after providing for the expense of collection, would be undoubted: and we should in that case content ourselves with claiming the benefit of the principle laid down in the Act of 18 Geo. 3, c. 12, 1778, by which Act the revenues of the North American colonies were declared, as a matter of principle, to be at the disposal of the colonies themselves; a principle which we believe is recognised with reference to all the present colonies of the Empire. But the claims of the Isle of Man stand, we humbly conceive, on the higher footing of its having been an ancient and independent kingdom, with peculiar laws, and a constitution which it had enjoyed from its earliest period, and by which it is governed at the present day.[71]

The delegates were scheduled to discuss the case with Russell on 20 June, but the death of William IV intervened: the interview was cancelled, and the assimilation proposals (along with all other government business) were shelved.

Despite the proximate role of circumstance, Manx politicians were to persist in the belief that their efforts and arguments had prevailed, that Russell was on the verge of acceding to the authority and wisdom of the delegation. Thereafter, whenever Manx privileges seemed under threat, there was a prompt re-activation of the 'pressure' mechanisms – public meetings, petitions, delegations – which had proved their worth in 1837. However, the unity displayed on that occasion (sullied at the outset by proverbial Manx factionalism) was not to be repeated. As the rhetorical premises of the campaign against Customs assimilation were called into question, petty jealousy and rivalry deepened into political and economic division.

The gravamen of the constitutional case, no taxation without representation, exposed the vulnerable position of the self-elected House of Keys. Manx 'public opinion' came to stand apart from the members of the Island's ancient legislature. Elected at open public

---

71] The letter was reprinted in PP 1852–3 (605) XCIX, Letter by Agent of the Isle of Man to the Secretary of the Treasury.

meetings, people's delegates were to claim a higher authority, justified historically by the precedent of 1643: in convening the Insular legislature, the seventh Earl of Derby had also ordered the election of four men in each parish, representatives of 'the whole Commons of the Isle' to assist the Keys to 'adjust various grievances'.[72] At the same time the increasingly hegemonic force of British arguments for free trade and commerce steadily undermined the commitment to the existing fiscal regime and the static socio-economic system it sustained. Manx reformers sought a new arrangement which, while preserving political independence and fiscal differentials, would enable the Island to participate in commercial and industrial growth. Hard bargaining with the British Treasury was accompanied by a determination to eradicate the 'feudal' institutions and practices which prevailed on the Island at the expense of its economic development.

While they could still unite against specific British threats to the Island's independence and privileges, Manx politicians were increasingly divided, albeit without any party system, into conservative and liberal camps with opposite views of how best to secure Manx autonomy. Fearful of undermining historical legitimacy, conservatives cautioned against any change, an attitude personified by G.W. Dumbell and broadcast by the *Manx Sun*. Liberals, by contrast, sought to eradicate historical anomalies and anachronisms. Urged on by Robert Fargher and *Mona's Herald*, they propounded a pre-emptive programme of reform (beginning with an elective House of Keys and abolition of the licence system) to safeguard Manx independence in the modern world. By reforming itself, the Island would be left alone, free from critical gaze and the threat of incorporation into the United Kingdom.

Campaigns for Reform

In the aftermath of the Customs campaign Fargher hoped to engage broad-based support for political reform. Much in line with the radical project in England, his brand of reform sought to extend and redefine, not to challenge and subvert, the constitutional heritage. Through appeal to history and principle he sought to purify and modernise the 'present anomalous constitution, with all its monstrously absurd, and glaringly, unjust usurpations of our primal rights as free British subjects'. He called upon the Keys to 'amend themselves, to lead a new

---

72] See, for example, the historical arguments in PP 1864 (553) LVIII Correspondence and Petitions of Inhabitants of Isle of Man on Appropriation of Customs Revenues for Construction of Harbour and Redress of Grievances, 1854–64.

political life, and become *de facto*, what they now unjustly and falsely
assume themselves to be, the true and just representation of the insular
state'.[73] Although property-based, the proposed suffrage qualification
in the 'Plan for an Elective House of Keys' was low: 'all men paying
One Pound Lord's Rent per year and upwards, all Tenants of Land, or
whole Houses, paying Five Pounds Rent per year and upwards'.
Perhaps the most radical suggestion was for meetings of the Keys, at
least in its judicial or appellate capacity, to rotate between the four
towns.[74] Printed petitions in favour of such reform, held in abeyance
after the failure of an earlier series of public meetings, were recirculated
in every parish in the autumn of 1837. Given the delicate stage of
negotiations for retention of the bishopric and the commutation of
tithes, and in light of the withdrawal of Customs assimilation, the
Manx Sun considered the antics of Fargher and his 'discordant band of
agitating Manx troubadours' untimely and unwise: 'the interest of the
Island would be best cultivated at this moment, by a respectable
tranquillity, and a cautious silence on the contending politics of the
Island'.[75]

The reform petitions revealed divisions previously concealed by
united opposition to customs assimilation and ecclesiastical annexation. Even among the stranger-residents there were pronounced
differences of political opinion. At this stage Hillary and his entourage,
the new social elite, kept distant from political reform, dismissing the
proposed restoration of a representative House of Keys as

> a revolution of piddling importance ... Whether it would be worth
> while, for the sake of form, to maintain the principle, and go through
> the tumult of electing twenty-four people from the four winds of
> heaven to manage the local affairs of a mere parish, is the question to
> be asked.[76]

Political reform was a more urgent consideration, however, for less
successful (or over-indulgent?) in-comers, particularly those whose
disillusionment and debts were compounded by entanglement in the
vagaries of Manx law. Beyond all anomalies in the Island the self-

73] *Mona's Herald*, 17–31 Oct 1837.
74] A handbill of the 'Plan' is enclosed in Ready to Maule, 9 Mar 1838 (PRO: HO98/
80). For brief details of the campaign see R.E.C. Forster, 'The reformist movement in
1837', *Proceedings of the Isle of Man Natural History and Antiquarian Society*, VI
(1963), 379–87.
75] *Manx Sun*, 9 Mar 1838.
76] Welch, *Six Days' Tour*, 97.

Tynwald Fair *Without the benefit of loudspeakers, crowds cluster round Tynwald hill to hear the reading of the new Acts. This 1857 engraving of the Tynwald ceremony at St John's shows clearly that little has changed in almost a century and a half. (MNHL)*

elected House of Keys stood condemned as the bastion of archaic and unjust laws which

> can only have been made in feudal times and when this island was the refuge of the swindler, the reprobate and the outlawed of other countrys [*sic*], and not as it now is, the haunt of the respectable, civil, military and naval Resident of large and also limited Incomes, who prefer a domicile here to spending their means in a Foreign Country.[77]

77] J.T. Thomson to Peel, 12 Jan 1835 (PRO: HO98/78). For sustained exposure of the inequities of the Manx legal and political system see J.T. Thomson, *Important to Stranger-Residents, and Landlords and Tenants of the Isle of Man. The Trial at Common Law, 'Thomson v. Kelly', at Castletown, 9th October 1833* (Liverpool, 1833).

Joseph Train, busily engaged in drafting the contemporary chapter of his *Historical and Statistical Account of the Isle of Man*, took a keen interest in the campaign, and reported to Lord John Russell that 'it is generally strangers who have been domiciled for a few years in the island who are most active in opposing the vested powers of the constituted authorities':

> I have not the smallest interest in advocating the cause of the people of Man, excepting the interest a Historian naturally feels in his desire to record facts in the light of truth ... while the House of Keys was at one time a popular assembly, elected by the 'whole commons of Man', it was also declared by the Deemsters and by the House of Keys themselves to be one of the prerogatives of the King of Man *to dispense altogether with the House of Keys* ... It might therefore be a question for your Lordship's consideration, whether our most Gracious Queen as in right of the ancient Kings of Man, might not dispense with the Manx Parliament altogether.[78]

The campaign ended in controversy. First there was dispute over the number and 'weight' of the petitioners, as Ready questioned the means by which the signatures (1,032 in total) had been secured, adding that 'a great many of the respectable and wealthy Inhabitants are favourable to the existing Constitution and desire no change'. The deputation, however, claimed that at least three-quarters of the landed proprietors had signed, the principal exceptions being Members of the House of Keys and the holders of public office. Furthermore they took exception to Ready's impolitic conduct in rejecting the petitions. As his correspondence with the Home Office reveals, Ready was anxious to isolate the reformers, to 'silence the persons who are agitating the question'. Hence he chose to express some plain truths as he understood British policy: an elected House of Keys would not be accorded control of the surplus revenue; and reform might well lead to incorporation – 'I have further to inform you that if a reform in the House of Keys is found to be really wanted, that a Representation for the Island in Parliament may be the measure of reform adopted.' The deputation refused to accept these points as British government policy unless confirmed in writing by the Home Secretary. In the end Ready was compelled to forward the petitions to the Home Office, where they were to rest unattended.[79]

78] Train to Russell, 14 June 1838 (PRO: HO98/80). Train, *Historical and Statistical Account*, i, 219–20.
79] Ready to Maule, 9 Mar, 13 Apr and 8 May: Deputation to Ready, 6 Mar, 21 Apr and 2 May (PRO: HO98/80); Maule to Ready, 21 Apr and 12 May 1838 (PRO: HO99/18 f 296–7 and 300–1).

Fiscal Reform

Although political reform proved divisive and contentious, the economic agenda of liberalism began to resonate, boosted by the readiness of the free-trade ideologue Dr John Bowring, philosophic radical and MP for Bolton, to champion the Island's interests in the Commons.[80] There was increasing criticism from merchants and reformers, both English and Manx, of harbour dues and fiscal duties which impeded trade and commerce. The ad valorem duties (ranging from 2.5 to 15 per cent) on imported goods of British manufacture were condemned as 'a form of taxation ... detrimental to the manufacturing and other trading interests of the united kingdom, whose goods should go free into that part of Her Majesty's dominions'.[81] The most trenchant criticism, however, was directed against the licence system, the mechanism which underpinned (and undermined) Manx fiscal privilege. Bowring's lucid exposition of the origins and operation of the system merits quotation at length:

> On the final sale of the island to the crown, the power was exercised by parliament of introducing such fiscal laws as were necessary to the protection of the British revenues ... the arrangement made was to prohibit the importation of all articles subject to high duties in Great Britain except under licence; and the quantity to be introduced under licence was defined by act of parliament, the distribution of the licences being left to the lieutenant-governor ... Monopoly and privilege thus assumed a strange form in the legislation of the Isle of Man. They were represented by the word *Licence*, – the most important articles of consumption being imported under licence alone, – and licences being granted under the authority of the ruling powers only, none but those in favour with the ruling powers could obtain them. Licences were given solely to the opulent and influential. The rich man revelled in cheap tea, cheap sugar, cheap spirits, cheap tobacco; – while the poor man paid double price for all the articles that he consumed, either to the privileged party who possessed a licence, or to the party who purchased licences of others. The trade in licences was an important one. They were sold by auction, – they were made the instrument of extorting higher rents, – they were employed in all ways for purposes of oppression and

80] Unfortunately there are only brief references to Manx matters in Sir John Bowring, *Autobiographical Recollections* (London, 1877), 19, 82 and 212–13.

81] See the memorial from several mercantile houses in Leeds, reported in *Times*, 27 Dec 1842. This and other criticism was rejected by the Keys in a letter to Ready, 5 July 1843 (MNHL: House of Keys Journal: Legislative ii, 9191/2/2, f 402–3).

corruption. The unprotected consumer paid a high price for what he wanted, that high price being caused by the licence monopoly.[82]

Sensitive to mounting criticism of what Train called 'huxtering in surplusages',[83] the British government put forward a package of measures in 1844 (one of Peel's 'first free trade experiments') by which an increase in fiscal duties (sufficient to render smuggling uneconomic, but stopping short of assimilation) would allow the abolition or suspension of the ad valorem duties and of the licence system other than for tobacco, spirits and eau-de-Cologne. Considerable care was taken to explain the underlying principles, a combination of conventional financial rectitude and 'single-market' free-trade optimism:

> In the first place they have deemed it desirable that the trade with the Isle of Man should be placed in all particulars where it is practicable upon the footing a Coasting Trade.
>
> Next they have been desirous to avoid the adoption of any measure which would have the effect of materially increasing the pressure of Taxation in the form of Import duties upon the Inhabitants of the Island.
>
> Thirdly, they have deemed it most of all important to avoid incurring the risk of converting the Isle of Man into a Depot for Contraband Trade.
>
> Lastly they have sought in all cases where it could be done without serious objections to give to the Trade of the Island what may be practicably termed an entire freedom.[84]

Reaction on the Island was predictably mixed. Despite annual complaint at the 'very anxious and laborious duty' of distributing licences in 'a just and impartial manner' (so as to exclude 'hucksters, petty publicans and petty retailers'), Ready defended the system by which 'the Island has derived many moral and political advantages; has produced a large amount of revenue and illicit trade is extinguished'. Hence he argued for increased quotas rather than abolition of licences.[85] The House of Keys remained locked in the gloomy rhetoric of 1837, oblivious to any potential commercial benefit:

82] Bowring, 'Free trade recollections: number II – The Isle of Man', *Howitt's Journal*, 30 Jan 1847, 58–61.
83] Train, *Historical and Statistical Account*, ii, 325.
84] Lefevre to Manners Sutton, 29 Feb 1844 (MNHL: House of Keys Journal ii, f 405-10).
85] Ready to Maule, 21 July 1838, 5 Oct 1839, and to Manners Sutton, 22 Apr 1842 and 6 June 1844 (MNHL: Letterbook iv, f 328–32, 372–4, 468–72 and 525–9).

The Keys most earnestly desire to call the attention of Her Majesty's Government to the poverty of the Isle of Man, without Trade or Manufactures ... The continual drain of capital from the Island is only supplied and can only be supplied by the small Incomes of British Residents, and the money expended by persons annually visiting the Island. But if by any alterations of Duties the Strangers be driven from the Island, an injury will be inflicted upon the country from which it can never be expected to recover.[86]

The Council was prepared to accept an increase in duties on the understanding that 'any surplus revenue created by alterations in the duties ought to be applied to the benefit of the Island and not to augment the revenue of Great Britain'. This was a carefully circumscribed proposal, avoiding any wider reference to political representation or insular autonomy: sums were to be allocated for specific improvements, such as harbour works and an asylum for the lunatic poor.[87]

Outside the Insular legislature the Peelite proposals were received with both greater enthusiasm and harsher criticism, reflecting, as Dr Buck observed, their character as 'half free trade, half monopolist, half conservative, half liberal'. Looking to the commercial benefits, speakers at the public meeting at Douglas Court House on 11 April 1844, chaired by Sir William Hillary, encouraged the government further towards free trade, recommending entire abolition of the ad valorem duties and the licence system, and calling also for the removal of the harbour dues (measures which Hillary had advocated privately as an ideal to Bluett in 1837). Much of the meeting, however, was sharply critical in tone, condemning the proposed increase in duties on the constitutional, political and economic grounds previously rehearsed in the anti-assimilation campaign of 1837. Once again John James Moore called upon his fellow Manxmen to take a united stand against imposition, oppression and injustice. Citing the hallowed historical precedent of the great inquest of 1643, he looked to delegates, duly elected at parish and town meetings, to stiffen the resolve of the Keys:

Did the Legislature and the delegates co-operate together – and he had no doubt if they did so, they would be backed by the country – they could not fail of success ... Let them firmly maintain their

86] John Moore to Graham, 10 Apr 1844 (MNHL: House of Keys Journal ii, f 411–16).
87] Ready to Manners Sutton, 21 Mar 1844 (MNHL: Letterbook iv, f 515–20, and Council Book ii, f 384–90).

inalienable rights; let the Legislature put themselves in a position to become a shield of the people and then duties might be modified as circumstance might require.

Fargher, of course, favoured a more radical course, looking to the election of parish commissioners (a kind of anti-parliament) to take command of the surplus revenue. While all speakers demanded Insular control of the surplus revenue (public wealth which rendered unnecessary the proposed increases in duty), none was prepared to second Fargher's amendment denying financial authority to the Keys as it was 'a self-elected irresponsible body'.[88] With the prospect of the virtual abolition of the licence system and other benefits, Manx politicians had no desire to entertain contentious political issues (or to persist too strongly in opposition to duty increases which still preserved a favourable differential). Thanks to astute lobbying by Bowring (assisted by a London delegation including R. Duff, T. Garrett, Jun, and S.S. Rogers), the Bill was amended in a most satisfactory manner to include abolition of the harbour dues and an annual grant of £2,300 out of the Customs revenue for use by the Harbour Commissioners. Bowring eagerly awaited the benefits of 'Manx commercial emancipation': 'The grand secret of commercial prosperity was to invite intercourse, not repel it. Their Fiscal laws and oppressive harbour duties had hitherto shut the gates of mercy.'[89]

In retrospect the Fiscal Bill of 1844 marked an important watershed in Manx economic and political development. Despite gloomy predictions to the contrary, there was no reversion to smuggling and no decline in population (emigration was a necessary safety valve of the traditional economy). 'The success has been most complete', Bowring observed in 1847:

> the revenues have greatly increased, – commercial transactions have been wonderfully augmented, – the value of the lands and houses, and all other property in the island, has been much elevated, – and a satisfaction almost universal (the exception being only among the few who lost the pride and privileges of monopoly) pervades the Manx community.[90]

Although hit badly by the potato blight, the Manx economy displayed considerable resilience. When a parish-by-parish survey

88] *Mona's Herald*, 17 Apr 1844.
89] 'Free trade in the Isle of Man', *Economist* 21 Sept 1844. Bowring's speech at Ramsey reported in *Mona's Herald*, 9 Oct 1844.
90] Bowring, 'Free trade recollections'.

confirmed that conditions were not as bad as elsewhere, the Keys accepted Hope's advice to withdraw their request for extraordinary measures of public relief and for the despatch of a parliamentary commission to investigate distress. External intervention, Hope feared, might undermine the distinctive virtues of the Insular economy: the voluntary basis of its poor relief (adequate for the needs of the small number of 'actual paupers'); and the stoic self-sufficiency of its workforce:

> The almost total failure of the potato crop and the partial failure of the crops of oats and barley, together with the deficiency of the produce of the Fishery during last year followed by an unusually severe Winter, has fallen very heavily upon a class of the people, who in ordinary years are well off, but who in case of a failure of their crops have no money or other resources to fall back upon but the produce of their labours ... I must add that under all the privations they are suffering, the conduct of the people has been most exemplary. There has been little complaint, and indeed it is not the nature of the people to complain. There has been no disturbance of any kind and the amount of crime has been very small and the number of Committals to Gaol less than has been usual at this period of the year.[91]

Having withstood the worst horrors of the 1840s, this solid subsistence economy provided the foundation for commercial expansion.

Guide books and other promotional literature were soon expatiating on commercial growth and potential, not least in mining, hoping to attract a more entrepreneurial type of in-comer. Colonel Johnson's *Brief Sketch of the Isle of Man* (1851), a publication funded by the Steam Packet Company and a 'Town Committee', offered an enticing prospectus:

> Aside from our fisheries, it cannot be boasted of native Manxmen, that they are emulous or illustrious for enterprize. They have hitherto left the field open, that others may step in and reap the harvest ... in no place in the Kingdom or in Europe could capital be introduced and invested in shipping, manufactories, and commerce, with a certain prospect of a good return, better than on the Isle of Man ... the extent of our natural resources, now hid in the recesses of the mountains,

91] Hope to Grey, 9 Feb, Goldie Taubman (Speaker, House of Keys) to Hope, 9 Mar and 9 Apr 1847 (MNHL: Letterbook v, f 285–91, 312–14 and 335–6). For details of the survey, but not alas its precise findings, see report of Tynwald, 10 Apr 1847 (MNHL: Council Book ii, f 495–9).

might convert his little Isle into an European Potosi, or an insular California, thereby doubling the value of real estate.[92]

Commercial development brought economic costs: there was steady upward pressure on Manx prices as the Island adjusted to the wider 'single' market facilitated by the new legislation (and by continued improvement in steam transport). Such a rise in the cost of living was unwelcome to those who still identified the Island's economic fortunes with the presence of the straitened and superannuated gentility. As price differentials were eroded, the need to defend the remaining Manx fiscal privileges became all the more important. However, for those who favoured commercial growth, the political priority shifted from retention of fiscal privilege to control of the surplus revenue, the means by which harbour and other necessary improvements could be funded. As defence of Manx autonomy was critical to both economic camps, economic and ideological division was exposed less in negotiation with the British than in Insular politics.

Bowring and Reform

During his triumphal tour of the Island in autumn 1844, celebrating the end of the licence system – 'the poor man at Laxey being now enabled to purchase on precisely the same terms as the rich man at Castletown' – Bowring carried the free trade struggle into politics. Free trade required free institutions, the removal of the 'incubus of bad institutions and bad laws' which impeded commercial progress. As a first step the Keys had to be reformed so as 'to harmonize with the spirit of the age':

> They needed to reform their House of Keys and not overturn them ... I will not lend my aid to overturn any of your venerable institutions ... Their insular affairs required a local legislature; and if they could be as successful in reforming the House of Keys as they had been in obtaining the Fiscal Bill, then their Keys would soon become the House of the people of the Isle of Man.[93]

Thus encouraged, reformers mounted a major petitioning campaign for an elected House of Keys, co-ordinated (not without regional friction) by the newly formed Ramsey-based Northern Association 'to secure representation of the People in the legislature by Election by Ballot'.[94]

92] Colonel Johnson, *A Brief Sketch of the Isle of Man, Showing its Advantages as a Retreat to Visitors and Place of Residence to Strangers* (Douglas, 1851), 21.
93] See the extensive reports in *Mona's Herald*, 1 and 9 Oct. 1844.
94] Ann Harrison, 'Reform from the North, 1844-1847', *Proceedings*, VIII (1982), 402–12.

The effects of mining on fishing *Because the run-off from the Foxdale mines had destroyed the lugworm on Peel shore, the Peel men used to walk to Douglas to dig for bait. (Major F.C. Harris (MNHL))*

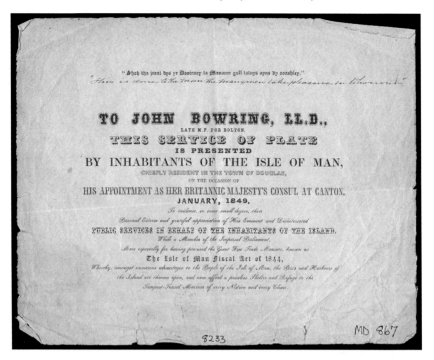

Printed address of presentation of plate to Dr John Bowring *Dr John Bowring MP actively supported reform of the House of Keys by encouraging three petitions which were presented to Lieutenant-Governor Colonel Ready in 1845. (MNHL)*

Throughout the campaign, as R.E.C. Forster has observed, support was strongest in 'commercial centres where the growth of a wealthy and politically conscious trading class bred resentment of a self-elect, land-dominated legislature' and in that area 'most geographically isolated from the Clique, Ramsey and the North'.[95] In January and February 1845 three petitions were presented to Ready signed by 5,386 inhabitants out of a total adult male population calculated as eight thousand by J.J. Moore.[96]

The signatories, Ready assured the Home Office, 'represent a small portion of the real property and intelligence of the Island ... no member of the Manx legal profession appears to have signed the Petitions except one, and none of the Manx Clergy but two, a Vicar

95] R.E.C. Forster, *A study of the constitutional and financial movements of the Isle of Man 1833–1866*, unpublished BA dissertation, University of Birmingham, nd.
96] The petitions are printed in PP 1845 (106) XLV.

and a Curate'. Ready provided brief biographical details of the eighteen figures most prominent in the campaign, four of whom were identified as recent in-comers (Torrance, Rogers, the American 'Colonel' Johnson, and Dr Buck, former chaplain of Liverpool gaol). Most were engaged in the retail sector: four grocers (Torrance, R. Duff and the Garrets, senior and junior, who also owned twenty acres of land), one shopkeeper (J. Duff), one draper (Cubbin), one druggist (R. Kelly), one tallow chandler (W. Kelly), one general dealer (Duggin) and two tailors (Hales and Kerruish); there were two newspaper editors (Fargher and 'Colonel' Johnson); one farmer (J.J. Moore, whose stock and effects 'were lately advertised for sale by the officers of the law'); one merchant (William Callister, 'possessed of considerable personal property'); and two landowners (Rogers and Clucas, a former captain in the merchant navy, now qualified by his considerable landed property for membership of the House of Keys).[97]

The Keys despatched a report to the Home Office, denigrating the 'system of agitation' which

> appears to have originated with a few shopkeepers, to have been adopted by some stranger residents, who, under a plea of 'reform', desire to subvert the constitution of the country where, for reasons best known to themselves, they have sought an asylum; and who, by means of false representations, and by holding out advantages not likely to be realized, have induced some landowners to join in the agitation now in question.

For good measure the petitioners were accused of malpractice, swelling the numbers by adding the names of 'common labourers, illiterate people unable to write', as well as the signatures of Irish fishermen in port. The rest of the report upheld the virtues of the established order, insisting that substantial landowners alone possessed the independence, integrity and education to discharge the legislative and judicial capacities of the Keys. While the general principle of popular election was unobjectionable, its implementation would be detrimental

---

97] Ready to Manners Sutton, 14 Feb 1845 (PRO: HO45/943, and MNHL: Letterbook iv, f 536–42). Some leaders described themselves in slightly different terms at the heads of the petitions. For further biographical details see the notes to 'Hunt the Keys', a squib by John Kelly, High Bailiff of Castletown, originally published anonymously in 1837 and reprinted in *Manx Society*, XVI (1869), 112–20. The section on 'Reformers' in A.W. Moore, *Manx Worthies* (Douglas, 1901), 185–91 is disappointing: of those involved in the petition campaign only William Callister and Robert Fargher are accorded entries.

it would necessarily entail a considerable expense upon the people, and, from the isolated position and very limited extent of the island, would engender a degree of bitter animosity among neighbours, highly prejudicial and strongly contrasted to the hitherto peaceable state of society.

Furthermore, as the Keys formed the highest court of appeal in civil cases from the common law courts, it 'would be impracticable to have the Keys returned by popular election, without making other and extensive alterations in the constitution of the island'. However, seemingly oblivious of any contradiction, the Keys announced its willingness to embrace the elective principle if this would secure access to the surplus revenue!![98]

There was angry reaction when details of the report, drawn up behind closed doors (and before all three petitions had been presented), became public.[99] Particular exception was taken to the defamation of stranger-residents, an 'unmerited insult on a most respectable class of men who have never expressed sentiments unsuited to British subjects, and who are frequently the most extensive capitalists on the island'. There was ardent defence of the signatures of the 'illiterate' in line with Manx custom: 'although such a mode of signing is not customary in England, yet in the Isle of Man, a person wishing his name to be written for him, and evidencing his consent thereto by merely touching the pen, is considered sufficient even in our courts of law'. As for the Irish fishermen, they were a figment of the Keys' imagination.

Through meticulous point-by-point refutation of the calumnious, erroneous and inconsistent report, a procedure adopted in numerous memorials and open letters of protest to Ready, the Home Office and the Queen, the reformers turned the argument to their advantage. Not only was reform kept in the forefront of public attention, but, with the credibility of the self-elected House of Keys under question, the petitioners could claim the high ground. Their purpose – in line with Bowring's injunction – was to safeguard and revitalise the ancient constitution, 'to have it restored in its pristine purity'. 'Election of the Keys', J.J. Moore repeatedly emphasised, 'will not be an alteration, but a restoration of soundness to that constitution.' In vindication of the reformers' case, Colonel Campbell, nominated by the Keys and selected by the Lieutenant-Governor, refused to be sworn in to fill a vacancy in the self-elected chamber.[100]

98] Printed in PP 1845 (106) XLV.
99] All the relevant material can be consulted in PP 1846 (88) XXXIII.
100] There is additional material on the Campbell affair in PRO: HO45/943.

Presented in popular constitutional manner – the rhetoric also favoured by radicals in Britain – reform could attract a broad constituency.[101] As Ready feared, the reformers were able to draw upon considerable discontent, the consequence of unpopular legislation and the recent collapse of the Isle of Man Joint Stock Bank. The assimilation of Manx currency (with its fourteen-pence shilling) into that of Great Britain was still the cause of much complaint: on its introduction in 1840 there had been extensive rioting, most serious at Peel where the civil power had been 'set completely at defiance and driven from the field'.[102] Other legislation, recently passed or in process, proved no less contentious: the introduction of game licences;[103] the proposed registration of the medical profession, an 'insidious attempt at the establishment of an unjust and hateful monopoly', Fargher remonstrated, 'under the pretence of putting down quackery';[104] restrictions on the printing and publications of news-papers;[105] and laws for civil registration and the solemnization of marriage, so 'hostile to the principles of religious liberty and equality' as to unite Catholics, Presbyterians, Independents, Wesleyan and Primitive Methodists against the Anglican establishment.[106] The most

101] J.A. Epstein, 'The constitutionalist idiom' in his *Radical Expression: Political Language, Ritual and Symbol in England, 1790–1850* (New York, 1994), 3–28.

102] Ready to Maule, 26 and 29 Sept, 2 Oct 1840, 4 and 17 Jan 1841 (MNHL: Letterbook iv, f 411–18, 427–31). Ready was reprimanded for failure to liaise with the military in quelling the riots; see Maule to Ready, 26 Sept, 18 and 28 Oct 1840 (PRO: HO99/18 f 447–8, 455–6 and 464–5). See also *Times* 9 Oct 1840. See also J.B. Laughton's satirical song, 'The Copper Row', reprinted in *Manx Society*, XVI (1869), 118–20.

103] Money raised from the sale of licences was used for highway repairs.

104] *Mona's Herald*, 1 Apr, 7 Oct 1843, 29 June, 23 July and 13 Aug 1844. Minutes, 10 Mar 1843 (MNHL: Council Book ii, f 347–8). See also, M. Killip, *The Folklore of the Isle of Man* (London, 1975), 48–52, on the failure of the scheme. The Medical Society brought forward similar legislation in 1858, noting that 'the enactment of a Bill here might indirectly aid the movement in Britain for this Island is by nature intended to be an experimental garden to England', Mackenzie to Walpole, 29 June 1858 (MNHL: Letterbook viii, f 250–1).

105] Legislation passed in 1846 enacted that no person should print or publish a newspaper till they had signed a declaration specifying personal and business details; see *Statutes*, iii, 159–64.

106] Report of Tynwald, 5 July 1843, and subsequent consideration of Memorial presented by France (Methodist), Haining (Independent) and McGrath (Roman Catholic) (MNHL: Council Book ii, f 351–62). There is a vast amount of correspondence in the Letterbooks, particularly after Bowring took up the issue, see, for example, the enclosures in Manners Sutton to Hope, 26 Feb and Hope's reply, 3 Mar 1846 (MNHL: Letterbook v, f 98–108).

serious grievance, however, related to 'bank-director legislation', the close involvement of leading members of the Keys in the ill-fated affairs of the Isle of Man Joint Stock Bank.

In July 1842 James Holmes, manager of Mungo Murray's estates on the Island, reported his concern about 'Building Companies and other foolish Speculations ... Forbes has left the Island who was manager of the Share Bank, its [sic] stated we shall not see him back.'[107] A year later the Bank collapsed. To the anguish of ruined shareholders, the directors, all members of the House of Keys (as had been the fugitive manager), escaped the consequences of 'this most disgraceful of joint-stock bubbles'. To the Chartist Bronterre O'Brien, a recent arrival on the Island, the history of the bank, its formation, seven year existence and ultimate bankruptcy, was an instructive lesson in Manx procedures, revealing a 'system of falsehood, fraud, and wilful imposition'. The directors, having lived like princes in the Island through gross abuse of credit, were 'still continuing in the same position in society, still rolling in their carriages, without the law having been able to reach them or bring them to account for the satisfaction of those whom they have so grievously wronged'.[108] The collapse of the Bank, indeed, prompted Bowring into a full-scale critical examination of the inequities, inadequacies and constitutional improprieties of Manx law.

Ready was convinced that the strength of the reform movement, or rather the unpopularity of the Keys, stemmed from the bank failure: in listing the leaders of the petition campaign he underlined the names of those who were shareholders (Hales, R. Duff, J. Duff, Fargher and Cubbin). Unfortunately, Ready's rapidly declining health made matters worse, precluding his attendance at the Court of Chancery. In the absence of precedent, the Home Office refused to appoint a Deputy Governor or Chancellor pro tempore.[109] Pending consideration of suits and petitions by the Court, the estates and funds of the hapless shareholders remained 'under arrest'. Inundated by letters of protest at the 'serious delays which have almost the consequence of a denial of justice', Bowring implored Sir James Graham (then in the midst of the Maynooth controversy) to give urgent attention to the 'practical anomalies and absurdities' of 'Manx affairs'.[110]

107] Holmes to Mungo Murray, 12 July 1842 (SRO: GD190/3/351).
108] Extract from O'Brien's *National Reformer* in *Mona's Herald*, 20 Nov 1844. See also *Times*, 15 Aug, 8, 14 and 21 Sept 1843.
109] Ready to Manners Sutton, 22 Feb, 1 Mar and 7 May, and Manners Sutton's reply, 12 May 1845 (MNHL: Letterbook iv, f 543–7, 555–60).
110] Bowring's letters and enclosures to Graham, 25 Apr–6 May 1845 (PRO: HO45/943).

On appointment as Lieutenant-Governor following Ready's death in July 1845, Charles Hope, former MP for Linlithgowshire, was greeted with polite but strongly worded memorials from the regional groupings of reformers (north, south and Douglas), protesting at inattention to and misrepresentation of their earlier petitions, and repeating the demand for a popularly elected House of Keys. With pressure for reform intensifying, the Home Office instructed Hope to inquire into the justice of complaints against the Keys and the extent of support for constitutional change among respectable inhabitants. In asking for Hope's own opinion as to the desirability of change, the Home Office insisted he 'should not lose sight of the question of revenue ... to a proposition for the surrender of this revenue, or any part of it, the Government is not prepared to accede'.[111]

Hope delayed his reply until after he had met a deputation of the memorialists on 23 December. Boosted by Fargher's recent release from prison (whence he had been consigned on conviction for criminal libel against G.W. Dumbell, bank-director, attorney and leading anti-reformer in the House of Keys),[112] the reformers were further encouraged by Hope's seemingly favourable response to their case. This was to prove a serious misjudgment. Although by no means as crass and injudicious as the Keys' report of 27 January, Hope's letter to the Home Office on 30 December was of similar purport, dismissing the need for reform and questioning the strength of the stranger-originated movement in its favour. Hence, when its contents became public, there was recharged outrage.[113] Angered at being misled by Hope (an allegation he denied strenuously), the reformers despatched further memorials to the Home Office, claiming 'the people's rights as British subjects' to representative and responsible government. The Isle of Man, they rued, 'presents the anomaly of an enthralled islet in the very heart of the home empire (which acknowledges no other than free institutes), an evident foil to those countries, as a satire ... a drag upon the progress of modern civilization'.

'I am not prepared to deny that an anomaly is presented by the existence in an Island almost within sight of England, and forming part of Her Majesty's dominions, of institutions very dissimilar from those of this country', Sir George Grey observed in an important letter to

111] All the material was printed in PP 1846 (88) XXXIII.
112] Chappell, *Dumbell Affair*, 22–3.
113] All relevant material (on which the following analysis is based) was printed in PP 1847 (141) LIX Memorials and Correspondence on Reform of House of Keys.

Hope which, in outlining the fundamental British position, sought to take account of the reformers' grievances:

> I cannot, however, consider the Isle of Man in the light of British colony, entitled as such to a separate Legislature, based on a representative system. I regard it rather as a portion of the mother country, possessing, indeed, from accidental circumstances, peculiar customs and institutions, but from its position and constant intercourse with other parts of the kingdom, capable of being incorporated with the United Kingdom, and of being admitted, by such incorporation, to a participation in those free institutions of which the memorialists speak in terms of just admiration.

Not wishing 'to press or even suggest any such incorporation contrary to the wishes or inclinations of the inhabitants of the Island', he called upon Hope and the Keys to give careful consideration to what appeared serious grounds of complaint: the union of legislative and judicial functions in the House of Keys, and the large number of lawyers among its members; the absence of any effective check on the levying or expenditure of 'rates' (that is, the highway fund which was collected by a uniform tax on property, from beer, wine and spirit and game licences, and the dog tax); and the alleged enactment of laws without any opportunity for the expression of public opinion.

Hope and the Keys refused to acknowledge any just grievance: the union of functions and presence of members of the Manx Bar in the Keys led to 'no practical evil'; annual accounts were published of the 'trifling' amount raised for the highway fund; and all Bills brought before the Keys and/or the Council were ordered to be printed. While prepared to consider 'any mode by which the proceedings of the Legislature can be made more public', the Keys dismissed further refutation of the memorialists' arguments as a waste of time:

> but if any further proof was required, the Keys consider it is found in the fact of the rapid and continued increase in the prosperity of this island, and that hundreds and thousands of the inhabitants of Great Britain, although partakers of the benefits of 'popular election' (of which the memorialists are so enamoured), leave all the advantages to be derived therefrom, and enjoy in the island a happy and peaceful retreat.[114]

114] Hope's reply (26 Jan) to Grey's key letter of 18 Jan 1847, can be found in PP 1847 (141) LIX. For the Keys see Goldie Taubman, 9 Mar 1847 (MNHL: Letterbook v, f 304–11, and printed in *Papers Relative to the Political Condition of the Isle of Man* (PRO: HO45/943).

This was by no means the end of the matter. The reformers came forward with resolutions of no confidence in Hope accompanied by demands for the appointment of a parliamentary commission to investigate 'publicly on oath the circumstances under which this island is now politically suffering'.[115] Hope, the 'uncompromising enemy of the Reforming party', was roundly condemned at public meetings and in the press:

> Their memorials have been misconstrued; their objects perverted, their wills gainsayed [sic]; their motives impugned; and their inclinations thwarted by Governor Hope. *Clique* influence has been his law, opposition to Reform his motto, and contented degradation his text and his mandate; and all, forsooth, because he was a Tory.[116]

The demand for a parliamentary commission, a fitting culmination to Bowring's ceaseless lobbying at Westminster, gathered pace, fuelled by continuing controversy over civil registration and by outrage at the latest scandal, the most glaring instance of the absurdities and injustice of a 'Danish' system in which Tynwald lawyers 'commence as legislators, proceed as counsel and terminate as judges'. Acting in its appellate capacity, the Keys decided to increase the damages awarded to Grellier, editor of the *Manx Sun*, in his libel action against Penrice and Wallace, publishers of the *Manx Liberal*, from 40s to £100. As member (and secretary) of the House of Keys, G.W. Dumbell, counsel for the plaintiff in the inferior court, sat as one of the judges on appeal!

> No reformer on this island, by any efforts he might make, could so effectually subserve the cause of the people, and hasten on reform as has done the Secretary of the House of Keys in the present instance. He has made the Manx judiciary look supremely ridiculous by his persevering in a constitutional privilege.[117]

Appalled by improprieties of this order (even Hope considered Dumbell's conduct injudicious),[118] some reformers moved towards a more radical (and previously unthinkable) agenda. Where Bowring and his supporters looked to a parliamentary commission and emulation of the Channel Islands, the *Manx Liberal* began to advocate incorporation into England, the only means to ensure the 'disenthralment of the

115] All material related to this campaign can be found in *Papers relative*.
116] *Manx Liberal*, 28 Aug 1847.
117] *Mona's Herald*, 27 Jan 1847 (also in *Papers Relative*).
118] Hope to Somerville, 5 Feb 1847 in *Papers Relative*.

people of this island from the Scandinavian barbarisms under which they have hitherto suffered ... Annexation we hold to be infinitely preferable, and far more likely to promote the Island's welfare than any system of local Reform.'[119] The new *Isle of Man Times*, edited by William Shirrefs, announced itself 'decidedly in favour of Union with England': negotiations should commence forthwith to ensure retention of fiscal and postal privileges within an incorporation package.[120] A Scotsman who had first come to the Island in the 1830s, Shirrefs was the leading figure in the Manx 'unstamped' of the 1840s. Free of stamp duty, paper duty and advertisement tax, papers published on the Isle of Man were entitled to free postage throughout Britain, a privilege extended to include repostage in 1840. Papers could thus be sent post-free to mainland agents for wider distribution through the post at no further cost. Shirrefs exploited these arrangements to considerable 'niche-market' effect, providing inexpensive propaganda for temperance advocates, various 'faddist' and activist groups; cheap 'in-house' journals for affiliated friendly societies, amalgamated trade unions and political organisations; and repackaged news for journals suitable for the Victorian family home. The *Isle of Man Times*, with its progressive agenda of incorporation and improvement, was financed out of the profits from this off shore printing and publishing.[121]

Shirrefs's success was in marked contrast to the sad fate of Bronterre O'Brien, the schoolmaster of Chartism, whose estate in the Isle of Man was finally wound up in May 1848. A disaffected activist, O'Brien had left London for Douglas in 1844, seeking to use the publishing and postal privileges to challenge the 'demagogue-tyranny' of both Feargus O'Connor and Daniel O'Connell. By condemning the 'palliatives' pursued by trade unions, benefit societies, and other organised forms of working-class collective mutuality, he denied himself the printing, publishing and advertising revenue that Shirrefs was able to attract.[122]

119] *Manx Liberal*, 1 May 1847.

120] *Isle of Man Times*, 13 Feb and 5 June 1847.

121] John Belchem, 'Radical entrepreneur: William Shirrefs and the Manx free press of the 1840s', *Proceedings*, X (1992), 33–47. See also James Cowin, *Reminiscences of Notable Douglas Citizens and a Review of Manx Men and Manners Fifty Years Ago* (Douglas, 1902), 42.

122] John Belchem, 'The neglected "unstamped": the Manx pauper press of the 1840s', *Albion*, XXIV (1992), 605–16. See R.C.M. Fyson, 'Bronterre O'Brien: A Chartist in the Isle of Man, 1844–1847', *Proceedings*, X-4 (1998), 393–400. Unfortunately he has not been able to locate the first series (nos 1–75, Nov 1844–Apr 1846) of O'Brien's *National Reformer and Manx Weekly Review of Home and Foreign Affairs*, surely among the most important radical papers to have gone missing.

Furthermore he poured critical scorn on the 'sham-radical' Manx reformers, the 'new Liberal plutocracy' who refused to commit themselves to universal suffrage:

> the getters up of the agitation, are known to be insincere self-seekers, who, caring not a straw for the rights of the multitude, want just as much reform as may instal their own profit-mongering class in the House of Keys; but shall, at the same time, effectually exclude the working people from all chance of being represented in that or any other House. To pull down those above them, and to keep down those below them – such is the *bona fide* intent of the Manx Reform clique.[123]

Despite discordant voices on its fringes, the reform movement displayed considerable persistence, running in parallel with protracted legal actions over the bank collapse and newspaper libels. However, the motion for a parliamentary commission, finally presented on 2 March 1848, was a disappointing climax. Bowring, who 'appeared to be suffering from indisposition', called for the reform and modernization, not the abolition, of immemorial institutions 'to which the Manx people were fondly attached'. He decided to withdraw the motion, however, when Sir George Grey insisted that

> a complete remedy for the evils complained of was to be found, not in a separate legislature for a small island within a few hours' sail of the British coast, but, on the contrary, in the complete incorporation of the Isle of Man with the United Kingdom.[124]

Faced with the explicit threat of incorporation, the movement collapsed. 'However anxious we might be to conceal the fact', the *Manx Liberal* was soon forced to acknowledge, 'the circumstance that Reformers, if not Reform, is on the wane, is too obvious not to be admitted.'[125] Bowring continued at his post, lobbying on the Island's behalf and presenting petitions (while engaging with Dumbell in the press). Such efforts, however, lacked the public support previously enjoyed.[126] Bowring, the *Manx Sun* observed, stood alone as 'Self-Installed Protector of the rights and liberties of all and sundry, Her Majesty's *dis*contented lieges in the Isle of Man; and Grievance-Monger General of the United Kingdom of Great Britain and

123] Extract from O'Brien's *National Reformer* in *Manx Sun*, 27 Sept 1845.
124] *Parliamentary Debates*, xcvii, cols 125–7.
125] *Manx Liberal*, 29 Apr 1848.
126] *Manx Liberal*, 29 Apr 1848. *Isle of Man Times*, 29 July–2 Sept 1848.

Ireland'.[127] In the absence of 'pressure from without', the *Isle of Man Times* was reduced to sophistry, arguing the case for reform on the basis of the Britishness of the 'Celtic' Manx at a time of rising and revolution elsewhere:

> If more proof were wanting of the loyalty of the Manx people than their perfect quiescence and obedience under every reign for four hundred years, it would now be found in their peaceable and orderly conduct, while all is convulsed around them. Having much of the blood of the Celts flowing in their veins, and many of them descended from Irish families, nevertheless they feel no sympathy with Irish repeal; no commotion, no rising, no brawling, no discontent other than, as being men and Britons, they have hitherto been treated by their rulers as slaves and serfs, having no part in representative rights. Could her Majesty know our loyalty and attachment to her throne and person – could she know how discreetly and orderly we should exercise the elective franchise, sure we are that she would no longer withhold it from us.[128]

Immune from the revolutions of 1848, the Isle of Man returned to normality, advertising its virtues (superior to those of Jersey and Guernsey) as safe haven for genteel refugees, for 'English and Irish families who have flocked from the Continent owing to its revolutionary movements'.[129] Tranquillity seemed assured when legislation was introduced to remove the postal privileges of the Manx unstamped, 'snuffing out Adventurer Shirrefs, and his crew of Socialists, Chartists, Communists and Jacobins of every hue'.[130]

Insular Politics

Following the collapse of the campaign for a parliamentary commission, Manx politics became more inward-looking, but no less contentious, driven by tension and rivalry between town and country, commercial and landed interests. Controversy over the Towns Bill 1848, permissive legislation enabling the towns to elect commissioners and levy rates for paving, cleansing, sewerage, lighting and other improvements marked the transition. In an apparent reversal

127] *Manx Sun*, 10 May 1848. The leading conservative Manx unstamped paper had previously dismissed Bowring as 'one of that small *coterie* who live upon grievances, real or imaginary ... How he came to be the patron saint here we know not', *Church of England Journal*, 30 Sept 1846.
128] *Isle of Man Times*, 29 July 1848.
129] *Manx Liberal*, 22 Apr 1848.
130] *Manx Sun*, 2 May 1849.

of roles, this progressive (and much-needed) measure was promoted by the Insular legislature but rejected decisively in Douglas in a public campaign organised by William Kelly and other prominent reformers, long-time advocates of municipal improvement.[131]

Applauding the intention of the measure, the Douglas reformers sought at first to amend the proposed ways and means of its implementation. Their amendments, however, were dismissed by the Keys in 'contumelious, unbecoming, contemptuous and offensive language'. Thereafter there was resolute opposition: to the reformers the Towns Bill symbolised the inequities of a political system dominated by 'landed proprietors residing in the country', exposing the underrepresentation and over-taxation (in the highway fund) of the towns. Boundaries were redrawn to ensure that, among others, Colonel Goldie-Taubman, the Speaker of the Keys, and Dumbell, its Secretary, would be exempt from the proposed urban rates, a 'glaring specimen of the partial legislation imposed on Manxmen by their self-constituted legislators'. This town/country antagonism was compounded by rivalry within the urban hierarchy. In recognition of its demographic and commercial growth and pre-eminence, Douglas demanded 'an entirely independent municipal constitution':

> The Bill, possibly, may suit the town of Peel, for instance, consisting, as it does, of 'five streets and some narrow lanes', and containing less than 2,200 inhabitants. But it does not follow that it is an eligible Bill for the flourishing town of Douglas, with its population of nearly 12,000, and its numerous, enterprising, public-spirited and intelligent citizens.

'I have a tremendous task before me', Bluett confided to his diary on appointment in September 1851 as High Bailiff of Douglas: 'The Town is in a most wretched state and none but general measures can remedy the evil, but the people are so opposed to all taxation that I fear they will hardly ever consent to any Towns Bill.'[132] As the refusal to adopt the Towns Bill evinced, English rate-based models of municipal improvement were inapplicable. Indeed rejection of rates was aggravated by fierce contention over the highway fund, resented as a disproportionate 'poll-tax' charge on urban householders. Dispute over disparities in the fund (and its irresponsible management by the Keys) continued for many years, as Douglas-based reformers demanded

131] The following analysis is based on Correspondence relating to Towns Bill, May 1848–Jan 1852, PP 1852 (322) XXVIII.
132] J.C. Bluett: autograph diary (MNIIL: MD10141A), 20.

proper accountability and a more equitable distribution.[133] Such internal political divisions cut across the external struggle with the British for control of the surplus revenue. At an annual average of £20,319 over the last twenty years, the surplus stood at £406,398 by the early 1850s.[134] For the rate-resisting Manx the surplus revenue became imbued with 'some of the marvellous productive qualities of the widow's cruse of oil – that, however, frequently it might be called upon to provide funds for public works, this surplus revenue should never diminish'.[135]

Through hard bargaining in 1853 and 1854 the Manx made limited advance towards application of the revenue to Insular purposes. In 1853 the British government announced its intention to abolish the last remnants of the licence system and the ad valorem duties, again relying on modest increases in duty to prevent smuggling.[136] As in previous negotiations Manx politicians sought to moderate the duty increases (J.J. Moore again proposed a self-adjusting system based on 'the relative portion of the English duties upon importations into the island, instead of a fixed amount of duty'), and to gain insular control of any additional revenue raised. However, anxiety was heightened when the Treasury decided to incorporate the new duties into the General Customs Consolidation Bill, a utilitarian measure to regularise all laws and regulations on trade and Customs in the United Kingdom and British possessions abroad into one act. The Manx were outraged at this denial of separate status and privileges: however, one disgruntled former stranger-resident, an acquaintance of Shirrefs, implored the Treasury to ignore the pertinacious grumbling of the Manx and proceed with incorporation, 'treating this island (bought and paid for by our Government in hard cash) as you would Wight or Skye'. In order not to delay the global matters covered by the Bill, the Treasury readily agreed to amend its title to be 'a consolidation of the Customs Acts of the United Kingdom *and the Isle of Man*'. This was sufficient to satisfy the reform delegates (Fargher, Duff, Clarke, Harris and their

---

133] *Brown's Directory*, 43–52. The most persistent critic of the fund was F. Cubbin: see, for example, his letters to Insular and Whitehall officials of 30 Sept 1857, 14 and 27 Jan and 7 July 1859 (MNHL: Letterbook viii, f 206–7, 474–80 and 570–2).

134] PP 1852–3 (501) XCIX Return of Gross Revenue Collected at Isle of Man, 1805-53; Gross Income from Crown Lands in Island, 1828–53.

135] Loch's speech at the Great Manx gathering in Liverpool, *Isle of Man Times*, 27 Jan 1883, extract in SRO: GD268/119.

136] All material was presented in PP 1852–3 (982) XCIX Treasury Minutes and Correspondence between Treasury and Authorities of Isle of Man on Customs Reform. It includes items previously printed in PP 1852 (662), (746) and (847) XCIX.

chair, J.J. Moore, who was now permanently based in London, at Pump-Court in the Temple). In similar manner to Hope and the Council, they largely refrained from further criticism other than on minor financial detail. There was general appreciation of the benefits to be derived from eradication of the licence system, abolition of the 15 per cent ad valorem duty, and (much applauded in Ramsey) the opening up of trade to all ports on the Island.

The Keys, however, decided to take a stand on constitutional principle. Dumbell and Callister were despatched to London as an official delegation to remind the British government that the Isle of Man was neither part of the United Kingdom nor a British possession abroad:

> The Isle of Man has all the essence of an independent state. She is not indebted to Great Britain for her constitution ... true the constitution has been encroached upon, though not demolished; but so much the more does it behove the people, to whom the remnant has been transmitted, jealously to protect it against any further aggression.

To the annoyance of the Treasury (which was prepared to concede some of the additional revenue from increased duties to the insular authorities), Dumbell and Callister prolonged these strictly fiscal negotiations by raising 'inadmissible' constitutional arguments concerning an extraneous matter, the annual and accumulated surplus revenue. As champions of Manx rights, the vulnerability of the Keys' stance was soon exposed. Fargher and the reform delegates disavowed their credentials as representatives of the Manx people. Running short of patience, Wilson at the Treasury read them a political lesson:

> if the House of Keys had been a representative body, elected by the people of the island, the Lords of the Treasury would have been disposed to have taken a much more favourable view of your proposal to entrust to it the administration of these funds, and the control of the improvements and works to be effected thereby.

Caught unawares by such bluntness, one of the delegates immediately returned to the Island to confer with other members of the Keys. They drew up a letter to Palmerston, the Home Secretary, seeking confirmation and assurance of the British position:

> The House of Keys are the constitutional guardians of the rights and privileges of the Isle of Man; the only representatives of the people ... it would ill become the House of Keys to seek to withhold from the people a voice in selecting their representatives, and most especially when those Representatives claim upon constitutional principles a

right to impose taxes for local purposes, to control the imposition of duties by the Imperial Parliament, and to disburse the revenue of the Island after providing for the expenses of Government there.

We now beg leave respectfully to request that your Lordship will be good enough to state whether in case an Act of Tynwald is passed to provide for the election of the House of Keys by the people, your Lordship will deem it consistent with your duty to recommend the Royal Assent to be given to such Act?[137]

Hope interrupted his vacation to express concern at such irregular and unauthorised conduct. Still opposed to reform, he admitted to some perplexity as the two essential premises of his position apparently no longer applied: the refusal of the Treasury to surrender any of the revenue; and the unequivocal hostility of the Keys to constitutional change. The revenue, he reminded the Home Office, bore no relation to the needs of the Island 'as the duties are laid on not to provide for certain expenditure, but for the protection of British commerce against illicit traffic':

> If therefore the claims of the Insular Legislature were successful, this would place very large funds at the disposal of an assembly elected by a small community, where of course personal and local interests must have great weight in the disposal of those funds. It is probable also that an assembly so elected would claim far greater and more arbitrary power than the present House has ever attempted to exercise. I have no doubt that these claims would in a very short time place an elected House of Keys at issue with the British Government and with any Council consisting of Members nominated by the Crown – and would probably result before long in the necessity for some further interference by Government and by Parliament.[138]

There was to be no further reference to constitutional change. Dumbell and Callister continued to test the patience of the Treasury until a final settlement was imposed: the Island was accorded one-ninth of the gross annual revenue to be expended on public works, 'it being clearly understood that the necessary improvements in the harbours shall take priority to other works; such works to be determined by the Court of Tynwald, the Lieutenant-Governor having a veto, and to be executed under direction of the Lords Commissioners of the Treasury'. As a

137] Dumbell and Callister to Palmerston, 2 Aug 1853 (MNHL: Letterbook vi, f 567–72). There is no reference to this in the Parliamentary Papers.
138] Hope (Featherstone Castle) to Fitzroy, 26 Aug 1853 (MNHL: Letterbook vi, f 578–95). This too does not appear in the Parliamentary Papers.

further safeguard and check, Palmerston subsequently advised Hope
that the Keys 'should do nothing in the way of expending money on
Harbours without the sanction of the Lords Commissioners of the
Admiralty'.[139]

Despite these extensive negotiations, matters were far from settled.
Within a year, the Manx were again locked in dispute with the
Treasury, their sensitivities provoked by a hastily announced change in
the Public Revenue and Consolidated Funds Charges Bill. Henceforth,
in defiance of past practice and constitutional right, the gross Customs
revenue of the Island was to be paid into the Exchequer *before*, instead
of after, the deduction of the expenses of government. In protesting
against this ominous change, the Manx regrouped in united assertion of
their 'constitutional right' to the surplus revenue.[140] This time the Keys
kept in the background. Empowered by memories of 1837, the force of
'pressure from without' gave expression to the true and united will of
the Manx people. At public meetings held in every parish, delegates
were elected to a Surplus Revenue General Committee whose tasks
were to co-ordinate an Island-wide petition (3,252 signatures were
secured in all, including 95 for a separate Castletown petition); to
appoint an agent to visit the neighbouring seaports to secure their
support for the construction of a harbour of refuge; and to select two
delegates for a delegation to London. James Aikin of Liverpool had to
retire before the petition was forwarded, leaving the veteran reformer
J.J. Moore as the sole 'Delegate and Agent from the Inhabitants of the
Isle of Man'. Moore compiled a vast array of historical and other
material in (prolix) justification of claims based, as in 1837, on both the
Manx and the British constitution. It was to no avail. The
administrative convenience and financial requirements of the Treasury
prevailed over Manx sensibilities, rights and privileges:

> my Lords are unable to recognise the proportion of the public
> revenue derived from the Isle of Man in any other light than that in
> which they regard the revenue derived from any locality of the
> United Kingdom ... With regard to improvements, my Lords are of
> opinion that they can only be considered upon the same principle as
> is applicable to all other places. Those which are of a purely local
> character must be undertaken from local sources, and those which
> are of a public and Imperial character must be provided for by votes
> of the Imperial Parliament, in relation to their urgency as compared

139] Fitzroy to Hope, 7 Oct 1853 (MNHL: Letterbook vi, f 600–1).
140] All relevant material was printed in PP 1864 (553) LVIII

with other works of a like nature in other parts of the Kingdom, as parliament may decide.[141]

Constrained by these financial parameters and devoid of local rate income (with the exception of permissive and limited assessment for elementary education after 1851),[142] the Manx authorities were hindered in their efforts to effect a range of necessary improvements, most notably harbour works and the provision of proper facilities (a lunatic asylum) for the mentally ill. Until Loch's reforms energies were expended in complex negotiations conducted on two fronts: while seeking loans from Whitehall (on the security of the one-ninth allowance of 1853) for 'local' improvements, the Manx had continually to remind the British of the financial obligations of their 'imperial' responsibilities.

Harbour Improvements

The harbour improvements required by the expansion of trade since 1844 were beyond the means of Harbour Commissioners and their annual grant of £2,300 (in lieu of the old harbour dues). In December 1846, as the potato blight took hold, the Keys asked the British government to sponsor harbour improvements which, while providing work for distressed labourers ('not only natives but a great number of Irish labourers who from time to time come over to this island for employment'), would prove 'highly advantageous to the shipping interest of England, Ireland and Scotland'. Such arguments failed to impress the Treasury. The Harbour Commissioners, already under criticism from commercial and mercantile interests, were left to do the best they could with their fixed allowance, 'without the power of imposing a duty on shipping, or borrowing money'.[143]

In composition and procedures the self-elected Harbour Commissioners, an appendage of the Insular establishment, belonged to the old precommercial order: the office of one of their number, the Receiver-

---

141] Waddington to Hope, 20 Sept 1854 (MNHL: Letterbook vii, f 114–15).
142] Hinton Bird, *An Island that Led: The History of Manx Education* (2 vols, Port St Mary, nd), i, 269–74. Having made some exaggerated claims for the pioneer status of the 1851 Act for making better provision for parochial and other schoolmasters, Hinton Bird acknowledges that 'the feature of the age was not so much the involvement of the wider community in education though assessment, as the turning of the old parochial schools into unmistakably Church Schools through affiliation to the National Society'.
143] PP 1851 (651) LII Correspondence on Improvement of Harbours of Isle of Man, 1846–51.

General, had, indeed, been rendered redundant by the 1844 Act. Business was conducted behind closed doors, 'not open to the public, or even to those interested in the shipping, the fisheries or the mercantile affairs of the island'. Geographical rivalry also intruded: jealous of the attention accorded to Douglas, Ramsey regularly petitioned for its own Harbour Commissioners.[144] While acknowledging the validity of much of the criticism, Hope cautioned against change. Separate boards would be 'very objectionable ... In a small place like this Island, it appears to me that the general interests of the whole should be considered in preference to those of the separate ports.' British elected models, premised on rate-finance, were inappropriate as 'there are no ratepayers ... and to say they were to be elected by the merchants and shipowners of the place would, I fear, provide a very undefined and uncertain constituency'.[145]

After 1853 the annual grant of £2,300 was supplemented by the allowance of one-ninth of the gross Customs revenue, computed at £3,411 a year. The arrangements were unduly complex. Subject to the veto of the Lieutenant-Governor and the Treasury (and, in practice, the Admiralty), Tynwald determined the work to be undertaken, while the Harbour Commissioners were responsible for its effectuation. Even so, funds fell short of requirements. At Hope's instigation negotiations commenced in 1854 for a Treasury loan to be granted without the need for further legislation, the money 'being borrowed on the Security of the Revenue already devoted to the improvement of the Harbours'.[146] In eager expectation the Harbour Commissioners appointed the naval engineer James Walker to draw up plans. A number of difficulties ensued. There was unwarranted delay before Walker's plans, drafted in full recognition of income restraints and Insular priorities (low-water landing facilities at Douglas and provision of shelter), were finally dismissed by the Admiralty as 'small and trifling alterations ... whatever money is expended, should be devoted to real and substantial improvements'. Their grandiose (and uncosted) alternative proposals would require a substantial government grant, Hope insisted.[147] Impatient at the delay in getting work started, he proposed

144] Petition from Ramsey Harbour Committee 17 July 1856, and Waddington to Hope, 31 Mar 1857, enclosing petition dated 17 Mar 1857 (MNHL: Letterbook vii, f 449–51, and viii, f 45–6).

145] Hope to Treasury, 29 May 1855 and to Waddington, 1 Apr 1857 (MNHL: Letterbook vii, f 239–40 and viii, f 59–72).

146] Hope to Fitzroy, 26 Sept 1854 (MNHL: Letterbook vii, f 119–21).

147] Phinn (Admiralty) to Waddington, 8 Dec, and Hope to Waddington, 31 Dec 1856 (MNHL: Letterbook vii, f 547–8, 582 91).

either that the matter should be dealt with as one affecting the Isle of Man alone, and the funds belonging to the Island applied to secure the advantages required for the Island alone, or that, if a more extended plan is to be undertaken for Imperial interests, H.M. Government should provide funds for this purpose otherwise.[148]

At this stage a further problem arose. The Harbour Commissioners were informed that legislation would be required to enable them to borrow against the security of the one-ninth of gross revenue allocated by 16 and 17 Vict. c. 107. 'The case of the Isle of Man is somewhat peculiar', the Treasury informed the Public Works Loan Commissioners as work began on drafting the Bill. To Hope's ill-concealed annoyance, it proved a lengthy and contentious process, protracted by the Admiralty, who first insisted on the insertion of clauses to defend their jurisdiction over the shores of the Isle of Man ('powers committed to them by prescription') and then refused to accept conciliatory amendments proposed by Tynwald and the Harbour Commissioners and approved by the Treasury.[149] When the Bill was finally passed and the loan granted (the exact sum was itself a matter of controversy, the Treasury having to concede a miscalculation and an initial underpayment of nearly £2,500),[150] the Admiralty exerted its influence to ensure the selection of Abernethy's plans for the Douglas breakwater. This was a volte-face from their earlier stance. The only merit of Abernethy's proposal – a creosoted wooden superstructure on a sloping foundation of loose rubble – was its low cost, undercutting Walker's amended plans. In a scathing and prescient report Walker warned that the 'Blyth system of construction' favoured by Abernethy, endorsed by the Harbour Commissioners and finally approved by Tynwald in December 1861, 'is quite inapplicable to Douglas and if persisted in, it will result in a total failure'.[151]

Provision for the Mentally Ill
Similar difficulties, obstacles and misunderstandings, aggravated by the absence of poor rates on the Island, beset the funding of proper provision for the mentally ill. The criminally insane, recognised as a

148] Hope to Hamilton, 26 July 1858 (MNHL: Letterbook viii, f 380–6).
149] PP 1860 (513) LXII Correspondence on Clauses to be Inserted in the Isle of Man Harbours Bill.
150] Pigott to Treasury, 29 June and 16 Aug and Treasury reply 30 Sept 1861 (MNHL: Letterbook ix, f 298–300, 317–19 and 324–5).
151] Walker, Burgess and Cooper to R. Quirk, 2 Feb, and Pigott to Admiralty, 26 Dec 1861 (MNHL: Letterbook ix, f 219–24 and 364–5).

charge upon the imperial purse (paid out of the Fine Fund), were removed to asylums in England and Scotland. The pauper insane were confined in Castle Rushen gaol, an unsatisfactory arrangement which exposed the inadequacy of the Island's voluntary provision. 'I have been for some time endeavouring to prevail on the Church Wardens of the parishes to which these unfortunate persons belong to devise sufficient Funds for their maintenance', Ready reported in 1840, 'and I have reason to believe this desirable object will be speedily accomplished, and the afflicted objects removed to a proper Lunatic Asylum.'[152] Such optimism was misplaced. The matter became more urgent in 1847 when the Attorney-General ruled that the removal of criminal lunatics to asylums in England and Scotland contravened the law.[153] Thereafter the close confinement (and inadequate segregation) of the criminally insane, the pauper insane and common prisoners in Castle Rushen gaol gave rise to much concern. In 1850 Hope gained British government approval for a joint initiative by which the Treasury agreed to cover half the cost of building a lunatic asylum (for both the criminally and pauper insane), once the Manx had raised the other half through voluntary subscription (similar arrangements had led to the construction of the Douglas House of Industry in 1837, maintained thereafter entirely by subscription and donation).[154] Unfortunately, sufficient subscriptions were not forthcoming. The Treasury refused to cover the shortfall:

> Every county is bound by Law to provide at its own expense a Lunatic Asylum, the cost being defrayed out of County Rates; and there seems to be no good reason why the Isle of Man should not do the like. Therefore the offer of the Lords Commissioners of the Treasury to defray half the expense out of the general Revenue of the United Kingdom was a more liberal proposal than the People of the Isle of Man had any right to expect.[155]

Chastened by the Towns Bill fiasco, Hope saw no prospect of Insular approval for rate-finance. Hence he let the matter drop until 1858 when, in the hope of securing a more sympathetic response (at least for some temporary provision), he drew the attention of the new Home

152] Ready to Maule, 4 Nov 1840 (PRO: HO98/82).
153] Ogden to Hope, 11 Dec 1847 (MNHL: Letterbook v, f 438).
154] Hope to Bouverie, 8 Nov (MNHL: Letterbook vi, f 159–60), and Waddington to Hope, 28 Nov 1850 (PRO: HO99/19 f 235). On the House of Industry see Maule to Ready, 18 July 1836 (PRO: HO99/18 f 218–19).
155] Hope to Fitzroy, 6 Dec and Waddington to Hope, 17 Dec 1853 (MNHL: Letterbook vii, f 12–17).

Secretary, Spencer Walpole, to the now scandalous conditions in Castle Rushen.[156] Walpole promptly agreed to reinstate the joint funding arrangements, but insisted that the Island raise its share through a rate. After discussion he offered an amended (and more acceptable) proposal to hasten construction of the asylum and enable the Manx authorities to phase in rate-finance: they were to apply to the Public Works Loan Commissioners for a loan to cover their half, to be repaid through annual instalments once rates were introduced. However, once the Public Works Loan Commissioners had been disabused of the assumption that the Isle of Man could be treated in like manner to an English county, they insisted that legislation would be required before a loan could be granted. Fortunately, it was agreed that clauses covering the asylum could be appended to the Bill for the harbour loan. Without further delay, Tynwald began to draft legislation for the provision of the asylum. As amended by the Keys (against Hope's advice), the Bill implied that the Treasury was to be responsible for half the maintenance, not just the construction costs, and that Crown property on the Island would not be rate-exempt. At this point, after critical scrutiny by various British government departments, the joint loan arrangements broke down. Undeterred, Tynwald decided to proceed by raising its share through rates, but this was to court controversy and delay. Construction of the asylum could not commence until a full-scale valuation had been completed and approved; and the Treasury declined to seek parliamentary approval for the British contribution until the necessary calculations were finalised on the Island. In the absence of specified funds, the Treasury and Home Office responded negatively to the repeated efforts of Hope's successors to secure interim joint finance for a temporary asylum (a costly and legally complicated proposal as no suitable premises were available within Castle Rushen itself).[157]

Disafforestation

A further complication in negotiations between the Insular authorities and the British government was the intervention of HM Commissioners of Woods and Forests, who administered Crown property on the Island

---

156] The following analysis is based on PP 1864 (428) LII Correspondence on Question of Proposing to Parliament Vote for Half of Expense of Lunatic Asylum in Isle of Man.
157] Pigott to Clive, 16 Nov 1861 (MNHL: Letterbook ix, f 342–4); Waddington to Pigott, 6 Jan 1862 (PRO: HO99/19 f 452–3): Loch to Drinkwater, 22 Dec and to Ogden, 22 Dec 1863 and 15 Jan 1864 (SRO: GD268/942 f 81–95); Waddington to Loch, 6 Feb 1864 (PRO: HO99/20, f 14–15).

in single-minded pursuit of 'the greatest improvement in revenue which can be legitimately obtained'. They hoped to maximise Crown revenue (and boost agricultural productivity) through enclosure of the 'unappropriated lands or forest of Man which the Crown acquired by purchase from the Duke of Atholl ... more than 26,000 acres, which still lies waste and unenclosed'. They were convinced that 'the principal landowners would rejoice to see a scheme carried into effect for a general division and allotment of the wastes'.[158] As it was, there was much antagonism, even physical resistance when the Crown endeavoured to enclose the commons. A particular flash-point was the grant of a licence to T.A. Corlett, the Vicar-General, to enclose 342 acres at Lezayre (for a sum of £320), a grant which the great inquest (charged to protect public ways, watercourses and turbaries) refused to ratify. On the advice of the Attorney-General, however, the Commissioners of Woods proceeded with the grant, and duly instructed John Jefferson, a Douglas surveyor, to survey the land. As he set about his task, Jefferson was accosted and manhandled by aggrieved commoners for whom Thomas Cowley, coroner of Michael Sheading, was the menacing spokesperson. Outraged by this atrocity, Howard, the Commissioner of Woods, called the Manx authorities to account. While refusing to condone violence, Hope reported (not unsympathetically) on the inhabitants' fears, especially in the north where the commons were most valuable, that 'the present proceedings are intended to deprive them of rights which they have long enjoyed and to which they believe themselves to be legally entitled'. As tension persisted in the north – 'no-go' territory controlled by the Sulby Cossacks[159] – Hope called repeatedly for some form of legal settlement or 'amicable arrangement':

> How the value of the waste lands was calculated, I do not know but they certainly were producing no value to the Duke of Atholl nor do they at present produce any to the Crown. Therefore any arrangement which gave the Crown free disposal of these or any portion of them, would be a decided gain, while the people whatever their legal rights may have been have long enjoyed certain advantages some of which they may lose.

In response Howard offered a non-negotiable 'compromise' package which proposed, following the valuation of the waste land, that 'one-third part in value be allotted to the Crown, discharged of all rights and

158] Howard to Massey, 28 May 1857, in PP 1859–2 (216) XV Correspondence as to Forests in Isle of Man, on which the following analysis is based.
159] Douglas, *This is Ellan Vannin*, 126–9.

claims over it, and that the remaining two-thirds shall become the property of the inhabitants'. A good deal at face value, Howard's offer was premised on recognition of Corlett's claims and legal prosecution of Cowley and others, conditions which were unacceptable to the Keys. There were other points of dispute, such as mineral and turbary rights. Here too Howard was obdurate, dismissing as impractical and inappropriate the proposals of a delegation of the Keys despatched to London in the hope of reopening negotiations.

Having withdrawn his 'compromise' package, Howard proceeded to draft legislation to resolve the matter by full judicial process. However, provided there was unconditional acceptance of the heads of his draft bill, he was prepared to have it presented as an Act of Tynwald, thereby avoiding the expense and inconvenience of Westminster legislation. Having gained some reassurance over turbary rights (of vital importance to the 'poorer classes in the island to whom no other fuel is accessible'), Hope advised the Keys to comply. When they chose to move relatively minor amendments, Howard announced his intention to reroute the legislation through the imperial Parliament.[160] Hope and the Council tried to retrieve matters, fearing not only the expense but also the constitutional consequences of a Westminster-imposed settlement:

> They are matters concerning the internal regulation of the Island, and the Interests of the people of the Island, which can be and always hitherto have been settled by Acts of the Insular Legislature and it will be quite contrary to the usual course followed in such matters not only in the Isle of Man, but, as the Council believes, in all the Dependencies of the Crown having independent Legislatures, that they should be regulated by Acts of the Imperial Parliament.[161]

Howard was unmoved, reminding Hope that the imperial Parliament – whose reputation for impartiality and speedy efficiency Tynwald was unable to match – had not hesitated to legislate 'in regards to questions affecting the Imperial Revenue derived from the Isle of Man or the other Dependencies of Great Britain'. As for the expense of appearing before a Select Committee at Westminster, the Manx were no worse placed than inhabitants on the fringes of the United Kingdom. A lengthy correspondence ensued as Hope insisted that the 'the cases of Ireland or the islands of Orkney and Shetland, which have no separate Legislature of their own, are represented in the British Parliament,

160] Correspondence in PP 1859–2 (216) XV ends at this point.
161] Hope to Howard, 14 Dec 1859 (MNHL: Letterbook viii, f 632–8).

cannot form any precedent for dealing with these questions in the Isle of Man'. The bickering continued, but Howard agreed to delay presentation of his Bill to allow Tynwald to draw up a measure of its own, subject to his approval. Significantly, there was a proposal to deploy the proceeds of the Commoners' Allotment 'towards the erection and maintenance of a Lunatic Asylum so as to relieve to that extent the parties, who would be entitled to a share on a division, from the payment of rates'. Howard rejected this on grounds of impracticality, but Loch was later to contemplate its introduction. A stern critic to the end, Howard finally agreed that the much-amended Act of Tynwald (its remaining inconsistencies notwithstanding) should proceed to the Royal Assent.[162]

The Insular legislature was allowed no say in the appointment of the Disafforestation Commission, three barristers selected respectively by the Lord High Chancellor, the Treasury and the Inclosure Commissioners of England and Wales. In conducting their task it seems they misunderstood Tynwald's intentions and local circumstance. There was a storm of protest when they chose to regard unfenced intacks (unenclosed but licensed private property) as part of 'the forest'. To remedy this injustice Tynwald drew up a Compensation Act by which those who had lost property were to be recompensed out of a fund of £5,000, half of which was to be provided out of the remaining sale of the commoners' allotment, and the other half out of the capital of the land revenues of the Crown. Having previously discussed the matter with Howard in London, Loch, the newly appointed Lieutenant-Governor, managed to secure reluctant British approval for the compensation package. Ironically, these concessions displeased the veteran reformer J.J. Moore: the scourge of the Commissioners, he feared that compensation legislation might prejudice his application to the Privy Council in condemnation of their 'unjust and inconsistent proceedings and defalcation of duty'.[163] When forwarding the petition presented by delegates from fifteen parishes against the Compensation Bill, Loch cast doubt on the regularity of their procedures and the pretensions of their

162] Howard to Hope, 21 Dec and Hope's reply, 23 Dec 1859 (MNHL: Letterbook viii, f 641–7). Thereafter they were in regular correspondence until July 1860: see, in particular, Hope, 12 May, and Howard's reply, 19 May (MNHL: Letterbook ix, f 81–2, 86–7).
163] PP 1865 (6) XXX Report by Commissioner of Woods, Forests and Land Revenues in Isle of Man to Treasury, relating to Isle of Man Disafforestation and Acts of Tynwald; PP 1865 (169) XXX Papers Respecting Isle of Man Disafforesting Act. See also Loch's 'private' letters to Howard, 27 June and 14 July 1863 (SRO: GD268/942 f 6–9, 15–19).

leader. Moore, he informed the Home Office, has 'for a great length of time represented himself as an agent for the inhabitants of the Island, but I believe has no claim whatever to such a title'.[164]

Governor Loch

Once the Compensation Act was passed, Moore redirected his energies to political reform. He presented Loch with a petition to forward to the Queen, condemning the culpable conduct of the irresponsible self-elected Keys in three specific areas: the injustices of disafforestation; the impropriety of rate-financing for the asylum; and the incompetence and inadequacy of the Douglas harbour works, Abernethy's 'bird-cage'. The petition campaign developed out of a series of public meetings in August 1862, all addressed by Moore, the 'agent of the inhabitants of the Isle of Man, elected by them in 1854, to obtain by all constitutional means their rights'. Delegates were elected, a co-ordinating committee appointed, and some 3,373 signatures duly collected in support of the appointment of a select committee to investigate the grievances (separately listed in a 'concise statement' for distribution to MPs) of the Manx people:

> Latterly, the people have not only been prevented from being represented in Tynwald Court, but it has enacted laws to tax them for objects in direct opposition to their will, even after it has been strongly expressed; and also statutes to deprive them of their property, under the pretence that such was a Royal Forest, where none ever existed, by which means some members of the House of Keys have acquired possession of large portions of land that have been enjoyed by the people since time immemorial, such being a violation of all the principles of British legislation.[165]

In a point-by-point refutation of the alleged grievances (a practice he inherited from his predecessors) Loch displayed no sympathy for the petitioners' case. A select committee, he opined, would 'find no grievances existing in the Island that cannot and will not very shortly be removed by the action of the Insular Legislature'.[166] Events were soon to disabuse him of such complacency.

On disafforestation Loch was unable to gain further concessions from Howard. His proposals for revaluation and reallotment to facilitate local smallholder purchase (and funds for the lunatic asylum)

164] Loch to Waddington, 12 Feb 1864 in PP 1864 (553) LVIII.
165] For full details of the campaign see PP 1864 (553) LVIII; and PRO: HO45/7548.
166] Loch to Waddington, 2 Aug 1864 (PRO: HO45/7548).

Sir Henry Loch and family *After an eventful career in the Middle and Far East, Henry Brougham Loch was appointed Lieutenant-Governor in 1863 at the unusually young age of 35. His three children were born during his period of office on the Island, the eldest being christened Douglas. (MNHL)*

were summarily dismissed, as was his later suggestion that the Commoners Allotment should be vested in the Crown in return for the Crown abandoning the lords rents, alienation fines and abbey rents.[167] Violence ensued as the sales and enclosure proceeded, not helped, Loch observed caustically, by the provocative behaviour of Howard's agents.[168] Before Loch took up office vast numbers of aggrieved commoners had been involved in the destruction of over a mile of newly constructed (enclosing) wall at Parc Llwellyn, but, despite repeated offers of substantial rewards and legal immunity, no information on the perpetrators was forthcoming.[169] Later there were

167] Loch to Howard, 27 Sept 1863 (SRO: GD268/942 f 32–5); Loch to Howard, 8 Nov 1864 (MNHL: Letterbook x, f 462–8); and Loch to Grey, 8 Nov, Howard to Waddington, 1 Dec 1864 (PRO: HO45/6366).
168] Loch to Howard, 20 Oct 1863 (SRO: GD268/942 f 44–8).
169] Pigott to Waddington, 28 Nov 1862, and Howard to Loch, 6 Mar and 5 Aug 1863 (MNHL: Letterbook ix, f 523–5, 556–7, 655–8).

violent clashes in the southern mountains when Skrimshire, the local Crown Agent, endeavoured to fulfil Howard's instructions to remove all sheep, geese and cattle from Crown lands in Rushen and Glenfaba. At first Loch refused to adopt extraordinary measures. Captain Goldie, the Head Constable, was instructed to protect the Crown officials, but not to assist them in their task. Having taken the names of ringleaders who were encouraging the commoners to violent resistance, the police were to withdraw, allowing the matter to be resolved on the morrow by the arrest and conviction of the identified troublemakers. When the police went to serve the arrest warrants, however, they were repulsed by angry crowds. Denied the speedy resolution he had promised Howard, Loch hastily marshalled all the resources at his command. The next day he attended the scene in person, accompanied by a large police and military force:

> Between 200 and 300 people were collected, but on seeing the force I had with me they offered no resistance. It appears from their statement that a curious misapprehension as to the state of the Law existed amongst them; they considered if they could maintain possession of the Commons by force the law would confirm them in possession.[170]

Major clashes were avoided thereafter, but destruction of walls and other 'depredations' continued, causing some Crown lessees to demand partial or total remission of rent in compensation. Having discussed the matter with the Acting Attorney-General, Skrimshire informed Howard that there was no summary and effectual remedy for preventing the continuance of such criminal practices. When Howard duly lectured Loch on the inadequacies of Manx law, Loch pointed to clauses he had recently inserted in the Petty Sessions Act so that 'the Law in this respect now nearly resembles that existing in England and Ireland for the punishment and prevention of such offences'.[171] While holding his own against Howard, Loch applied to the Home Office for a complete set of English statutes (the only set in the Island being kept by the Clerk of the Rolls in Castletown). 'I am desirous of introducing into the Insular Legislature a Bill to amend the present Criminal Code of the Isle

170] Skrimshire to Loch, 14 May, Loch to Goldie, 19 May, to Sir George Grey, 20 and 25 May, and to Howard, 23 May 1864 (MNHL: Letterbook x, f 225–6, 232–3, 240–5, 247–50). Loch to Grey, 1 June 1864, in PP 1865 (169) XXX.

171] Howard to Loch, 24 Dec, enclosing Skrimshire's report, 20 Dec 1864, Loch to Howard, 2 Jan and Howard to Loch, 7 Jan 1865 (MNHL: Letterbook x, f 519–22, 526–31).

of Man which is greatly in need of revision', he explained to Whitehall: 'I am anxious to assimilate the law as far as possible with that existing in England.'[172] In the process the duties and functions of legal officers required redefinition. Emoluments were withdrawn (such as the interest previously enjoyed by the Clerk of the Rolls on funds paid into the Court of Chancery), salaries were fixed and residence requirements enforced. As his agenda became interventionist, Loch could not rely on the Acting Attorney-General, 'being only a member of the Manx Bar'. When the post of Attorney-General fell vacant on Ogden's death, Loch stressed the need for permanent residence so that he could benefit from 'the advice and assistance of the Attorney General respecting any Bills it may be necessary to introduce into the Insular Legislature and also of his opinion on any legal question that may arise'.[173]

While seeking interim provision – he travelled to London to talk directly to the Treasury about 'renting and fitting up a temporary building'[174] – Loch tried to expedite construction of the long-delayed permanent asylum for the mentally ill. As a matter of principle he believed the Manx contribution should be funded through rates (although he suggested that the burden might be lessened through virement from enclosure income):

I should be sorry however to abandon a small rate, for I think it a good thing that the people should feel that they are responsible for the support of an Establishment of this nature which is for the public good, and I wish it to get them out of the habit of thinking whenever any public improvement is to be carried out, the Government must find the means. I want to make them feel their responsibilities which they are rather apt to forget.[175]

172] Loch to HO, 24 Jan and to Waddington, 7 Mar 1865 (MNHL: Letterbook x, f 538, 616).
173] Loch to Waddington, 8 July, to Clerk of the Rolls, 30 Nov 1865, and to HO, 1 Mar 1866 (MNHL: Letterbook xi, f 176–80, 408–10, 521–4).
174] Loch (Rutland Gate, London) to Ogden, 15 Jan 1864 (SRO: GD268/942 f 93–5).
175] Loch to G. Wingrove Cooke, 9 Aug 1863 (SRO: GD268/942 f 22–5). When the temporary asylum opened, the British Treasury was charged with costs on a 10:32 ratio, there being 10 criminal lunatics and 22 pauper lunatics housed; see Loch to Grey, 20 Feb 1865 (MNHL: Letterbook x, f 592–4). There was an unforeseen delay when the Commons rejected the vote of supply to cover the British contribution for construction of the permanent asylum. Through persistent lobbying Loch gained compensation for Manx expenses incurred in anticipation of a favourable vote, and an assurance that the measure would be reintroduced as soon as parliamentary convention allowed; see Loch to Grey, 4 and 28 June, to Waddington, 8 July, and Waddington's reply, 11 July 1864 (MNHL: Letterbook x, f 283–5, 316 17, 323 8).

Manx opposition to rates for such insular projects continued undiminished, but at municipal level there were now Town Commissioners (elected for Douglas in 1860, followed by Ramsey in 1861) with limited powers to levy an improvement rate. To Loch's dismay, further development was hindered by several factors: continuing criticism of the Keys' mishandling of the highway fund (a matter Loch was determined to amend by prompt and proper publication of accounts); on-going disputes about the respective needs and contributions of rural and urban areas; and the open hostility of the Keys to the new Douglas Town Commissioners. When they applied for an extension of their powers in 1864 the Commissioners were traduced by the Keys as 'mere tradesmen', fit only to control donkeys on the beach. Such obloquy prompted the editor of the recently revived *Isle of Man Times*, James Brown (an in-comer of mixed-race Liverpool stock, who had served his apprenticeship under O'Brien and Shirrefs) to respond in kind. For his damning indictment of the despotic Keys, Brown was called before the Bar of the House where, after his legal counsel was refused a hearing, he was sentenced to six months' imprisonment for contempt. From his cell in Castle Rushen he refused to be silenced, 'casting back into the very teeth of these insolent braggarts and sneerers against respectable tradesmen, their ribald jests, their coarse buffooneries and their illiberal and dogmatic assertions'. When his son entered an appeal in the British courts, the Queen's Bench ruled that the Keys, sitting in its legislative and not in its judicial capacity, had no powers to commit for contempt. Released amidst fervent public demonstrations, the martyred Brown promptly sued for wrongful imprisonment and was awarded £520 damages and costs.[176]

The disaster which finally prompted Loch out of his initial complacency was the destruction of Abernethy's breakwater at Douglas. Hope had written to Loch on his appointment, briefing him on a number of matters, not least the 'unwise course' adopted for harbour improvements: 'For this however, the Admiralty are more responsible than the Island authorities.'[177] A few months later the first signs of weakness were apparent. For the next year or so there was a

176] *Brown's Directory*, 46–56. M. Faragher, 'The Browns of the "Times": an instance of Black social mobility in the 19th century', *North West Labour History*, XX (1995–6), 44–9. See also the correspondence between the Douglas Town Commissioners, 18 Feb, and Loch, 7 Mar 1864, on their proposal to abolish the (vacant) post of High Bailiff and to become the mayor and corporation of the town (MNHL: Letterbook x, f 143–5, 153–5).
177] Hope to Loch, 28 Feb 1863 (SRO: GD268/115).

determined effort to repair, reinforce and complete the structure (and thereby avoid political embarrassment) until such action proved futile. The ill-fated breakwater was finally swept away in a storm in January 1865, leaving, as Loch reported,

> a dangerous mass of ruin in the middle of Douglas Bay, impossible to repair, and the Insular Government had no funds available for its removal – the balance unexpended of the borrowed £45,000, and the unmortgaged portion of the one-ninth of the Revenue, being wholly inadequate for that purpose.[178]

The financial implications of this disaster compelled Loch into negotiations with the British government, hard bargaining which led to his famous reforms.

In conduct and content the negotiations ran counter to previous practice.[179] Loch took personal and absolute charge of the discussions, refusing to involve Tynwald until the final package had been agreed between himself and the Treasury. Remarkably, his starting-point was Customs assimilation, the spectre which haunted the Manx. In a lengthy letter to Sir George Grey on 21 March 1865 Loch proposed to raise revenue (to be 'mortgaged and applied to the construction of a breakwater, wharves, etc at Douglas, and to other public works') through increases in duty up to British levels. Such assimilation was to apply to luxury items – spirits, tobacco, eau-de-Cologne, liquors and wine – where consumption levels would be maintained through the growth of tourism. Existing differentials were to remain on tea, coffee and sugar. By an ironic twist of fate, these proposals, so much in line with the ambition of previous British governments, were subverted by the Treasury. Loch's careful fiscal calculations were undermined by 'assimilation' of a different order. As part of the new 'social contract' of Gladstonian finance – the promise of the 'free breakfast table' through gradual elimination of taxation on the necessaries of life – the Liberal government announced a reduction of duties on British tea, down in fact to the level in force on the Island. Applied in this way 'free trade' represented a substantial threat to Insular revenue, as local grocers were the first to admit: 'it will be to the interest of the Manx importer to pay the duty in England, and without bond or entries import the tea

178] *Brown's Directory*, 80–1. Loch to Waddington, 4 Mar 1865 (MNHL: Letterbook x, f 612–13); Loch to HO, 17 Nov 1873 (MNHL: Printed Confidential Documents, 1873–82), 2.
179] This analysis is based on PP 1865 (115) XXXIX Correspondence Relative to Financial Measures for Isle of Man.

into the island under the head of "duty-paid" goods. The consequence will be, that the duty so paid will not appear in Manx customs revenue accounts.'[180] It was evident, the Treasury noted, that 'the difficulty which had been occasioned by the equalization of the tea duty would occur again, and would result in still greater inconvenience if the alterations in the tariff proposed by the Lieutenant Governor should be adopted'. Forced back to the drawing board, Loch put forward a new and more complex scheme on 21 June based on rises in duty (sugar included) but short of assimilation. His 'complicated calculations' displeased the Treasury since they 'gave to the island the benefit of prospective improvement in the revenue, without a corresponding liability to loss from any unexpected diminution of consumption'. While accepting his proposed new rates of duty the Treasury insisted that the 'effect upon the revenue should be at the risk of the island, and not of the United Kingdom; and that, instead of a proportionate amount of the gross receipt being paid to the former, the sum going to the Exchequer should be fixed by law'. In calculating the fixed sum in a Minute of 21 December, the Treasury went back to the £220,000 expended on revestment:

> Considering the military and naval defence of the island is entirely at the expense of the Government of the United Kingdom, and that its inhabitants enjoy the privileges of British citizenship without its burthens, my Lords are of opinion that a contribution at the rate of £10,000 per annum, or 4½ per cent on the capital invested, will be a very moderate return to ask from the island.

Despite repeated insistence that the sum of £10,000 'must be considered final', Loch produced detailed calculations and projections in a determined effort to persuade the Treasury to amend the figure downwards (and to adjust the various other deductions from the Insular revenue).[181] The Island, he reminded them, 'was not purchased as land investment, but to stop smuggling; the result was a saving of £350,000 a year ... besides the income derived from lands and customs'. For his pains Loch was censured for the increased costs of civil government which, Childers complained, had risen by 13 per cent in the year 1864/5 (up to £12,182 4s 3d from an average over the last

---

180] See the memorial from Douglas merchants enclosed in Loch to Treasury, 6 June 1865, in PP 1866 (115) XXXIX.

181] The following analysis is based on Loch to Childers, 14 and 28 Nov 1865, 14 and 22 Feb, 3 Mar 1866; and Childers to Loch, 26 Nov 1865, 1 and 6 Mar 1866 (SRO: GD268/961, and in printed form at GD268/939).

fifteen years of between £10,300 and £10,600): 'I certainly thought I had gone to the very verge of liberality in allowing you £11,000 a year for the cost of your Government.' Having queried the figures and justified the increase (mainly the cost of police reform), Loch pressed Childers for a final agreement:

> Upon the faith of repeated assurances from the Treasury that an early decision should be arrived at, I have for nearly a year declined to give any information to the public here as to the steps I have been taking to obtain money for the Harbour works.

'You must remember', Childers replied testily, 'that twice after it was entirely settled you reopened it on questions of figures involving careful inquiry.' In March 1866 the final package was at last ready for presentation to Tynwald.

The Isle of Man Customs, Harbours and Public Purposes Act (1866) was a landmark reform separating Manx finances from those of the United Kingdom. Beyond the essential costs of government (which now included the new post of Treasurer) and certain statutory expenses (carried forward from 1844 and 1853), and after payment of the annual fixed sum of £10,000, the Manx at last gained access to the 'surplus revenue'. However, Tynwald's new powers were carefully circumscribed: deployment of surplus Customs revenue on public works required the approval of the Treasury and was subject to the veto of the Lieutenant-Governor.[182]

Under Loch's judicious guidance the arrangements worked well. Extensive harbour works, including new deep-water landing facilities for steamers, were finished ahead of schedule, precipitating what Loch proudly described in a report on his first ten years in office as 'a very marked change in the condition of the Island':

> The steamers by landing their passengers at the pier at low water, instead of their being landed, as formerly in boats, which was the work of hours, have been enabled, by making repeated passages, to bring to the Island nearly double the number of visitors … The increased rapidity and frequency of communication with Liverpool has had the effect, in one sense, of bringing it nearer the Isle of Man, and likewise of enhancing the value of all description of produce. This is, of course, severely felt by those who have fixed incomes; but, the increased wealth being otherwise proportionately

182] Kermode, *Devolution at Work*, 31.

distributed, the result has been a very general progressive prosperity.[183]

This optimistic assessment took insufficient account of the adverse
aspects of change. Loch's reforms were to squeeze out the gentlemanly
rentiers, pensioners and half-pay officers whose year-round presence
(albeit on fixed incomes) had kept the economy afloat. Their departure
imposed a new seasonal pattern which brought at best, its critics
bemoaned, a brief ten-week period of tourist prosperity. A.W. Moore
noted a 'new problem in the way of pauperism as distinct from
poverty'.[184] Addressing the Liverpool Manx Society in 1883, Laughton
called for a return to the old fiscal-economic system:

> By some mistake or other, we have to give £10,000 a year out of our
> poor revenue to help you to pay your debts ... If we got that £10,000
> a year, we could cheapen our duties, we could make the Isle of Man
> a cheap place for half-pay officers, and others of reduced income, to
> come and live in. We could reduce our taxation, and then we would
> have a resident population.[185]

Loch's financial measures confirmed an important turning-point in
the Island's image, identity and economic rationale (a successful
'rebranding' to use today's political jargon). Having lost its tax
attraction for a resident gentility, the Island abandoned its role as
outpost of the fiscal-military state (itself much reduced in scale by
Gladstonian retrenchment and reform). As Lancashire textile workers
led the way in the transition from day excursions to an annual seaside
holiday, the Isle of Man adjusted to become, in Spencer Walpole's
words, 'the play-ground of Northern England'. Blessed by natural
beauty and the 'winds of the Atlantic', the Island offered seasonal
delight to 'operatives whose lives are spent in arduous toil in dreary and
unhealthy factories'.[186]

'The Isle of Man is not now what it was even five-and-twenty years
ago', Hall Caine noted in 1891:

> It has become too English of late. The change has been sudden ...
> God forbid that I should grudge the factory hand his breath of the

183] Loch to HO, 17 Nov 1873 (MNHL: Printed Confidential Documents, 1873–82),
3–4.
184] Moore, *History*, ii, 687.
185] Press cutting in SRO:GD268/119.
186] Spencer Walpole, *The Land of Home Rule: An Essay on the History and
Constitution of the Isle of Man* (London, 1893), 242. Review of Walpole in *Edinburgh
Review*, CLXXVII (1893), 53.

sea and glimpse of gorse-bushes; but I know what price we are paying that we may entertain him.[187]

The new visitors, as *Punch* observed on a visit while the fiscal negotiations were still in progress, seemed oblivious of the physical and natural attractions of 'Manxland':

> The natives call them 'cotton balls', and seem to hold them in contempt, although many a Manx pocket is richer for their coming … All they seem to do all day is to ride about in cars, smoking bad tobacco, and playing at All-Fours, and you see them at their ride's end, with the prettiest views accessible, sitting in inn-yards and playing All-Fours still: and this is, I presume, how they enjoy the scenery.[188]

Mass tourism accentuated seasonality and aggravated cultural, social and geographical tensions within the Island. The issue of Sunday opening of public houses, a question which divided commercial urban tourist interests from religious and rural opinion, had already caused Hope considerable anxiety.[189] Where the Island had offered domestic repose and prodigal indulgence for the gentlemanly bon viveur, it now had to control the public saturnalian excesses of the working-class holiday-maker. Not surprisingly, extra policing was Loch's first priority:

> the class of visitors from whom any disturbances may be feared and for whom an increase in Police is urgently required is that from whom the Island derives little or no advantage, and unfortunately it comprises a large portion of the visitors .. These are composed to a great extent of the working classes – large numbers of mechanics come from Manchester and other manufacturing towns, these come for a cheap holiday, and although generally very well behaved, amongst so great a number a considerable amount of drunkenness is inseparable from the degree of licence they allow themselves during these pleasure trips.[190]

187] Sir Thomas Henry Hall Caine, *The Little Manx Nation* (London, 1891), 155–6.
188] 'Mems from Manxland', *Punch*, 16 Sept 1865, 111. A fortnight later *Punch* advocated incorporation: 'Could Manxland pardon the indignity of being spoken of as Manxshire, and put up with the affront of being treated and regarded as a simple English county, the Manxshiremen would soon find English capital flow in for them more freely than it now does, and supposing that their hearts made heavy by the change, they would be consoled by feeling their pockets heavy too.'
189] Hope to Waddington, 13 June 1857 (MNHL: Letterbook viii, f 148–60).
190] Loch to HO, 2 May 1863 (MNHL: Letterbook, ix, f 589–95).

The financial measures were accompanied by (and were indeed dependent upon) political reform, the House of Keys Election Act 1866. Here too negotiations were conducted in private, but were less contentious and quickly settled through 'verbal communication' with the Home Office. Having at first rejected Moore's petitions for reform, Loch soon found himself unable to endorse a self-elected House of Keys. Already subject to pressure for the elective principle to apply to the new 'subordinate' bodies responsible for the highway fund, the lunatic asylum and urban improvements, he realised that the new financial arrangements would be unacceptable without the introduction of representative government:

> deputations waited upon me to press upon me the importance that any public body that had control of public moneys should be an elected body. But I saw the difficulty that if I acquiesced in this, that the subordinate bodies holding their position direct from the people, would consider themselves superior to the legislative body, and, therefore, in my opinion, it was beginning at the wrong end; and the body that should be elected was the one that had power and control over the subordinate bodies. When the question of increased taxation arose, I was not prepared to accede to it without representation; and I could not admit that her Majesty's subjects residing in the Isle of Man were not to enjoy those rights which were enjoyed in other parts of the United Kingdom.[191]

As agreed in the Whig–Liberal confines of discussion between Loch and his patron, Sir George Grey, political reform was moderate and cautious, far short of the Disraelian 'leap in the dark' upon which Britain was soon to embark. There was a high property qualification for members of the House of Keys (£100 a year in real estate, free of mortgages, or £50 in real estate and a £100 a year clear derived from personal property); and the franchise, restricted to adult males, was fixed at £8 in the towns and £14 in the country, a high qualification, *Brown's Directory* observed, given the low rental of houses especially in the country: 'reform of the Manx House of Keys was conceived in an eminently conservative spirit ... the franchise was carefully limited to the narrowest circle possible, and included only a very small proportion

191] Loch to Grey (Confidential), 21 Mar 1865 (MNHL: Letterbook xi, f 25–6). Report of Tynwald, 5 June 1866, and press cuttings of his speeches to the Manchester Manx Association, 1874 (SRO:GD268/119, Loch Scrapbook). In Loch's original scheme life members of the Keys were to be replaced gradually by elected members over a four-year transition period.

Arriving in Douglas *The peaks of the Island's tourist industry were just before the outbreak of the First World War when there were almost 650,000 arrivals, and in the years on either side of the Second World War, by which time there were rather more facilities for holiday-makers arriving in Douglas than there were at the time of this photograph. (MNHL)*

of the population'. The first elections, held in April 1867, led to the return of 'a thoroughly conservative house; 13 of the 24 members elected having sat in the old self-elected House, and a majority of the 11 new men being pledged to conservative views'.[192] The final component of the reform package, the Appellate Jurisdiction Act – 'to provide a Court of Appeal for causes which have hitherto been dealt with by the House of Keys' – was delayed the Royal Assent until 1867 to allow time for critical scrutiny by the law officers and the Commissioners of Woods.[193]

The conservative outcome of the reforms was to disappoint Loch, hindering his agenda of responsible and progressive government (even so, he managed to complete some seventy to eighty measures in his first ten years of office, including the introduction of compulsory education, a policy he was proud to pioneer).[194] The representative principle gave voice to Manx parsimony and frugality, values at odds with Loch's commitment to 'improvement':

> There is an absence of any similar public opinion to that which exists in England and that tends so much towards controlling abuses, promoting efforts for the amelioration of the poor and working classes, the enforcement of sanitary regulations, and the adoption of those principles of legislation that have for their object the protection of women and children from excessive work. The members of the Legislature, being in the majority of cases small landowners, are perhaps in too many instances opposed to measures however desirable and advantageous they may be that could by any possibility involve a future liability or charge upon land.[195]

The absence of support for proper poor law provision was a case in point. Concerned at the manifold inadequacies, Loch commissioned an inquiry into local and voluntary arrangements. To his dismay, the report's recommendations were kept to the minimum, 'without departing from the voluntary system of charitable relief so dear to the heart of every Manxman':[196]

> Although there was quite sufficient evidence taken before the Commission to prove the necessity for the adoption of immediate

192] *Brown's Directory*, 61–2.
193] For the Election Act and the Appellate Jurisdiction Act see PRO: HO45/7827.
194] Loch to HO, 17 Nov 1873 (MNHL: Printed Confidential Documents, 1873–82), 5. Letter to his brother George on compulsory education, 19 Nov 1869 (SRO: GD268/279).
195] Loch to HO, 13 Sept 1879 (SRO: GD268/936). This important report (not in MNHL) also reflects on the ill-fated Port Erin breakwater scheme, a long-running matter of dispute between the island and the British Treasury; see Kermode, *Devolution at Work*.
196] *Medical Aid and Poor Relief Commission (Isle of Man) Report* (Douglas, 1879), xxvii and *passim*.

steps for improving the existing system under which relief is now administered, and for providing medical aid where none at present exists, I have reason to believe that much stronger evidence might have been laid before the Commissioners with regard to the suffering and distress that prevail, but that it was suppressed by those who merely looked upon the enquiry as a probable precursor to a rate being levied in the event of a necessity for the same being clearly proved to exist.[197]

Under pressure from Loch, the charities in Douglas (notorious for indiscriminate provision) adopted an Elberfeld-system of co-ordinated relief, but to little effect. In his final report Loch made clear that, had he been staying in post, he would have introduced legislation for rate-funded local poor law boards backed up by 'Government inspection to ensure that an equitable system of relief and medical aid was provided throughout the whole Island'.[198] As it was, the Manx were to continue to take pride in freedom from poor rates, government intervention and dependency, 'ethnic' symbols of their self-sufficiency:

the absence of a poor law appears to have diminished pauperism, assisted thrift, and raised the self-reliance of the Manx … Habits of self-support have thus been ingrained in these islanders for generations, whilst in England three centuries of public relief have caused the poor to believe that they are not bound to provide for the future, and to look to the State for provision when disease or age has put an end to their powers of work … To many this social feature will be of more interest than quaint legends or customs which have had their origin in distant ages, and it is one which redounds to the honour of the Isle of Man as a community. It is a characteristic of the people, who are undoubtedly self-reliant, dogged, and industrious.[199]

The reforms of 1866 notwithstanding, there were limits to what Loch could achieve within the Manx political system and culture. In a series of reports towards the end of his term of office he mounted a sustained critique of the constitution, the workings of which precluded the responsible government to which he aspired. The Lieutenant-Governor possessed 'very extensive powers, greater in some respects than those exercised by Governors of Crown Colonies', but these were

197] Loch to HO, 29 Jan 1880 (MNHL: Printed Confidential Documents, 1873–82), 2–3.
198] Loch to HO, Apr 1882 (MNHL: Printed Confidential Documents, 1873–82), 2.
199] *Edinburgh Review*, CLXXVII (1893), 54.

most readily exercised in negative manner, by veto or inaction. There was neither assistance nor support for an imperial agenda of improvement:

> In the Isle of Man the position of the Lieut.-Governor is unique, for he is not only the representative of the Crown, but in the absence of any constitutional system of responsible government is likewise Prime Minister without colleagues or a party ... The members of Council disclaim any obligation to support the Lieut.-Governor, even if he is acting under express instructions from the Imperial Government ... In the House of Keys there is no representative of the Government to take charge of bills passing from the Council – they are merely read by the Secretary without explanation. This gives great opportunity for an opponent to a measure to obtain its rejection, as no member is officially interested in its passing.[200]

To make matters worse, he was under pressure to open the doors to the public at meetings of Council:

> The whole question hinges upon the necessity that exists for the Lieutenant-Governor having some portion of the Legislature on whose support he has the right to rely. Hitherto, from the mode of conducting business, I have been able to do by persuasion what, under the proposed altered condition of affairs, would be hopeless for me or any other Governor to attempt to do in future.[201]

Drawing upon Crown colonial models, Loch persisted in opposition to the public conduct of Council business, endeavoured to secure the pledged support of Crown appointees in the Council (to the outrage of Deemster Drinkwater and others who insisted on the independence of the judiciary) and lobbied for the appointment of a Colonial Secretary to take charge of all government measures.[202]

Viewed in perspective, Loch's vaunted position in Manx historiography is not without irony. His financial reforms conceded the

---

200] Loch to HO, 13 Sept 1879 (SRO: GD268/936), 4–10.
201] Loch to HO, 30 Apr 1881 (MNHL: Printed Confidential Documents, 1873–82), 3.
202] Loch to HO, 4 and 30 Apr 1881, Mar 1882 (enclosing his 'Strictly Confidential' Minute to members of Council, 27 Dec 1881, followed by their individual replies), and his final report, Apr 1882 (MNHL: Printed Confidential Documents, 1873–82).

Close of poll, 1867 *In December 1866 the Keys passed a Bill making the House an elected assembly, with the first election taking place the following April. Considerable excitement was generated, as is shown in this early action photograph of the close of poll in Athol Street, Douglas. (MNHL)*

principle of assimilation, defying the logic of previous Manx negotiations with the British government. He secured an elected House of Keys, but, in contrast to the reform movements, his politics (reminiscent at times of enlightened absolutism) eschewed consultation and participation. Although technically a pioneer exercise, the grant of 'parliamentary' suffrage to women in 1881 – the House of Keys Election Act of 1881 extended the franchise to all males, spinsters and widows over 21 who owned, or in the case of the former, occupied property of £4 a year – was limited in impact, less of an advance than that secured contemporaneously by 'ladies elect' in English municipal elections.[203] No democrat, Loch stood for active and responsible aristocratic rule, the Foxite legacy upheld by Russell and his Whig Liberal patrons, relatives and friends. Alone on the Island, he looked for assistance in this role to the clergy, a body he intended to rejuvenate through shattering another Manx shibboleth, the independence of the see of Sodor and Man. Loch lobbied hard first for a new bishopric at Liverpool, and then on its establishment for Manx annexation to it. Amalgamation would improve the quality and status of the Manx clergy (previously the concern had been to appoint Manx speakers),[204] befitting them for leadership of responsible public opinion. 'In a small place like the Isle of Man', he explained to Gladstone, 'the people are much more dependent upon the example and influence of the Clergy than in England.'[205] Such was the force of (misguided) local reaction – a rerun of anxieties about annexation to Carlisle, the 1830s scare which first raised the spectre of outright incorporation into England – that Loch was compelled to abandon the proposal.

In assessing Loch's achievement due account must be taken of his obvious ambition, his determination (amply revealed in private correspondence with relatives, well-connected friends and patrons) to secure higher colonial office. His brother George, a Scottish MP, and a constant source of advice, gossip and intelligence, underlined one great virtue of the Isle of Man posting, its permanency:

203] M.A. Butler and J. Templeton, *The Isle of Man and the first votes for women* (Occasional Paper, Dept of Political Studies, Sheffield City Polytechnic, nd).
204] Minutes of meeting, 21 Dec 1837 (MNHL: Council Book ii, f 95–6), on efforts to pursue a similar language policy to that of the Church of Wales. See also T. Hill (ed), *Letters and Memoir of the Late Walter Augustus Shirley, D.D.* (London, 1849), 463–5, and 474–6.
205] Loch to Gladstone, 7 Oct 1871 (SRO: GD268/117). There is much correspondence on the bishopric with high-placed individuals GD268/116–18 and 951–2.

This is a merit in any office, too little valued ... There are no doubt positions to which you might fairly aspire, so superior to the Isle of Man, as to justify an attempt to reach them, even though to be enjoyed only for a time, but they are few in number, and would in any cases be accompanied by the drawbacks of going to bad climate, etc, ... At the same time I am quite clear that no scruple need deter you from applying to the present people, should an occasion for doing so present itself.[206]

Over the following years Loch despatched lengthy and informed reports on a range of issues – conditions in the antipodes, plans for global reorganisation of military resources – to remind Whitehall of his experience and ability.[207] Principle and career advancement were neatly combined in one particular issue, his persistent effort to secure a pension for the Lieutenant-Governorship. The absence of pension arrangements – the reason which had compelled the octogenarian Smelt to remain in post[208] – neatly symbolized the Island's anomalous position. It stood outside United Kingdom superannuation provision and was not included within Crown colonial arrangements. Loch disabused Cross, the Tory Home Secretary, of any impression that he had accepted the governorship of the Island 'upon conditions that deprived me of any claims either to Pension or other employment in the Public Service':

The Government of the Isle of Man resembles that of a 'Crown Colony' a system that centres nearly all power and control in the hands of the Governor, and as the training and experience acquired in the administration of the Government of the Isle of Man might fairly be considered as affording a claim for consideration for Colonial employment, I venture to renew the suggestion ... that the Isle of Man should be brought within the Colonial Governor Pension Acts.[209]

Pending a colonial appointment, Loch secured various other improvements in terms and conditions of service. (At the same time

---

206] Letters from his brother George (including 5 Nov 1867) occupy two files (SRO: GD268/278–9).

207] See, for example, Loch to Bruce, 8 Nov 1869, and to Russell, 5 Aug 1870 (SRO: GD268/115); his correspondence with Grey in GD268/118, and with Northbrook, Governor of Calcutta, in GD268/116.

208] Smelt to Melbourne, 14 Nov 1832 (PRO: HO98/77).

209] SRO: GD268/396 contains 43 items on the pension issue, 1873–6. See also Loch to Cross, 5 Aug 1874 (SRO: GD268/117). See also PP 1876 (215) III Bill to make provision respecting Superannuation Allowances or Pensions of Persons Employed in Service of H.M. Govt of Isle of Man.

he made use of personal connections to the wealthy and powerful to promote investment in Insular railways.)[210] Soon after appointment he was accorded a salary increase to £1,200 a year in recognition of the increased cost of living since 1837 (when Ready's salary had been raised from £700 to £900) and in acknowledgment of the additional expense of residence in Douglas.[211] The decision to reside in Douglas was taken after careful consideration and much helpful advice from First Deemster Drinkwater. Although he had applied for the post himself, Drinkwater was delighted by Loch's appointment and supplied him with information 'you will not find in the Guide Books': candid assessment of the calibre of individual members of the Council and the Keys; critical commentary on the 'very limited' society and 'dreary' countryside around Castletown: and, without wishing to influence Loch's decision, annotated details of suitable properties in the Douglas area.[212] The controversy surrounding the location of the Governor's residence (and its implications for the seat of government) exemplified the main political tensions of the period since Ready's appointment: internal rivalry between Castletown and Douglas, aggravated by the commercial dominance of the latter; and the external difficulty of extracting adequate funding from the British Treasury to cover the cost of government on the Island.

After the sale of the 'Lord's Garden' at Castle Rushen there was no official residence for Ready on his appointment to the post in December 1832.[213] Having been granted an annual allowance of £150 to rent suitable premises, he took out a lease in September 1834 on Lorn House, Castletown, an arrangement which was to last for the next twenty-five years until the owner required the property back for his own use. As he sought alternative accommodation, Hope came under considerable pressure to decamp to Douglas, but he preferred to remain in Castletown, the seat of the law courts, and duly requested the Treasury to sanction the purchase or construction of a permanent residence there. The Treasury refused to authorise a special charge on the Customs revenue on the grounds that accommodation costs were included within the 'fixed proportion of the revenues of the island allotted to the support of its government'. This led to yet another fiscal-constitutional dispute as Hope insisted that financial arrangements

210] Much of the correspondence with his brother George concerned the involvement of the Duke of Sutherland and others in Insular railway investment.
211] Waddington to Loch, 26 Dec 1863 (PRO: HO99/20, f 9).
212] Drinkwater to Loch, 31 Jan and 7 Feb 1863 (SRO: GD268/116).
213] Smelt to Melbourne, 14 Oct 1831 (PRO: HO98/77).

were not determined by any 'fixed proportion': the legislation decreed that the first charge on the Customs revenue was to defray the necessary expenses of the Insular government and 'only the balance remaining, after payment of these charges, was to be paid into the Exchequer'. Furthermore, the building of a residence for the Lieutenant-Governor fell outside the specific terms of reference for the allocation of one-ninth of the revenue on harbour improvements and public works. Such arguments were to no avail: the Treasury offered no advance on the 1834 arrangements. As it happened Hope retired and left the Island as the lease expired. Pressure was then renewed by the Douglas lobby to persuade his successor (Pigott) to rent in Douglas, prior to the transfer of the courts and seat of government. Significantly, the leading protagonist was G.W. Dumbell, now distanced by commercial (and other) success from the old Castletown 'clique':

> Everything has been done for Castletown that could be accomplished, through the influence of a little party that has passed away, but without success; the town has dwindled into insignificance; without steam communication of any kind; without the telegraph; situate at the one end of the Island; the Governor, instead of being alive to what is passing in the island, and without exercising the personal influence he ought to do, is buried in seclusion, and is subject to be greatly misled in consequence. Douglas, on the other hand, has constant communication by steam and the telegraph wire, and is essentially the proper place for the Governor's residence, both as respects position for himself, and for the great benefit of the public.[214]

Pigott (previously MP for Reading) promptly decided on Douglas but was unable to find anything suitable within the annual allowance of £150: he took out a lease for the Villa Marina on Douglas Bay at £250 a year. However, it was not until the end of his first full year of office (he had decided not to commit himself earlier) that he recommended the transfer of the seat of government: 'the circumstance of its being the chief Port and Market, the large population and the central position of Douglas naturally points it out as the proper place for the holding of

---

214] PP 1860 (521) XXXIX Copy of Correspondence between the Secretary of State for the Home Department and the Lieutenant Governor of the Isle of Man Relative to the Removal of the Official Residence of the Latter from Castletown to Douglas; continued in PP 1861 (290) LVII together with Correspondence with the Treasury and the Board of Works on the same subject. On one occasion, at least, Hope experienced the geographical inconvenience of Castletown: when the royal party anchored off Ramsey, rather than in Douglas Bay as intended, Hope was unable to reach the vessel and present the loyal address to the Queen before she set sail; see *Manx Liberal*, 28 Aug. 1847.

The Villa Marina *Before the 8-acre gardens and the purpose-built two-thousand-seat Royal Hall became the home for shows, concerts, ballroom dancing, festivals, conferences and bathing beauty competitions, the original Villa Marina had been a private house and a school. A handsome colonnade between the Promenade and the Gardens links the Villa with the Art Deco Arcade and Matcham's gloriously restored Gaiety Theatre. (MNHL)*

the chief Courts'.[215] Led by M.H. Quayle, the Clerk of the Rolls, the Castletown clique protested vigorously at such a rash and unwise decision. After much consultation with legal officers, the Home Office accepted the clique's objections: not a matter for the Lieutenant-Governor alone to decide, the transfer would require special legislation and the approval of Tynwald. On Pigott's sudden death from cancer in January 1863, the clique acquired further influence as Quayle was appointed Deputy Governor.[216] Having chosen to live at Bemahague on the outskirts of Douglas, Loch heeded Drinkwater's advice and proceeded with the utmost caution and care in lobbying for the

215] Pigott to Lewis, 20 Nov 1860, and to Grey, 21 Dec 1861 (MNHL: Letterbook ix, f 183–4, 360–2).
216] Letters and enclosures in Pigott to Grey, 22 Apr and June, Waddington to Pigott, 28 Apr 1862 (MNHL: Letterbook ix, f 408–15, 428, 439–43). Quayle to Grey, 24 Jan 1863, and all other items in PRO: HO45/7434.

transfer of the seat of government. However, where Hope and Pigott failed, he persuaded the British government to provide financial subsidies and other assistance to institute a daily postal service and repair the telegraphic link, improved communications which reinforced Douglas's claims to capital status.[217]

By the time Douglas became the official capital and Loch left the Island with a knighthood – destined not yet for high colonial office but by curious irony to take up the post of Commissioner of Woods and Forests – the Isle of Man had become recognisably 'modern'. As this chapter has suggested, this was not a unilinear or uncontested process. Given the evidence available, however, it is unlikely that historians will be able to reconstruct the complex ambiguities, contradictions and tensions of 'premodern' Man:

> When I arrived in the Isle of Man, in the beginning of 1863, I found that the official correspondence in the Governor's office had not been kept with great exactness, and that the recorded correspondence upon general questions with the Home Office, Treasury, etc, was very meagre, while there appeared to be little, if any, record preserved of the correspondence that must have passed on local questions between former Governors and the various subordinate officers, and there was much difficulty in tracing and ascertaining the position of many questions affecting the interests of the Island.[218]

It is to be hoped that this chapter will encourage others to rise to the challenge, to scour the archives in search of nineteenth-century Man.

217] Loch's speech to the Manx Society, Liverpool 1879 (SRO: GD268/119). There was some embarrassment over the telegraph repair: Loch secured the services of the *Lightning* from the Admiralty, but the replacement cable ordered by the company was found to be too short; Loch to Dumbell, 7 Oct 1863 (SRO: GD268/942).
218] Loch to HO, 17 Nov 1873 (MNHL: Printed Confidential Documents), 1. Loch progressed to be Governor of Victoria (1884–9), and Governor of Cape Colony and High Commissioner for South Africa (1889–95).

Constitutional Development and Public Policy, 1900–79

DAVID KERMODE

INTRODUCTION

This political survey of the Isle of Man between 1900 and 1979 has a dual focus: the political and constitutional development of the Island from strict colonial rule to self-government, and the changing role and purpose of government in Manx society. It will make only passing reference to internal political conflicts during elections and in the House of Keys, as this requires further research. Although the works of Samuel Norris[1] and Jeffrey Vaukins[2] throw considerable light on elections and policy-making, both focus on the Raglan era. Research in progress by the author into elections and policy-making over the whole of the century does, however, warrant a number of general observations.

First, although there were differences of opinion both during and between elections over the pace and direction of constitutional reform, there was broad support within the Keys for the leading advocates of reform. The major exceptions were where reform related to the respective powers of Tynwald and local authorities and the distribution of seats for elections to the House of Keys, which invariably polarised opinion. Second, throughout the period up to 1979, decisive majorities were generally willing to support the development of the welfare state along UK lines and major initiatives in support of the Manx economy. Third, such internal political dissent as was manifest cannot readily be explained by reference to any single set of socio-economic, religious or cultural divisions. The few political groupings or parties that participated in Manx politics were never able to make significant

1] *Manx Memories and Movements* (Douglas, 1938).
2] Jeffrey Vaukins, *The Manx Struggle for Reform*, M Phil dissertation, University of Lancaster, 1984.

inroads into the independence of members of the House of Keys (MHKs). Every vote in the Keys was a free vote, and even Manx Labour Party (MLP) members frequently found themselves taking opposite sides on an issue. Different areas of controversy produced different patterns of voting. Finally, given the small size of constituencies and electorates, candidates seriously interested in being elected or re-elected could ill afford to alienate significant groups or interests. This encouraged a predominance of relatively bland manifestos, and electors were often left to choose between personalities rather than policies.

A brief word of explanation of the periodisation may be helpful. With the agreement of Alistair Ramsay, the twentieth century has been divided into five discrete periods. In this chapter a brief discussion of the Island's position during the latter part of the nineteenth century will be followed by a study of the Raglan era from 1902 to 1919. Lord Raglan's appointment coincided with the start of the Keys' struggle for constitutional reform; his resignation in 1919 came as the Island was about to embark on a major programme of constitutional, electoral and social reform. Focusing on the interwar period makes eminent sense, given the major political developments of 1919 and war in 1939. Combining the years of the Second World War with the postwar period up to 1958 is perhaps more controversial. However, the war did see the resumption of the Keys' campaign for an Executive Council and the removal of UK Treasury control and the promise by the UK of progress on both fronts. Parliament's Isle of Man Act 1958 marked the culmination of the negotiations to give effect to that promise. Constitutionally the next two decades were dominated by internal political reform, with MHKs setting out to achieve fully representative and responsible government in time for the celebration of Tynwald's Millennium in 1979. The transition to a ministerial system of government after 1979 is the subject of the next chapter, by Alistair Ramsay.

The Myth of Home Rule, 1866–1902
Although legislation in the UK Parliament in 1866, 1872 and 1878 enhanced the freedom of the Island to manage its own affairs, the reserve powers kept by the UK authorities were considerable. Spencer Walpole's description of the Isle of Man in 1893 as 'The Land of Home Rule'[3] and similar references to self-government during this period are misleading because of their neglect of those reserve powers and the pivotal role of the UK-appointed Lieutenant-Governor.

3] Spencer Walpole, *The Land of Home Rule* (London, 1893).

The House of Keys in session *Although the 24 Members of the House of Keys are popularly elected every five years, they in turn elect eight of the 11 Members of the Upper House, the Legislative Council. The branches meet separately during the year to enact legislation, coming together as Tynwald Court for up to three days a month. This nineteenth-century view shows the House of Keys in session, with members sitting in the seats allocated to their constituencies. (MNHL)*

The Isle of Man Customs, Harbours and Public Purposes Act 1866, which had been passed on condition that the House of Keys became an elective chamber, separated Manx finances from those of the UK and gave Tynwald a share in determining the expenditure of the surplus Customs revenue left after meeting the essential costs of government and certain statutory expenses. However, because the expenditure of this surplus was subject to the approval both of the Lieutenant-Governor and of the UK Treasury, the actual powers of Tynwald remained subject to the good will of the colonial authorities. In conflict with a Lieutenant-Governor or the UK Treasury, Tynwald remained extremely weak.

Following the reforms of 1866, relations with the UK authorities were for the most part cordial and the Island was fortunate in having broadly sympathetic Lieutenant-Governors. A series of developments, both formal and informal, resulted in further increases in the authority of Tynwald. In addition to the right to decide what harbour works should be undertaken, which had been gained in 1866, an Act of the Imperial Parliament in 1872 gave Tynwald control of the Island's harbours and the right to vote on the Lieutenant-Governor's nominations for membership of the Harbour Board. In 1888 Lieutenant-Governor Walpole, while reserving the rights of the UK authorities and his successors, gave an undertaking that he would not increase the costs of government without first consulting Tynwald and that he would defer to any objection that was supported by a majority in Tynwald.[4] Although this was an informal change, guaranteed only as long as Walpole was Lieutenant-Governor, the Isle of Man (Customs) Act 1887 (an Act of Parliament) empowered Tynwald to impose, abolish and vary Customs duties by means of resolutions. However, Tynwald was still able to propose changes only indirectly through and with the support of the Lieutenant-Governor. Moreover, in most instances the Island chose to follow the UK tariff very closely, and there is good reason to believe that the Treasury would have disallowed greater departures from the UK for fear of a recurrence of illegal trading.[5]

Thus, when Lord Raglan became Lieutenant-Governor in 1902, the constitutional authority of Tynwald was still severely constrained. The UK Parliament retained the right to legislate for the Island on any matter, and all Manx legislation required the Royal Assent, which was by no means a formality. The Crown, through the Home Office and Lieutenant-Governor, remained responsible for the good government of the Island and continued to appoint and control such officers as were necessary for carrying on the insular government, including the judiciary, the law officers, the police and civil servants. The Lieutenant-Governor was the Island's sole executive and Chancellor of the Exchequer. He presided over Tynwald and dominated the Legislative Council, made up as it was almost exclusively of Crown-appointed officials. The Council enjoyed parity of powers with the House of Keys and provided an effective means for the colonial government to control the legislature without recourse to such extreme measures as denial of Treasury approval or the Royal Assent. While members of the House of Keys could reject legislation and refuse to sanction financial resolutions,

4] A.W. Moore, *A History of the Isle of Man* (London, 1900), 813–14.
5] See D.G. Kermode, *Devolution at Work* (Farnborough, 1979), 49, n 36.

positive initiatives depended for their success on a sympathetic Lieutenant-Governor and the backing of the UK authorities.

The Role of Government in Manx Society: Social Policy

The late nineteenth century saw a major extension in the role of the state in Manx society as governments began to respond more positively to the social needs of the Island. The response to social problems was by no means a comprehensive one, but it is possible to see in a series of nineteenth-century initiatives the foundations of a welfare state.

The Poor Relief Act of 1888[6] marked the first small step by government as opposed to charitable endeavours to address the problem of poverty. It provided for the establishment of a poor asylum and empowered local authorities to set up poor relief committees and levy a district poor rate to cover the costs of maintaining the poor from that area. The legislation was permissive, with the Island's 21 local authorities free to decide whether to provide a rate-funded public service. Only Douglas and Ramsey chose to appoint poor relief committees immediately; Castletown and four parishes followed suit between 1894 and the turn of the century, when the committees were renamed boards of guardians.[7] The poor asylum operated as 'the hospital and infirmary of the destitute';[8] it was redesignated the Home for the Poor in 1900.[9] The total number of people on relief in the late 1890s was around a thousand, two-thirds based in Douglas.[10] Poor relief was to remain the Island's only form of social security until after the First World War.

Without doubt the most extensive and expensive social intervention by the state in the latter part of the nineteenth century was in the field of education,[11] where the Island felt obliged to follow English

6] *Statutes*, vi, 55–62.
7] *Report of the Poor Law Commission*, Mar 1940, Douglas, para 39. The poor relief committees became board of guardians in 1900 under section 12 of the Poor Relief Amendment Act of that year; see *Statutes*, vii, 340–6.
8] *Isle of Man: Annual Report of the Asylum Board Year Ending 31 March 1896* (Douglas, 1896).
9] Under section 12 of the Poor Relief Amendment Act 1900; *Statutes*, vii, 340–6.
10] See Moore, *History*, 691. The total cost of state poor relief in the year ended 31 Mar 1900 was £5,537, of which two-thirds was spent by the Douglas Board of Guardians; see *The Reports and Annual Statement of Accounts of the Isle of Man Asylums Board and Assessment Board for the Year ended 31 March 1900* (Douglas, 1900), 74–86.
11] For a detailed discussion of the history of education in the Isle of Man from 1872 see Hinton Bird, *An Island that Led: The History of Manx Education* (Port St Mary, 1995), ii.

developments very closely. The Education Acts of 1872 and 1892[12]
provided first compulsory and later free elementary education. Local-
authority-based school committees were empowered to remedy
deficiencies in the availability of elementary schools by public
provision, and to waive school fees for the poor and enforce attendance
of children aged seven to 13 (five to 13 after 1878). The revenue costs
were to be borne partly by fees and voluntary subscriptions, partly by a
school rate and partly by Insular government grants, the latter not to
exceed other sources of revenue and conditional on adhering to
Whitehall regulations. The capital costs were to be covered half by
borrowing and half by similarly conditional government grants. Under
the Acts the Island was formally tied to the English educational system
by making grant aid conditional on adherence to the Educational Code
prevailing in England. It was also significant for future educational
progress that local responsibility was divided between a relatively weak
Board of Tynwald and 21 powerful school committees. The legislation
encouraged an expansion of the state sector at the expense of the
voluntary sector, and by the turn of the century 63 per cent of the 8,154
elementary school pupils were in state schools. By 1900 both levels of
attendance and standards of achievement were comparable with those
of England.[13] Government spending on public education more than
trebled between 1878 and 1900, accounting, in the year ended 31
March 1900, for 20 per cent of revenue expenditure by Tynwald
(£14,493).[14]

The latter half of the nineteenth century saw a serious response by
Tynwald and the commissioners elected under the Towns Act 1852[15] to
the squalor and disease prevalent in the Island's towns, involving
legislation in three broad areas: water supply, the quality of food and
drink and local government. Between 1857 and 1886 the Douglas
Waterworks Act 1834 was followed by six similar measures regulating
the activities of private water companies in Castletown, Ramsey, Peel,
Port Erin and Rushen.[16] In each case subsequent legislation empowered
the local authorities to purchase and operate the waterworks as public

12] *Statutes*, iv, 57–94, and vi, 379–88.These measures were consolidated, and amended
to raise the school-leaving age to 14, by the Education Act 1893; *Statutes*, vi, 454–508.
13] Bird, *An Island*, 61–5.
14] See Moore, *History*, 696, and *Financial Statement for the Year Ended 31 March
1900* (Douglas, 1900), 9.
15] *Statutes*, ii, 297–303.
16] The Castletown Waterworks Act 1857, the Ramsey Waterworks Act 1859, the Peel
Water Act 1862, the Port Erin Waterworks Act 1885 and the Rushen Waterworks Act
1886.

utilities.[17] By 1900 water supply in Douglas was in local authority hands, while in Port Erin and Rushen it was under the joint control of the Port Erin Commissioners and the Rushen Water Company.[18]

A second group of measures was designed to safeguard against the adulteration of food and drink and followed similar legislation in England, albeit with local variations and an elapse of time. In 1869 it was made illegal to adulterate food and drink; complaints could be heard in the courts and products analysed; and the Lieutenant-Governor was empowered to appoint public analysts.[19] Subsequent legislation extended the scope of the original Act to include tobacco and increased the powers of the authorities in respect of food and drink.[20] The Bread, Flour and Corn Act 1880 regulated the composition and sale of bread.[21] This combination of regulation, analysis and the threat of prosecution proved a vital if relatively inexpensive contribution to public health.

The final set of legislation provided for the development of local authorities whose main responsibilities were in the area of public health. The Douglas Town Act 1860 and a series of amendment Acts[22] empowered Commissioners to exercise a wide range of public health functions including the paving, cleansing and lighting of streets, making and keeping in good repair drains and sewers, ordering the cleansing of premises, removing refuse, the erection and maintenance of public urinals, the maintenance of a public fire service and the regulation of house-building. The Ramsey Town Act 1865,[23] the Castletown Town Act 1883[24] and the Peel Town Act 1883[25] did likewise for the other three towns. Most of this early local government provision was repealed and extended by the Public Health Act 1884.[26] This in turn

---

17] The Castletown Town Act 1883, the Ramsey Town Act 1862, the Peel Town Act 1883 and the Port Erin Waterworks Act 1900. The latter dealt with both Port Erin and Rushen.

18] In the case of Douglas the option of full public ownership was exercised in 1890 at a cost of £144,000; see 6 *Reports of Debates in the Manx Legislature* (hereafter *Manx Deb*), 11 May 1890, 472–9.

19] *Statutes*, iii, 497–500.

20] *Statutes*, iv, 316–29, and vi, 75–84.

21] *Statutes*, v, 77–82.

22] *Statutes*, iii, 1–13. Amending legislation was passed in 1864, 1874, 1882, 1884, 1886, 1889, 1890, 1891 and 1892.

23] *Statutes*, iii, 196–203. Amending legislation was passed in 1874, 1882, 1885, 1886, 1889, 1891 and 1892.

24] *Statutes*, v, 267–84.

25] *Statutes*, v, 286–303.

26] *Statutes*, v, 374–400.

Members of legislature, 1886 *This collage shows the generally be-whiskered members of the Island's legislature twenty years after the first elections. Acts passed around this time set up the 'Insular Public Museum', improved conditions relating to public health and made 'further provision for the Protection of Women and Girls, the Suppression of Brothels, and other purposes'.*

was repealed and modified by the Local Government Act 1886.[27] The legislation of 1884–6 formally recognised the Commissioners of the four towns as sanitary authorities and enabled ratepayers in other areas to petition Tynwald for similar recognition, Port Erin gaining recognition in 1884, Port St Mary in 1890 and Laxey and Onchan in 1896.[28] Armed with extensive powers under these Acts, urban local

27] *Statutes*, v, 512–630. Amending legislation was passed in 1889, 1890, 1894 and 1897.
28] Port Erin acquired this status in 1884 prior to the first published volume of the *Manx Debates*. For Port St Mary see 6 *Manx Deb*, 23 Jan 1890, 35–6; for Laxey and Onchan see 12 *Manx Deb*, 5, 9 and 23 July 1895, 539–40, 564–6 and 633–4.

authorities were able to transform sanitary conditions for much of the Island's population, building modern sewers and sewage works, enforcing the provision of privy accommodation for houses and factories and their proper drainage into sewers, cleansing streets, removing refuse, restricting the establishment of offensive trades and responding to complaints about 'nuisances' injurious to the public health. Local government, at least in the towns and larger villages, had begun to accept responsibility for environmental health, and this was reflected in rapidly increasing levels of expenditure and debt.[29] Between 1880 and 1895 total expenditure by the four towns, Port Erin and Port St Mary increased more than fivefold from £13,634 to £72,591, while their debt escalated from £45,201 to £370,353.[30]

Progress was much slower in the rural areas and much of the Island remained without a local public health authority. The Local Government (Amendment) Act 1894[31] went some way towards remedying this. First, it provided for a Local Government Board of Tynwald that was to become the key player in public health provision, especially through powers of inspection and reporting to Tynwald. Second, it introduced elective local government to the rural areas by creating Parish Commissioners, albeit with few responsibilities, a reluctance to spend and parish boundaries that were to prove inappropriate for major public health purposes.

While the state assumed responsibility for environmental health, the treatment of ill health was, with few exceptions, left to the voluntary sector. The exceptions were in the areas of mental health, infectious diseases and medical treatment for the poor. The Lunatic Asylum Act 1860[32] provided for the erection and maintenance of an asylum for criminal and pauper lunatics, funded partly out of the general revenue and partly by a lunatic asylum rate. The asylum opened at Strang in the parish of Braddan in 1868. Major outbreaks of infectious diseases resulted in a series of public initiatives for prevention and containment. The Vaccination Act 1876[33] empowered the Lieutenant-Governor to appoint general practitioners as public vaccinators with authority to vaccinate all persons resident in a district. The Public Health Act 1884[34]

29] For further detail see Moore, *History*, 705–6; G.N. Kniveton (ed), *Centenary of the Borough of Douglas 1896–1996* (Douglas, 1996), 8 and 28–30; Constance Radcliffe, *Shining by the Sea: A History of Ramsey 1800–1914* (Douglas, 1989), 111–21.
30] Moore, *History*, 732.
31] *Statutes*, vi, 562–79.
32] *Statutes*, iii, 43–73.
33] *Statutes*, iv, 468–77.
34] *Statutes*, v, 374–400.

authorised the Lieutenant-Governor to make, alter and revoke regulations for the prevention of disease, on such matters as the treatment of infected persons, the interment of the dead, provision of medical aid and accommodation and cleansing areas. The Public Health (Amendment) Act 1885[35] gave sanitary authorities the power to establish fever hospitals and provided for up to 50 per cent grants from the general revenue towards the costs of purchasing suitable premises. This led to the establishment by the Douglas and Ramsey Commissioners of isolation hospitals at White Hoe in 1888 and Cronk Ruagh in 1896. In practice these hospitals served the whole Island, other authorities being charged for their use. The Local Government Act 1886[36] provided for the establishment of boards of health in the various districts operating under the Act with the responsibility for ensuring the enforcement of government regulations for the prevention of diseases;[37] half of their operating costs were to be borne by the general revenue and half by local rates. Following its appointment in 1894 the Local Government Board began to assume responsibility in this area and in 1897 formally replaced the Lieutenant-Governor as the regulatory authority under the Local Government (Amendment) Act 1897.[38]

The Island's first public sector housing was built in Douglas under the Douglas Town Improvement Act 1889.[39] Promoted in Tynwald by the Douglas Commissioners and modelled on English local authority schemes,[40] the Act gave the Commissioners powers, subject to schemes being approved by Tynwald, to improve 'unhealthy' districts and to provide for the accommodation of displaced working-class persons in suitable dwellings. In 1892 the Commissioners petitioned Tynwald for authority to clear and rebuild the James Street, King Street and Lord Street area and to erect artisans' dwellings for the 970 persons who would be displaced by the scheme. Initially the intention was that the housing should be undertaken by private enterprise, but the Committee of Tynwald that reported on the proposal recommended public housing. Tynwald approved the recommendation, and between 1895 and 1899 a total of 66 tenement flats was erected in four blocks on what

---

35] *Statutes*, v, 431–2.
36] *Statutes*, v, 512–630.
37] The Lieutenant-Governor's powers to issue such regulations under the Public Health Act 1884 were incorporated in the 1886 Act.
38] *Statutes*, vii, 224–30.
39] *Statutes*, vi, 118–30.
40] Developed under the Artisans and Labourers Dwellings Improvement Acts 1875 and 1879 (Acts of Parliament).

became James Street and King Street. The second phase of the programme in Lord Street proved much more controversial.

Government Support for the Manx Economy

With increased economic powers after 1866 and reasonably supportive colonial authorities, the Manx authorities were able to provide support for the economy in a variety of ways, in particular by paving the way for private enterprise by means of legislation and regulation; investing in infrastructure, social policy and public buildings; and providing economic support for local industries. Notable areas of increased enabling and regulatory activity covered traditional local industries, urban development, transport and the private utilities and services. While agriculture remained for the most part in private hands, a series of legislative measures between 1851 and 1900 dealt with land drainage, land settlement, farm sales, leases and improvements, cattle diseases and the adulteration of agricultural products.[41] Sea fishing was also the subject of legislation and attempts at regulation, although, because of the unwillingness of the UK government to restrict fishing by non-Manx fishermen in Manx waters, these proved of little practical value in limiting the steady decline of the industry. Between 1860 and 1897 Tynwald legislated extensively on the subject of local government, empowering new local authorities and, after 1894, the Local Government Board to regulate aspects of urban and rural development. The private development of a network of steam railways and electric tramways between 1870 and 1898 was facilitated by legislation, regulation and inspection.[42] In a similar vein Tynwald authorised and regulated the private supply of water and gas, further legislation in the case of water providing for public ownership and control.[43] The expansion of Manx trade also brought with it regulatory measures relating to the operation of companies, financial transactions, sale of goods and weights and measures.[44] Tourism, the Island's major growth industry in the latter years of the nineteenth century, benefited directly or indirectly from most of this enabling and regulatory activity.

Although regulatory endeavours made relatively few demands on the

41] See Moore, *History*, 939–40.
42] See G.N. Kniveton, *The Isle of Man Steam Railway: Official Guide* (Douglas, rev ed 1993), 1–11; G.N. Kniveton and A.A. Scarffe, *The Manx Electric Railway: Official Guide* (Douglas, rev ed 1994), 1–16.
43] The activities of gas companies had been regulated since the passing by Tynwald of the Douglas Gas Act in 1835 and the Peel Gas Act, the Castletown Gas Act and the Ramsey Gas Light Act in 1857.
44] See Moore, *History*, 710–11.

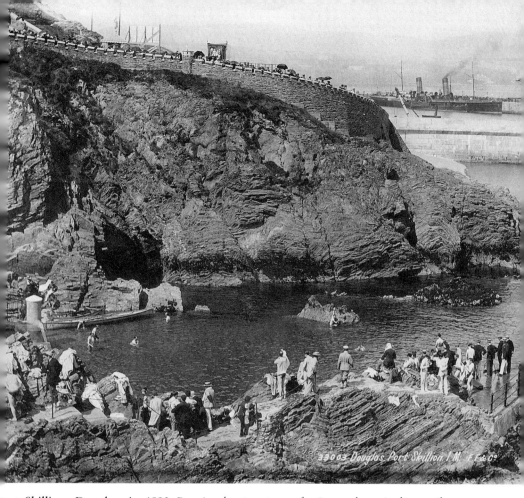

Port Skillion, Douglas, in 1893 *Rowing-boats, steam ferries and an incline railway gave holiday-makers access to Douglas Head with entertainments which included concert parties, a camera obscura, the light house, the Marine Drive railway and Port Skillion, a popular creek for bathers. Open-air services on Sundays were known to attract up to ten thousand worshippers.* The Ward Lock Guide *notes that 'it is considered very bad form to be in Douglas many hours without "doing" the Head'. (MNHL)*

public purse, investment in infrastructure, public buildings and social policy was a different proposition. Between 1866 and 1900 total capital expenditure on harbours amounted to 'more than £400,000', all but the £45,000 spent on the Port Erin breakwater being productive investment of benefit to commerce, fishing and tourism.[45] During the same period the government also spent more than £146,000 on public buildings.

45] Moore, *History*, 718–22; see also Kermode, *Devolution*, 33–5, for a discussion of the Port Erin Breakwater.

Local authorities too invested in public buildings, Douglas building a town hall, a library and new market halls within a few years of achieving borough status in 1896.[46] Policy commitments in the fields of education, public health, water supply and, in the case of Douglas, housing also made heavy demands both on Tynwald and on local government. Thus, although in 1880 local authority debt was a mere £50,402, by 1895 it had increased almost eight-fold to £396,304.

Government spending in direct support of local industries was minimal before 1900, and, generally speaking, only tourism benefited directly from public subsidies. Following a petition to Tynwald in April 1893, the Advertising Rate Act 1894[47] enabled the Government to levy a rate for the purpose of publicizing the Island and to supplement the rate by a grant from the revenue of £750 a year. Although government funding in this area was initially turned down by the UK Treasury, conditional approval in 1894 marked the beginning of a role for government that was to increase dramatically in the next century.[48]

Manx Finances at the Turn of the Century

Although Manx finances were separated from those of the UK after 1866, there remained an extremely close financial relationship with the UK. Although the government derived revenue from a miscellany of sources (for example fees, fines, rents and interest on loans) and could borrow on the security of that revenue, the main sources of current revenue were Customs and Excise duties. After 1866 these sources constituted the general revenue of the Island. Any surplus over current requirements became part of the Isle of Man Accumulated Fund and was available for expenditure in subsequent years. In the year ending 31 March 1900 current government revenue totalled £84,759, of which £78,230 or just over 92 per cent came from Customs duties.[49]

Although free to establish and maintain duties at a different level from the UK, the Island tended to follow changes in the UK tariff fairly closely either because it needed the extra revenue or to allay UK fears of illicit trade. The practice of maintaining duties at UK levels, paying revenue into a 'common purse' and dividing it between the Island and

---

46] See Kniveton (ed), *Douglas Centenary*, 15–17.
47] *Statutes*, vi, 611–12. For further details see J.G. Beckerson, *Advertising the Island: The Isle of Man Official Board of Advertising 1894–1914*, MA thesis, University of East Anglia, 1996; see also 10 *Manx Deb*, 28 Apr 1893, 748–9 and 14 July 1893, 1015–28; and 11 *Manx Deb*, 16 Mar 1894, 228–34.
48] See Kermode, *Devolution*, 113–14.
49] See *Financial Statement for the Year ended 31 March 1900*, 8.

Port Erin Breakwater under construction. *The building and financing of the breakwater was the subject of prolonged negotiations between the UK and the Manx authorities between 1861 and 1879. While other harbour projects undertaken during Loch's governorship proved of immense value to the Manx economy, the Port Erin Breakwater was subject to repeated storm damage and was finally destroyed in 1884.*

the UK originated with tea in 1890 and was quickly extended to include tobacco, wines and a few less important items where duty was already at the UK level.[50] By 1900 some 41.6 per cent of total Customs revenue was accounted for by the Common Purse Arrangement. The Island's share was based on its resident population plus a fiscal equivalent for visitors. Increases in the volume of trade and keeping or coming into line with a rising UK tariff proved an indispensable source of funding for new or more expensive services. For example, bringing the tobacco duty up to the UK level in 1891 enabled Walpole to find an additional £3,000 a year to meet the costs of free elementary education.

A significant proportion of revenue spending was also accounted for by the practice of emulating UK policies. Again colonial control was a significant factor, legislative constraints and gubernatorial power combining to limit the scope for independent initiatives. The Isle of Man Customs, Harbours and Public Purposes Act made it clear that the first calls on Customs revenue should be the cost of collection and other necessary expenses of government as determined by the Lieutenant-Governor, statutory payments for harbours and public buildings and an annual contribution of £10,000 to the UK for defence and other common purposes. In 1899/1900 these items accounted for 75 per cent of a total expenditure from the general revenue of £72,635. A further 20 per cent was spent on public education, where levels of funding were largely determined by English policy. The Island authorities were, subject to UK Treasury approval, able to determine priorities within these areas of expenditure, including the commitment of funds from the Accumulated Fund or through borrowing for capital purposes,[51] but the scope for independent initiatives was very limited indeed.

Between 1900 and 1979 total spending by Tynwald other than that incurred through borrowing increased from £86,411 to £32,716,691, a 23-fold increase in real terms. By 1999 the level of spending had reached £265,374,000, a 58-fold increase over 1900 in real terms.[52] One of the

---

50] See Kermode, *Devolution*, 117–18.

51] In the Isle of Man during this period capital expenditure by the Isle of Man government came partly from savings in the Accumulated Fund and partly through borrowing. Although at the end of 1867/8 there was no Manx national debt, between then and 1893/4 the net debt rose steadily to a high of £219,531 before falling to £186,322 in 1899/1900; see Moore, *History*, 729.

52] The current expenditure figures were obtained from the *Financial Statement for the Year Ended 31 March 1900*, 11, the *Accounts of the Government Treasurer for the Year ended 31 March 1979*, 1, and the Isle of Man Government, *Digest of Economic and Social Statistics 2000* (Douglas, 2000), table 16.1. Grateful thanks are due to Martin Caley of the Economic affairs Division of the Manx Treasury for supplying the price

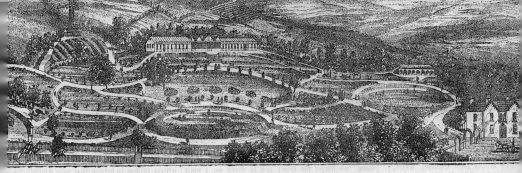

que Glen, unsurpassed in Romantic Beauty by any in the Kingdom, is now fitted up with Rustic Seats, Bowers, Walks, Shrubberies, Croquet Grounds, B
Alleys, Quoits, Swings, &c., &c.   Forming an unequalled resort for Pic-Nic Parties, and all classes of Pleasure Seekers ; and should be visited by all who
healthful and invigorating outing Dinners, Teas, Confectionary, and Refreshments, at Moderate Prices. Admission 3*d*.

DOUGLAS

AQUARIUM BATHS,

VICTORIA ST., near the PROMENADE,

CLEANLINESS, ORDER, & CIVILITY, THE RULE.

BATHS AT REDUCED PRICES.

Two good large separate PLUNGE or

SWIMMING BATHS,

PROPERLY HEATED,

Supplied with FRESH SEA WATER Every Day.

SMALL SWIMMING BATH, 70 ft. long. Admission 6d.
LARGE SWIMMING BATH, 80 ft. long, fitted up with Spring-
boards, Swings, &c. Admission 9d.

SWIMMING BATH RESERVED FOR LADIES

Open every MONDAY and THURSDAY.

LADIES' AND GENTLEMEN'S

PRIVATE BATHS,

Supplied with Hot and Cold Sea or Fresh Water.

ADMISSION ONE SHILLING EACH.

DOUCHE BATHS, 1s. 6D.

All these Delightful Baths, under New Management, are NOW OPEN
to Visitors and Residents.

Every Week Day, from   ...   .   6 a.m. to 9.30 p.m.
Sundays   ...   .   6 a.m. to 10 a.m.

Female and Male Attendants.

BY ORDER,

THOMAS LIGHTFOOT & SON, Proprietors,
And Proprietors of the DOUGLAS BAY TRAMWAY, &c.

Advertising the Island *The visiting industry produced some interesting advertisements, sometimes including claims that would not be allowed today. The artwork and copy-writing was sometimes of a very high standard, including contributions by Hall Caine and John Miller Nicholson.* (MNHL)

primary aims of this and the next chapter is to describe and explain this massive increase in expenditure.

THE RAGLAN YEARS, 1902–19

The weakness of Tynwald when confronted with a hostile Lieutenant-Governor was revealed during the governorship of Lord Raglan between 1902 and 1919. While the Liberal government in the UK was embarking on a major programme of social reform, members of the House of Keys became embroiled in a serious constitutional confrontation with their conservative Lieutenant-Governor, both over his powers and those of the Legislative Council and over the question of financial control. The conflict dominated Manx politics between 1903 and Raglan's resignation in 1919 and was a major factor in delaying the introduction of Liberal reforms in the Isle of Man, although this delay was in part due to the conservatism of members of Tynwald and to the war itself after 1914.

Constitutional Conflict, 1902–19

During the early years of his appointment Raglan interpreted his role firmly in the colonial tradition. He was responsible for the good government of the Island and was implacably opposed to the ideology of government that had given the Liberals such an overwhelming victory in the British elections of 1906. He believed in the superiority of the colonial administration and had a jaundiced view of the ability of the elected members of Tynwald. His appointment at a time when members of the Keys were anxious to expand their role was to prove a recipe for constitutional conflict.

Following an extra-parliamentary initiative by journalist and printer Samuel Norris, the establishment of the Manx National Reform League (MNRL) made constitutional and social reform central issues in the general election of 1903.[53] The MNRL programme was influenced by Liberal demands for political change in the UK and built on the spirit of reform among progressives already in the Keys – evidenced by Hall Caine's radical programme of reform when contesting the Ramsey by-

---

index printed as the Statistical Appendix to this chapter. It has been used throughout this chapter to calculate real changes in the levels of spending. The resultant figures should be treated cautiously as the index is a retail price index and not one that can accurately portray the changing value of items that loom large in government spending, such as labour.

53] For details see S. Norris, *Manx Memories and Movements* (Douglas, 3rd ed 1941), ch 12.

election in 1901; attempts to remove the Archdeacon and the Vicar-General from the Legislative Council in 1903; the widening of the franchise by the House of Keys Election (Amendment) Act 1903; and substantial minorities in favour of following UK legislation on employers' liability and factories and workshops and in opposition to the taxation of food.[54] Norris was successful in welding together these disparate strands into a programme acceptable to the MNRL.[55] The League's contribution was to attract support for the reform programme from the overwhelming majority of successful candidates. Although Norris and the League campaigned in a similar fashion at elections in 1908 and 1913, after the 1903 election the real impetus for reform shifted to the House of Keys.

On 27 February 1907 the House of Keys shifted its focus away from Lord Raglan to petition the Home Secretary with a view to obtaining for the Manx people 'fuller control of insular affairs than they have yet enjoyed'.[56] They sought to limit the power of the Lieutenant-Governor by means of a fixed term of office, the appointment of an Executive Council to assist in all questions of government and finance and the transfer of responsibility for the police to a board of Tynwald. They wanted a majority of members of the Legislative Council to be elected, with only a minority appointed by the Crown. They also asked for economy and fairness in the administration of justice, notably the involvement of an English barrister in hearing appeals (in place of the judge whose decision was being challenged), the replacement of the four High Bailiffs by a single stipendiary magistrate; and measures to prohibit the Attorney-General from engaging in private practice. Forwarding the petition to the Home Office on 1 March 1907,[57] Raglan indicated his strong opposition to the proposals, saying that it would be quite inappropriate to grant financial control to a legislature 'which does not enjoy responsible government'. Opposing changes to the composition of the Legislative Council, he argued that 'there is not a

54] A Factories and Workshops Bill had been passed by the Legislative Council in January 1901, but fell at second reading in the Keys. An Employers' Liability Bill had been passed by the Council in February 1901, but was narrowly defeated in the Keys. The Financial Statement delivered in Tynwald on 29 May 1903 by Deputy Governor Sir James Gell was followed by a controversial resolution to impose a tax on sugar; a minority of eight MHKs voted against what they saw as an inequitable tax on consumption.

55] The full programme is included as appendix A to Norris, *Manx Memories*.

56] See *Isle of Man Examiner*, 14 Jan 1911, where the petition is reprinted in full.

57] The details in the rest of this paragraph are taken from PRO: HO45/10492/113941.

man in the House of Keys and hardly one outside it in the Island, who would strengthen the Council if summoned to its deliberations'.

The Home Office response to the petition was delivered shortly after the Manx general election of 1908, during which a clear majority of the successful candidates had expressed their support for the petition. The Home Office indicated its acceptance of a fixed term of office for future Lieutenant-Governors and the introduction of a minority of indirectly elected members on the Legislative Council, but were unwilling to see any dilution of colonial control over finance. This did not go far enough for members of the Keys and, in spite of a Home Office deputation to the Island to consider the matter further, no agreement was reached.

Matters came to a head two years later over the question of financial control. A proposal by a member of the House of Keys, to increase a financial vote for advertising the Island without prior consultation with the Lieutenant-Governor, was ruled out of order in Tynwald and led to a refusal on the part of the Keys to participate in any further business until the matter was settled. Initially the Home Office supported the ruling made by Raglan, but, in the face of the Keys' continuing to refuse to do business, on 9 March 1911 announced the appointment of a departmental committee under Lord MacDonnell to inquire into the subject of Manx constitutional reform.[58]

The MacDonnell Committee reported to the Home Secretary on 31 August 1911. It opposed any reduction in the powers of the Lieutenant-Governor or the Legislative Council, but recommended a fixed term of office for future Lieutenant-Governors and the introduction of indirectly elected members to the Legislative Council. It supported a reduction in the number of Deemsters from three to two and the number of High Bailiffs from four to two, the removal of the Lieutenant-Governor from the judicial bench and measures to guarantee the independence of those hearing criminal and civil appeals. On finance the Committee felt that Tynwald should be allowed a greater measure of financial control. It suggested an altera-tion in the form of the Manx budget, Part 1 of which (the necessary costs of government)[59] should not be discussed in Tynwald, while Part 2 (all other items including increases in Part 1), should be subject to the

---

58] See *Report of the Departmental Committee on the Constitution, etc. of the Isle of Man, 31 August 1911*, Cd 5950 (1911). Evidence to the Committee was published in a separate volume, Cd 6026 (1912).

59] The cost of collecting revenue, the servicing of public debt, the grant of £2,300 for harbours and £10,000 for the Imperial Exchequer, pensions, the cost of audit and of the

scrutiny and vote of Tynwald. To enable Tynwald to perform this new financial role the Committee proposed the establishment of a Finance and General Purposes Committee of Tynwald with freedom to initiate expenditure policy, subject to not raising estimated expenditure above estimated revenue 'by a larger sum than is available from the accumulation of realised surpluses'. It also argued that, as long as it maintained a reserve of £20,000 in the Accumulated Fund, Tynwald should be free to frame its budget 'according to its income and available surplus'.

In the face of outright opposition from Raglan and objections by the Treasury to the proposed financial role of Tynwald, the Home Office announced three major outcomes, in a Government Minute on 17 July 1913.[60] In future Lieutenant-Governors were to be appointed for a fixed term of seven years. Tynwald was to introduce legislation to provide for the reform of the Legislative Council, the result being the Isle of Man Constitution Amendment Act of 1919. This provided for a Council with four ex-officio members (the Bishop, the two Deemsters and the Attorney-General), four members to be elected by the House of Keys from among their own members or the electorate and two to be appointed by the Lieutenant-Governor. On the subject of finance the Home Office accepted the Treasury view that the initiation of expenditure should remain the prerogative of the responsible executive and rejected the idea of a Finance and General Purposes Committee, but accepted the Committee's recommendation that, so long as there was £20,000 in the Accumulated Fund, there should be no restriction in framing the budget according to income and available surplus, subject to the rule that there should be no budgeting for a deficit. The Committee recommendation regarding the form of the budget was implemented by means of a further Government Minute on 11 December 1913.[61] This divided the estimates into two parts: the reserved services over which Tynwald had no control, and the voted services, in respect of which a vote of Tynwald was necessary. On the insistence of the Treasury the recommendation that increases in the

---

decennial census, the salaries of the Lieutenant-Governor, judges and their office expenses and of the Secretary to the Government and his office expenses.

60] The minute also contained controversial recommendations for the reform of the judiciary and the centralisation of the administration of education and poor relief. After considerable delays the judicial reforms were implemented by the Isle of Man Judicature (Amendment) Acts of 1918 and 1921 and the educational reform by the Education Act 1920; the local boards of guardians survived until 1951.

61] *Government Office Minute No. 3 G.O. 2847*, 11 Dec 1913 (Douglas, 1913).

reserved services should be the subject of a vote in Tynwald was not accepted.

Although the position of the House of Keys was improved by these changes, after a protracted delay in the case of the reform of the Legislative Council, the main objects of the 1907 petition had been defeated. The Lieutenant-Governor remained a strong executive, invariably supported in Tynwald by the 'official' majority on the Council and thus able to defeat even a unanimous House of Keys. In the field of finance real power still resided with the Lieutenant-Governor and the UK Treasury. As the Keys pointed out in a letter to the Home Office on 17 August 1917, it remained theoretically possible for every penny of Manx revenue to be spent 'not only without the consent, but without any reference to the representatives of the Manx people'.[62]

Simultaneously with this struggle for financial control, members of the Keys had begun to campaign for the selective adoption of the social reforms introduced in the UK from 1906 onwards.[63] Here too the House found itself powerless in the face of Raglan, a Lieutenant-Governor who made no secret of the fact that he was ideologically opposed to social reform. He also made it clear that, even without the additional cost of emulating the social policies of the UK, the Island had nearly run out of money and needed to find new sources of revenue. Addressing Tynwald on 5 October 1915, he urged members to accept the principle of direct taxation. While members responded positively, the Keys insisted on clauses stipulating that the expenditure of the proceeds of the new taxation should be determined by Tynwald without reference to the UK Treasury. Thus began another stage in the Keys' long struggle for financial control. Tynwald's first move was to approve an Estate Duty Bill. The UK Treasury objected to the legislation, insisting that Manx finances remain subject to Treasury control. As neither party was willing to modify its stand, the Bill was lost. The same constitutional principle lay at the heart of the conflict over the Income Tax Bill that was introduced in 1917.

When in 1917 the circumstances of war led the British government to subsidise flour in the UK in order to reduce the price of a loaf from 1s to 9d, Tynwald voted £20,000 from the Accumulated Fund to provide for a similar subsidy. In order to provide funding for the subsidy after the initial six months, the government introduced its Income Tax Bill. As

---

62] *Government Office Minute No. 6 G.O. 9220/14*, 14 Nov 1917 (Douglas, 1917).
63] For a useful summary of these reforms see Kathleen Jones, *The Making of Social Policy in Britain 1830–1990* (London, 1994), 2nd ed.

with the Estate Duty Bill, the Keys decided to insert a clause providing that the expenditure of all income tax revenue should be determined by Tynwald.[64] Once again the Treasury objected, and financial deadlock ensued. In his budget speech on 28 June 1918 Lord Raglan announced that the bread subsidy was to be stopped immediately, given the deadlock and the refusal of the Treasury to sanction further expenditure on the subsidy out of the Accumulated Fund. At a private sitting later that day the Keys demanded that the subsidy should continue to be funded out of the Accumulated Fund and decided not to agree to taxation of any sort until the matter of the subsidy had been resolved. A deputation met with the Lieutenant-Governor, who advised that the Keys' demands would not meet with Treasury approval. Both Tynwald and the House of Keys then adjourned until 2 July 1918. Before either could meet, the Island's bakers had announced their decision to increase the price of bread to 1*s*; the Lieutenant-Governor responded by issuing a proclamation fixing the maximum price of bread at 10½*d*; the bakers immediately refused to bake any more bread until the subsidy had been restored. On 2 July 1918 the Keys unanimously reaffirmed its decision not to support any taxation measures until the subsidy issue had been settled. Two days later the Island was facing a general strike with trade union leaders campaigning for the restoration of the subsidy. On 5 July 1918 Lord Raglan, on his own initiative, capitulated and made immediate arrangements for the restoration of the subsidy.

Following meetings with the Lieutenant-Governor, the UK response was to blackmail the House of Keys into submission, by threatening to impose UK rates of income tax.[65] By the end of July the Income Tax Act 1918 had been passed and given the Royal Assent. Although the entire Manx budget was to remain subject to Treasury control, the revenue from income tax was at least reserved for use 'for such purposes as may be determined by Act of Tynwald'.[66] A mechanism was now in place for Tynwald to identify policy priorities and, subject to the approval of the Lieutenant-Governor, to earmark funds for such purposes. The way was open for Tynwald to overcome some of its longstanding frustrations in the arena of social policy.

While the Keys was engaged in its own struggle for constitutional

---

64] 35 *Manx Deb*, 20 Nov 1917, 100–13. The ensuing details are taken from Kermode, *Devolution*, 43.

65] See Norris, *Manx Memories*, 444. The Home Office files for this period contain only newspaper reports of the discussions; see PRO: HO45/11015/348878.

66] *Statutes*, x, 292–321.

and fiscal reform during the war years, the distress caused in the Island
by the collapse of the visiting industry gave rise to a very different
challenge to established authority, including the Keys, from outside
Tynwald. Once again Samuel Norris was involved in establishing and
organising an extra-parliamentary protest movement. It began life in
December 1915 as the War Rights Union (WRU), with the limited goal
of obtaining relief from the distress being experienced by boarding-
house keepers and others dependent on tourism and by local authorities
suffering a serious loss of rate income, but in conflict with Raglan and
Tynwald transformed to become the Redress, Retrenchment and
Reform Campaign with much broader constitutional and political
goals. The political tactics employed and the constitutional solutions
offered did not endear the movement to most members of Tynwald, but
they did attract mass support, highlight the undemocratic nature of the
Manx political system and provide an impetus to the cause of
constitutional change.

Tynwald's initial response to the distress in June 1915 had been to
reduce rents and rates for boarding-house keepers by two-thirds and
offer them the option of a loan against the security of furniture and
other assets. It was the lack of help for traders, shopkeepers and local
authorities and the harsh terms of the loans that provided the impetus
for the WRU with its demands for fair rents and rates and help for local
authorities, the encouragement of passive resistance by local authorities
and ratepayers by refusing to collect or pay more than a fair rate (one-
third of the full amount) and requests for Home Office intervention.
Tynwald did eventually respond by passing the War Emergency (Relief
of Rates) Act 1916, but this was seen as too little and too late. Although
it did provide for rates to be reduced to one-third and grants to local
authorities in respect of another third, the balance was to be obtained
by ratepayers taking out loans against the security of furniture and
other assets, the relief would only be available from 1916/17 onwards
and, to add insult to injury, the funding of the relief would be obtained
by increasing the duty on tea. Public meetings followed, culminating in
a mass demonstration on Tynwald Hill on 5 July 1916 and a memorial
to Tynwald seeking 'Redress, Retrenchment and Reform', the redress
of grievances relating to war distress and taxes on food, retrenchment
in government and reform of the Manx political system, including the
replacement of Lord Raglan by a financially able and sympathetic
Lieutenant-Governor. Immediately after the Tynwald ceremony the
demonstrators approved the appointment of a Redress, Retrenchment
and Reform Committee. The strength of feelings expressed at the
demonstration, the refusal of Tynwald to discuss the memorial, which

was ruled out of order on a technicality, and the prosecution of the Douglas members of the Reform Committee, including Norris, for refusing to pay the balance of their rate demand for 1915/16 opened up a more militant phase of the struggle.

In July 1916 petitions were sent to the Home Secretary and the House of Commons demanding the replacement of the Lieutenant-Governor, drawing attention to the unfairness of taxation, the inadequacy of war relief, the urgent need for social reform and the use of the Manx courts to crush the reform movement and seeking, in the absence of local action, the suspension of the Manx constitution and a period of direct rule. When members of the Reform Committee had goods seized by the coroner for failing to pay outstanding rate demands, they attempted to persuade people attending the auction on 6 October 1916 not to buy the seized goods. As a result they were found guilty of contempt by a court presided over by the Lieutenant-Governor, the very man they were campaigning to replace. While other members were simply fined and threatened with prison if they did not pay, Norris received an open-ended prison sentence – until such time as he had purged his contempt. A further petition to the Home Secretary reiterated earlier demands, drew attention to the parody of justice that had led to Norris's imprisonment and demanded his immediate release. Ironically the Home Secretary referred the petition to Raglan, the Lieutenant-Governor being responsible for the exercise of the prerogative of pardon in such cases, provoking Norris to observe: 'Lord Raglan had prosecuted me; Lord Raglan had presided over the Court which sentenced me to prison; Lord Raglan alone was now capable, according to the Home Secretary, of giving me my release … He was Caesar in the Isle of Man.'[67] Raglan refused to pardon Norris, but did agree to convene a court to hear a petition for release and, after four weeks in prison and an apology for contempt, Norris was released.

The various petitions for reform and UK intervention were unsuccessful, the Home Secretary honouring the constitutional status of the Island and accepting that the lack of progress with reform was the result of the war. Nevertheless, the Reform Committee's campaign and the publicity generated especially by Norris's imprisonment did much to highlight the case for constitutional and social reform. Taken with the Keys' own campaign, it made the Home Office more sympathetic to Manx demands for reform and a sympathetic Lieutenant-Governor and almost certainly influenced Raglan's decision to resign once the war was over.

67] Norris, *Manx Memories*, 237–425.

The Absence of Social Reform

The Raglan years were characterised by a relative lack of major innovations in the social field. Circumstances combined to frustrate demands for social reform, and the Island emerged from the First World War with the role of the state little changed.

When Parliament passed the Old Age Pensions Act in 1908, Tynwald was very quick to respond. On 27 July 1908 W.M. Kerruish MHK moved a resolution urging the Court to follow the UK example in providing pensions for the over-70s. He argued that it was the duty of the Government to see that the old were not impoverished and provided figures which suggested that a third of the Manx people who were over 70 were dependent on charity, relations or poor relief. He stressed the importance of keeping in line with the UK given the close links and movement of people between the islands. In spite of general support for the resolution in both the Keys and the Legislative Council, Raglan repeatedly refused to introduce legislation as 'he did not see his way to obtaining the money'.[68]

Frustrated at waiting for the government to act, the House of Keys introduced and passed two Bills, one to provide for pensions on English lines, the other to levy estate duty to pay for them.[69] However, the Legislative Council gave its backing to Raglan and effectively quashed the Bill by agreeing on 5 April 1910 to adjourn consideration *sine die*. Raglan had expressed serious doubts about the Island's capacity to fund a pensions scheme similar to that of its wealthy industrial neighbour and suggested that death duties were unlikely to raise enough revenue to cover the costs of collection, let alone pensions. Two years elapsed before the matter was raised again.

By this time Parliament had passed the National Insurance Act 1911. Within weeks, members of Tynwald were asking the Lieutenant-Governor not only about his plans to introduce an old-age pensions scheme but also about national insurance. On 15 May 1912, nearly four years after Tynwald had urged him to introduce old-age pensions, Raglan announced the appointment of a commission to investigate the likely costs of a pensions scheme. The Commission, chaired by Deemster Callow, reported that it would cost approximately £20,085 a year to provide for pensions for the 2,262 people aged 70 or over.[70]

68] 27 *Manx Deb*, 2 Nov 1909, 5.

69] For details of the debate on the Old Age Pensions Bill see 27 *Manx Deb*, 15 and 22 Mar 1910, 682–94 and 807–35; for the Estate Duties Bill see 27 *Manx Deb*, 1 and 15 Feb and 8, 15 and 22 Mar 1910, 353–409, 621–44, 656–82, 774–803 and 809.

70] *Isle of Man: Report of the Commission on Old Age Pensions* (Douglas, 1913).

However, in his budget speech on 4 March 1913 the Lieutenant-Governor identified the costs of a range of social reforms – old-age pensions, health insurance, medical inspection in schools and the appointment of a medical officer of health – that had been requested by Tynwald and the 'crushing taxation' that would be necessary to meet them. To cover additional annual expenditure in excess of £31,000 on these items, it would be necessary both to raise certain Customs duties into line with those of the UK and to legislate for new forms of taxation. Following two inconclusive debates in Tynwald during 1913, the following year Lord Raglan appointed a commission to investigate the matter. At this point war intervened and the Commission effectively ceased operations for the duration of the war. Protests in Tynwald fell on stony ground, the Lieutenant-Governor refusing to contemplate major additions to the Island's financial burden while hostilities lasted.

In the meantime the Island's poor, many of whom were the elderly, had to rely on charitable endeavour and poor relief. The period saw two major changes in the operation of the poor law. The Poor Relief Amendment Act 1908 extended the responsibility of the family for the maintenance of the poor. Fathers, mothers or children with appropriate means who failed to maintain poor relations became liable to imprisonment with hard labour for up to three months. Second, the number of local authorities choosing to appoint boards of guardians increased from seven in 1900 to 16 in 1918.[71] As a result of these changes and the social instability immediately after the war, total expenditure on poor relief rose from £5,537 in 1899/1900 to £10,288 in 1918/19.[72]

Although by contrast public education remained a relatively expensive service, for most of the period the Island visibly failed to keep pace with developments in England. Hinton Bird refers to the period as 'the wasted years', progress being frustrated in much of the Island by the division of responsibility for education and the hostility of many of those in power to any expansion of provision.[73] The Education Bill passed by the Legislative Council in 1905 was designed to improve elementary education and extend public provision into the secondary or 'higher' sector along the lines of the English Act of 1902. It was also designed to end the fragmentation of responsibility in public education

---

71] See *Report of the Poor Law Commission, March 1940*, para 39.
72] See *The Reports and Annual Statement of Accounts of the Isle of Man Asylums Board and Assessment Board for the Year Ended 31 March 1919* (Douglas, 1919), 61. Douglas accounted for 51 per cent of total expenditure.
73] Bird, *An Island*, 176.

by establishing an all-Island authority. Debate in the Keys focused exclusively on the replacement of the 21 school boards either by a single authority or by five district authorities. Both proposals were narrowly defeated, and the whole Bill was lost. Opponents were suspicious that a single authority would favour the interests of the Douglas area at the expense of the rest of the Island; they were also opposed to public funding of secondary education, being more interested in economy and the availability of children for work.

Two years later the Island did attempt to make good the loss of the 1905 Bill in so far as secondary education was concerned. The Higher Education Act 1907 provided for the establishment of four higher education boards with powers to supply or assist with the supply of secondary education in their district, raising to 25 the number of local education authorities. However, the impact of this legislation outside the Douglas-dominated Eastern District was very limited, and even there progress, including the establishment of a new secondary school, was frustrated by the war, leaving Douglas struggling to manage with temporary additional accommodation and the Island as a whole with 'very inadequate' provision.[74]

Although many in the Island were only too well aware of the urgent need for educational reform, it was perhaps the mainland Education Act of 1918 that proved a catalyst for action. The Fisher Act was seen as a means of establishing a national system of education available for everyone by imposing on the education authorities the duty to provide for 'the progressive development and comprehensive organization of education in their areas'.[75] Moreover, the prospect under the Act of compulsory education for the 14–18 age group 'more or less compelled the Isle of Man to review its system of education'.[76] That review was under way before the end of the war, and, although real progress had to wait until the 1920s, the 1914–18 period did see progress on a number of longstanding issues.

The Education (Provision of Meals) Act 1915 empowered the school boards to provide meals for children at school and to levy a halfpenny rate to provide free meals for children in need. The Act was based on Parliament's Education (Provision of Meals) Act 1906, one of the few social reforms of the prewar period to find its way on to the Manx statute book during the Raglan administration. More significant was the Education (Aid Grant) Act 1918. This empowered the Council of

---

74] Bird, *An Island*, ii, 184.
75] Education Act 1918, s. 1.
76] Bird, *An Island*, ii, 181.

Education to award grants for elementary and secondary education at the rates laid down in Parliament's Education Act 1902, overcoming a serious hindrance to the progress of education on the Island. It also enabled teachers in the Isle of Man to benefit from the level of grant aid in support of salaries that had been available in England and Wales since 1902. One result of the Act was to increase national spending on public education from £14,764 in 1917/18 to £22,538 in 1918/19. Finally, in February 1918, a conference of the school and higher education boards carried a resolution in favour of their replacement by a single central authority, paving the way for the postwar Tynwald to remove the major structural obstacle to educational progress since 1872.

Fragmentation of responsibility was an obstacle to progress also in the field of public health, especially in the rural areas. Small local authorities often lacked the powers and resources to tackle problems such as water supply and sanitation. Local authority boundaries often meant that solutions to such problems required co-operation between authorities, the creation of ad hoc authorities or even the modification of boundaries, none of which was easily achieved. Local authority commissioners frequently prided themselves on keeping budgets low and encouraging self-reliance and voluntary endeavour. Reporting in 1918 on the need for local government commissioners to be more active in the public health arena, the LGB Inspector, Herbert Faragher, regretted to say 'that the majority of the Boards of Parish Commissioners are inert and are, in some cases, dead'.[77] Even so, the Island generally was able to build on the public health achievements of the latter part of the nineteenth century. The Factories and Workshops Act 1909 made registration of factories and workshops compulsory and provided the LGB with powers of inspection in respect of sanitation, safety and working hours. The Children Act 1910 consolidated existing legislation concerned with the protection and welfare of children and brought the Island into line with recent UK legislation. There were improvements to water supply and sanitation in urban areas and enhanced awareness of public health in local government circles as a result of the appointment of medical officers of health and sanitary officers in every local authority and campaigns by the LGB. These advances were offset by the lack of progress with the appointment of an all-Island medical officer of health,[78] improving

77] *Summary by the Local Government Board of the Annual Report of their Inspector as to the Public Health in the Isle of Man for the Year Ended 30 September 1907*, 26 Nov 190/ (Douglas, 1907), 8.

water supply and sanitation in the rural areas, tackling housing that was unfit for human habitation and reducing the incidence of tuberculosis.[79]

Public policies regarding the treatment of ill health did not change markedly. With the exception of the mental hospital, the two isolation hospitals and expenditure on poor relief, medical treatment was left to the voluntary sector. Although Tynwald expressed a desire to adopt a national health insurance scheme and the medical inspection of schoolchildren, the necessary legislation was not forthcoming because of the refusal of the Lieutenant-Governor to give such measures priority in a period of financial hardship and war.

Housing was an area of great social need, especially in Douglas, where the older parts of the town 'abounded' with housing that was unfit for human habitation.[80] For the most part housing was left to the private sector. Government's only routine involvement was that of regulation, inspection and associated action. Douglas was the exception, having pioneered the development of public housing in the 1890s with remarkably little opposition. In contrast, the Lord Street phase of the same development provoked considerable hostility within both the Council and Tynwald. Because of the value of the land and the strength of commercial interests in the Council, petitions were presented to Tynwald initially for permission to build shops on the ground floors and tenements above and subsequently for permission to sell the land for private development and build in another part of town. After prolonged argument the Lord Street tenements were eventually completed in 1911. Even with this development, insanitary conditions and overcrowding remained a problem for the Island, both in urban and in rural areas. The complete absence of building work during and immediately after the war made matters much worse, making arguments in favour of public investment in housing irresistible. Although there was no public investment in new housing until after the war, 1918 did see the introduction of rent control for working-class housing. Initially UK legislation restricting rent increases on houses with an annual rental below £26 was applied to the Island, before

78] On 1 April 1913 the Local Government (Medical Officer of Health and Inspection of Dairies) Bill was defeated in the Keys because of strong rural opposition to the licensing of dairies. The Island had to wait until 1934 for the licensing of dairies and 1949 for the appointment of an all-Island Medical Officer of Health.

79] Tuberculosis was a major cause of death and illness, with between 120 and 160 deaths a year between 1900 and 1918.

80] Kniveton (ed), *Douglas Centenary*, 15.

becoming the subject of Manx legislation in 1921.[81] Although this helped to prevent profiteering at a time of housing shortage, it in no way removed the need for additional housing.

The Protection and Promotion of Manx Economic Interests

The early years of the twentieth century did not see any major changes in the role of government in the economy, although rising prices and distress during the war led to a reduction in spending on infrastructure and advertising and new spending on relief. Perhaps the most important area of difference between the late nineteenth and early twentieth centuries was the extent to which Tynwald provided for the public regulation of private enterprise. Between 1900 and 1919 the scope of such legislation included the operation of companies and financial institutions, conditions in factories and workshops, landlord–tenant relationships, gaming and betting, licensing and a range of individual traders (brewers, pharmacists, pedlars and street traders, dental practitioners, money-lenders, conveyancers and boarding-house keepers). Tourism continued to benefit. The Highways (Light Locomotives) Act 1904 provided for the Island's first motor racing on public roads. The Advertising Rate Act was amended in 1904 and 1917 but continued to provide for the public funding of advertising the Island as a holiday resort.[82] The Villa Marina Act 1910 enabled Douglas Corporation to purchase the Villa Marina estate, open the Villa Marina Park and, with funding from the Noble Trustees, build the Villa Marina Royal Hall. The Ramsey Mooragh Improvement Acts of 1912 and 1915 were simply the latest in a series of measures enabling the Ramsey Commissioners to 'improve' the Mooragh for the benefit of the town and its visitors.[83]

Public investment by the Island's authorities was on a smaller scale than in the later years of the nineteenth century and the war brought to an end public works that might otherwise have provided both employment and other benefits. Capital spending by Tynwald was almost exclusively on harbours and public buildings. Between the turn of the century and March 1919 over £171,000 was spent on

---

81] The Increase of Rent and Mortgage Interest (War Restrictions) Act 1915 (5 and 6 Geo. 5 c.97) was extended to the Isle of Man by SRO1918/469 and remained in force until its repeal by SRO1921/1287 and replacement by Manx legislation; *Statutes*, xi, 79–90.

82] The 1904 Act renamed the Advertising Committee the Board of Advertising, and the 1917 Act modified the composition of the Board to include local authority representatives.

83] During the 1880s the Commissioners had purchased the Mooragh and adjacent lands for the purpose of housing and tourist developments; see Radcliffe, *Shining*, 111–15.

improvements and repairs to harbours and almost £43,000 on public buildings. Investment by the local authorities during the same period declined in the urban areas as major water and sewerage projects were completed and as local debt imposed a growing burden on ratepayers. Capital spending in the rural areas remained extremely limited.

Government expenditure in direct support of local industries was negligible. Apart from minor spending on improving the breed of horses and cattle, planting trees, the Port Erin Fish Hatchery and, after 1916, the Labour Exchange, Tynwald's only significant commitment was grant-aid towards the cost of advertising the Island, rising from £750 a year in 1899/1900 to £2,550 in 1914/15, when the grant was stopped for the duration of the war. Local authorities too were concerned to make their areas more attractive to visitors. Although a wide range of local authority activity was of direct benefit to the tourist industry, authorities also invested explicitly in tourist projects. Douglas was prominent in this respect.

The pattern of public spending between 1914 and 1919 was radically altered by the war. Capital investment declined rapidly as scarce resources were directed towards the relief of distress caused by the collapse of the tourist industry and rampant inflation. On 22 June 1915 Tynwald adopted a report of a committee set up to investigate the impact of the war on local industries. Although the committee acknowledged that, with the possible exception of agriculture, the entire Manx economy was adversely affected, it targeted its recommendation at boarding-house keepers. In December that year Tynwald voted £25,000 for loans to enable boarding-house keepers to retain their tenancy and render the sale of furniture unnecessary. Between December 1915 and March 1919 the War Distress (Loans) Committee authorised £12,500-worth of such loans. After a long campaign by the War Rights Union and the Island's rating authorities, Tynwald passed its War Emergency (Relief of Rates) Act 1916. Between the granting of the Royal Assent in May 1916 and March 1919 Tynwald provided needy authorities with £57,072 in grants and £25,029 in loans, and in the final eighteen months of the Raglan administration subsidisation of flour cost the Island £46,511. At the end of the war the Island followed the UK in voting moneys for demobilised service personnel who were without employment. In 1918/19 the 'out of work donation' scheme cost the Island £4,500. In the same year the total committed to these war-related schemes was £67,781, a massive 42 per cent of total expenditure.[84]

84] The total referred to here is of expenditure out of the General Revenue, the Accumulated Fund and the Income Tax Fund.

Manx Finances, 1900–19

A close financial relationship with the UK continued to dominate, characterised by tight colonial control and Tynwald's lack of real success in challenging that role. The one major change was the introduction of income tax in 1918. For most of the period the lion's share of the Insular revenue came from Customs duties; even with the introduction of income tax, they accounted for 71 per cent of total revenue in 1918/19. Moreover, the proportion of Customs revenue derived from the practice of keeping in line with the UK tariff had risen from 41.6 per cent in 1899/1900 to 47.8 per cent in 1918/19. Although the 'reserved services', over which Tynwald had no control, accounted for only 23 per cent of total spending in 1918/19, the major items of 'voted' expenditure – education, the relief of distress and the subsidization of flour – and several lesser items were the result of pursuing UK policies, albeit with the blessing of Tynwald. If the Keys had had its way over social policy, the extent of UK influence would have been even greater. The scope for genuinely independent initiatives remained extremely small. Changes in the level of spending in this period are summarised in Table 1. Prior to the war there was a modest increase in spending, from £86,411 in 1899/1900 to £88,002 in 1913/14, representing an 11.7 per cent reduction in real terms. By 1918/19, following a period of rapid war-induced inflation and expenditure, the level of spending had risen to £191,819, but was still just over 10 per cent below the 1899/1900 figure in real terms.

THE INTERWAR YEARS, 1919–39

A new Lieutenant-Governor, Major-General Sir William Fry, a reform-minded House of Keys and a reconstituted Legislative Council worked together to deliver a package of social and economic reforms that were to transform the role of the state in Manx society. Although the recession of the 1920s and 1930s undoubtedly limited the extent and impact of the reforms, a successful tourist industry, buoyant Customs revenue and a flexible income tax base gave the Manx government the capacity to consolidate its welfare role and extend its economic work in tackling unemployment. Although the role of government changed quite dramatically in this 20-year period, the change was not matched by any formal diminution of UK control.

Limited Progress in the Struggle for Financial Control

Constitutionally the interwar period was dominated by the question of financial control. Although the financial authority of Tynwald continued to be severely constrained by that of the colonial power,

Table 1   Manx central government expenditure, 1899/1900 to 1918/19

Financial year to 31 March	Total expenditure (£)	Expenditure at 1999 prices (£)
1900	86,411	4,549,107
1901	82,602	4,383,853
1902	88,047	4,784,474
1903	81,517	4,248,748
1904	92,779	4,928,977
1905	89,519	4,736,540
1906	84,311	4,342,438
1907	91,716	4,655,137
1908	82,277	4,128,002
1909	79,897	3,951,706
1910	81,793	4,305,992
1911	78,959	4,199,040
1912	85,647	4,486,361
1913	96,094	4,925,106
1914	88,002	4,014,915
1915	98,461	3,912,249
1916	105,718	3,578,237
1917	162,863	4,377,595
1918	134,415	3,232,546
1919	191,819	4,076,729

Notes

The sources of the raw expenditure data were the annual *Financial Statements* up to 1918/19. The level of spending at 1999 prices was calculated with the help of the Price Index supplied by Martin Caley of the Economic Affairs Division of the Manx Treasury. The real expenditure figures should be treated with caution as they are derived with the help of an index designed for a different purpose.

To avoid double counting, expenditure facilitated by borrowing is not included in the totals:
i) 1899/1900–1917/18 The sum of expenditure from the General Revenue Account and the Accumulated Fund.
ii) 1918/19   The sum of expenditure from the General Revenue Account, the Income Tax Fund and the Accumulated Fund.

the fact that a major programme of expensive social legislation was passed and implemented was indicative of a change in attitude on the part of the colonial authorities. There was a consensus between the elected and official members of Tynwald and the UK authorities in favour of these UK-based social reforms; however, in conflict with the Lieutenant-Governor and the UK authorities, members of the Keys were very conscious of their and Tynwald's weakness, in matters of both finance and legislation.

Following an increase in the number and salaries of government officials in 1919 without its knowledge, the new House of Keys decided on 21 January 1920 to refrain from meeting in Tynwald until its rights to consider and approve increases in salaries were recognised and its demands for increased financial control were met. This action was taken in response to an eve-of-resignation decision by Lord Raglan. Following a meeting with a five-member deputation from the House of Keys and consultations with the Lieutenant-Governor and the Treasury, a way forward was suggested by the Home Office and accepted by the Keys on 1 June 1920. It was agreed that in future the Lieutenant-Governor should secretly put all financial proposals to both Houses for private discussion and response, that the responses would be considered by the Lieutenant-Governor and if necessary discussed with a deputation in order to reach agreement and that, in the event of disagreement, the matter would be referred to the Home Office. It was also accepted that proposals from the Keys for expenditure from the surplus revenue should be made in the form of a declaratory resolution, submitted to the Lieutenant-Governor and dealt with in a similar manner.[85] Accordingly the House of Keys set up a standing Finance Committee to undertake this new role. In 1928, on the suggestion of Lieutenant-Governor Sir Claude Hill, the Keys appointed a five-member Consultative Committee which he could consult on matters relating to the government of the Island. On the initiative of the Keys in 1929 the two committees were amalgamated to become the Consultative and Finance Committee. Although these informal developments led to improvements in the role of the elected representatives with regard to finance and their working relationship with the Lieutenant-Governor, they fell short of their aspirations for a more democratic system of financial control. At informal discussions with the Home Office in 1928 a committee of the House of Keys proposed the removal of Treasury control and the transfer of financial power to an Executive Council or Committee responsible to Tynwald. However, the Home Office was unwilling to discuss such a radical proposal. Further demands for constitutional change in 1937 met with a similar response.

The constitutional weakness of the Island in the area of finance was further highlighted in the early 1930s as it sought to modify its laws on taxation. For example in 1931 the Isle of Man government drafted estate duty and surtax Bills only to be told by the Home Office 'to drop any idea of resorting to super-tax or estate duty' and to 'refrain from

---

85] See *Report of the Deputation from the House of Keys to the Home Secretary on Financial Control* (Douglas, 1920), 50–2 where the Home Office proposals are recorded in full. For the reactions of the Keys to the proposals see 37 *Manx Deb*, 1 June 1920, 777–88.

suggesting them in any way' to the Legislative Council or the Consultative and Finance Committee of the House of Keys, as this would
result in a significant loss of revenue for the UK. Even though this
reasoning was challenged, the Island was obliged to abandon both Bills.
In rather different circumstances and with the aim of financing
contributions to the UK government towards the cost of rearmament,
surtax was eventually introduced in 1939.

The Island's experience of Treasury control during this period was in
part a reflection of the unfavourable economic circumstances of the
interwar years. The attitudes of the Home Office and Treasury were
clearly influenced by their own experience of recession and were
probably less favourable to the Isle of Man than at any time since 1866.
The tightness of control was a regular source of controversy and
without doubt was one of the factors that led to wartime demands for
radical constitutional reform, in particular an end to Treasury control.

Social Policy: Reform and Consolidation

The political circumstances of 1919 were generally favourable to the
cause of reform. The UK authorities had already introduced reforms
and were unlikely to object in principle to the Island following suit.
Indeed, the immediate postwar period saw an extension of reform in
such key areas as social security, education and housing. The new
Lieutenant-Governor, Sir William Fry, was sympathetic to the aspirations of Tynwald and wasted no time in responding to the demands for
social action. Reform-minded candidates in the Manx general election
of November 1919 emerged with a majority in the House of Keys and
included the first four members of the Manx Labour Party[86] and
Samuel Norris, a longstanding campaigner for both constitutional and
social reform. The Legislative Council now included four members
chosen by and sympathetic to the House of Keys and Crown-appointed
officials who were known to favour reform. War served to highlight the
poverty and poor health of many volunteers and conscripts and their
families and led to a political determination to respond to these social
needs. The healthy state of the Island's finances immediately after the
war meant that it could afford the high cost of reform.

The first priorities were old-age pensions and national insurance. In
December 1919 Tynwald agreed to introduce a temporary pensions
scheme on UK lines pending the introduction and implementation of
legislation for the longer term. The first old-age pensions (10s per week
or less depending on means) were paid out of the General Revenue with

86] T.G. Bridson, J.R. Corrin, C.R. Shimmin and A.J. Teare.

effect from January 1920. When legislation was introduced the Lieutenant-Governor made it clear that it should be passed as a matter of urgency. Under the Old Age Pensions and National Insurance Act 1920, old-age pensions were to be paid to persons aged 70 or over at the prevailing UK rate and subject to a similar means test. Tynwald agreed subsequently that two-thirds of the cost should come from the Income Tax Fund and one-third from the General Revenue. The Act also provided for national health insurance (NHI) along UK lines, covering all employed persons aged 16–70 with earnings up to £200 and all manual workers whatever their wage. Contributions from employees and employers were to be the main source of funding for the scheme, with two-ninths of the cost of benefits and administration being borne by Tynwald out of the General Revenue. Benefits were to include financial payments in respect of sickness (initially 15s per week for men and 12s for women) and disability (initially 7s 6d per week), and medical attendance and treatment. Both contributions and benefits were to be at the prevailing UK rate. Although the Act did not include provision for unemployment insurance, in other respects it marked the beginning of a long period of harmony and reciprocity with UK policy in this area.[87] Thus the Island followed the UK with the introduction of a contributory pensions scheme in 1929,[88] enabling voluntary contributors to participate in both the contributory pensions and NHI schemes in 1938[89] and opening up NHI to young employees between the ages of 14 and 16 in 1938.[90]

The outstanding difference between the UK and the Isle of Man was in respect of unemployment insurance. In 1927 a report on Manx unemployment concluded that the mainland scheme was unsuited to a small island with a very different occupational structure and a

87] Although it proved impossible to negotiate reciprocity in respect of the non-contributory pensions intoduced in 1920 because of minor differences between the UK and Manx schemes, reciprocal arrangements were agreed in respect of national health insurance and the contributory pensions introduced in 1929; for details see the *Annual Reports of the Old Age Pensions and National Health Insurance Board* for the interwar period.

88] The Widows, Orphans and Old Age Contributory Pensions Act 1929 extended the insurance principle to the provision of pensions, which were to be paid at the age of 65 to insured persons and the wives of insured men. At the age of 70 and above the original non-contributory scheme would apply but without the restriction of means testing; *Statutes*, xv, 495–540.

89] By means of the Widows, Orphans, and Old Age Pensions (Voluntary Contributors) Act 1938; *Statutes*, xv, 56–73.

90] By means of the National Health Insurance (Juvenile Contributors and Young Persons) Act 1938; *Statutes*, xv, 31–4.

distinctively seasonal unemployment problem.[91] Even though the 1931 Commission on Unemployment Insurance disagreed, arguing that a sound insurance system was 'a necessary and desirable part of any good scheme for abating the hardships of unemployment',[92] the Island continued to rely on non-contributory methods – in particular public works investment and poor relief. With rising unemployment causing a steady increase in the financial burden on the local boards of guardians, in 1928 Tynwald agreed to fund 50 per cent of the costs incurred in the relief of unemployment. Even with this support from Tynwald, net expenditure by the boards continued to rise, from £12,650 in the year ending March 1920 to £20,841 by 1930 and £29,148 by 1940. The figures for Douglas alone were £6,359, £9,592 and £13,642 respectively, with a growing proportion accounted for by unemployment.

The changes to the Island's social security provision in this period involved a significant proportion of the Island's population. By 1939 over 8 per cent of the Manx population (4,287 persons) were in receipt of pensions and a further 35 per cent (18,390) were paying contributions for pensions and health insurance.[93] During the same period expenditure by Tynwald on social security rose from nothing in the year ended 31 March 1919 to £45,109 in 1921, the first full year of provision, and £87,905 in 1939, making social security the most expensive public service funded by Tynwald.

Public education was also subject to radical change during this period, which Hinton Bird characterised as one of 'remarkable progress'.[94] With the passage of the Education Act 1920, the Island's education laws were brought into line with those of the UK, political responsibility for education was centralised, the quality of provision was greatly improved and a school medical service was developed. Behind this progress was a generosity of funding that was, perhaps, surprising given the world wide recession. The outstanding achievement of the 1920 Act was the creation of an all-Island authority that was able to transcend 'the pettiness of local politics and parsimony'

91] See *Isle of Man: Report of the Commission on Unemployment* (Douglas, 1927).

92] *Report of the Commission on Unemployment Insurance, 12 November 1931* (Douglas, 1931). Legislation to implement the Commission's recommendations for a scheme targeted at seasonal unemployment was rejected by the House of Keys in 1933; see PRO: HO45/15178/557114.

93] *Nineteenth Report of the Health Insurance and Pensions Board, Year ended 31 December 1939* (Douglas, 1940). The pensions data are in the main body of the report and those relating to contributors in Appendix G.

94] Bird, *An Island*, ii, 233.

associated with the the 25 local education boards it replaced.[95] The directly elected Education Authority was made responsible for policy, subject to the consent and control of the Council of Education. Under these new arrangements the Island invested heavily in both elementary and secondary education. With the disappearance of the school boards, a programme of rationalisation of elementary provision saw the amalgamation of schools, the closure of uneconomic ones and the building of new schools serving more than one local authority area. New secondary schools opened in Douglas in 1927 and Ramsey in 1931, and opportunities for secondary study increased across the Island by the late 1930s. The pay and conditions of teaching staff were improved, with all teachers being placed on the Burnham scale following a mass resignation of teachers in 1920[96] and with the Island subsequently resisting the reductions in pay imposed in the UK at the height of the recession. Private education continued to decline as public provision improved and the proportion of free places at secondary schools increased from the 25 per cent figure laid down in 1907 to well over 50 per cent by the mid-1930s. The private grammar schools in Douglas, Ramsey and Castletown had closed by 1931, and the Peel Clothworkers Schools were transferred to the public sector in 1936; one result of this was the emergence of a unitary secondary school system that was to provide the basis for the postwar adoption of comprehensive education.

   The funding of Manx education increased dramatically during this period. Tynwald's 50 per cent contribution to revenue spending almost trebled from £22,538 in the year ended 31 March 1919 to £63,688 in 1939. This increase occurred in spite of reservations by the UK authorities over levels of spending that would not have been tolerated at home. Fortunately for Manx education the Island's wishes were generally if somewhat reluctantly respected. 'Unlike us they have the money to spend' was the private response of the Home Office to Treasury criticisms of the 'lavish' expenditure estimates for 1923/4.[97] These and other controversially high estimates (by English standards) were eventually approved, but only after a lengthy exchange of correspondence and a spirited defence by the Island of its rights and

95] Bird, *An Island*, ii, 209.
96] The mass resignation involved all teachers except those in Douglas and Onchan, where the school boards had agreed to increase pay in line with the Burnham scales. Faced with this threat and the inability of the remaining school boards to fund the increase, Tynwald agreed to a request from Lieutenant-Governor Fry to vote the necessary funds. See PRO: HO45/12567/211309/17.
97] In a letter to the Treasury dated 20 July 1923, PRO: HO45/12567/211309/39.

needs. The increase in capital spending, which had been negligible before 1919, was also the cause of friction between the Isle of Man and the UK. Here the cause of conflict was not so much the level of spending as the proportion to be borne by the rates and associated borrowing. Section 58 (1) of the Education Act 1920 provided that half of all capital expenditure should be borne by the education district concerned and the UK authorities objected to a series of capital projects where it was proposed that the full costs be borne by Tynwald. After a lot of hard argument, approval was given during the 1920s for 100 per cent capital funding of new secondary schools in Douglas (because they served the whole Island) and elementary schools in Laxey and Rushen (because they served rural areas unable to bear the cost) and in 1939 for 75 per cent of the capital costs of new elementary schools in Douglas, Ramsey and Peel.

Progress in the field of public health was partly the result of the actions of local authorities and the LGB under legislation passed before 1919 and partly the result of new legislation concerning both the protection and promotion of public health and its treatment. Between 1919 and 1939 a programme of legislation provided for an increase in the LGB's powers of regulation and inspection – with respect to drainage (1922);[98] the quality and standards of food and drink (1922 and 1925);[99] the notification, treatment and prevention of tuberculosis (1922 and 1929);[100] town improvement (1922 and 1936);[101] the safety of mechanical contrivances (1923);[102] urban housing (1924–8 and 1936);[103] rural housing (1929 and 1934);[104] the registration of dairies and the sale of milk (1934);[105] and the extermination of rats (1938).[106] The Local Government (No. 4) Act 1938 empowered the LGB, subject to the approval of Tynwald, to issue orders enabling or requiring joint action by authorities in carrying out any of the

98] The Local Government Amendment Act 1922; *Statutes*, xi, 339–63.

99] *Statutes*, xi, 339–63, and the Adulteration Act 1925, *Statutes*, xii, 83–108.

100] The Local Government Amendment Acts 1922 and 1929; *Statutes*, xi, 339–63 and xiii, 35–42.

101] Douglas Town Improvement and Artisan Dwelling Act 1922; *Statutes*, xi, 283–9, and the Housing Act 1936; *Statutes*, xiv, 434–60.

102] The Mechanical Contrivances Act 1923; *Statutes*, xi, 404–6.

103] The Housing Acts 1924 and 1936; *Statutes*, xii, 7–13 and xiv, 434–60. The Acts of 1927 and 1928 merely extended the provisions of the 1924 Act for a further period.

104] The Housing (Rural Workers) Acts 1929 and 1934; *Statutes*, xiii, 11–20, and xv, 158.

105] The Local Government (Milk and Dairies) Act 1934; *Statutes*, xiv, 279–82.

106] The Local Government (Extermination of Rats) Act 1938; *Statutes*, xv, 110–12.

provisions of the Local Government Acts. During the same period powers given to the four town authorities by the Local Government Act 1916 were gradually extended to the rest of the Island (1922, 1931 and 1938).[107] In addition local authorities were given enhanced powers of regulation and inspection over private housing and common lodging houses (1922)[108] and the opportunity to become housing authorities (1922, 1924–8 and 1936). Not all legislative initiatives were successful, a majority of members of the House of Keys resisting a series of attempts to increase the powers of central government at the expense of local authorities.

In spite of the improvements in water supply and sanitation recorded in the Annual Reports of the LGB Inspectors, public health remained a source of serious concern in the late 1930s. The LGB was pressing for further centralisation to achieve a more effective service. Parliament's Local Government Act 1933 and Public Health Act 1936 raised the possibility of a new set of responsibilities for local government in the field of welfare. Both members of Tynwald and the LGB were anxious to see greater investment in public housing and regretted the complete lack of response by local authorities to the slum clearance provisions of the Housing Act 1936. In 1938 Lieutenant-Governor Leveson-Gower responded to these concerns by appointing a public health commission. Unfortunately, war intervened, the work of the Commission was suspended and the much-needed policy developments had to wait until hostilities ceased.

In relation to health treatment, the interwar period saw the evolution of a limited but fragmented public service. While general hospitals and medical practice remained in private hands, public access to treatment was greatly enhanced by the introduction of national health insurance, the School Medical Service (SMS) and increased state funding of specialist medical services. Provision for NHI was made in 1920 and people began to receive medical benefits in January 1921. Initially these were restricted to attendance and treatment by the Island's 21 GPs, but, following negotiations with GPs in 1921, Tynwald agreed to fund additional benefits that were not available in the UK, access to special surgical and X-ray treatment at local hospitals and part-time medical and surgical consultants. Between 1921 and 1939 the range and quality of benefits were increased, dental treatment being included from 1927 and pathological and electrocardiographic examinations from 1938. As

---

107] Under the Local Government Amendment Acts 1922 and 1931; *Statutes*, xi, 339–63, and xiii, 224–5; and the Local Government (No. 3) Act 1938; *Statutes*, xv, 113–16.
108] The Local Government Amendment Act 1922.

in the UK, benefits did not include hospital or maternity treatment. Benefits were open only to insured persons, some 20 per cent of the Manx population in 1921 (12,101 out of 60,284) rising to 35 per cent by 1939 (18,390 out of 52,029). Dependent relatives were not included in the scheme.

From 1923 onwards some of those dependants gained access to medical and dental treatment through the new SMS, provision for which had been made, with the unanimous support of both branches of Tynwald, in the Education Act 1920. Fifty per cent of the costs were to be paid by Tynwald out of the General Revenue and the balance by the Education Authority. Initially the SMS was targeted solely at school-children. It provided free medical and dental inspections, free treatment of minor ailments and means-tested treatment for other ailments. In 1932 the scope of the service was extended to include pre-school children and young persons up to the age of 21. As with NHI, the nature of the treatment available improved with time, a major advance occurring in 1932 when Tynwald agreed to fund the full costs of a comprehensive orthopaedic service for children and young persons up to the age of 21. The proportion of the population gaining access to a medical service through the SMS rose from 13.5 per cent in 1924 to 32 per cent in 1939.[109]

The third strand of state provision involved services such as the mental hospital, the isolation hospitals and poor relief dating from the late nineteenth century and others resulting from initiatives by Tynwald in the interwar years, of which the most important related to the treatment of tuberculosis. The Local Government Amendment Act 1922 empowered the LGB to make regulations and orders concerning the notification, treatment, general supervision and prevention of the disease. Tynwald also agreed to fund a special TB consultancy service, a state sanatorium at Cronk Ruagh and a TB dispensary at Murray House in Douglas.

A major public health problem during this period was the poor quality of working-class housing. Overcrowding, poor sanitation and inadequate water supplies were endangering not only health but also the image of the Island as a resort. The seriousness of postwar conditions persuaded Tynwald of the need for a series of housing initiatives throughout the Island. The first of these was to replace

---

109] These figures must be regarded as approximations as they are derived from census data for 1921 (5–14 age group) and 1931 (0–21 age group) rather than actual SMS figures for the years in question; *Isle of Man: Census 1921* (London, 1924); *Isle of Man: Census 1931* (London, 1933).

wartime rent controls on rents for private accommodation with peacetime controls. The Increase of Rent and Mortgage Interest (Restrictions) Act 1921 was the first of a series of interwar measures regulating rents on both unfurnished and furnished accommodation and the circumstances under which tenants could be evicted. It applied to two-thirds of the Island's dwellings. Apart from the period between May 1924 when the Act expired and June 1925 when a replacement measure came into force, rent control remained a feature of the Manx housing scene throughout this period.

The second initiative came in Tynwald on 1 February 1921. A committee was appointed to devise a national housing scheme and issued three reports, one on 12 July 1921 resulting in the Douglas Town Improvement and Artisan Dwellings Act 1922, the second on 8 March 1922 leading to the more broadly based Housing Act 1924, and the third on 30 January 1923 resulting in a scheme to provide government aid to private builders. Initially Douglas was the only authority prepared to undertake a building programme, so Tynwald agreed to authorise a Douglas scheme. The 1922 Act enabled the Corporation to carry out a street improvement scheme between the pier and the railway station and to provide housing for displaced artisans. The Act was the first to provide for the payment of government grants in support of housing, in this case to cover one-third of the cost of the street scheme and half the net costs of the housing. The Housing Act 1924 placed a duty on local authorities to prepare housing schemes to meet local needs and provided the LGB with default powers in the event of their not doing so. Under the scheme the Government was to meet 50 per cent of the net costs, up to a maximum of £250 per house, although, under pressure from the UK Treasury, this maximum figure was progressively reduced to £125. Between 1922 and 1939 a total of 904 public sector houses were built by eight local authorities, Douglas accounting for 76 per cent of the total. Under the private enterprise scheme, finalised in 1923, Tynwald agreed to provide low-interest loans to Manx residents wishing to build their own house (repayable over 20 years) and to builders building private houses for sale to Manx residents (repayable on the sale of the house). Further encouragement to home ownership was provided by the Income Tax Act 1927,[110] section 6 of which introduced mortgage interest tax relief.

The next initiative came with the Housing (Rural Workers) Act 1929, which aimed to provide financial assistance towards the improvement

110] Between 1927 and 1966 tax relief on mortgage interest payments was deductible from income payable in respect of the gross value of residential property of housing for agricultural workers. Local authorities were to submit improvement schemes to the LGB for approval and the authorisation of up to two-thirds of the cost up to a maximum of £100 per dwelling. Between 1929 and 1938 some 56 agricultural cottages were improved under this scheme.

But despite these improvements, the housing problem persisted. Tynwald's response was to pass the Housing Act 1936, which empowered local authorities to clear or improve 'unhealthy' areas or houses, the precise amount of financial subsidy being a matter for negotiation with the Lieutenant-Governor. Despite the continuing social need, however, not a single authority had come forward with a clearance scheme prior to the outbreak of war in 1939. Those where the need was greatest were unwilling to add to their already heavy rate burden. Other authorities were either unwilling to see housing as a priority or too poor to raise their share of the net costs. Real progress had to await the much higher levels of national funding made available after the war.

The Protection and Promotion of Manx Economic Interests

The interwar years saw a massive increase in government spending, a reflection of the more interventionist role adopted immediately after the war. The role of government became absolutely pivotal to the health of the Manx economy, as regulator, provider of welfare, investor in infrastructure, owner of public utilities and supporter of local industries. Legislation enabling and regulating private and public enterprise remained an important feature of government activity, well over a hundred Acts of Tynwald in this category being passed between 1919 and 1939. New social policies brought a large increase in public spending, most notably on education, pensions and national health insurance. In addition Tynwald committed unprecedented levels of capital expenditure on housing, schools and public health, providing both sought-after facilities and much-needed employment. Between 1922/3 and 1938/9 Tynwald's share of expenditure on public housing totalled £258,370, over three-quarters of this being committed between 1924 and 1930. Over the same period Tynwald's share of spending on schools amounted to £161,147. During the 1930s Tynwald also agreed to assist with a range of water supply and drainage projects for the villages and rural districts, committing a total of £176,925 between 1930/1 and 1938/9.

The Isle of Man government's responsibility for infrastructure accounted for even higher levels of spending. Harbours continued to be a major call on public funds, a total of £430,415 over the 20-year period. However, the biggest single call on central funds was highways. From 1920/1 Tynwald agreed to fund 50 per cent of the cost of the upkeep of public roads, and from 1933/4, 75 per cent of the cost, through grants to local authorities and the Highways Board. The total grant-aid for the period amounted to £1,539,904.

Public ownership was hardly to the forefront of Manx politics in the interwar period. However, Tynwald did agree to extend public ownership in order to progress the development of much-needed utilities. In the case of electricity the Douglas Corporation Electric Light and Power Act 1921 and the Isle of Man Electric Light and Power Act 1932 gave the power to provide electricity to Douglas Corporation and the Isle of Man Electricity Board respectively, the two undertakings eventually amalgamating in 1984. In the case of water Tynwald established and funded special boards under the Water (Supply) Acts 1929 and 1934. The Northern Water Board was set up in 1936 to serve the five northern parishes of Andreas, Ballaugh, Bride, Jurby and Lezayre which were still without a public water supply, filling a vacuum left by private and local authority provision. To combat the financial difficulties facing existing suppliers and obstacles to be overcome by small local authorities in supplying hitherto neglected areas, in 1939 the Southern Water Board became responsible for supplying Castletown, Port Erin, Port St Mary and the parishes of Arbory, Malew, Rushen and Santon; a total of £74,384 was paid in compensation to the Castletown Water Company (£14,798), the Rushen Water Board (£50,266) and the Malew Commissioners (£9,320). Although on the outbreak of war responsibility for public water supply was still fragmented and shared between the private and public sectors, the industry was heading towards supply outside of Douglas by a single public board.

Capital spending on infrastructure and social policy, including water supply, became important planks in the Island's battle against unemployment. Part of that spending was committed with the explicit purpose of providing 'winter work'. Although dependence on the tourist industry constituted a fundamental weakness in employment structure, the Island's employment problem was seen as essentially a seasonal one. Although some members of the House of Keys did press for action to diversify the economy, there was no investment in diversification until after the war. In the meantime the main thrust of the Island's policies was directed towards the relief of seasonal unemployment and the strengthening of established industries. Provision of work for the unemployed became one of Tynwald's highest priorities. Pressures from radical members of the Keys and support from other members of Tynwald resulted in the annual adoption of 'winter work' schemes to absorb surplus labour. Initially these schemes did provide work for most of the unemployed, but rising costs – from £54,675 in 1921/2 to £124,000 in 1926/7 – prompted Lieutenant-Governor Hill to appoint a special commission on unemployment which resulted in a more broadly based strategy.

The 'winter works' approach was retained, with Tynwald providing 75 per cent of the wages bill. Unemployment relief for the minority not obtaining work was to be administered through the poor relief system, with Tynwald footing 50 per cent of the bill (75 per cent from 1934/5). A third outcome was the establishment of a Juvenile Employment Committee and the development of policies to help school-leavers find work. The maximum numbers on the unemployment register for the winter months rose from 1,282 in 1928/9 to 1,878 in 1931/2 and remained at that level or slightly above for the rest of the decade. The 'winter works' schemes provided employment for between 50 and 60 per cent of those on the register, the rest being obliged to claim poor relief.

Economic circumstances resulted in increased levels of support for local industry, especially for agriculture and tourism. Separate boards of Tynwald were established to provide assistance to agriculture, forestry and fishing, although the financial support given to fishing was very small. Support for tree planting rose steadily during the 1930s from just under £1,000 in 1920/1 to £4,976 in 1938/9. Support for the improvement and protection of agriculture increased steadily throughout the period from just under £2,000 in 1920/1 to £14,761 in 1938/9. In addition the Agricultural Rates Acts of 1924 and 1929 and the Agricultural Rates and Improvement Fund Act 1934 relieved the industry of much of the burden of rates. The cost of such relief under the 1924 Act was around £5,000 a year, rising to around £15,000 under the 1929 Act and £20,000 under the 1934 Act. The other major beneficiary of government support was the tourist industry. The level of the grant for advertising the Island was increased from £2,550 in 1919/20 to £11,300 in 1938/9. In addition, starting in 1929/30, Tynwald agreed unanimously to provide up to £5,000 a year in support of the TT and other races.

The Tynwald ceremony *After the completion of the business on Tynwald Hill, the processions return to the Royal Chapel of St John's for the Captioning Ceremony. This photograph from 1934 shows the Sovereign's personal representative on the Island, HE Sir Montagu Butler, preceded by the Sword-Bearer with the Manx Sword of State, which is believed to date from not later than the twelfth century, and 'signifies the duty of the Sovereign, acting through Tynwald, to protect and defend the people from the incursions of their enemies, in peace and war'. (Tynwald Souvenir Programme, 1995, 16)*

Manx Finances, 1919–39

The financial relationship between the Isle of Man and the UK became even closer in the interwar period, partly as a result of social legislation by Tynwald and partly because of the further development of the Common Purse Arrangement. Manx Government spending was heavily influenced by colonial controls and UK-based policies. Although the 'reserved services' accounted for a diminishing proportion of the total budget, most major items of 'voted' expenditure were the result of emulating the UK. Education, pensions and national health insurance each fell into this category and, although the support for law and order, housing, roads and agriculture were distinctively Manx, in each case the Island had adapted UK legislation.

In so far as sources of revenue are concerned, the average ratio of Customs to income tax revenue was four to one; the total revenue share in 1938/9 was 73 and 19 per cent respectively. More important from the point of view of UK influence, the proportion of Customs revenue attributable to the Common Purse Arrangement had risen to over 90 per cent by 1938/9. The buoyancy of Customs revenues enabled the Island to manage with much lower rates of income tax than the UK. On introduction, rates ranged from 7.5 to 13.125 per cent. However, for most of the period they were lower and, when in 1938/9 surtax was introduced on incomes over £2,000, the range was from 3.75 to 13.125 per cent. Ironically, given the Keys' struggle for financial control, the policies for which the Income Tax Fund was used were heavily influenced by the UK – the flour subsidy until 1921/2, two-thirds of the cost of old-age pensions and national health insurance from 1921/2, contributions towards the cost of the First World War from 1922/3 to 1933/4 and towards rearmament in 1938/9 and part of the costs of servicing Isle of Man debt from 1933/4.

Changes in the level of spending – the sum of expenditure from the General Revenue, the Accumulated Fund and the Income Tax Fund – for the period are shown in Table 2. There was a major increase in spending during the 1920s from £191,819 in 1918/19 to £524,597 in 1926/7, representing a real increase over the eight-year period of 244 per cent. Between 1926/7 and 1937/8 spending fell slightly below the 1926/7 figure, before rising to a new height of £591,623 in 1938/9, a real-term increase over 1918/19 of 333 per cent.

WAR, SOCIALISM AND DEVOLUTION, 1939–58

The period from the outbreak of war in 1939 to Parliament's Isle of Man Act in 1958 saw both the achievement of Island self-government and a major expansion in the role of the state. There was no postwar socialist victory in the Isle of Man: the Manx Labour Party won only two seats in

Table 2   Manx central government expenditure, 1919/20 to 1938/9

Financial year to 31 March	Total expenditure (£)	Expenditure at 1999 prices (£)
1920	273,454	5,432,711
1921	489,898	9,288,466
1922	304,377	7,477,325
1923	318,354	8,265,107
1924	398,304	10,224,487
1925	416,562	10,633,578
1926	442,326	11,750,832
1927	524,597	14,017,756
1928	486,542	13,556,033
1929	431,862	11,887,433
1930	430,451	12,216,629
1931	463,082	14,106,403
1932	417,889	13,078,672
1933	453,007	14,299,985
1934	495,902	16,185,249
1935	471,483	15,279,349
1936	509,456	15,944,444
1937	499,285	15,108,863
1938	522,548	15,305,953
1939	591,623	17,668,820

Notes

The sources of the raw expenditure data were the annual *Financial Statement* for 1919/20 and the *Accounts of the Government Treasurer* from 1920/21 to 1938/39.

To avoid double counting, expenditure facilitated by borrowing is not included in the raw totals, which are the sum of expenditure from the General Revenue Account, the Income Tax Fund and the Accumulated Fund.

the 1945 general election. It was a liberal/conservative Tynwald that felt obliged to emulate UK policies. The irony is that, as steps were being taken towards the formality of Island self-government in 1958, the real freedom of Tynwald was being progressively constrained by what it saw as a necessary harmonisation of major social and economic policy.

Towards Island Self-government

During the war the House of Keys renewed its demands for constitutional reform. Following an initiative by Samuel Norris, the Keys agreed on 1 December 1942 to appoint a committee to consider the issue of reform. As amended the resolution reads:

> This House believes that freedom of thought, freedom of speech, freedom from fear and freedom from want, and that government of the people by the people and for the people are as essential and as much the right of small peoples as for the biggest nations with whom

we are now fighting as allies ... This House is determined to secure these liberties under Manx Home Rule, and to bring about as great a measure of social service and housing and economic and industrial conditions as is provided for the people of Britain through Parliament, but asserts that it is necessary to bring into operation the same principles of democratic government as are enjoyed in England.[111]

This declaration of principle revealed an interesting combination of belief in the Island enjoying both the same democratic rights as the people of the UK and equivalent social and economic benefits. While the Committee of the House of Keys concentrated on the former, the decisions of Tynwald during and immediately following the war revealed a determination to provide for the Island a similar programme of social and economic reform to that introduced by the coalition and Labour governments.

The central constitutional demand was for an Executive Committee presided over by the Lieutenant-Governor and responsible to Tynwald. Already a number of informal developments had improved the position of the Keys in the decision-making process. In November 1939 the War Consultative Committee had been established to advise the Lieutenant-Governor, Earl Granville, on 'the problems of the day'. Although the Committee was chaired by Deemster Cowley, an ex-officio member of the Legislative Council, five of the seven members were selected from the Keys.[112] This Committee played a central role in decision-making during the war; though circumstances precluded its development as a responsible executive, all proceedings being strictly confidential. In a letter to the Keys on 16 April 1943 the Lieutenant-Governor indicated his readiness, if requested, to meet the Keys' Consultative and Finance Committee to discuss taxation proposals and certain other budget items before they were brought formally before Tynwald.[113] These developments, while beneficial to the House, were not enough. The Keys believed that its proposals for an Executive Committee, five of whose seven members would be from the House, would retain the advantages of an experienced administrator, combine in one body the responsibility for good order and government, including finance and the law and order services, and bring to an end the humiliation of being deemed incapable of self-government.

111] 60 *Manx Deb*, 1 Dec 1942, 111.
112] All seven members were elected by Tynwald with the chambers voting separately and agreeing six names and together to arrive at a seventh.
113] See R.B. Moore, *Memorandum on the Constitutional Position of the Isle of Man with Relation to the Imperial Government, 10 October 1944* (Douglas, 1944), 9.

On 4 January 1944, acting on its Committee's recommendations and freshly concerned at the appointment of a new Government Secretary without any reference to its members, the House agreed unanimously to petition the Home Secretary to receive a deputation to discuss the proposal. The petition was forwarded to the Home Secretary by the Lieutenant-Governor, who argued privately that such radical reforms did not have the support of the Manx people.[114] Before a reply had been received and because of a desire on the part of Tynwald to present a united front at any talks with the UK government, the Keys agreed to moderate its proposals in favour of an advisory Executive Council. That agreement meant that when a deputation was eventually received by the Home Secretary, Herbert Morrison, on 17 October 1944, it was representative of Tynwald and not just the House of Keys.

The outcome of the talks was a letter from the new Labour Home Secretary, Chuter Ede, to the Lieutenant-Governor, providing for the establishment of a seven-member Executive Council drawn primarily from among the Chairmen of the major Boards of Tynwald and appointed by the Lieutenant-Governor on the recommendation of Tynwald. The letter itself was to provide the necessary authority for the appointment of such a Council. The idea that one member might be made responsible for finance was rejected; the whole issue of financial control would be dealt with later by the Treasury. Tynwald accepted this statement unanimously, and on 16 October 1946 the first Executive Council was appointed. Consideration of financial matters was delayed because of the need for legislation at Westminster. In explaining the delay, the Home Office did make clear on 13 April 1949 that the government was prepared to sanction a major transfer of power to the Manx authorities, including the long-sought removal of Treasury control.

The negotiations over the next eight years culminated in two agreements dated 30 October 1957 and the passage at Westminster of the Isle of Man Act 1958 and in Tynwald of the Isle of Man Contribution Act 1956, the Finance Act 1958, the Customs (Isle of Man) Act 1958, the Import Duties Act 1958 and the Loans Act 1958. The details of these negotiations are well documented in a series of reports to Tynwald between May 1949 and September 1956.[115] While

114] In a letter dated 28 Jan 1944; see PRO: HO45/24990/689462/17.
115] See *Report of the Committee Appointed by Tynwald on 3 May 1949 with Reference to Financial Relations between the Isle of Man and the Imperial Government, 29 May 1949* (Douglas, 1949); *Report and Recommendations of the Consultative and Finance Committee of the House of Keys re the Constitutional*

much of the detail had been agreed after the first two years of negotiation, full agreement was delayed by events both in the Isle of Man and the UK. In the Isle of Man there was a major disagreement over the financial role of the Keys and the ineffectiveness of the Executive Council. The House complained that the Council was rarely consulted on the initiation of fresh legislation, police matters, official salaries and establishments and fiscal policy and that the government was invariably fully committed to schemes long before proposals came to their Consultative and Finance Committee. The two branches of Tynwald eventually agreed to concentrate on the transfer of powers from the UK on the understanding that internal constitutional reforms would be tackled following the removal of Treasury control. In the UK a change of government in 1951 was followed by a congested parliamentary timetable and a lengthy process of inter-departmental and inter-governmental consultation.

The first of the two agreements concerned the payment of an annual contribution to the UK. The amount was to be determined from time to time by Tynwald in accordance with the provisions of the Isle of Man Contribution Act 1956 and after consultation between representatives of the two governments. In the first instance the contribution would be 5 per cent of net Common Purse receipts, and this remained the level until the agreement was replaced by the Customs and Excise Agreement in 1979. The effect of the second agreement was to increase the Island's control over its own affairs. The UK government agreed to repeal the 1866 Act. Tynwald was to proceed with legislation on finance, the police, loans, the civil service and harbours as soon as the UK measure became law. Further, the Isle of Man agreed to follow UK changes in Customs duties and not to introduce any fresh differences in duties without first consulting the UK government. The Island would keep its laws on Customs administration in line with those in the UK, and the Commissioners of Customs and Excise would continue to collect all duties as before. The proceeds of 'unequal' duties would be paid straight to the Island, while those of 'equal' duties less the costs of collection and audit would be shared under the terms of the Common

Position, 26 June 1951 (Douglas, 1951); *Further Report of the Committee Appointed by Tynwald on 3 May 1949 ...*, 15 September 1951 (Douglas, 1951); *Report of the Deputation Appointed by Tynwald on 18 May 1954 to Interview the Home Secretary on Matters Relative to the Constitution of Man, 30 October 1954* (Douglas, 1954); and *Final Report of the Committee of Tynwald with Reference to the Constitutional Development of the Isle of Man, 26 September 1956* (Douglas, 1956).

Purse Arrangement. There was provision for the review of the Agreement at the instance of either government. Of the legislation which followed this Agreement the most important was Parliament's Isle of Man Act 1958, which provided for a major devolution of power. It repealed the Isle of Man Customs, Harbours and Public Purposes Act 1866 and enabled Tynwald to legislate on such matters as customs, harbours, loans, mines and government officers, hitherto the preserve of Parliament at Westminster. The most significant change was the removal of formal Treasury control over Manx finance and with it a situation where a large portion of Manx revenue was expended without reference to Tynwald.

Although the Isle of Man Act was an important milestone in the campaign for self-government, it was by no means the end of colonial rule. The Finance Act 1958 left financial power in the hands of the Lieutenant-Governor. Although, with the exception of Crown salaries and pensions and the interest and sinking fund payments in respect of Government borrowing, all expenditure had to be approved by Tynwald, the Lieutenant-Governor remained the Island's Chancellor of the Exchequer; Tynwald's final controlling power was essentially a negative one. The Executive Council remained an advisory body, whose role depended on the good will of the incumbent Lieutenant-Governor. The Act also provided for revenues from income tax and surtax to form part of the General Revenue and for surpluses to be transferred to the Isle of Man Accumulated Fund, £500,000 of which would in future be set aside as a strategic reserve, the Isle of Man Reserve Fund. The Customs (Isle of Man) Act 1958 made provision for Tynwald to impose, abolish and vary Customs duties and provide that such resolutions might have retrospective effect. It empowered the Lieutenant-Governor by Order to bring Manx duties into line with those of the UK. Such Orders required the approval of Tynwald. On paper this Act clearly represented an increase in Tynwald's powers. In practice the change was of little immediate significance as Tynwald had agreed not to use this power without first consulting the UK government and continued to impose, vary and abolish duties in complete accordance with the UK tariff, only beer remaining outside the Common Purse Arrangement. A further piece of Customs legislation, the Import Duties (Isle of Man) Act 1958, merely gave legal effect to the Island's pledge to follow the UK tariff in respect of all protective duties, Imperial preference duties and other duties imposed in accordance with international agreements. The third Manx Act resulting from the 1957 Agreement and passed before the internal constitutional review undertaken by the Commission on the Isle of

Man Constitution, was the Loans Act 1958. This made it possible for loans to be raised just with the approval of Tynwald instead of Tynwald and the UK Treasury and to be charged against all or part of government revenues instead of just Customs revenue. Extensive use would be made of these powers once the outstanding constitutional issues had been resolved.

Set against the democratic ambitions of the wartime House of Keys, the immediate impact of the financial reforms of 1957/8 was limited, given the powers of the Lieutenant-Governor and the continued operation of the Common Purse Agreement. Real progress was to await the outcome of the internal constitutional review that was set in motion in March 1958 under the chairmanship of Lord MacDermott.

The Welfare Revolution

While the branches of Tynwald were divided over constitutional matters, there was remarkable consensus over social policy. Postwar social policies reflected a determination on the part of most Manx politicians to provide their people with the social benefits being made available to UK citizens. The Island adapted UK policy to meet its own particular needs, but without challenging the fundamental principles underpinning the welfare revolution: social insurance backed by the state, free education up to the age of 15 and improved access to higher education, renewed emphasis on the public health role of local government, a comprehensive national health service free at the point of delivery, public sector housing for those in need, and a commitment to government action to ensure full employment. During the war the Island followed a series of improvements in social security provision initiated by the coalition government under Sir Winston Churchill, lowering from 65 to 60 the age at which women could receive pensions, providing for the payment of supplementary pensions on proof of need, extending the scope of the NHI scheme to include non-manual workers earning between £250, the previous limit, and £420 a year, and providing for the payment of family allowances. Keeping in line with the Labour government after 1945 ushered in a much more radical transformation of the Island's social security system. In addition to substantial increases in pensions introduced simultaneously with the UK in 1946,[116] there were two major reforms. Based on the UK Act of

---

116] The Old Age, Widows and Orphans Pensions Act 1946 empowered Tynwald to increase pensions by resolution in order to accelerate the process of conforming with UK rates; *Statutes*, xvi, 306–17. The first use of this power saw the Island increasing the basic pension to 26s (42s for a married couple).

1946, the centrepiece was the National Insurance (Isle of Man) Act 1948. It provided for the compulsory insurance of everyone over school-leaving age and under pensionable age except for unemployed married women, who were to be covered under their husbands' insurance. The insured would be eligible for unemployment benefit, sickness benefit, maternity benefit, widows' benefits, guardians' allowances, retirement pensions and a death grant. Notwithstanding the importance of the legislation it provoked very little debate in Tynwald. One member of the Legislative Council and a minority of the Keys did object to the introduction of unemployment benefit on the grounds that the existing Manx system was to be preferred to an insurance-based approach, but otherwise the provisions were accepted without division. The scheme was radical both in respect of the numbers compulsorily insured – 23,147 in 1951, almost 42 per cent of the total population – and in the scope and level of benefits, the most notable additions being benefit for uninsured married women and unemployment benefit. The National Assistance Act 1951, based on the UK Act of 1948, replaced local poor relief and a range of supplementary national schemes with a single national assistance scheme. Assistance was to be primarily by way of financial aid to those in need, with residential accommodation and welfare services also available for the elderly and infirm. While this measure engendered considerable debate, this was mainly due to the distinctively Manx components of the system being replaced and the extent of adaptations deemed necessary for the scheme – devised to be administered by local authorities in the UK – to operate in the Isle of Man. A handful of members of the Keys did speak against it on the grounds of expense and the adequacy of existing provision, but the second and third readings were approved without division. The result of this legislation was a comprehensive system of social security, providing for people in need 'from the cradle to the grave'.[117] Legislation in the 1950s provided for further increases in national insurance benefits and contributions and in family allowances in line with the UK. The radicalism of the changes over the period as a whole can be seen by reference to the spending on the service, rising from £87,905 in 1938/9 to £486,824 in 1957/8, a real increase of some 151 per cent.

Wartime improvements in the funding of education, including

117] This was a phrase coined by Sir Winston Churchill in responding to the Beveridge Report and quoted by Deemster Cowley during the second reading of the National Insurance Bill. See Nicholas Timmins, *The Five Giants: A Biography of the Welfare State* (London, 1996), 48; and 65 *Manx Deb*, 9 Dec 1947, 186.

substantial increases in teachers' salaries, were automatically followed in the Isle of Man. Parliament's landmark Education Act 1944, as amended by the Education Act 1946, provided the impetus for the major educational reform of the postwar period. Tynwald's Education Act 1949 followed the UK in providing for free compulsory education from the age of five to 15, in primary schools up to the age of 11 and secondary schools up to the age of 15, subsidised milk and school meals and free medical inspection and treatment. It required the Education Authority to provide further education opportunities for persons over compulsory school age. Manx educational institutions were to remain subject to Ministry of Education regulations and inspection by HMIs. In one respect the Island chose a distinctive path, opting for a fully comprehensive system of secondary education, a logical extension of the prewar practice of catering for all ability levels in the same secondary schools. The cost of a greatly improved educational service was very high. Tynwald's share of revenue spending on education – between two-thirds and three-quarters of the total – increased from £63,688 in 1938/9 to £338,203 in 1957/8, a real increase of 141 per cent. During the same period Tynwald's share of capital spending, mainly in the ten years from the end of the war, totalled £250,943.

The creation of the Manx National Health Service was perhaps the most radical of the postwar reforms and certainly the most expensive. The impetus for the National Health Service (Isle of Man) Act 1948 was provided by Parliament's Act of 1946, and a determination on the part of a majority in Tynwald that the Island should follow the UK. At the second reading of the Bill a minority of members in the Keys disagreed because of the expense involved or because they believed that a better way forward would be to reform the NHI scheme to include wives and children, although they did not carry their opposition to the third reading which was approved without division. Under the Act the Health Services Board was given the responsibility of providing 'a comprehensive health service', free at the point of delivery. While the existing public hospitals[118] became the responsibility of the Board, the voluntary hospitals,[119] unlike their counterparts in the UK, were allowed to continue as long as they co-operated 'fully' with the Board. A series of specialist committees, with medical interest group representation, were given responsibility for making arrangements for the general medical,

118] The Ballamona Mental Hospital, the White Hoe Isolation Hospital and the Cronk Ruagh Sanatorium.
119] The Noble's Isle of Man Hospital, the Ramsey Cottage Hospital and the Jane Crookhall Maternity Home.

dental, pharmaceutical and ophthalmic services. Specialist services were to be purchased from the UK and the entire service funded by Tynwald. The special arrangements for the voluntary hospitals and the involvement of medical interest groups in planning the detail of implementation went a long way towards avoiding the bitter conflict that had accompanied reform in the UK. There were short-term difficulties with these groups as a result of Tynwald's decision to bring the service into effect on 5 July 1948, simultaneously with the UK, before it had voted funds for the new service and before the Health Services Board had clarified an interim modus operandi. It was only the good will of the medical profession in deciding to stop charging patients on 5 July 1948 that enabled the Manx NHS to start on time.[120]

Between inauguration day and 1958 the Island developed its health service along UK lines, providing or paying for a similar range of services, paying staff at the same rates as their UK colleagues and, after 1951,[121] following the UK in imposing limited charges for dental treatment, spectacles and prescriptions. The main service remained free at the point of delivery, becoming the most expensive of all public services. In 1948/9 estimated expenditure in areas that were to become part of the comprehensive service amounted to approximately £80,000.[122] In 1949/50, the first full year of operation, revenue spending on the Manx NHS totalled £454,890, the increase resulting partly from extra spending on established public services, but primarily from the funding of the general medical service and the three voluntary hospitals.[123] By 1957/8 spending had risen to £606,869, a 9 per cent reduction in real terms. The first ten years saw very little capital spending on the Health Service; although in 1956 Tynwald did agree in principle to a £395,000 hospital modernization programme, it was two years before work got under way.

120] See C.G. Pantin, *An Account of the Introduction of the Health Service on the Isle of Man in 1948* (unpublished).

121] Under the National Health Service (Isle of Man) Act 1950, *Statutes*, xvii, 962. This amending legislation was based on the Health Services Amendment (Northern Ireland) Act 1950.

122] This figure covers Tynwald's share of the cost of medical benefits under the NHI scheme, the miscellaneous health and welfare services managed by the LGB and the state hospitals at Ballamona, White Hoe and Cronk Ruagh and calculated with the help of the detailed estimates for the Social Services, Local Government and Mental Hospital Boards presented to Tynwald in March 1948; see 65 *Manx Deb*, 16 and 17 Mar 1948, 526–7 and 566–73.

123] The general medical service accounted for 39 per cent of the estimate and the voluntary hospitals 23 per cent; see 66 *Manx Deb*, 26 Apr 1949, 607–21

The war delayed any response by government to the appalling housing conditions at the end of the interwar period. Although housing stock did not suffer the war damage experienced on the mainland, a six-year period of neglect certainly exacerbated the problem. Everybody concerned accepted that the housing crisis could not be resolved without massive public investment. The outcome was a five-pronged attack: a public authorities housing scheme, a temporary housing programme, investment in rural housing, assistance to private enterprise and a modified rent restriction scheme. The proposal for a public authorities scheme was presented on 6 February 1945 and amended on 17 April 1946, following advice that the new Labour government was prepared to sanction higher levels of funding by Tynwald. The scheme was welcomed in Tynwald and approved unanimously. Housing was to be provided solely for the working classes, a restriction removed in the UK in 1948 but which survived in the Isle of Man until 1955.[124] The LGB was to assume overall responsibility. Town, village and parish authorities were to be invited to submit schemes for working-class housing; where authorities did not submit schemes, the Board would become the functioning authority. Functioning local authorities were to receive 75 per cent of the net costs from Tynwald, the remaining 25 per cent to be rate-funded. Tynwald's share of the net costs was to be five-sixths in the case of non-functioning town and village district authorities and 100 per cent in the case of non-functioning parish authorities. Following the invitations, nine local authorities – the four towns, the village districts of Onchan, Port Erin and Port St Mary and the parishes of Braddan and Malew – became functioning housing authorities. The LGB became the functioning authority for Michael and the remaining 16 parishes. Between 1945 and 31 March 1959 a total of 2,117 new houses were built, 1,221 by the local authorities and 896 by the LGB or other government boards. In addition existing housing stock was maintained and upgraded as in the case of the 66 flats built by Douglas Corporation before the First World War.[125]

As it was impossible to meet demand for houses overnight, the government proposed to purchase and convert into temporary housing huts built for the armed services during the war. On 13 August 1946 Tynwald approved the development of the Royal Navy camps at

124] See Timmins, *The Five Giants*, 144. The Manx change came with the Housing Act 1955; *Statutes*, xviii, 544–614.
125] On 25 October 1949 Tynwald granted a petition from the Corporation for permission to borrow £8,000 in order to supply each of these flats with a hot water supply, bath, new sink and tiled fireplace; 67 *Manx Deb*, 26 Oct 1949, 93–4.

Castletown and Ballasalla for this purpose and on 8 July 1947 the Air Force camps at Andreas and Glen Maye, providing temporary housing for 329 families, all but 22 of these having been rehoused by 1958.

Under the Rural Housing Act 1947 the LGB was required to inspect agricultural workers' dwellings from time to time, prepare improvement schemes for approval by Tynwald and authorise financial assistance in the form of grants and loans. The Board was also given the power to require owners to repair or demolish unfit dwellings. The Rural Housing Act 1949 extended the Board's powers so that it could authorise and assist the construction of new dwellings. Both measures were approved without division. Between 1947 and 31 March 1959 assistance was provided in respect of 219 farmhouses and 132 agricultural workers' cottages.

The assisted private enterprise scheme, approved by Tynwald on 16 October 1945, was designed to encourage individuals to build their own house with the help of grants covering 10 per cent of costs and interest-free loans covering a further 20 per cent of costs, subject to a maximum grant and loan of £250 and £500 respectively. The scheme ran for nine years and 532 houses were completed, just over a third of the 1,484 private houses built between 1945 and 31 March 1959. Mortgage interest tax relief provided an additional incentive for home ownership. The renting of private accommodation remained subject to statutory control. The major innovation came with the Rent Restriction Act 1948. This provided tenants with security of tenure, including the right to continue in possession of a property when a contractual agreement came to an end, and security from eviction except by court order, as well as the security against excessive rents that had been provided since 1918.

As a result of these schemes, net expenditure by Tynwald on housing rocketed from £197 in 1946/7 to a high of £380,556 in 1950/1 before declining gradually as demand for housing was met. Between 1946/7 and 1957/8 Tynwald committed a total of £1,563,920, of this three-quarters in the five years from April 1947. By the end of the decade the LGB was able to report that demand for housing had been 'substantially met', the outstanding need being more bungalows for the elderly. A total of 3,601 houses had been built since 1945, of which 53 per cent were in the public sector and a further 17 per cent had been built with the help of public funds.

The Protection and Promotion of Manx Economic Interests

Although the traditional role of government as regulator and developer of infrastructure remained important, the economic role of the state was transformed by the special measures taken in response to the war, the extent of intervention resulting from radical social policies and the dramatic increase in support for the local economy in response to war, UK policies and fear of the consequences of laissez-faire.

The war necessitated an exceptional degree of intervention and regulation. With the approval of Tynwald the Emergency Powers (Defence) Act 1940 was applied to the Isle of Man. The requisitioning by the UK authorities of personnel, land and holiday accommodation for the armed forces, ships for the supply of goods and hotels and boarding-houses for the accommodation of internees, prisoners of war and refugees was accompanied by a flood of regulations, emergency action and special legislation. Although the end of the war brought a gradual relaxation, 'emergency' economic services were still being provided, albeit on a smaller scale, throughout the 1950s and other rationales for intervention soon took over. The welfare revolution brought huge increases in both revenue and capital spending as well as much-needed employment and an increase in people's spending power. By 1958 revenue spending on the three main social services – education, health and social security – had risen to over £1.4 million. The high levels of capital investment in education, housing and public health were crucial in terms of employment, as became evident in the 1950s when they proved unsustainable. Infrastructural investment on harbours, highways and local authority roads was also important in employment terms. After relatively low levels of spending during the war, almost £1 million was spent on harbours and £1,775,114 on highways in the 13 years to 1958. The increase in economic support for local industries was partly in response to the war and partly out of concern to protect vital industries and diversify a vulnerable economy. During the war the Island funded an extremely expensive programme of 'emergency services', the expense resulting primarily from subsidising staple foods – cereals, meat, potatoes and milk products – in line with UK policy.[126] The Island continued to follow UK policy on food subsidies after the war, as a result of which 'emergency services' expenditure remained one of the largest budget items. By 1947/8 annual expenditure had risen to £359,165 and continued to rise to £474,088 in 1951/2 before falling in the late 1950s; the figure for 1957/8 was £251,802. Other schemes for the relief of local economic difficulties included the War Emergency (Relief of Rates) Act 1940[127] enabling

---

126] Expenditure increased from £5,946 in 1939/40 to £251,995 in 1945/6; see the *Accounts of the Government Treasurer* for the period.

127] *Statutes*, xv, 473–5; grants over the seven years in which the scheme operated totalled £63,983.

local authorities to apply for grants and loans to cover the loss of rate revenue, the War (Local Conditions) Act 1940,[128] designed to safeguard the assets of the tourist industry by providing loans and grants to those in financial need, and the relief of individual distress due solely to the war emergency.[129]

Influenced by the parlous state of Manx agriculture, the higher levels of assistance available in the UK and the recommendations by the Island's Commission on Agriculture in 1939, Tynwald agreed to an increase in agricultural subsidies. When the UK increased the level of subsidies during the war as part of the push for food, the Island readily followed suit. Similarly, when the Labour government's Agriculture Act 1947 provided for the extension of subsidies into peacetime, the Island agreed to keep in line.[130] The developing policy of subsidisation provided the main reason for the steady rise in spending on economic support for the industry from £14,765 in 1938/9 to £80,539 in 1947/8 and to £209,524 in 1957/8, representing over the twenty-year period a real increase in spending of 543 per cent. Agriculture also continued to benefit from rate relief. Under the Agricultural Rates and Improvement Fund Act 1934 the industry was assessed for rates at only a quarter of rateable value and the government paid an equivalent sum into an Agricultural Improvements Fund. The Rating and Valuation Act 1948, which provided for the complete derating of agricultural land and buildings, brought the Island into line with the mainland, where derating had been introduced in 1929, and was broadly welcomed in Tynwald as 'long overdue'.

In peacetime tourism reverted to being the Island's main source of income and employment. Issues of access, mobility, health and the cost of living were clearly important for visitors, while the Island recognised the need for explicit measures to protect and promote the industry in a rapidly changing world. After a six-year gap Tynwald resumed its funding for the industry at slightly above pre-war levels. From 1946/7 to 1957/8 there was a steady increase in the funding of the Publicity Board (after 1952/3 the Tourist Board) from £18,885 to £84,000, a real increase over 1938/9 of 134 per cent. Much of this was in response to falling numbers of visitors during the 1950s. Low-interest loans for the

---

128] *Statutes*, xv, 476–84; grants amounting to £69,233 were made over a period of ten years.

129] A total of £35,035 was spent on such relief; see *Accounts of the Government Treasurer* for the period 1939–47.

130] After 1947 most of the subsidy schemes operating in the Isle of Man were based on similar UK schemes; see, for example, 65 *Manx Deb*, 16 Mar 1948, 531–45.

modernisation of tourist premises had been discussed during the war by the War Consultative Committee, but, with immediate postwar demand for accommodation being as high as ever, ten years elapsed before the Hotel and Boarding House Improvement Act 1954 and the Tourist Accommodation Improvement Act 1957 made such loans available. Over the first four years of the scheme a total of £37,431-worth of loans was approved. Of much greater significance in the longer term was Tynwald's approval in February 1955 of a resolution in the name of J.C. Nivison proposing the establishment of a commission to inquire into the state of the visiting industry. The wide-ranging report of the Visiting Industry Commission proved a catalyst for a much higher level of state involvement. After a lengthy debate on 17 and 18 April 1956 Tynwald accepted without dissent that steps should be taken to extend the length of the season, improve the state of the Island's natural amenities, provide support for the development of sport, register and grade hotels and boarding-houses, help to improve the facilities of tourist accommodation, extend shopping hours, preserve the Manx Electric Railway (MER) and increase the powers of the Tourist Board. The Commission's proposal to liberalise the licensing laws for limited Sunday opening was rejected as a result of opposition in the House of Keys. For the longer term the critical measure was the Tourist (Isle of Man) Act 1958, which required the Board to encourage, develop, protect, promote and facilitate tourism by means of publicity, advice, financial support, regulation and inspection, the latter in co-operation with the LGB. This was very much an enabling Act, paving the way for the development of the Tourist Board as the vehicle for a massive expansion of state involvement.

Public ownership did not assume the significance that it had in the UK under a Labour government ideologically committed to nationalisation. However, the Island was not averse to public ownership or nationalisation where the private sector or local authorities had been unable or unwilling to provide the quality of service or level of investment required: similar motives led to an extension of public ownership to include further water undertakings, Ronaldsway airport, Crown lands and the MER. Each purchase was deemed to be in the national interest. On 16 October 1946 Tynwald agreed to the establishment of the Isle of Man Water Board with full responsibility for public water supply outside the Douglas area. The new Board took over the public water undertakings of the Northern and Southern Water Boards and local authorities other than Douglas and the private undertakings of the Ramsey and Peel Water Works Companies for a total of £416,300. Both the water and electricity services received subsidies from Tynwald for much-needed development work after the war, a total over the thirteen-year period of £911,077 for improvements to water supply and drainage and £312,078 for the supply of electricity to villages and farms. During the war the private airfield at Ronaldsway was taken over and developed by the Admiralty for military purposes. In 1945 it was offered to the Island for £1 million, considerably less than had been spent on it but more than the Island was prepared to pay. In March 1947 the Labour government announced that it was no longer willing to subsidise the Manx airport at the expense of the British tax-payer and that it should be purchased and run by the Manx government. On 8 July 1947, with scarcely a word of debate, Tynwald agreed to acquire the airport for the negotiated price of £200,000, knowing full well that it would have to subsidise its operation. The Isle of Man Airports Act 1948 provided for the establishment of an Airports Board to operate Ronaldsway as a commercial service. In the event Tynwald found itself having to approve an annual subsidy, which rose from £21,437 in 1950/1 to £97,128 in 1957/8, a real increase of 255 per cent.

In a similar vein Tynwald agreed to purchase all the Crown's property interests in the Island for £75,000, resulting in the transfer of common lands, forest, minerals, quarries and foreshore throughout the Island. The Forestry, Mines and Lands Act 1950 placed responsibility for these lands in the hands of a new Board of Tynwald. Although the new Board, like its predecessors, engaged in commercial activity, gaining receipts for example from rents and the sale of trees, some measure of public funding was taken for granted. By 1957/8 net spending by the Board had risen to £47,500, compared with £4,883 on forestry alone in 1939/40 and £15,000 on the extended service in 1951/2. Between 1952 and 1958 the Board also received £13,420 of funding for the purchase of seven national glens, Ballaglass and Tholt-y-Will Glen in 1952, Colby Glen and Molly Quirk's Glen in 1955, Dhoon and Laxey Glens in 1956 and Glen Helen in 1958.

The needs of the tourist industry were also paramount in Tynwald's decision to purchase the Manx Electric Railway in 1957. Faced with mounting losses and deteriorating track and rolling stock, the MER Company gave notice to the government that it would have to cease operations after September 1956 and that it was willing to sell the MER for £70,000. After lengthy investigation, negotiation and debate and in spite of warnings of the extremely high cost of restoring and operating the railway, on 12 December 1956 Tynwald agreed by a substantial majority to purchase the MER for £50,000 and in doing so committed the Island to an estimated subsidy for capital renewal and maintenance of £25,000 for the next 20 years. It now fell to the new MER Board, set up under the Manx Electric Railway Act 1957, to deliver Tynwald's ambitious plan in the face of a declining tourist industry and rapidly changing transport needs.

While supporting tourism, the government and Tynwald were anxious to become less dependent on it. The Development of Industry Act 1949 empowered the Lieutenant-Governor to provide financial assistance for the development of light industry, subject to funding not exceeding £100,000 in any one year without the approval of Tynwald. The immediate results were not very promising: only one successful development in the first three years. As a result Tynwald agreed to offer a more attractive package of financial inducements: appropriate new industries would be offered relief from taxation and rates (other than water rates), subsidised freight and electricity, key worker housing, help in obtaining raw materials and access to sites purchased and developed by the government. By 1958 the growth of the Island's manufacturing sector was well under way, new industries employing 380 men and 218 women. There was, moreover, every prospect of further development and higher levels of employment in manufacturing.

The Isle of Man emerged from the war with a commitment to full employment. In spite of the best endeavours of government, however, unemployment remained a problem. Continuing dependence on the tourist industry left the Island with persistent seasonal unemployment. The decline of tourism and the building industry in the 1950s gave rise to year-round unemployment. The recruitment of recent immigrants or personnel from outside gave rise to demands for preference to be given to Manx workers. Towards the end of the 1950s increases in the number of school-leavers, the result of higher birth rates during and immediately after the war, and the prospect of the end of national service in 1960, gave rise to serious concern about youth employment. In pursuance of a resolution of Tynwald, the Lieutenant-Governor's Unemployment Advisory Committee was replaced by a committee of Tynwald. Under the chair of Alfred Teare, an MLP member of the Keys, the Employment Advisory Committee became instrumental in keeping unemployment high on the political agenda. Initially the chief concern was to provide for the large number of men registering unemployed during the winter season, which rose from 481 in 1946/7 to 2,347 in 1953/4 before settling at around two thousand for the rest of the decade. The short-term response was to maximise the amount of public work that could be organised in the winter and to fund special 'development' schemes, although help was also given by the Employment Exchange to find other work both on the Island and on the

The proclamation of the accession of HM Queen Elizabeth II *According to traditional constitutional practice, the Lieutenant-Governor Sir Geoffrey Bromet, along with 'the Deemsters and Keys being here assisted with other officers ... with one voice and consent of tongue and heart, publish and proclaim that the high and mighty Princess Elizabeth Alexandra Mary become our only rightful and liege Lord' was made from Tynwald Hill on 12 February 1952. A similar proclamation was made from Douglas Town Hall. There was newspaper speculation as to whether the new Queen would use the title 'Lord of Mann', as opposed to 'Lady of Mann', as there was no precedent, the title having been introduced during the reign of George VI. (MNHL)*

mainland. Between 1946 and 1958 roughly a third of the men registered were found work on the special 'development' schemes, another third found other employment, often in the UK, leaving a further third to claim unemployment benefit.

After 1952 male unemployment during the summer added to the problem, and attention turned to the longer-term strategies of diversifying the economy and regulating employment. The Employment Act 1954 enabled the Lieutenant-Governor to regulate the engagement of workmen by employers. Under the Regulation of Employment Order 1954 all male workers, except those exempted under the terms of the Order and Isle of Man workers resident in the Island for at least five years, had to obtain a work permit. Exemptions covered the police, civil servants, clergy, doctors and dentists and all employment of a temporary nature not exceeding two weeks. Female unemployment received considerably less attention. Fewer registered unemployed during the winter – between five and six hundred throughout the 1950s with about a third of those receiving benefit – and almost none remained unemployed during the holiday season. Those who registered were helped to obtain work by the Employment Exchange and some gained employment in the new industries, but there was no special winter work and no protection under the Employment Act 1954.

In 1957 Tynwald modified its approach to the unemployment problem. Responsibility for co-ordinating winter work schemes was transferred to the Board of Social Services, leaving the Employment Advisory Committee to organise training, place people in private employment, explore the possibilities of UK employment and devise means of creating new employment. In its Annual Report for 1957/8 the Committee made it clear that, although limited progress was being made, both seasonal and year-round unemployment were proving persistent. Moreover, it warned that matters were likely to get worse, as the numbers of children leaving school increased and national service ended. It fell to a government and Tynwald with their authority greatly enhanced by the Isle of Man Act 1958 to come up with the answers.

Manx Finances, 1939–58

Expenditure continued to be influenced by both UK controls and the practice of emulating UK policies. The expensive social services education, health and social security each fell into this category, as too did the policies of subsidising agriculture and food. Much other expenditure was committed under legislation modelled on that of the UK. On the revenue side UK influence over the Island's indirect taxation became even stronger: it remained the most important source of revenue, although less dominantly so. Whereas in 1938/9 it accounted for 73 per cent of total revenue and income tax only 19 per cent, by 1957/8 the figures were 60 and 30 per cent respectively. In absolute terms, of course, the revenue from indirect taxation increased substantially, as did the UK Chancellor's influence. When purchase tax was introduced in 1941 to raise extra war revenue, the Island promised to keep rates in line with the UK in return for its inclusion in the Common Purse Arrangement. Tynwald also agreed that all duties other than those on beer should be kept in line with the UK. Under the Customs Agreement of October 1957 the Island agreed not to deviate further from UK levels of taxation without prior consultation, in return for which the Common Purse Arrangement would continue. In 1957/8 the CPA accounted for 92 per cent of total Customs and purchase tax revenue. Direct taxation remained at the level necessary to fund the shortfall in revenue from indirect taxation. Increases during the war were followed by temporary reductions in the late 1940s before rising again during the 1950s when the standard rate of tax was between 22.5 and 25 per cent. As in the interwar period expenditure from the Income Tax Fund was almost exclusively on items where the Island was determined to follow the UK.

Focusing on the level of government spending, Table 3 illustrates the magnitude of the change that occurred. There was a major increase in spending during the 1940s, rising from £591,623 in 1938/9 to £2,740,004 in 1949/50, a real increase of 208 per cent. Over the next five years spending levelled out and fell well below the 1949/50 figure in real terms as spending failed to keep pace with inflation, before rising to the new height of £4,137,228 in 1957/8, a real increase over 1938/9 of 217 per cent.

THE CONFIRMATION OF ISLAND SELF-GOVERNMENT, 1958–79

The Isle of Man Act 1958 provided for a major devolution of legislative power to Tynwald but did nothing to meet the aspirations of the House of Keys for more democratic and responsible government. The period between 1958 and the celebration by Tynwald of its Millennium saw a lengthy but ultimately successful campaign by the Keys for a transfer of power within the Island, from the Lieutenant-Governor to Tynwald and within Tynwald to the elected chamber. The Island was able to safeguard its newly won constitutional status in the face of threats posed by UK policies on devolution and Europe. The real value of the Island's special status after 1958 was that it could choose when to follow the UK, when not to and when to develop distinctive Manx policies. The

Table 3   Manx central government expenditure, 1939/40 to 1957/8

Financial year to 31 March	Total expenditure (£)	Expenditure at 1999 prices (£)
1940	571,204	14,581,124
1941	600,777	13,935,022
1942	898,443	20,526,727
1943	963,998	22,135,322
1944	1,739,848	39,750,307
1945	1,718,892	38,883,055
1946	1,394,891	31,397,601
1947	1,716,419	38,446,069
1948	2,044,179	43,244,606
1949	2,753,524	56,543,281
1950	2,740,004	54,339,759
1951	2,526,251	47,705,723
1952	2,895,661	48,899,027
1953	2,798,944	45,113,379
1954	2,678,250	42,680,592
1955	2,877,232	44,355,408
1956	3,277,080	47,458,672
1957	3,915,289	55,174,252
1958	4,137,228	55,989,106

Notes

The sources of the raw expenditure data were the *Accounts of the Government Treasurer* from 1939/40 to 1957/58.

To avoid double counting, expenditure facilitated by borrowing is not included in the raw totals, which are the sum of expenditure from the General Revenue Account, the Income Tax Fund and the Accumulated Fund.

conflicts between successive governments that dominated UK politics were seen to be of limited relevance to the Island. The Island chose not to follow UK legislation in such areas as race, sex and abortion. Perhaps the most significant use of the Island's right to be different was in the way it sought to diversify the economy and assist tourism.

The Confirmation of Special Status
Despite the consensus between the UK and the Isle of Man over the extent of devolution delivered by 1958, controversies surrounding the issue dominated the relationship between the two territories well into the 1970s. In 1966 the UK government used the occasion of converting the Post Office into a public corporation to offer the Island the opportunity to assume responsibility for its own postal and telecommunications services. Although initially turning down the offer, after four years of negotiation, during which the UK authorities agreed to deal with postal and telecommunications services separately, Tynwald agreed to assume responsibility for Manx postal services. This was seen as having

tremendous potential in financial and publicity terms, whereas the tele-communications sector, which was undergoing capital-intensive mod-ernisation, seemed likely to be a major financial and technical burden. The Isle of Man Postal Authority began operations on 5 July 1973.

On 18 January 1977 Tynwald appointed a Select Committee to report on the Common Purse Agreement. The outcome of extensive discussions between the two governments was that a new Customs and Excise Agreement should replace the CPA with effect from 1 April 1980 and that an Isle of Man Customs and Excise Service be established with responsibility in the Isle of Man for functions hitherto carried out by UK Commissioners.[131] The Island agreed to keep in line with UK rates of duty and indirect taxation, save in respect of beer, and to ensure that the Manx Customs and Excise Service corresponded to that of the UK with regard to management, collection and enforcement. Many people associated with the tourist industry were disappointed with the outcome of the negotiations, having seen differences in VAT rates or complete abrogation as a means of revitalising the tourist industry and the economy generally. The issue continued to exercise the minds of the Island's politicians throughout the 1980s and 1990s.

Controversies over commercial broadcasting, the European Econom-ic Community and judicial corporal punishment illustrate well the vulnerability of the Island in those areas which transcend the boundaries of the Isle of Man either physically or as a result of international agreements entered into by the UK on the Island's behalf. The struggle in the 1960s for permission to establish a powerful commercial radio station resulted in the Royal Assent being refused to the Wireless Telegraphy (Isle of Man) Act 1962 and the application of the UK Marine etc. Broadcasting (Offences) Act 1967 to the Isle of Man without the concurrence of Tynwald. The Royal Assent was refused on the grounds that broadcasting could not be considered 'solely domestic to the Isle of Man' and that Tynwald's plans were incompatible both with UK policy and with international obligations accepted with membership of the International Telecommunications Union (ITU). The Island had to be satisfied with a strictly local commercial station. But Manx Radio had hardly commenced operations when on 5 July 1964 the high-powered Radio Caroline began transmitting off the Manx coast in defiance of the regulations of the ITU. Early in 1965 the Island was asked by the Home Office to co-operate in combating pirate radio stations. In spite of

---

131] For details of the negotiations and final decision see Kermode, *Devolution*, 57–8. The Agreement was followed by enabling legislation at Westminster, the Isle of Man Act 1979 and in Tynwald by the Customs and Excise (Transfer of Functions) Act 1979.

warnings that UK legislation would be extended to the Island if it did
not pass its own, MHKs were unwilling to pass the Island's Marine etc.
Broadcasting (Offences) Bill without first being granted greater
transmitting power for Manx Radio. On 7 March 1967 the Bill was
discharged at second reading by an overwhelming majority of 19 votes
to three. On 1 September the UK Marine etc. Broadcasting (Offences)
Act 1967 was duly applied to the Island, the Home Office reiterating that
this was not a domestic matter for the Isle of Man and that the UK was
under an international obligation to outlaw pirate radio stations.

Two days later the Minister of State at the Home Office, Lord
Stonham, arrived in the Isle of Man to establish a Joint Working Party to
examine the constitutional relationship with a view to resolving differences of opinion over what was and what was not domestic to the Isle of
Man. The Joint Working Party met on seven occasions, and the main
result of its one report in 1969 was the establishment of the Standing
Committee on the Common Interests of the Isle of Man and the United
Kingdom, comprising three members elected by Tynwald and three
members of the UK government with a joint secretariat. It was to meet in
London and Douglas alternately at six-monthly intervals or at the
request of either side and would keep under review the practical working
relationship between the two governments. While the outcome of
meetings over the first ten years was mixed – favourable in connection
with the EEC, completely unproductive in respect of Manx Radio – the
new machinery undoubtedly helped create a much better working
relationship between the UK government and Tynwald. The Stonham
Working Party did not resolve the problem of defining what was
domestic to the Island. When the Isle of Man was included in the terms of
reference of the Labour government's Commission on the Constitution
in 1969, Tynwald pursued its campaign for a formal agreement reserving
to Tynwald the right to legislate on all domestic matters, including the
purely local aspects of matters transcending the frontiers of the Island.
The Kilbrandon Commission saw this proposal as a 'wholly impracticable' means of reconciling the Island's acknowledged autonomy in
internal affairs with the UK's responsibility for international relations.

The most serious threat to the Island's special relationship with the
UK arose following the UK's application to join the European
Economic Community.[132] The Home Office made it clear that,
although arrangments might be made to exclude the Isle of Man
from the EEC, there was very little prospect of negotiating a special

---

132] For details see Kermode, *Devolution*, 9–10 and Mark Solly, *Government and Law
in the Isle of Man* (Castletown, 1995), 147–77.

relationship. The choice facing the Island seemed very much one between evils. Entry with the UK seemed likely to jeopardise rights of self-government, the source of much of the Island's prosperity, while exclusion appeared to threaten serious uncertainty for an economy and society so closely integrated with the UK. Thanks to France's vetoes of UK membership in 1963 and 1967, the Island did not have to face up to the dilemma, but following De Gaulle's resignation as French President in 1969 the political climate proved much more sympathetic to the special problems facing dependent territories. The Conservative government was successful in negotiating special terms for both the Channel Islands and the Isle of Man. At a meeting on 28 July 1971 the EEC negotiators indicated that they were willing to adapt Article 227 of the Treaty of Rome to accommodate the islands' concerns. On 9 November 1971 special terms were proposed by the Community under which the islands would be included in the EEC solely for the purpose of free movement of industrial and agricultural products. To that end they would be required to apply the common external tariff, the agricultural levies on imports from third countries and certain parts of the common agricultural policy. Other parts of the Treaty of Rome would not apply. Tynwald approved these terms, well satisfied that a major threat to its special relationship with the UK had been avoided.

Tynwald was far less happy with the decision of the European Court of Human Rights in the *Tyrer* case on 25 April 1978,[133] which involved an appeal to the Court at Strasbourg against the UK for allowing judicial corporal punishment in the Isle of Man. The Court confirmed the preliminary opinion of the European Commission of Human Rights that such punishment was 'degrading' within the meaning of Article 3 of the European Convention of Human Rights. By implication the Acts of Tynwald providing for corporal punishment were declared incompatible with the Convention. Tynwald saw the decision as a gross infringement of the Island's freedom to manage its own affairs. Short of negotiating withdrawal from the Convention, which it was not prepared to do, it had little choice but to accept the consequences of an earlier delegation of authority to a supranational institution.

Towards Representative and Responsible Government
In parallel with Tynwald's struggle to safeguard its authority, the House of Keys conducted a long and eventually successful campaign to

133] Council of Europe, European Court of Human Rights, *Tyrer Case: Judgement 25 April 1978* (Strasbourg, 1978), 16; see also Kermode, *Devolution*, 165 and 168–9, and *The Manx Law Reports 1978 80* (Oxford, 1986), 13–44.

transfer power from Crown-appointed officials to the elected representatives of the people. Having shelved their demands for internal constitutional reform so that Tynwald could present a united front during the devolution negotiations, members wasted no time once the Agreements of October 1957 had been signed. On 26 November Tynwald approved a resolution in the name of E.C. Irving MHK, asking the Lieutenant-Governor to set up a constitutional commission. On 18 March 1958 and following consultations with the Home Office, the Lieutenant-Governor, Sir Ambrose Flux-Dundas, announced the appointment of a five-member commission under the chairmanship of the Chief Justice of Northern Ireland, Lord MacDermott.

The Keys' demands to the MacDermott Commission were for modifications to the composition and powers of the Legislative Council and less power in the hands of the 'outsider' at the head of the Manx government. On 14 March 1959, almost exactly a year after its appointment, the Commission reported.[134] Its recommendations were largely in sympathy with the Keys and ushered in the first phase of reform between 1961 and 1965. The reforms dealing with the composition and powers of the Legislative Council were watered down and delayed by opposition from members of the Council, whereas those providing for the transfer of powers from the Lieutenant-Governor met with broad support in both chambers. This was to be the pattern for the next phase of reforms. Although the driving force for reforms in both areas came from the House of Keys, the initiative for further reform of the Legislative Council came from the House's own Constitutional Development Committee, whereas that for the further transfer of power from the Lieutenant-Governor came from Tynwald's Select Committee on the Duties and Powers of the Lieutenant-Governor. Change was gradual, but taken together the constitutional legislation between 1961 and 1980 effected a major transformation of the Manx system of government.

The Isle of Man Constitution Acts 1961–80[135] effected changes to both the membership and powers of the Legislative Council. They

134] *Report of the Commission on the Constitution of the Isle of Man, 14 March 1959* (Douglas, 1959), hereafter referred to as the MacDermott Report.
135] The Isle of Man Constitution Acts 1961, 1965, 1968, 1969, 1971, 1975, 1978 and 1980; see relevant volumes of *Statutes of the Isle of Man* and the more recent annual volumes of *Acts of Tynwald*. For detail on the background to this legislation and its progress in the face of opposition from the Legislative Council, see Kermode, *Devolution*, 72–9 and *The Changing Pattern of Manx Devolution* (Studies in Public Policy No. 52, Centre for the Study of Public Policy) (Stathclyde, 1980), 24–5; see also Solly, *Government and Law*, 251–61.

provided for the gradual reduction in the official and nominated majority from seven, including the Lieutenant-Governor, to two, the Lord Bishop and the Attorney-General as a non-voting member. The year 1961 saw an increase in the number of indirectly elected members from four to five, 1965 the removal of the Second Deemster, 1969 the replacement of the two nominated members by two indirectly elected members, 1971 the loss of voting rights by the Attorney-General, 1975 the replacement of the First Deemster by an eighth indirectly elected member and 1980 the removal of the Lieutenant-Governor and his replacement by a President chosen from among the nine voting members. The Isle of Man Constitution Acts of 1961 and 1978 brought to an end the formal parity of legislative power between the two chambers. Under the 1961 Act the House of Keys was empowered to override the Legislative Council after it had rejected a Bill in three successive sessions, a two-thirds majority being required in respect of constitutional legislation. This left the Legislative Council with the power to delay legislation for two years. With the passing of the 1978 Act the power to override became available after rejection in two successive sessions, reducing the Council's power of delay to one year.

Side by side with this legislation came moves to transfer executive power away from the Lieutenant-Governor to bodies with a majority from the House of Keys and responsible to Tynwald. The first phase of legislation in the 1960s followed the Report of the MacDermott Commission and moderated the executive authority of the Lieutenant-Governor by establishing a much more formal advisory structure than had previously existed. The second phase between 1970 and 1980 followed recommendations of Tynwald's Select Committee on the Duties and Powers of the Lieutenant-Governor and provided for the formal transfer of power to these advisory bodies. The Isle of Man Constitution Act 1961 placed the Executive Council on a statutory basis for the first time with the duty of advising the Lieutenant-Governor on all matters of principle and policy. Amending legislation in 1968 guaranteed the recruitment of five of the seven members from the House of Keys and made the Speaker ineligible for membership. Additionally Tynwald's system of boards was extended into three areas previously reserved to the Lieutenant-Governor. The Finance Board Act 1961 provided for a Finance Board comprising a chairman and two members, with the role of advising the Lieutenant-Governor on all financial matters. The Police (Isle of Man) Act 1962 set up a Police Board with a chair and two members appointed by Tynwald and two further members appointed by the Lieutenant-Governor, its duties being to provide and maintain a constabulary in the manner required by the Lieutenant-Governor. The Isle of Man Civil Service Act 1962 resulted in the establishment of the Manx Civil Service and transferred to the Civil Service Commission most of the powers of appointment previously reserved to the Lieutenant-Governor. During the 1960s Lieutenant-Governors acted increasingly on the advice of the Executive Council and the new boards, paving the way for a formal transfer of power during the 1970s.

Tynwald's Select Committee on the Duties and Powers of the Lieutenant-Governor was established in 1970 and chaired by the Speaker of the House of Keys, Charles Kerruish. Its terms of reference were to make recommendations for the further transfer of power to Tynwald, fulfilling the broad constitutional objective of promoting Manx self-government. Its recommendations on finance, general functions, the police and membership of the Executive Council met with overwhelming support in Tynwald and no objections from the UK authorities. On 17 February 1976 Tynwald resolved that legislation should be introduced to transfer the financial powers of the Lieutenant-Governor as Chancellor of the Exchequer to the Finance Board. All bills and motions involving public expenditure required the concurrence of both the Lieutenant-Governor and the Finance Board, but formal responsibility for presenting the Island's budgets rested with the Lieutenant-Governor. The main purpose of the Governor's Financial and Judicial Functions (Transfer) Act 1976 was to make the Finance Board solely responsible for those financial functions that in the UK are the responsibility of the Treasury. The Act marked the end of a long struggle by the Island for full control of its own finances. Tynwald also committed itself in February 1976 to legislation transferring a wide range of general executive functions, but action was delayed until after the general election in November. The Governor's General Functions (Transfer) Act 1980 transferred a wide range of functions to boards of Tynwald or other appropriate authorities. Where there was no appropriate body the functions were transferred to the 'Governor in Council', defined as 'the Governor acting on the advice and with the concurrence of the Executive Council'. The Act excluded the Lieutenant-Governor's responsibilities in respect of certain constitutional and ecclesiastical matters, the civil service and the police.

On 13 December 1977 Tynwald committed itself to the transfer of police powers. As far back as 1907 the House of Keys had petitioned the Home Secretary to have the police placed under a board responsible to Tynwald. However, when the Police Board was established in 1962 its powers fell far short of what the Keys had sought. The Lieutenant-Governor retained responsibility for appointments, promotions, discipline and disposition. The Police Board's role was restricted to that of a 'quarter-master's department', looking after 'pay, clothing, housing, equipment and so on'.[136] On 21 June 1978, in the wake of several officers of the Manx force being found guilty of criminal and disciplinary offences, Tynwald asked the Police Board to carry out a full review of the Police (Isle of Man) Act. A divided Board reported to Tynwald in July 1979, the majority favouring the transfer of powers to the Governor in Council, a minority of one preferring to see the Police Board assume full responsibility. The Police (Amendment) Act 1980 implemented the majority recommendation, but only after the narrow defeat of amendments in favour of 'democratic devolution'.

On 19 June 1979 Tynwald accepted the recommendation of its Select Committee on Constitutional Issues that the Lieutenant-Governor should no longer chair the Executive Council, and this was given effect by the Constitution (Executive Council) (Amendment) Act 1980. While the Lieutenant-Governor continued to attend and participate in meetings, this Act ushered in a new era in which real executive leadership was firmly in Manx hands. The combined effect of the constitutional reforms between 1958 and 1980 was a remarkable trans-formation of the pattern of Manx devolution. Whereas in 1958 the Lieutenant-Governor was the Island's chief executive and a dominant force in the legislative process, by the end of this period the Island's leading campaigner for reform, Charles Kerruish, was prepared to describe him as a 'rubber stamp'.[137] The chief beneficiaries of the reforms were the elected members of the House of Keys and the people they represented. The Manx political system underwent a process of democratisation, the reforms finally delivering the representative and responsible government that had been at the heart of the Keys' petition to the Home Secretary in 1907.

Expansion of the Welfare State

Although there were differences between the two major UK parties over both the principle and detail of policy, there were important areas of bipartisan agreement and a common commitment to improving welfare services. For the most part the Isle of Man chose to continue harmonising policy with the UK. There were important differences of detail in the way particular services were developed, but a policy of expansion prevailed. In the case of social security there were few differences even of detail, save in the field of non-contributory benefits,

136] E.C. Irving; see 95 *Manx Deb*, 21 June 1978, T945.
137] In an interview with the author, 15 Sept 1978.

where absence of the constraints of reciprocal agreements left room for local discretion. The Island still ended up following the UK, but after an interval of years and an evaluation of UK experience in relation to Manx needs. Thus the Labour government's introduction of supplementary benefit in place of national assistance grants in 1966 was not followed until 1970, and the Conservative government's family income supplement scheme, initiated in 1971 to help poor families, was not taken up until 1975. By contrast, Labour's replacement in 1977 of family allowances, which were payable only to second and subsequent children, by child benefit, payable to mothers in respect of every child, came into effect simultaneously in the Isle of Man. Total revenue spending by Tynwald on social security rose steadily from £486,824 in 1957/8 to £1,758,772 in 1973/4, before rising sharply to £5,605,037 in 1978/9. This represented a real increase over the period of 169 per cent.

Spending on education also increased dramatically. School buildings were modernised and new schools built to meet rising UK standards; improvements in the numbers, training and pay of teachers mirrored those of the UK; grant aid for education was maintained at or above UK levels and opportunities for post-secondary education were improved with investment in training, a new College of Further Education and support for Manx students to attend British institutions of higher education.[138] In one important area, that of raising the school-leaving age to 16, the Island chose not to follow the UK's 1973 initiative, at least not until 1987. Tynwald did agree in principle to the change on 13 December 1967 and the Education (Compulsory School Age) Act 1971 enabled the change to be introduced once an 'appointed day' had been decided. However following the general election in 1971, the Board of Education twice failed to obtain agreement to proceed on grounds of cost, lack of preparedness and the denial of choice to the group of children concerned.

Tynwald also turned its attention to two long standing issues that were not UK-related. Since 1920 responsibility for Manx education had been shared by a council or board responsible to Tynwald and a directly elected authority, a duality of control that had led to conflict over policy, duplication of effort and debates about their respective mandates and accountability. After several unsuccessful attempts to address this problem, the Education Act 1968 provided for the merger of the two authorities. A new Board of Education was established with five members of Tynwald and 24 elected repesentatives, the former being given a built-in majority on the Board's finance and executive

138] For a detailed discussion, see Bird, *An Island*, ii, 235–90.

committee to retain for Tynwald the financial control previously exercised by the old Board. Both outgoing authorities supported the change, and, although a minority in the Keys would have preferred a smaller Board with one elected member for each of the Island's 13 constituencies, the general reaction in Tynwald was favourable. Much more controversial was the campaign between 1962 and 1974 by the Board of Education and its chair until 1971, G.V.H. Kneale to abolish the education rate, which was seen as a regressive tax on property and an inappropriate vehicle for funding a rapidly growing national service. Eventually in 1971, following yet another rejection of abolition by a clear majority in both chambers, Tynwald agreed to stabilise the rate for a period of five years.[139] Further attempts at abolition were made by Kneale in 1973 and 1974, by which time the share of grant-borne expenditure had risen to over 80 per cent and looked set to rise further as a consequence of stabilisation policy. The first attempt, on 21 February 1973, was narrowly approved by the Keys but rejected by the Council. The second, on 19 March 1974, was amended in favour of a phased abolition, in five equal stages commencing in 1975/6, and carried by an overwhelming majority. Since 1980 the entire education budget has been funded by Tynwald.

Revenue spending on education by Tynwald increased steadily but substantially from £338,203 in 1957/8 to £1,977,248 in 1973/4, before rising rapidly to £6,567,476 in 1978/9, a real increase over the period as a whole of 353 per cent. After relatively modest levels of capital expenditure over the ten years prior to the abolition of the Education Authority in 1968 – a total of £419,647, including 75 per cent of the cost of the new Castle Rushen High School – the next 11 saw extremely high levels of borrowing – a total of £6,250,360 including the cost of rescheduling Education Authority debt and the full cost of a series of school extensions and improvements, new schools including the Queen Elizabeth II High School at Peel and a new College of Further Education in Douglas. While the increases in revenue and capital spending have to be seen in the context of rising school rolls and the declining share of rate-borne funding after 1971, the main factors were undoubtedly the expansion and improvement of the service.

There was similar expansion in public health, especially in relation to the Manx National Health Service. Every attempt was made to keep abreast of developments on the mainland and, where necessary, provide

139] 88 *Manx Deb*, 16 Mar 1971, T555–67. The resolution was only carried in the Legislative Council with the casting vote of the Lieutenant-Governor. At the time approximately 25 per cent of expenditure on education was rate-borne.

Manx people with access to specialist services in the UK. The period as a whole saw improvements in hospital buildings and facilities, in the availability and pay of consultants, doctors and other health service workers, in the quality of general medical, pharmaceutical, dental and ophthalmic services, and in the provision of services that in the UK were the responsibility of local authorities: the ambulance service, maternity care, health visiting, home helps, care in the community for the physically and mentally disabled and the vaccination and immunisation service.[140] Although insulated from many of the conflicts over pay and conditions that plagued the UK service during this period, the Manx NHS accepted the main outcomes of such disputes and kept pay and conditions in line with the UK.

In one important area where Tynwald had decided not to follow the UK in 1948, a decade of experience brought about a change of heart. The 1948 Act had allowed the three voluntary hospitals to continue, with their own management committees but almost 100 per cent public funding. Difficulties experienced in devising a coherent hospital policy, the waste and duplication resulting from separate management and concerns about the lack of public accountability convinced the Health Services Board and most members of Tynwald that these hospitals should be transferred to the Board. The National Health Service (Isle of Man) Act 1963 provided for this transfer, ending the voluntary status of Noble's Isle of Man Hospital, the Ramsey and District Cottage Hospital and the Jane Crookhall Maternity Home. The 1963 Act also provided for the transfer of the functions of the LGB in relation to nursing to the Health Services Board, further integrating the political management of health and welfare services. In the UK the postwar reforms had left the three main arms of the service under separate management; in the Isle of Man a single Health Services Board was now responsible for managing the entire hospital service, the general medical services and those health services that in the UK had remained the responsibility of local government. The Island was able to use its special status to avoid the bitter conflict between the Labour government and consultants over plans to outlaw private beds from public hospitals by choosing not to follow the short-lived National Health Services Act 1978.[141]

The Manx NHS remained the Island's most expensive service

140] Expenditure on the services provided under Part 111 of the 1948 Act increased from £32,035 in 1958/9 to £408,260 in 1978/9; see 75 *Manx Deb*, 16 Apr 1958, 773, and *Isle of Man Digest of Economic and Social Statistics 1980* (Douglas, 1980), 212–15.
141] For a discussion of the conflict see Timmins, *The Five Giants*, 330–41.

throughout this period, revenue spending increasing from £606,819 in 1957/8 to £1,353,942 in 1968/9 and £7,730,652 in 1978/9, a real increase for the whole period of 197 per cent. Work also began on the hospital modernisation programme approved by Tynwald in 1956, the main part of which, a new wing and facilities for Noble's Hospital, had been completed by 1961. This was followed by fairly low levels of spending until the late 1960s. In the ten years to March 1968 total spending amounted to £541,119, of which over two-thirds had been committed to the 1956 scheme. The next eleven years saw much higher levels of spending, a total of £3,260,623 on hospital improvements and extensions, including new psycho-geriatric and therapeutic community units at Ballamona Hospital and a new geriatric day hospital and ward at Noble's Hospital.

Circumstances prevailing in the Isle of Man combined to keep housing high on the political agenda, resulting in an expansionary programme of state involvement. Public sector housing remained the responsibility of the LGB, acting on behalf of rural authorities, and those local authorities that had opted to provide a service since 1946. The funding arrangements agreed in 1946 continued until 1974, when Tynwald agreed without division to take on full responsibility for housing deficiency payments in recognition of 'the urgent need' to accelerate the programme of public building. Between April 1961 and March 1979, 2,075 new dwellings were completed. In 1958/9 net revenue spending by Tynwald on public sector housing, was £20,905 and remained around that level for the next seven years before rising to £562,963 in 1980/1, a real increase for the period of 372 per cent.

In 1962 Tynwald approved two schemes to encourage home ownership. The Housing Advances Scheme provided residents with up to 95 per cent mortgages on houses with a maximum value of £7,000. In 1975 the maximum value was increased to £10,000 and preferential interest rates were introduced for those on low incomes. Up to December 1978 when the scheme was replaced, 4,195 persons were assisted with loans. The Building by Private Enterprise Scheme, a modified version of the postwar scheme that ran until 1954, was designed to help private individuals build their own house with the help of grants covering 10 per cent of the costs, interest-free loans covering a further 10 per cent and low-interest loans a further 20 per cent. To be eligible the cost of the proposed house had to be between £2,000 and £5,000. Between 1963 and 1978 when the scheme expired, help was given to 998 persons.

In 1978 the two schemes were replaced by the House Purchase Scheme, increasing the maximum value of a house eligible for a government mortgage from £10,000 to £15,000 and providing grants of up to £1,000 for low-income first-time buyers. In the first year of the new scheme help was given to 178 buyers. Between 1963 and March 1979 the three schemes provided £365,368 in grants and £24,232,866 in loans. Throughout the period Tynwald retained the additional incentive to home ownership of 100 per cent mortgage interest tax relief.[142] On a much smaller scale support was provided also for home improvement in the private sector, initially under the Rural Housing Acts 1947–55 and subsequently, following similar UK initiatives, under the Urban Housing Improvement Act 1969 and the Housing Improvement Act 1975. The latter brought together the rural and urban schemes under one legislative umbrella, providing grants and loans to enable home owners to bring their dwellings into line with minimum standards. Between April 1958 and March 1979 the three schemes together provided £102,237 in grants and £408,237 in loans.

The role of government in controlling housing rents varied widely between the public and private sectors. The LGB in consultation with the housing authorities determined rents in the public sector and from May 1971 operated a rent rebate scheme for tenants of modest means. In the private sector, however, government had very little involvement. The Island had followed the UK in retaining and strengthening rent control immediately after the war, the Rent Restriction Act 1948 providing for both security of tenure and security against excessive rents. In 1959 the decision not to renew the Rent Restriction Act was clearly influenced by the UK Rent Act of 1957 and was instrumental in removing security of tenure and rent control, save for the controls over the rents of furnished accommodation. Security from eviction without a court order was subsequently provided by the Landlord and Tenant (Miscellaneous Provisions) Act 1975, but between 1959 and 1981 rent control was confined to furnished accommodation.

Economic Support Operations

Faced with declining population and undue dependence on tourism, members of Tynwald set about using their newly acquired political autonomy to create an economic environment that was more conducive to economic growth and diversification. There was a reduction in support for agriculture and heavy investment in tourism, the public

---

142] Between 1927 and 1966 such relief was set against income payable in respect of the gross value of residential property. Although in 1966 such income ceased to be income for income tax purposes, section 2b of the Income Tax Act 1966 (*Statutes*, xvi, 383–462) provided for the retention of mortgage interest tax relief.

utilities and economic diversification. For agriculture and fisheries there was general commitment to provide support on similar lines to the UK, a policy reiterated following UK membership of the EEC. Initially the result was a continuing increase in spending from £218,918 in 1957/8 to £604,007 in 1961/2. Thereafter, the overall trend in real terms was sharply downwards, the 1978/9 figure of £743,031 representing a real reduction over 1961/2 of almost 70 per cent. With tourism the trend was the reverse: the Island did its utmost to stem the decline of what was still seen as its most important industry. Revenue spending by the Tourist Board alone increased steadily from £88,000 in 1957/8 to £221,411 in 1970/1 before rising rapidly to £1,160,271 in 1978/9, a real increase over the whole period of 208 per cent. The Board was also instrumental in funding loans and, after 1974, grants under the Tourist Accommodation Improvement Act 1957 and the Tourist Premises Improvement Acts 1961–74. After an initial burst of lending in the three years following the 1961 Act, applications and loans remained at a low level until 1974. In the five years from 1974/5 to 1978/9 the Board approved £1,278,669 in loans and £528,697 in grants for improvement purposes, a clear indication of Tynwald's growing concern to promote the industry in the years leading up to the Millennium celebrations.

Tourism was also the *raison d'être* of other spending by Tynwald. Much of the work of the Forestry, Mines and Lands Board and the Manx Museum and National Trust was tourist-related. The former remained responsible for the care, maintenance and control of the national glens and some 20,000 acres of open hill land; the latter for the various branches of the Manx Museum, the principal ancient monuments and the lands of the Manx National Trust. Other tourist investments made by Tynwald in this period included the purchase of the Ballaugh Curraghs and the development on site of the Wildlife Park between 1963 and 1966, the purchase of the Laxey Wheel in 1965, support for local authority swimming pools in Douglas, Castletown and Ramsey, substantial grants to Douglas Corporation for the Derby Castle Development Scheme (Summerland) both before and after its destruction by fire in 1972, the purchase and repair of the Gaiety Theatre in 1971, and the funding of the celebration of the Millennium of Tynwald in 1977/9.

The role of government in facilitating and providing transport to and from and within the Island was also crucial to tourism. Access to the Island was promoted as ever by investment in harbours, including the building of the sea terminal in the 1960s and the roll-on roll-off facilities at Douglas in the late 1970s. With effect from 1969/70 Tynwald subsidised the Isle of Man Steam Packet service from Llandudno by providing an annual grant towards the upkeep of Llandudno pier. Between 1973 and 1979 generous loans were provided to the Steam Packet Company for the reconstruction of the Princes landing stage in Liverpool to safeguard the Liverpool-Douglas service. Access by air also depended on public subsidy, the Airports Board receiving an average subsidy of £88,690 in the ten years up to 1967/8, when the level of support rose sharply from £107,493 to £451,869 in 1975/6 before falling equally sharply to the first ever profit of £30,864 in 1978/9.

Within the Island the fact that both Douglas Corporation and the private sector were finding it increasingly difficult to sustain economic services in the age of the motor car persuaded Tynwald to support the idea of an integrated national transport service. Already subsidising the bus/air terminal in Douglas (from 1966/7 onwards), the purchase of new buses and the operation of rural bus services (both from 1974/5), Tynwald agreed in principle to the purchase and amalgamation of the undertakings run by Douglas Corporation and Isle of Man Road Services Ltd. In spite of reservations about nationalisation expressed by a minority of members, the resolution was approved without division and provided the basis for the establishment in October 1976 of the publicly owned and managed Isle of Man National Transport. As with the MER twenty years earlier, the clear undertaking was to provide a subsidised service. In 1978/9, the first full year after nationalisation, Tynwald paid £261,003 towards the cost of vehicles, plant and equipment and £227,605 to cover the deficit incurred by Isle of Man Transport. Simultaneously with these moves, concern was being expressed over the gradual demise of the steam railway. Since the late 1950s services had been cut, winter services withdrawn and the lines to Peel and Ramsey closed. By the 1970s the remaining line to Port Erin was under threat. In 1977 Tynwald agreed to bring the railway into public ownership as a means of preserving a unique tourist attraction. Responsibility for the steam railway was vested in the MER Board. The annual subsidy to Manx railways increased from the £25,000 that had been agreed in 1957 to £127,529 in 1976/7, and, following the purchase of the steam railway, to £370,003 by 1978/9, a real increase over the period as a whole of 245 per cent.

Subsidies were paid also to the public utilities, electricity and water, although not on the scale of the immediate postwar period. Both remained in public ownership. Under the Water Act 1972 the supply of water for the whole Island became the responsibility of the Isle of Man Water Authority, Douglas Corporation relinquishing the independent status it had enjoyed in respect of water supply since 1890. In the case of gas, the role of government had previously been one of regulation rather than ownership. Financial problems experienced by some gas companies meant that they were unable to continue supplying gas. Once again Tynwald embarked on a programme of nationalisation, not out of ideological commitment but because of the failure of private enterprise. Between May 1965 and January 1967 Tynwald authorised the purchase of the undertakings of the Peel Gas Company, the Castletown Gas Works Company and the Port Erin and Port St Mary Gas Company as a means of ensuring that gas supplies were maintained. Under the direction of the Gas Committee of Tynwald from 1967, the Isle of Man Gas Authority from 1972 and the Isle of Man Water and Gas Authority from 1974, a major programme of investment was undertaken and a subsidised service provided to the south and west of the Island. The rest of the Island continued to be serviced by the private sector.

The decisive economic change in this period came in the management of the economy with the explicit purpose of attracting new residents, industry and wealth. This was achieved by establishing the Island as a low-tax centre and providing additional incentives to invest in the Island. In 1956 Tynwald had supported a proposal from Lieutenant-Governor Dundas to appoint an Income Tax Commission to review policy on direct taxation. With four members of Tynwald and three income tax experts, the Commission paved the way for a radical shift in taxation policy. On 21 June 1960 Tynwald accepted the Commission's recommendation to abolish surtax as a means of attracting well-to-do residents, investment in industry and generally 'strengthening the economy of the Isle of Man'. The proposal was approved, after a strongly argued debate, by 15 votes to nine in the Keys and seven votes to one in the Legislative Council, with MLP members strongest in their opposition. Surtax was formally abolished by the Income Tax (No. 2) Act 1960. In 1960/1, the final year in which surtax was levied, the standard rate of income tax was 22.5 per cent and surtax, paid in addition to income tax on income over £2,500, was charged on a progressive ten-point scale ranging from 3.75 to 37.5 per cent on income over £20,000. The revenue from surtax in 1960/1 was £120,694 or 13.5 per cent of total revenue from direct taxation. Between 1961 and 1979 the policy of low direct taxation continued, the standard rate being lowered to 21 per cent by 1978/9.

Policy on diversification was informed by the reports of three major economic surveys in 1960, 1971 and 1975. The 1960 Report by B.A. Williams of Liverpool University[143] resulted in the establishment in

143] *Report of the Isle of Man Industrial Survey 31 May 1960* (Liverpool, 1960).

April 1961 of the Industrial Advisory Council and the Industrial Office, the former with the task of advising Tynwald on industrial policy and the latter having responsibility for implementation. It also persuaded Tynwald to fund a more generous package of incentives for both existing and new industry. Priority would be given to established Manx industries, providing work for the unemployed and attracting new industry compatible with the preservation of the Island as a holiday resort. In addition to the benefits of low income tax and the absence of surtax and company taxation, the Industrial Office was able to offer prospective investors grants and loans for the acquisition of property, the erection or improvement of factories and workshops, the purchase of plant and machinery, housing for workers and the cost of training personnel. Between 1962/3 and 1972/3 Tynwald provided £244,342 in grants, £397,830 in loans and £628,578 for the purchase, erection and repair of buildings. The success of the policy was limited by housing and labour shortages and competition from the UK development areas. Even so, existing firms did expand, new firms were attracted to the Island and between April 1961 and April 1971 the number of people employed in manufacturing rose from 2,189 to 3,111, from 11 to 13 per cent of the total workforce.

Following the 1971 Report by PA International Management Consultants,[144] Tynwald appointed a firm of development consultants, Polecon Company Ltd, to advise on industrial development. The result was a remarkably generous package of incentives, comprising investment grants of up to 40 per cent towards the cost of new buildings, plant and machinery, first-year grants of up to 40 per cent of non-recurring initial expenditure, transfer grants of up to 40 per cent, training grants of up to 50 per cent to employers operating an approved training scheme, loans of up to 50 per cent of the venture's working capital requirement, sites zoned for industrial development, depreciation allowances and the taxation of profits solely at the standard rate of income tax.[145] In the six years from 1973/4 the development of manufacturing industry really gathered momentum, helped by £1,760,461 in grants, £755,627 in loans and £99,738 towards the purchase of sites and the erection of buildings. Between 1971 and 1981 the number of full-time employees in manufacturing increased from 3,111 to 3,467, from 13 to 15 per cent of the total workforce.

One of the recommendations of the 1975 report by PA International

144] *An Economic Appreciation of the Isle of Man* (London, 1971).
145] See *Twenty Fourth Bi-annual Report of the Industrial Advisory Council* (Douglas, 1973); Industrial Office, *Man is an Island* (Douglas, nd [1973]).

was that the Island should endeavour to reduce its dependence on the UK. While Tynwald's response was varied, including attempts to attract European investment and find new markets for Manx goods, the replacement of the Common Purse by the Customs and Excise Agreement and the serious marketing of the Island as a resort in Europe, the most important changes related to the financial sector. The Island's position as a low-tax centre had been greatly enhanced by the ending of the sterling area in 1972. This had left the Isle of Man and the Channel Islands as virtually the only scheduled sterling territories outside the UK, giving them enormous investment appeal. Between 1975 and 1979 the Island embarked on a programme of legislation that was to provide the basis for the rapid expansion of the financial sector. The Banking Acts of 1975 and 1977 aimed to create a more favourable environment for the international banking community and resulted in the incorporation of several new banks, a development accelerated by the UK's abolition of exchange controls in 1979. The Income Tax Act 1978[146] provided for the underwriting profits of captive insurance companies to be exempt from income tax, the first in a series of steps designed to develop the Island as an insurance centre. The Usury (Repeal) Act 1979 abolished the centuries-old practice of fixing maximum rates of interest on borrowing by Act of Tynwald, removing a long standing obstacle to investment in the Isle of Man. Between 1961 and 1981 the number of persons employed in insurance, banking, finance and business services more than tripled from 370 to 1,515, from 1.9 to 5.8 per cent of the total workforce.

These policies on taxation and diversification were the decisive factors behind the remarkable transformation of the Manx economy that occurred after 1961. In the twenty years from 1961 the population increased by 37 per cent from 48,133 to 66,101. There were 19,359 new residents, including 2,092 Manx persons returning to the Island, and a 36 per cent rise in the number of persons in employment from 18,999 to 25,864. Between 1960/1 and 1978/9 the revenue from income tax (and surtax in 1960/1) increased from £896,337 to £16,665,395, a real rise of 351 per cent. Although national income data are not available for the whole of this period, in the ten years from 1969/70 the total income generated from Manx sources rose from £31,109,000 to £140,245,000, a real increase of 55 per cent. Much of that increase was attributable to the financial sector, whose share more than doubled from 12 to 26.5 per cent. By 1978/9 the sectoral composition of national income revealed an

146] Sue Stuart, *Offshore Finance Handbook: Isle of Man 1996–97* (Narberth, Pembrokeshire, 1996), 28.

Island no longer dominated by tourism, the three major sectors – finance, manufacturing and tourism – accounting for 26.5, 13.7 and 11.4 per cent respectively.

One of the overriding considerations behind public policies was the postwar goal of full employment. The expansion of government activity and the economy generally in the 1960s and early 1970s brought the Island close to its achievement. Unemployment remained a problem but a much less serious one as more employment became available outside the tourist sector. After 1974 the Island felt the effects of recession in the UK and beyond, unemployment reaching levels not experienced since the early 1960s. Employment Exchange data for January and July of each year reveal a steady decline in winter unemployment from 1,209 in 1960 to 461 in 1974, a rapid rise to 968 in 1977 and a fall to 781 by 1979. Summer unemployment remained below 250 throughout the 1960s before rising to 547 in 1977 and returning to below 250 in Tynwald's millennial year. One of the most interesting aspects of these changes is the decline in the seasonal variation. While in 1960 the monthly unemployment rate ranged between 9.0 and 3.1 per cent, by 1964 the range had narrowed to 4.7 and 1.4 per cent. The 1978 figures of 3.8 to 1.5 per cent marked the lowest seasonal variation of the postwar period. Employment policy reflected these trends. Winter works schemes were an important ingredient of policy until the late 1960s, re-emerging at the height of the recession on the recommendations of the House of Keys Committee on Unemployment in January 1977. In addition to winter work in the public sector, between 1958 and 1962 Tynwald funded the Private Enterprise Employment Scheme, providing contributions to the wages of additional men taken on during the winter months (October to April inclusive). Similar incentives were made available under the 1958 Farm Labour Scheme and the 1962 Improvement of Tourist Accommodation Scheme. From 1958 onwards additional funding was provided for training and apprenticeships, and 1965 saw the establishment of the much-needed Youth Employment Service.

The Employment Act 1954 enabled the Island to give preferential treatment to resident male workers. The special status negotiated when the UK joined the EEC left the Island free to regulate the movement of labour, prompting an immediate review of the 1954 Act; this led to a major extension of powers to regulate employment. The Control of Employment Act 1975 extended the work permit system to include female workers and the self-employed and changed the residential qualification for Isle of Man worker status from five to ten years. Exempted employments were unchanged. However, the rapid rise in year-round unemployment after 1975 convinced Tynwald of the need to limit the exemption in respect of temporary employment. On 16 November 1977 the exemption in respect of temporary employment was reduced from two weeks to three days.

Manx Finances, 1958–79

UK influence remained a dominant feature of Manx expenditure. The Island continued to harmonise policy with the UK in such high-spending areas as police, agriculture, education, health and social security, which together accounted for two-thirds of total revenue spending in 1978/9, and much other expenditure was committed under legislation adapted from the UK. On the revenue side UK influence over indirect taxation remained almost total. By the time the Common Purse Agreement gave way to the Customs and Excise Agreement in 1979, it had been modified to include pool-betting duty in 1961, the Continental Shelf Agreement in 1966 and value added tax (VAT) in 1973 and accounted for 94.4 per cent of revenue from indirect taxation. Between 1958/9 and 1978/9 the revenue from indirect taxation increased from £2,338,998 to £18,393,920. Notwithstanding this 86 per cent increase in real terms, its share of total revenue fell from 65 per cent to 48.4 per cent. The main reason for the decline was the massive increase in the revenue from income tax, whose share more than doubled from 22 per cent in 1958/9 (including revenue from surtax) to 44.8 per cent in 1978/9. As can be seen from Table 4, devolution in 1958 did not usher in an immediate increase in the real level of spending. On the contrary, economic and demographic circumstances combined to limit the postwar expansion. After the constitutional changes of 1958 the real level of spending fell below the postwar high of 1957/8 for seven out of the next eight years (1961/2 being the exception), before rising steadily for the rest of the period. Taking this inflationary period as a whole, expenditure rose from £4,137,228 in 1957/8 to £32,215,373 in 1978/9, a real increase of 81 per cent.

CONCLUSION

Although there may have been controversy over the timing of Tynwald's celebration of its Millennium in 1979, few would dispute the significance of the occasion in relation to the Island's constitutional progress towards self-government. The goal of democratic and responsible government set by constitutional reformers during the first decade of the twentieth century was eventually achieved during the 1970s with the major transfer of power from the Lieutenant-Governor and the constitutional ascendancy of the elected chamber. However,

Table 4   Manx central government expenditure, 1958/9 to 1978/9

Financial year to 31 March	Total expenditure (£)	Expenditure at 1999 prices (£)
1959	3,970,994	52,814,220
1960	3,857,992	51,592,927
1961	4,129,246	53,750,395
1962	4,829,011	60,290,202
1963	3,979,001	48,145,912
1964	3,966,774	47,311,713
1965	4,232,278	48,319,917
1966	5,071,484	55,527,678
1967	5,595,295	59,198,221
1968	5,840,205	59,774,498
1969	6,605,914	63,614,951
1970	6,820,647	62,470,305
1971	7,993,056	67,309,524
1972	9,116,607	71,364,799
1973	10,080,789	72,944,589
1974	11,624,339	74,116,785
1975	16,126,145	84,871,901
1976	21,544,907	93,591,076
1977	24,391,003	92,856,548
1978	27,772,294	96,119,909
1979	32,716,691	103,352,020*

Notes

The sources of the raw expenditure data were the *Accounts of the Government Treasurer* from 1958/59 to 1980/81.

To avoid double counting, expenditure facilitated by borrowing is not included in the raw totals which are:
i) 1958/59 to 1961/62 The sum of expenditure from the General Revenue Account and the Accumulated Fund.
ii) 1962/63 to 1980/81 The sum of expenditure from the General Revenue Account.
* to nearest £10.

although the transfer of power left the executive arm of government in the hands of locally elected representatives, the end result was a fragmented executive, an Executive Council dominated by the chairs of the major spending boards and a multiplicity of boards of Tynwald and other statutory bodies, most of which were not represented in the central executive body. Moreover, in contrast to the UK there was no disciplined majority party to integrate the fragments. Dissatisfaction with this state of affairs led to demands for a rationalisation of the board system and the eventual adoption of a ministerial system.[147] In a

147] For a discussion of the operation of the Executive Council and the board system during the 1970s, see Kermode, *Devolution*, 93–8 and 124–30; for an analysis of the development and operation of the ministerial system see the next chapter.

similar vein, the moves away from equal bicameralism in 1961 and 1978 heralded a period of heart-searching about the future role of the Legislative Council, although to date it has survived with its 1979 membership and role largely intact.

In respect of social and economic policy, this chapter has shown an uneven but unrelenting increase in the role of the state in Manx society. While on the social front the major force for change has been the Island's desire to emulate the UK, on the economic it has been the determination, especially after 1958, to protect and promote the Manx economy. The period since 1979 has seen little relaxation of the role of the Manx state. On the contrary, at a time when the Thatcher and Major governments in the UK were seeking to push back the frontiers of the state by introducing free-market principles into welfare provision and privatisation and deregulation into the economy, in the Isle of Man both the welfare and economic roles of the state have continued unabated. A prosperous financial sector has provided the economic wherewithal to sustain and expand the real level of support for both welfare provision and the economy. The constitutional and political changes over the whole of the twentieth century will be discussed in more detail, in the light of ongoing research, in a full-length study by the author, entitled *Offshore Island Politics: The Constitutional and Political Development of the Isle of Man in the Twentieth Century.*[148]

STATISTICAL APPENDIX

Historical retail prices index 1900–99

	Index base (1900 = 100)	Factor to increase to 1999 prices
1901	100.0	52.645
1901	99.2	53.072
1902	96.9	54.340
1903	101.0	52.121
1904	99.1	53.126
1905	99.5	52.911
1906	102.2	51.505
1907	103.7	50.756
1908	104.9	50.172

148] As a Centre for Manx Studies monograph (forthcoming, Liverpool University Press).

	Index base (1900 = 100)	Factor to increase to 1999 prices
1909	106.4	49.460
1910	100.0	52.645
1911	99.0	53.180
1912	100.5	52.382
1913	102.7	51.253
1914	115.4	45.623
1915	132.5	39.734
1916	155.5	33.847
1917	195.9	26.879
1918	218.9	24.049
1919	247.7	21.253
1920	265.0	19.867
1921	277.7	18.960
1922	214.3	24.566
1923	202.8	25.962
1924	205.1	25.671
1925	206.2	25.527
1926	198.2	26.566
1927	197.0	26.721
1928	188.9	27.862
1929	191.3	27.526
1930	185.5	28.381
1931	172.8	30.462
1932	168.2	31.297
1933	160.1	32.873
1934	161.3	32.638
1935	162.5	32.407
1936	168.2	31.297
1937	174.0	30.261
1938	179.7	29.291
1939	176.3	29.865
1940	206.2	25.527
1941	227.0	23.195
1942	230.4	22.847
1943	229.3	22.962
1944	230.4	22.847
1945	232.7	22.621
1946	233.9	22.509

	Index base (1900 = 100)	Factor to increase to 1999 prices
1947	235.0	22.399
1948	248.9	21.155
1949	254.7	20.670
1950	265.5	19.832
1951	278.8	18.884
1952	311.8	16.887
1953	326.6	16.118
1954	330.3	15.936
1955	341.5	15.416
1956	363.5	14.482
1957	373.6	14.092
1958	389.0	13.533
1959	395.8	13.300
1960	393.7	13.373
1961	404.4	13.017
1962	421.7	12.485
1963	435.1	12.100
1964	441.4	11.927
1965	461.1	11.417
1966	480.8	10.949
1967	497.6	10.580
1968	514.4	10.235
1969	546.7	9.630
1970	574.8	9.159
1971	625.1	8.421
1972	672.6	7.828
1973	727.5	7.236
1974	825.6	6.376
1975	1000.3	5.263
1976	1211.9	4.344
1977	1382.8	3.807
1978	1520.9	3.461
1979	1666.4	3.159
1980	2017.8	2.609
1981	2254.1	2.335
1982	2525.6	2.084
1983	2681.9	1.963
1984	2811.6	1.872

	Index base (1900 = 100)	Factor to increase to 1999 prices
1985	3017.6	1.745
1986	3103.7	1.696
1987	3216.4	1.637
1988	3367.9	1.563
1989	3575.1	1.473
1990	3867.2	1.361
1991	4171.4	1.262
1992	4399.2	1.197
1993	4509.5	1.167
1994	4619.8	1.140
1995	4761.6	1.106
1996	4909.4	1.072
1997	5023.3	1.048
1998	5166.3	1.019
1999	5264.5	1.000

Note

From 1900 to 1914 the index is from E.H. Phelps Brown and Sheila V. Hopkins, 'Seven Centuries of the Prices of Consumables, compared with Builder's Wage Rates', *Economica* N.S. (1956). For the period from 1914–76 the United Kingdom General Index of Retail Prices has been used. The Isle of Man General Index of Retail Prices has been used for the period since 1976. From 1914 onwards the index for March has been used.

Tynwald Transformed, 1980–96

ALISTAIR RAMSAY

T he 1980s and early 1990s proved a period of major change for both the political structure and economy of the Isle of Man. A ministerial system of government replaced the traditional boards, concentrating executive power in the hands of a minority of Tynwald members. Unprecedented economic growth in the latter half of the 1980s, led by the financial services sector, allowed the new Council of Ministers to spend generously on public services and capital projects. But there were counter-effects. Organised opposition appeared in Tynwald for the first time, raising the prospect of party politics, and rapid development created social and environmental concerns. In the meantime the Island became increasingly aware of the international dimension, particularly with the development of the European Union, as an influence on domestic legislation and the economic future.

A Manx 'Cabinet'

The gradual diminution of the executive role of the Lieutenant-Governor culminated in his removal, by legislation of 1980, from the chair of Executive Council.[1] But the process of constitutional change throughout the 1960s and 1970s had left a 'vacuum' at the centre of government. Such was the view of the Tynwald Select Committee on Constitutional Issues in its third interim report, published in April 1983, on the future of the board system. Chaired by Executive Council chairman Percy Radcliffe, the committee contended that, in practice, each board of Tynwald could 'carry out its activities without reference to any other agency of the Isle of Man Government'. The report declared:

1] The Constitution (Executive Council) (Amendment) Act 1980.

> Though the present board system has undoubtedly served the Isle of Man well in the past, it is cumbersome and productive of rivalry between its several sectors . . . In times past, the Governor acted as the co-ordinating and stimulating force holding together the various statutory bodies, each carrying out its respective statutory functions in its own watertight container. In the vacuum created by his removal from day to day executive activity, no such co-ordination is possible, unless Executive Council can adopt a more cabinet style role.

The method of electing members to Executive Council did not ensure that it represented the whole of Tynwald or the views of the principal agencies of government. The report argued: 'Thus it has not always been capable of giving the lead in policy sought by Tynwald or of acting in the decisive way regarded as desirable.'

The committee recommended the introduction of a ministerial system with a chief minister elected by Tynwald heading a 'cabinet' of ministers in charge of the main areas of government. Other members would act as 'assistants' to the ministers, and no member would serve in more than one ministry. The detailed reorganisation of more than twenty individual boards into the eight new ministries would be considered by the Tynwald Select Committee on Boards' Responsibilities, originally established in November 1980.

The June 1983 sitting of Tynwald which debated the Constitutional Issues report heard more about why and how the system should change. Percy Radcliffe summarised the view of the committee that 'no changes vis-a-vis the Isle of Man's relationship with the United Kingdom can be made until the internal workings of the Isle of Man Government are rationalised and modernised'. Furthermore, the term 'chairman of the board' related more to local authority politics than to national government. Radcliffe said: 'Any member who has gone away from this Island to negotiate with officials of ministries at the Home Office will know that the term "chairman" carries less weight and authority with it than the term "minister".' Nor would the change be merely cosmetic:

> The chairman of a board speaks on behalf of his board but is subject to decisions taken collectively within that board. A minister will have ministerial responsibility. He will obviously be guided by the assistant ministers within his department but ultimately he will be the man responsible for the policy of the ministry.

What was proposed was 'a very radical change', but consensus politics would continue as the majority of members would still be involved in government. However, Radcliffe did see 'an opportunity for the Isle of Man to create a more efficient and authoritative government machine which will enable it to move with confidence into the future'.

Other arguments in favour of the ministerial system were voiced during the ensuing debate: it would clearly identify the executive responsible for making policy, leaving parliamentary select committees to their proper role of scrutiny; its greater accountability, co-ordination and efficiency would cut down on administrative error and waste; it would concentrate members' time and abilities within specific areas of government. Perhaps most persuasive of all, in the context of the recession and unemployment of the early 1980s, the new structure would better equip government to achieve economic development.[2]

But there was resistance: a minority of 'yes men' would carry the major load of responsibility, excluding the majority from power and influence; constitutional evolution should be a slow process; more detail was needed – the proposed scheme had not been thought through; it could succeed only under a party system; the cabinet's influence would create 'a one-party state'.

Nevertheless, the Third Interim Report of the Select Committee on Constitutional Issues was approved by 12 votes to nine in the House of Keys, with three for and three against in the Legislative Council, carried by the casting vote of the Governor.

This did not settle the matter, however. A joint report from the Constitutional Issues and Boards' Responsibilities committees on detailed implementation of the new system was rejected by Tynwald in February 1984. In March the former committee was successful in proposing a modified reform subsequently given effect by the Constitution (Executive Council) Act 1984, reconstituting Executive Council to consist of a chairman and the chairmen of eight major boards (finance, home affairs, industry, agriculture and fisheries, health services, tourism, local government, and education).

The demand for a full ministerial system was back on the Tynwald agenda in July 1985, when an overwhelming majority of members supported a call for appropriate recommendations to be produced. The

---

2] Thus R.E.S Kerruish's speech in the debate on the *Third Interim Report of the Select Committee on Constitutional Issues*, Tynwald, 21 June 1983: 'What is the problem we face at the present time? Very largely, to broaden and strengthen our economy, so that we can provide worthwhile job opportunities for the increasing population and particularly the increasing workforce we have to face in the future ... If we are going to meet that challenge, it is going to call for sound, co-ordinated policies and firm and sound leadership, and this is just what the new system is designed to provide.'

Select Committee on Boards' Responsibilities, working in conjunction with the Constitutional Issues Committee, duly reported in September, declaring: 'We remain convinced that the existing board system, under which a member may be required to serve on as many as five boards with unrelated duties, is no longer satisfactory and is unsuited to be the basis of the executive government of a modern country in the closing decades of the 20th century.'[3]

The committee, chaired by Dr Edgar Mann MLC (by then chairman of Executive Council), proposed a structure of nine 'departments', each headed by a 'minister' who would be a member of the 'Council of Ministers' (as Executive Council would be renamed). The chairman of Executive Council would become 'Chief Minister'. Thereafter the foundations of the new system were put in place with remarkable speed, given the magnitude of the change, and initial legislation had been passed by the time of the House of Keys general election in November 1986.[4]

The reorganisation of boards, their reduction in number and their transformation into 'departments' took place in stages. Meanwhile the Constitution (Executive Council) (Amendment) Act 1986 provided that Executive Council would comprise a Chief Minister, to be appointed by the Governor on the nomination of Tynwald after a general election, and nine ministers. Ministers would be nominated by the Chief Minister, each nomination requiring majority support in Tynwald, and would hold office for three years. The Chief Minister would hold office until the next general election.

The crucial move from the collective decision-making of the old board system to the vesting of power in individual ministers came with the Government Departments Act 1987. This gave ministers authority to exercise all the functions of their department, and the ability to delegate authority. Subsequently the Council of Ministers Act 1990 replaced and repealed the Constitution (Executive Council) Act 1984 and the Constitution (Executive Council) (Amendment) Act 1986. Under this new legislation the Chief Minister no longer required Tynwald approval for his choice of ministers, who remained in office at his pleasure. The 1990 Act dispensed with the fixed three-year term of office for ministers and formally renamed Executive Council as the Council of Ministers (a term that had been in unofficial use for some time).

3] *Report of the Select Committee of Tynwald on the Responsibilities of Boards of Tynwald etc*, Sept 1985.
4] Constitution (Executive Council) (Amendment) Act 1986.

The Prosperous and Caring Society

The House of Keys returned by the general election of November 1986 contained no fewer than 11 new faces. Five former MHKs had lost their seats and six had retired. Amongst the casualties of the polls was Dr Edgar Mann, formerly chairman of Executive Council, who was defeated in Garff after stepping down from the Legislative Council. The following month Tynwald chose Miles Rawstron Walker as the Isle of Man's first ever Chief Minister. Walker, a dairy farmer and chairman of the Local Government Board in the previous administration, was the only nomination for the post, in which he was to remain for the next ten years. His selection of ministers, approved by Tynwald by 18 votes to 14, comprised six MHKs and three MLCs, representing a broad range of political views, all independents except one member of the Manx Labour Party.[5]

The first policy document to be produced by a clearly identifiable Manx government appeared in October 1987 under the title 'The Development of a Prosperous and Caring Society'. This was a kind of post-election manifesto, reflecting priorities with which few in the Isle of Man could or did disagree – the economy, jobs, public services, protection of the Island's way of life. 'Our aim', it announced, 'must be to ensure that the management of the economy of the Isle of Man is conducted in such a way as to maximise the standard of living of the population, bearing in mind the need to safeguard the quality of life and overall environment':

> We must maintain and build a prosperous, law abiding and caring free enterprise society. A society which allows ample freedom for private enterprise to develop and flourish and encourages the creation of wealth; a society which nevertheless is caring – looking after the weaker members of society to ensure that they get the services and help they need. Caring also to ensure that prosperity as it develops is shared, not by means of penal taxation, but by reasonable redistributive measures and the provision of good public services. Caring, not just for people but for our way of life, our environment and our heritage.

The document went on: 'We propose a government committed to moderation, to stability and to evolutionary rather than revolutionary change; a government wise enough to follow what is good in the United

---

5] The Manx Labour Party member was Eddie Lowey, an MHK for Rushen, who was appointed Minister for Home Affairs.

Kingdom and elsewhere but bold enough to opt for differences where they are needed to suit the Island.'

It was obvious from this report that economic growth would be the cornerstone of policy, to provide jobs and revenue to fund public services. The achievement of the 'Prosperous and Caring Society' would require a sustained real increase in national income. At the time of the 1986 general election the Isle of Man's resident population was under 65,000.[6] The latest figures in 'The Development of a Prosperous and Caring Society' showed Manx GDP (gross domestic product) per head at just 57 per cent of the United Kingdom equivalent. Nearly a quarter (24 per cent) of residents were over retirement age, which was one-third more than the UK average and, said the report, was a 'considerable burden' on health and welfare services.

The recession of the first half of the 1980s had not halted the rise in government spending, which had increased twice as rapidly as income between 1981 and 1986.[7] Major capital schemes completed during the period included the new reservoir at Sulby and a new breakwater at Douglas. Unemployment had reached 11 per cent by 1984/5. The recession, which saw GDP fall an alarming 28 per cent in real terms between 1980 and 1982, combined with the Savings and Investment Bank (SIB) collapse of 1982 to concentrate minds on recovery. Much of the legislative and fiscal framework of the subsequent economic revival was put in place during this period: the 1981 Exempt Insurance Companies Act, designed to attract captive insurance companies; the creation of a new supervisory regime for financial services following the embarrassment of SIB; the 1984 Merchant Shipping (Registration) Act, to encourage ship management; and the 1984 Income Tax (Exempt Companies) Act, extending tax exemption for certain companies.

The 1987 policy report conceded that the Island's prospects were limited by its geographical isolation and small population, which constrained markets for goods and services. Room for fiscal manoeuvre was tightly restricted:

> There are limitations on our ability as a government to manage the economy effectively. It is difficult to contemplate change in the rate of direct taxation because of the need to remain competitive with other jurisdictions. The Customs Agreement with the United Kingdom fetters our discretion on changing indirect taxation.

6] The census carried out in April 1986 showed a resident population of 64,282.
7] 'The Development of a Prosperous and Caring Society', 1987, 5.

As a small, peripheral community the Isle of Man was vulnerable to external influences over which it had no control, such as international recession and standardising developments in the European Community. Yet the report was optimistic for the future. The Island's attractions included political independence and social stability, low tax, modern communications with the outside world and good public services. There was also the physical space to accommodate growth: 'Low population density gives us the scope and capacity to absorb some development and some increase in population without serious damage.'

The immediate economic goal (although without a target date) was set as per capita GDP parity with the UK. This was a substantial undertaking but the rewards of success would be considerable: 'We should be able to see increases in average earnings and a higher standard of living for all; higher government revenues and better and more sustainable public services.' However, with necessary economic development the public would have to accept some increase in population 'caused by the immigration of people willing to invest and work in or from the Island.' But there would be no laissez-faire approach to growth; indeed, managing its social consequences would be a preoccupation for government in such areas as housing, planning and public services. Nor would the climate of prosperity be for the exclusive benefit of a minority. Although government was committed to free enterprise and low taxation, the aim was to distribute the fruits of growth throughout the community, with a generous benefits system for those in need and a policy of removing those on modest incomes from the taxation net:

> To raise the living standards of the few and ignore the needs of the many would be both unjust and divisive ... Everyone must share in the benefits of progress ... Growing prosperity must be shared, good services must be provided and the elements which go to make up the quality of life must be protected.

Even as these words were being written the Manx economy, which had already started recovering, was entering a period of rapid growth unprecedented in recent history. The years 1987–9 saw the annual economic growth rate reach 17 per cent, driven by the burgeoning financial services sector. This sudden upsurge can be attributed to a variety of factors, both external and internal. It coincided with a finance-led boom in the UK and with mounting cost and capacity pressures in the rival offshore centres of the Channel Islands; the Isle of Man offered a cheaper and more spacious alternative. The Island had begun to build up a more respectable image with the development of a stringent regulatory regime for financial services. Some attractive commercial legislation was already in place.

Whatever the precise causes of the boom, the results were dramatic. In his end-of-term policy report of 1991 (published just before the general election of that year) Walker was able to look back on a period of 'very considerable progress'. National income had risen from £242 million in 1985–6 to more than £480 million, an increase of 58 per cent in real terms. In effect the Island's total wealth had grown by more than half as much again in five years. Despite a reduction in the lowest rate of income tax from 20 per cent to 15 per cent in 1988, and the raising of tax thresholds and allowances, government revenues soared. Its annual spending on public services grew by 31.7 per cent over the five years to £306.2 million, and its reserve fund was increased from £6.8 million in 1986 to £64 million in 1991.[8]

The Pressures of Growth

Income and expenditure were indeed prodigious, but the sudden immigration and inflation of the late 1980s made it an uncomfortable period for politicians. The Island's population increased by five thousand between 1986 and 1991, when the census revealed that the Manx-born had become a minority for the first time, albeit only just at 49.6 per cent of residents.[9] House prices shot up, the average rising from £34,614 in 1986 to £82,300 four years later.[10] Redevelopment, particularly in Douglas, led to a spate of evictions from private rented accommodation and lengthening waiting lists for public sector housing. Government struggled to keep on top of the situation, despite its ever more generous mortgage scheme to assist local first-time buyers. There was a feeling that the economy was over-heating and out of control. The vocal leader of local members of the Transport Union was quick to protest that the working class was missing out on 'The Prosperous and Caring Society' and warned, not for the first nor the last time, of a new militancy amongst trade unionists.[11] The sense of unease was heightened by the mysterious 'FSFO' (subsequently revealed to be an Anglo-Saxon instruction to the finance sector) campaign of daubing and arson, for which three young Manx nationalists were gaoled in March 1989.

8] *Isle of Man Government Policy Review*, Oct 1991.
9] Isle of Man Census Report. The resident population was 69,788 in April 1991.
10] Isle of Man Government, *Digest of Economic and Social Statistics 1996*, section 12.3.
11] TGWU District Officer Bernard Moffatt, reported in *Manx Independent*, Sept 1987.

Although legislative and fiscal developments in support of financial services continued, government decided early in 1988 to curtail its commercial marketing of the Island, 'a reaction to the onset of pressures affecting the labour market, housing, and property values, and to the visible impact of development on the urban and rural landscape'.[12] The year 1988 also saw the government's Social Issues Committee propose the introduction of a residence law to provide comprehensive control over immigration to the Island. This major piece of legislation had not been enacted by the time of the general election of 1996, but was still on the agenda. The policy report of that year stated:

> Government's population policy includes a commitment to ensure that the population does not, by virtue of its structure, size and rate of growth, prejudice the quality of life on the Island. This commitment requires there to be a facility which government can use to limit excessive immigration and powers to this end are to be provided in the Residence Bill which is included in the legislative programme.

The report added: 'It should be stressed, however, that it is not intended that the Bill should be brought into effect unless and until circumstances arise which make that necessary. Such circumstances do not exist at present, nor are they seen as likely to develop in the short to medium term.'[13]

A Generous Government

Economic growth slowed markedly and then revived in the first half of the 1990s, and in his final policy report in 1996, after a decade as Chief Minister, Walker produced some impressive statistics. The Island's GDP had risen 55 per cent in real terms since 1986–7, to around £600 million. The principal engine of growth was the finance sector, which had trebled its real income and contributed 36 per cent of national income compared with 22 per cent in 1985–6. The income gap with the UK had closed, with Manx national income per head at 77 per cent of the mainland equivalent by 1994–5, up 20 per cent since 1985–6. The annual earnings survey showed an 18 per cent increase in real average earned income per head between 1988, when the survey started, and 1995. The resident population had grown from 64,282 in 1986 to 71,769

12] From *Prosperity Through Growth*, the report of the Isle of Man Government's Central Economic Strategy Unit, Aug 1994.
13] *Isle of Man Government Annual Review of Policies and Programmes 1996*.

in 1996. The age profile had improved, so that there were an estimated 2.24 persons in employment for every retired person, compared with a figure of 1.9 in 1986. Unemployment in 1996, at 3.2 per cent of the workforce, was at the lowest level for five years. Annual government spending on public services had risen from £94.9 million in 1986–7 to £226 million – a real-term increase of 49.8 per cent. Sixty per cent of this higher level of public expenditure went to the Department of Health and Social Security and to the Department of Education. Since 1986 the reserve fund had been built up from £6 million to £110.6 million.

Thus an outstanding feature of the period 1986 to 1996 was a real increase of around 50 per cent in public service expenditure, made possible by economic growth at a similar rate. 'The growth in the economy has created more buoyant taxation revenues and has allowed government to provide more and improved public services', confirmed the 1996 policy report. Although linked to the UK system by reciprocal agreements for social security, the Manx government introduced a series of local benefit enhancements during this period. Areas in which Manx provision became more generous than its UK counterpart included: winter heating supplements and single payments for exceptional items, both paid under the supplementary benefit scheme; the Christmas bonus for pensioners and the needy; Child Benefit and One Parent Benefit. In addition the Island funded a number of special schemes with no equivalent in the UK. These included double unemployment benefit for qualifying claimants in their first 13 weeks out of work, free television licences for supplementary pensioners, and premiums and supplements for certain pensioners. In other areas of government student grants, rather than loans, were continued, and the Island retained free sight tests and dental examinations after these had been abolished in the UK. Dental charges and prescription charges remained lower than in the UK. Unlike its British counterpart, the Manx government, particularly after a change of minister in the relevant department in 1989, remained committed to the provision of additional public sector housing, completing 427 new units between 1990 and the summer of 1994. Local authority rates were lower than equivalent payments in the UK, and there was no attempt to introduce the community charge in the Isle of Man.[14]

Capital as well as revenue spending rose to unprecedented levels.

14] For a summary of Manx benefits see the report of the Council of Ministers Working Party on Low Incomes, Sept 1994.

Major schemes between 1986 and 1991 included a new power station at Pulrose, a National Sports Centre, new schools at Foxdale and Sulby, new sports halls at secondary schools, an extension to the Manx Museum, a new old people's home at Albert Terrace in Douglas, and extensions to both Ballamona and Noble's Hospital. A longer-term approach by departments, and the confidence engendered by swelling Treasury coffers, led government into major projects to update the Island's infrastructure, some of which, like the sewerage system, dated back to the Victorian era. Strategies were developed, and revisited, for a new hospital, the 'IRIS' all-Island sewerage scheme, and a refuse incinerator (first proposed in the 1970s but still unbuilt by 1996). Another aspect of the infrastructure in need of modernisation was the water supply. Ronaldsway airport was extended and refurbished, and harbour facilities at Douglas were improved.

Why did the government in the Isle of Man spend so freely on public services at a time when the very concept of state provision was being challenged during the Thatcher era in the UK? One answer is that it could afford to do so. Moreover, the absence of party government meant that there was no new regime correcting the errors of its predecessors, nor was there any objection in principle to public service. The continuing influence of the Manx Labour Party was also a factor. The Island did not have the experience of inefficient state industry, union militancy and public debt that paved the way for Thatcherite radicalism. (In any event, in their small constituencies Manx politicians are too close to their voters to survive the withdrawal of government support once it has been provided, even if they are philosophically motivated to do so.)

The pragmatic and ideologically neutral nature of the Manx government was demonstrated when the 1991–6 Council of Ministers found itself confronted with two privatisation proposals, from the prospective new owners of Manx Radio and the Manx Electricity Authority. In the former case the Council of Ministers seemed to accept the proposal but then retreated in face of public controversy. The latter plan was rejected after a consultation exercise and Tynwald Select Committee enquiry.

But this did not mean that the Council of Ministers favoured public ownership per se, and it maintained the Manx government's traditional resistance to periodic calls for the nationalisation of the Island's sea and air services. However, in 1995, after several years of negotiations, it concluded an agreement with the Isle of Man Steam Packet giving that company sole usage of the Douglas harbour linkspan, effectively a guaranteed monopoly on roll-on roll-off services, in return for certain levels and standards of service. Despite this rare intrusion into the running of an established privately owned service, the government showed no appetite for developing the precedent into a general regime of regulation of monopolies. A Council of Ministers report in 1996 accepted that the Island's small scale made monopolies unavoidable in various areas of business, but concluded that controlling them would present too many practical difficulties.

Organised Opposition, 1991–6

It was perhaps inevitable that the concentration of executive responsibility and power within the Council of Ministers would lead to the development of forms of opposition outside its ranks. Inevitable or not, the Alternative Policy Group (APG) emerged as Tynwald's first organised (but unofficial) opposition following the Keys general election of November 1991. It appeared for a mixture of reasons – as a result of personality clashes and ambitions as well as genuine differences of political style and policy, and a declared desire to redress the balance between executive and parliament.

The first leader of the APG was Dr Edgar Mann, the former Executive Council chairman, who had returned to the House of Keys via a by-election in September 1990.[15] Re-elected at the general election, he challenged Miles Walker for the position of Chief Minister, gaining ten votes to Walker's 23 in a Tynwald secret ballot. The APG formed soon after this vote, comprising Dr Mann and four other MHKs – Edgar Quine, David Cannan, Dominic Delaney and Adrian Duggan. Edgar Quine had been a regular critic of the previous Walker government and had always stood apart from it; Cannan and Delaney had been Treasury and Local Government Ministers respectively under Walker from December 1986 to December 1989, when they departed in a ministerial reshuffle. Over the next five years the APG became a thorn in the side of the Council of Ministers as it wrestled with a range of issues from the future of Manx Radio to reform of local authorities. In particular the group led opposition to the transfer of £44 million from the National Insurance Fund towards the proposed construction of a new hospital at Ballamona, a move it condemned as 'robbing the pension fund'. The APG also homed in on difficulties at the Tourism Department, where the minister resigned in 1994 after a series of much-publicised departmental embarrassments.

Resented by many of its members' colleagues as negative and

15] In his home constituency of Garff, following the elevation of Sir Charles Kerruish to become President of Tynwald.

headline-hunting, the APG nevertheless had its own policy programme for the future. In the approach to the Keys general election of November 1996 it set out its stall, offering leadership and competence in tackling difficult strategic issues such as the future of the Customs and Excise Agreement.[16] In this area it proposed the establishment of a commission of inquiry to find the best way for the Island to take control of its indirect taxation. While calling for stronger leadership, the APG also blamed the Council of Ministers for failing to maintain a consensus in Tynwald. The group wanted to return to the original requirement that the Chief Minister's selection of ministers be endorsed by Tynwald.

The APG's challenge was assisted, at least in terms of public perception, by the appearance of splits in the Walker regime towards the end of its term of office. In December 1995 the Minister for Agriculture resigned after being accused of attempting to undermine publicly a colleague, the Minister for Health and Social Security. Then in July 1996 the DHSS Minister's introduction of a Manx version of the controversial UK jobseeker's allowance prompted the resignation from the Council of Ministers of his Manx Labour Party colleague, the Minister for Trade and Industry (who was duly replaced by the former Tourism Minister). Amid much speculation as to whether he would seek a third term as Chief Minister, Miles Walker stood for the presidency of Tynwald only to be defeated by the incumbent Sir Charles Kerruish. In September 1996 Walker confirmed that he would stand for re-election to the House of Keys, but did not intend to do so for the position of Chief Minister.

In his final policy report Walker described the period 1987 to 1996 as 'certainly a decade of progress, but not a progress that has been without compassion or without soul' and declared: 'We have been true to the vision of a Prosperous and Caring Society.' He concluded:

> The Island can feel considerable satisfaction from the progress that has been achieved over the last ten years. We have, I believe, raised the standard of living of all our people without prejudicing the essentials of the quality of Manx life. We have provided a solid base on which the future can be built, a base which includes progressive policies, sound laws, satisfactory reserves and a community committed to progress and to the timeless values and qualities of

16] Edgar Quine, interviewed in *Isle of Man Examiner*, 19 Nov 1996, was quoted: 'The presentation and style of government would be quite different. There has been an unwillingness at the top of government to grasp nettles – a lack of certainty and confidence in dealing with these issues.'

Island life. As far as public services are concerned, important foundations have been laid across all areas of activity but most particularly for the substantial investments that will be needed for health, refuse and sewage disposal and improvements in the provision of water supplies.[17]

In the meantime the APG had published its own policy documents and was fielding a team of members and sympathisers as candidates in the House of Keys general election of November 1996. Within the Council of Ministers there was no declaration of a nominated successor to Walker, but the APG was clear that its candidate for Chief Minister would be its political leader, Edgar Quine.

The results of the general election confirmed the popularity of Miles Walker and some of his ministerial colleagues (but not all – two associated with unpopular policies lost their seats).[18] But the outcome was also encouraging to the APG in its ambition to become the first organised group in Tynwald to seize the reins of executive government. It seemed that the evolution of the ministerial system had brought the Island to the brink of something approaching party politics. This feeling was heightened as outline policy statements were produced by the two eventual candidates for Chief Minister – Quine and Donald Gelling, Walker's Treasury Minister for the previous six years, who was seen as broadly representing the status quo. Gelling was elected, quite comfortably, but faced an uncomfortable number of prospective opponents amongst the APG and its fellow travellers. Attempting to build a new consensus, he took the group's leader Edgar Quine and chairman Edgar Mann into the Council of Ministers and sought to make all members of Tynwald feel involved in the work of government.[19] The APG joined in, but continued to meet and function as a group.

Reviews were put in motion, and at the time of writing the future of the ministerial system itself was to be reconsidered both by a Council of Ministers subcommittee and by a Select Committee of Tynwald. The system seemed to be going into reverse, in practice if not yet in law, back towards the inclusiveness of the old board system.

17] *Isle of Man Government Annual Review of Policies and Programmes 1996.*
18] The Minister for Health and Social Security, associated with the new hospital plan and the jobseeker's allowance, and the Minister for Local Government and the Environment, associated with the proposed refuse incinerator.
19] Quine became Minister for Local Government and the Environment, Mann the Minister for Education.

The Modern World, the Outside World

The 1980s and early 1990s saw the Isle of Man fall into line with its larger neighbours in certain areas of modern social legislation. The initiative was sometimes local and voluntary, but where change was made under external pressure it provoked controversy over perceived constitutional constraints and outside interference. The period experienced the repercussions of the ruling of the European Court of Human Rights, delivered in 1978, that judicial corporal punishment in the Isle of Man was 'degrading' and thus contravened the European Convention on Human Rights. The effect of this ruling was confirmed by the Appeal Court in 1981 after magistrates in Douglas sentenced a youth to four strokes of the birch for malicious wounding. Quashing the sentence, Judge of Appeal Benet Hytner QC said that in the light of the European ruling Manx courts should always seek an alternative to birching. The Attorney-General, William Cain, expressed the view in 1982 that, while birching was still a lawful sentence, in practice it could no longer be imposed. More than ten years later the Criminal Justice (Penalties Etc) Act 1993 effectively removed birching from the statute book except for offences dealt with by the Court of General Gaol Delivery. The fact that it remained at all in the written laws of Isle of Man was a tribute to the sensitivity of members of Tynwald to public sentiment. Hanging, however, was erased from the statute book more cleanly, having been the mandatory sentence for murder in the Island but always commuted to life imprisonment by the British Home Secretary. The Death Penalty Abolition Bill was passed by the House of Keys in November 1992 with only three members voting against.

The right of residents of the Island to make individual petition to the European Court of Human Rights was allowed to lapse by the Manx Government in 1976 (following the initial application to the Court in respect of birching in 1972). In March 1987 a Tynwald motion calling for the restoration of the right of individual petition was deferred pending the introduction of a Sexual Offences Bill, after a warning that Manx law on homosexuality conflicted with rulings of the European Court.[20] The Court had made it plain, in relation to the law of Northern Ireland, for example, that legislation effectively criminalising consensual homosexual acts in private was contrary to the right of privacy under the European Convention.

Thus began the great 'Gay Debate'. Alleged public alarm at the prospect of more liberal buggery laws prompted a resolution, narrowly

---

20] The motion was tabled by the then Speaker of the House of Keys, Sir Charles Kerruish. The warning was sounded by the Chief Minister, Miles Walker.

approved in the House of Keys in May 1987, calling for the removal of the offending item from the Sexual Offences Bill. In March 1988 a House of Keys Select Committee reported that changing the law 'would not be acceptable to the vast majority of the people of the Isle of Man'. After a mysterious disappearance of two years, the Sexual Offences Bill resurfaced in March 1990, still containing the proposed reform. Chief Minister Walker said his ministers would have a free vote on the issue, which two months later was referred to another House of Keys Select Committee. The committee was split when it reported in March 1991, three of its five members contending that the status quo could be defended on health grounds, as a protection against the spread of AIDS. Their majority report was accepted by the House, despite a warning from the Chief Minister that control in this area of legislation might be taken over by the Parliament of the United Kingdom. In May the House of Keys finally voted 13 to 8 against the clauses in the Sexual Offences Bill which would have decriminalised private homosexual sex amongst consenting adults over the age of 21. In July gay rights activists from the UK demonstrated at the Tynwald Day ceremony. It was not until after the general election of November 1991 that the House, aware that legislation imposed by the UK might be even more liberal, and suffering from hostile British media coverage, voted 13 to 11 for the crucial section of the Sexual Offences Bill.

Another important social reform was morally controversial, but initiated without external prompting. Early in 1994 Tynwald approved a report from the Council of Ministers' Social Issues Committee proposing the legalisation of abortion in certain circumstances, but not abortion on demand. Twelve months later the House passed the second reading of the Termination of Pregnancy (Medical Defences) Bill with only one member voting against.

But it was in the field of employment and trade union law that the Manx government of the period achieved its most comprehensive modernisation. In December 1989 the House of Keys finally accepted the principle of redundancy payments, nearly 25 years after the UK, by giving an unopposed second reading to a Bill from the Department of Health and Social Security.[21] The following year, after extensive public consultation, the Social Issues Committee, advised by UK consultants Collinson Grant, produced the Trade Union Bill and the related Employment Bill. Despite protests from the trade union movement over restrictions on industrial action in 'essential services', the Bills were passed in 1991. For the first time the legislation introduced to the Island

---

21] Redundancy Payments Act 1990.

a modern code of employment law, including legal status for unions and the right to claim compensation for unfair dismissal. Tynwald also approved, in October 1991, a Social Issues Committee report recommending legislation to outlaw sexual discrimination in the workplace. By the time of writing this had still not been achieved.

In one other area, although not strictly within the definition of social legislation, the Island was arguably more progressive than the UK – but not for long. In the 1980s it replaced the old 'first past the post' method of voting in House of Keys elections with the Single Transferable Vote (STV) system of preferential voting. This was used for the first time in the 1986 general election, and again in 1991. But in 1994 Tynwald approved a motion to the effect that STV was not appropriate for the Island, and subsequent legislation returned the Manx system to 'first past the post' in time for the 1996 general election.

Meanwhile the essential framework of the Island's constitutional position remained in place throughout the period. Limited to Customs and for the free movement of goods, its special Protocol 3 relationship with Europe – by the terms of the United Kingdom's Treaty of Accession, the Isle of Man is neither a member state nor an associate member of the European Union – survived unchallenged through the introduction of the Single Market in 1992. Fears of increasing European influence over indirect taxation prompted renewed calls to end the Customs Agreement with the UK – most noticeably from the APG – but government continued to fight shy of breaking the VAT link with the mainland. Its grounds for caution included the costs of abrogation, particularly an immediate loss of revenue, and the traditional opposition of the manufacturing sector to the prospect of Customs barriers and red tape impeding their exports.

In respect of the constitutional relationship with the UK, Tynwald approved an historic agreement in July 1990 to extend Manx territorial waters from 3 to 12 miles.[22] Under the agreement the jurisdiction of Tynwald was extended over an additional 1,020 square miles of sea, with all gas, oil and mineral rights, at a cost to the Manx of £800,000. Coal rights were excluded, and there was disappointment that the UK retained the final veto on fisheries control, the deal being condemned as a 'sell out' by the Speaker of the House of Keys. However, the agreement came to be looked upon with almost universal favour a few years later when oil and gas companies started prospecting within the 12-mile zone,

---

22] This was done by Order in Council under the UK's Territorial Sea Act 1987. In July 1991 Tynwald passed the Territorial Sea (Consequential Provisions) Act 1990.

raising hopes, as yet unrealised, of a major boost to Manx government revenues.

An important constitutional change was made at the beginning of the period with the Royal Assent to Legislation (Isle of Man) Order 1981, delegating to the Lieutenant-Governor the Crown's power to grant Royal Assent to Bills passed by Tynwald. However, Article 3 of the order provides that the Lieutenant-Governor should reserve 'for the signification of Her Majesty's pleasure any Bill which he considers should be so reserved, or which he is directed to reserve by the Secretary of State'. Article 3 also lists certain subjects on which the Lieutenant-Governor must consult the Secretary of State, including defence, international relations, nationality and citizenship, the Governor's powers and remuneration, and the constitutional relationship between the UK and the Isle of Man. In deciding whether a Bill should be granted Royal Assent by the Lieutenant-Governor or reserved, His Excellency is assisted by the Royal Assent Advisory Committee, an informal body comprising the Chief Minister, First and Second Deemsters, the Attorney-General and Chief Secretary. One Bill that was reserved for Her Majesty was the Constitution Act 1990 which removed the Governor as the presiding officer of Tynwald, to be replaced by the first President of Tynwald elected by the members of the Court. This honour fell to Sir Charles Kerruish, previously Speaker of the House of Keys.

The process of devolving the Governor's powers seemed to have run its course by October 1993, when the Constitutional and External Relations Committee of the Council of Ministers produced its Second Interim Report on Future Constitutional Issues. 'This process has reached a point where it is difficult to see what further powers could be with advantage transferred', it noted. If the constitutional status quo was retained, it argued, 'the scope for greater independence is clearly limited'. But the report continued:

> However the policy of identifying areas of responsibility which can be transferred from the United Kingdom to the Isle of Man has not yet been exhausted. To a large extent this involves Tynwald legislating for matters which have previously been the subject of United Kingdom legislation.

'Substantial progress' had been made in such areas as Customs and Excise, telecommunications, merchant shipping, coastguards, copyright and civil aviation. The committee's recommendations included that consideration be given to whether in future the Attorney-General should be appointed by the Council of Ministers rather than the Crown. But on the question of full independence for the Isle of Man the committee concluded: 'Independence from the UK should not be pursued at this time'.

The report observed:

> The pursuit of independence should be a response to some widely-felt serious political, social and economic disadvantage which would be overcome by the achievement of independence. A clear understanding of the benefits to be secured must exist because to launch into the unknown for some ill-defined or speculative gain would be grossly irresponsible. There would seem to be little evidence of the sense of present disadvantage which is necessary. In the meantime progress can continue to be made within the existing constitutional framework by means of gradual change as opportunities arise. This approach continues the move towards more complete self-government and, should independence be the choice at some future date, the progress made will ensure that the final step is easier and the consequences more predictable than would otherwise be the case.

The committee pointed out, however, that 'in future, the opportunities for extending the Island's autonomy will be less frequent than in recent years, and change over the next generation is likely to be at a much slower pace than has taken place since 1945'.

Conclusion
After the celebrations of Millennium Year in 1979, Tynwald found itself confronted with the sobering realities of the early 1980s – recession, unemployment and the grave embarrassment of a bank collapse. The priority was economic recovery and work began on constructing the framework for the development of a healthier, more reputable, financial services industry. At the same time the final removal of the Lieutenant-Governor as the centre of gravity of Manx politics was followed by the introduction of the ministerial system, replacing the multitude of disconnected boards with a smaller number of much larger government departments, each represented on a central executive body. Of equal if not greater significance was the vesting of executive power and responsibility, previously held collectively between board members, with the ministers in charge of the individual departments. Thus the ministerial system had the effect of providing for more efficient co-ordination of the functions of government while concentrating authority and accountability within a group approximately one-third the size of the total Tynwald membership. This was a

monumental change from the traditional view – which made virtually no distinction between Parliament and executive – that Tynwald was the government of the Isle of Man. The objective was to introduce a greater sense of cohesion and direction. But this was more easily hoped for than achieved, given the absence of the discipline of party politics and the fact that the Council of Ministers had no guarantee of majority support within Tynwald. Nevertheless, one of the complaints against the system was the amount of patronage it placed in the hands of the Chief Minister, principally by his selection of ministers but extending through them to the choice of departmental members and even influencing nominations to the Legislative Council. All this combined, said critics, to create an unhealthy imbalance in favour of the executive at the expense of Parliament.[23]

The feeling inside the Council of Ministers was less secure. Government retreats, defeats and near-defeats were by no means unknown, and ministers ignored the mood of Tynwald, or perceived public opinion, at their peril. Arguably, this created a collective sense of vulnerability which in turn inhibited public debate. Controversial initiatives could be blocked by the Council of Ministers, never to see the light of day. Under the old system a board could bring its policy direct to the floor of Tynwald (specific spending proposals, but not general policy declarations, required the pre-approval of the Finance Board, an important central control at that time). The ministerial system gave the Council of Ministers the legal authority to progress policy but there remained little in the way of prior policy mandate, either from the public or from Tynwald, within which to exercise this. The Chief Minister was appointed personally by Tynwald, but with no direct mandate for the role from the people. The annual government policy document endorsed by Tynwald was a mixture of an objectives statement and administrative review, not a comprehensive programme of specific policies. In place of 'government policy' on issues there was the view of an individual minister or his departmental officers at any given moment in time. A change of minister could bring about significant shifts in direction, as with housing in the late 1980s or the IRIS sewerage project and new hospital plan in the early 1990s.[24]

23] Prominent amongst such critics were members of the APG.
24] A new Minister for Local Government and the Environment in December 1989 brought greater emphasis on public sector housing. At the Department of Health and Social Security the redevelopment of Noble's Hospital was dropped in favour of a new scheme at Ballamona, and plans for a centralised all-Island sewerage system were replaced by something less ambitious.

Without a clear mandate, and in the absence of party backing, the Council of Ministers had to feel its way cautiously, often relying on consultation exercises to sound out the opinion of the public and Tynwald.

But rivalry is a feature of politics, and consultation was not enough to deflect the APG in its challenge for leadership in 1996. As we have seen, the prospect of party-style politics loomed and then faded after the general election of that year as the APG was embraced within the wide consensus regime of the new Chief Minister, Donald Gelling. At the time of writing a watering down of the ministerial system, at least in relation to the appointment of ministers and their individual powers, was not beyond the bounds of possibility.

The first ten years of the ministerial system in the Isle of Man coincided with considerable economic growth, which was one of the main objectives of the Walker government alongside preservation of the Island's quality of life. Defining and maintaining the balance between the two was one of the great challenges facing Manx politicians in this period. Constrained in its freedom to adjust taxation, and with little stomach for radical solutions such as privatisation or spending cuts, the government was largely dependent on economic growth to pay for public service improvements and its ambitious programme of infra-structural renewal. With public and private sectors having strong vested interests in growth – for revenue and profit – there was a real question over government's ability to exercise control. On the related question of population growth, for example, its policy was vague. It did propose the introduction of residence legislation, to restrict immigra-tion if and when circumstances made this necessary, but this measure was first recommended in 1988 and ten years later had still not been enacted. Meanwhile the arrival of a Labour government in the UK and developments in the European Union, where EMU raised the prospect of tax harmonisation, prompted speculation over the long-term future of the offshore financial services industry, the source of much of the Island's new-found prosperity. The Labour and European social programmes also influenced the Manx agenda, posing the question of whether the Island should follow suit in such areas as the minimum wage, trade union recognition, the age of consent for homosexuals and the incorporation into domestic law of the European Convention on Human Rights.

Tynwald has been faced with important challenges at the dawn of the twenty-first century. Having emerged from the colonial era only in relatively recent times, it has sought to maintain and safeguard its independence in the new age of European integration and international obligations. At home it has had to encourage and manage economic growth to improve the standard of living and public services while protecting the Island's quality of life. It had to ensure that government was realistic in its commitments to expenditure to meet the rising expectations of the people. Was the internal machinery of Manx politics up to the task where difficult or unpopular measures proved necessary? The ministerial system had sought to introduce direction and discipline, but this did not come naturally in a non-party culture. Nor was the development of parties an obvious solution in a small community where personality was always more potent than policy. The scale of the Isle of Man – the closeness of the politicians to the people – remained both the strength and the weakness of its politics.

Economic History, 1830–1996[1]

DEREK WINTERBOTTOM

T he period from 1830 to the end of the twentieth century saw five main phases in the development of the Isle of Man's economy. The first, from 1830 to 1863, was a period in which most of the population lived in the countryside and struggled to feed and clothe themselves through the traditional occupations of agriculture, fishing and mining, though it was beginning to be apparent that the Island had its attractions as a holiday resort and, as is underlined in an earlier chapter, as a suitable residence for the genteel poor. A number of factors combined from 1863 onwards (the year of the appointment of Governor Loch) to make the period up to 1914 one of unprecedented growth, expansion and prosperity for the Island which during these years became one of the leading holiday resorts in the British Isles, with Douglas, in particular, expanding to meet the needs of hundreds of thousands of annual visitors. The third period, from 1914 to 1945, was one in which the Island's career as a holiday resort was drastically interrupted by two long wars during which it was used for the internment of enemy aliens and also for military training. From 1945 to 1970 tourism re-established itself as the mainstay of the economy, with manufacturing growing in importance and the traditional industries becoming far less significant. The fifth period, from 1970, was one in which the Island used its unique constitutional position to develop as an international offshore financial centre whose vigorous growth in the 1980s and 1990s replaced the ailing tourist trade as the main source of economic prosperity.

1] The author wishes to thank a team of specialist advisers who submitted detailed manuscripts: Richard Danielson, 'The Isle of Man Steam Packet Company since 1945'; Gordon Kniveton, 'Air Communications'; Chris Page, 'Agriculture since 1830'; Constance Radcliffe, 'Ramsey since 1914'; Fred Radcliffe, 'Fishing since 1830'; and Roger Rawcliffe, 'Financial Services in the Isle of Man since 1830'.

1830–63

Towns, Agriculture, Fishing and Mining
Towns

In 1831 the census revealed that the Isle of Man, some 30 miles long and 10 miles wide, had a population of 41,751. There were four towns, Douglas, Castletown, Peel and Ramsey, but more than 70 per cent of the population lived in the countryside. Douglas, with 6,776 inhabitants, was the largest and most prosperous town.[2] It had been the centre of the profitable smuggling trade in the eighteenth century and had a reasonably good harbour at the mouth of the combined rivers Dhoo and Glass. The town was concentrated on the North Quay, with few significant buildings in the vast sweep of Douglas Bay except for Castle Mona, the Duke of Atholl's magnificent seaside residence, built in 1804. In the centre of the town Duke Street and Strand Street were laid out in 1810 and a good many new houses were built between that year and 1829 when, for the first time, the streets were lit by a few oil lamps. Visitors from England around 1830 were not impressed by the narrow lanes, open gutters, dirt and bad smells, though Lord Teignmouth considered that many houses were 'respectable', while the shops were 'spacious and showy and worthy of any English country town'.[3]

Castletown was the historic capital but its population (2,062) was much smaller than that of Douglas. The town's heart was Castle Rushen, the formidable medieval fortress of the Kings and Lords of Man, and Castletown was also the seat of Tynwald, the Manx parliament. In 1830 the foundation stone of King William's College was laid on a site about a mile from the centre of the old town, and when the school opened in 1833 it brought business to the traders of Castletown, though not enough to arrest the gradual decline in the town's prosperity and importance.[4]

Peel, the only town on the west coast, had been an important fishing port since early times and had enjoyed prosperity in the 'smuggling'

2] A.W. Moore, *A History of the Isle of Man* (2 vols, London, 1900), ii, 646.
3] Lord Teignmouth, *Sketches of the Coasts and Islands of Scotland and of the Isle of Man*, etc (2 vols, London, 1836), ii, 184.
4] L. Earnshaw (ed), *King William's College Register, 1899–1989* (4th ed Castletown, 1990), 1.

The Market Place, Douglas, c.1900 *According to the Ward Lock Guide, the markets were seen at their best on Saturday, when they were 'devoted to the sale of fish, fruit, vegetables, butter, etc.'. At the height of the herring fisheries, a day's catch could be valued at as much as £10,000. (MNHL)*

years up to 1765. In 1831 it was the centre of the Manx fishing industry, with a population of 1,722 recorded by the census of that year. The same census found a comparable number of people (1,754) living in Ramsey, a small market town and fishing port at the mouth of the Sulby river.[5] Visiting Ramsey in 1828, Dorothy Wordsworth described it as 'a little fishing town now smelling of herrings in every crevice',[6] while Lord Teignmouth, the following year, found that 'the streets are narrow, but the houses are respectable, and appear neat and cleanly from the prevalence of whitewash, a customary precaution against typhus fever, which prevails here as in other towns of the Island'.[7] In 1829 a new North Pier was completed at the entrance to the harbour, which greatly improved its facilities.

According to the 1831 census 12,314 people lived in the four towns of Douglas, Castletown, Peel and Ramsey. The rest of the Island's inhabitants, some 29,437 people, were to be found in the countryside or in small inland villages like St John's or Kirk Michael, or in small coastal villages such as Port Erin and Port St Mary.[8] From an economic point of view the people were far from flourishing in 1831, whether they lived in the towns or in the countryside. Revestment in 1765 had made the smuggling trade far less profitable: the islanders had been thrown back on the traditional occupations of farming and fishing, with a little mining in Laxey and Foxdale. There was no coal on the Island, so an 'industrial revolution', such as the one that transformed life in Britain during the eighteenth century, was out of the question. Fortunately, debtors and retired army and naval officers found Douglas an attractive and inexpensive place to settle during the early years of the nineteenth century and between them they considerably increased the number of superior houses in the town and made a handsome contribution to its revenues. Elsewhere there was at first little sign of economic prosperity, though in the years between 1830 and 1863 there was a slow but gradual improvement in agriculture, fishing, mining and the early tourist trade.

Agriculture
In 1830 there were no great estates in the Isle of Man and 'absentee landlords' were not a problem. Thomas Quayle wrote in 1812 that 'the

5] Moore, *History*, ii, 646.
6] Quoted in Constance Radcliffe, *Shining by the Sea: A History of Ramsey 1800–1914* (Douglas, 1989), 18.
7] Teignmouth, *Sketches*, ii, 186.
8] Moore, *History*, ii, 646.

Laxey *A striking feature of many urban views is the pall of smoke from coal-burning fires.* *Pollution hangs over Laxey in this view down the valley from near the Great Wheel. The row* *of cottages on the right of the picture shows 'Dumbell's Terrace', which because of the large* *number of eating-places was known colloquially as 'Ham and Egg Terrace'. (MNHL)*

largest proportion of cultivated land is possessed by yeomen, farming from ten to one hundred and fifty acres, their own property ... it is probable that there are not in the whole Island more than sixty farms consisting of two hundred acres or above'.[9] Unfortunately, increased demand for agricultural goods during the Napoleonic Wars led to overproduction and a serious depression after 1815, when the wars ended. According to an article in the *Manks Advertiser*, 'many farmers, especially the smaller ones, were ruined, and they, with a number of the labouring class, long unable to obtain employment, emigrated to America, especially between 1825 and 1837'.[10] Another problem was the requirement to pay tithes to the Manx Church, effectively a tax on farm income. When Bishop Murray attempted to impose a new tithe on

9] Thomas Quayle, *General View of the Agriculture of the Isle of Man*, etc (London, 1812) in the facsimile reprint (Douglas, 1992), 25.
10] Quoted in J.W. Birch, *The Isle of Man: A Study in Economic Geography* (Cambridge, 1956), 79.

potatoes and turnips in 1825, there were serious riots. In 1839 Tynwald passed an act commuting tithes on agricultural products to an annual rent charge regulated by the average price of corn over the previous seven years.[11] When this new law was enacted in 1841 it marked the start of a significant recovery in the fortunes of Manx agriculture.

A further drag on agricultural improvement was the fact that most farm labourers doubled as fishermen and were frequently with the herring fleet just when they were most needed at harvest time. J.C. Curwen, in his report on Manx agriculture (1807), stated that the Manx people 'are become insensible of the riches to be drawn from the earth, by labour and exertion. To have a share in a herring-boat is the first object of their ambition, and is considered the only road to wealth.'[12]

A run of good harvests in the 1830s helped towards a reinvestment in the land. Optimism in farming was reflected in the foundation of the Isle of Man Agricultural Society in 1840, and the newspapers soon reported that 'the spirit of improvement has been awakened' in the Island's farms.[13] During the 1840s potatoes became more of a cash crop and regular shipments left Ramsey and Douglas for Workington and Liverpool. Potatoes were also a part of the staple diet of the labourers and small farmers and crofters. Failures in this crop immediately brought distress to the countryside, especially in 1845 when the Island was visited by the potato blight virus, a problem compounded by severe foot rot in sheep and an outbreak of murrain in cattle. In 1846 the potato blight resulted in a total loss of the crop and this, together with the news of gold finds in America and Australia, prompted another burst of emigration between 1847 and 1851.[14]

In 1860, following the report of a Royal Commission, the Disafforesting Act redistributed hitherto common land to the disadvantage of the crofting community which had relied upon common mountain land to graze their livestock. The crofters caused many disturbances over this issue, and in May 1864 the recently installed Governor Loch needed a garrison of soldiers and police to disperse a militant throng of crofters opposed to the removal of their sheep from what they considered common pasture. They lost their struggle and many crofters subsequently moved down from their hillside

11] Moore, *History*, ii, 665.

12] J.C. Curwen, 'Report of the Agricultural Society in the Isle of Man', *Rules and Proceedings of the Workington Agricultural Society*, (1807), quoted in Birch, *The Isle of Man*, 78.

13] *Manx Herald*, 4 Feb 1842, 2.

14] Moore, *History*, ii, 555

pastures to try their hand in the developing tourist industry in the towns.[15]

Fishing

Fishing fared little better during this period. Commentators at the beginning of the nineteenth century estimated that there were about four hundred Manx fishing vessels in use, operated by between three and four thousand men and boys – about a third of the working male population.[16] Like their ancestors for many centuries, they normally searched for the shoals of herring which appeared close to the coast between early summer and October. The normal pattern was for fishing to begin off the south-west coast and the Calf, often to be followed by the 'back fishing' off the east coast, near Douglas. There were also cod and ling to be found all round the Island between January and March. However, the number of vessels and men in-volved in fishing declined sharply as the century progressed. One reason was that from 1823 onwards up to three hundred Cornish boats began fishing in Manx waters and disregarded local regulations about the timing and location of their activities, so that the start of the season was gradually pushed back from the beginning of July to May. Another problem was the end, in 1833, of the bounty on herring catches formerly paid by the British government, and a third was the abolition of slavery in 1845 and the subsequent decline in the West Indian market for cured herrings. Fish curing had developed on the Isle of Man after revestment as an alternative to the prohibited smuggling trade, and by 1815 there were five large red herring houses in Douglas, and others at Derbyhaven, Port St Mary, Laxey and Peel.[17]

The arrival of the superior Cornish craft in 1823 prompted a change in the construction of Manx vessels: two-masted dandy smacks (or 'luggers') replaced the single-masted variety. George Quirk, a former Water Bailiff, described the Manx fleet around 1840 as consisting of some 220 vessels operated by 1,500 men. Nets had become longer and deeper, and each boat typically carried 15 or 20 pieces of net, handled by a crew of six or seven men. A completely fitted out boat, with nets, would have cost £250, Quayle estimated. He also noted that curing had declined sharply, with only one Manx firm fully operational in curing

15] Moore, *History*, ii, 896–901.
16] Birch, *The Isle of Man*, 136.
17] L.S. Garrad *et al*, *The Industrial Archaeology of the Isle of Man* (Newton Abbot, 1972), 141.

houses at Douglas and Derbyhaven.[18] So between 1830 and 1863 the numbers involved in both fishing and curing declined dramatically. However, in 1861 fishing boats ventured earlier in the year to Kinsale, in Ireland, to test out the spring shoals of mackerel there, and the results were promising for the future.

Mining
Though no coal has been found on the Island, the Manx slates have yielded good quantities of lead, zinc, iron and copper. Mining activities were recorded from the middle of the thirteenth century, with Foxdale being the major centre. However, by the middle of the eighteenth century most mining activity had ceased, and J. MacCulloch was able to write in 1819, with reference to the mines at Foxdale, Laxey and Braddan: 'It is now some time since they were abandoned, nor is there at present any prospect of their renewal.'[19] In 1829 the Crown's purchase of the Duke of Atholl's remaining feudal rights stimulated new interest in mining because a proportion of any profits would now go to the Treasury. The Foxdale mines, reopened in 1823, were developed subsequently by a syndicate, and in 1831 they produced silver-lead ore valued at £1,400 during a three-month period; by 1832 £100 shares in the Laxey mine were selling at £500. J.G. Cumming, writing in 1848, reported that the Laxey mine was raising 60 tons of lead, 200 tons of blende mixed with lead, and 5 tons of copper ore per month.[20] In 1850 George W. Dumbell became Chairman of the Laxey Mining Company and devoted his exceptional business talent to its development.[21] By 1854 £80 shares were changing hands at £1,200, and on 29 September that year the spectacular cast-iron waterwheel, named 'Lady Isabella' after the wife of Governor Hope, was ceremoniously set to work.[22] It was designed by a local man, Robert Casement, and many of its parts were made on the Island. Its function was to work the pumps that kept the mine free of water, and it was one of the biggest wheels of its type in Europe, symbolising the prosperity of the Manx mining industry and drawing international attention to the Isle of Man

---

18] Joseph Train, *An Historical and Statistical Account of the Isle of Man*, etc (Douglas,1845), 301–5 (Appendix on 'Manx Fisheries', written by George Quirk).

19] Quoted in Birch, *The Isle of Man*, 154.

20] Rev J.G. Cumming, *The Isle of Man, its History, Physical, Ecclesiastical, Civil and Legendary* (London, 1848), 308–10.

21] Connery Chappell, *The Dumbell Affair* (Prescot, 1981), 41–8.

22] Garrad *Industrial Archaeology*, 39–68 and 59–96. For more details about the Laxey wheel see A. Jespersen *The Lady Isabella Waterwheel of the Great Laxey Mining Company, Isle of Man, 1854–1954* (Copenhagen, 1954).

Snaefell mines *Between 1870 and 1900 the Great Snaefell Mining Company managed by Henry James produced 4567 tons of lead and double the quantity of zinc. The photograph shows the mine in operation c.1890, some years before the Island's worst mining disaster, when 20 men died as the result of carbon monoxide poisoning.*

as well as gratifying the ambitions of George W. Dumbell. In 1860 a row of houses in Laxey, built for mineworkers, was named Dumbell Terrace in the chairman's honour. The success of the Foxdale and Laxey mines led to a search for new veins of minerals all over the Island, though with little positive result. Nevertheless, between 1830 and 1863 these two mines brought great prosperity to the industry, with promise of more to come.

This period also saw a growth in manufacturing, which had been only of the localised cottage type at the beginning of the century. After 1830 the greatest progress was made by factory-based textile manufacturers producing woollen cloth and sail cloth, with main centres in Douglas and Union Mills. Shipbuilding became a growth industry, with a major yard established in Douglas in 1828, with others to follow. There were four yards in Castletown in the 1850s and a large yard at Ramsey was employing 250 men by 1863; it could build wooden or iron ships up to 2,000 tons.[23]

Despite the success of mining, textile and shipping operations, the Isle of Man was enjoying only limited economic prosperity, though the population had grown from 41,751 in 1831 to 52,469 in 1861, with a rise in the town population from 29 per cent to 39 per cent. The overall rise in the population can be attributed to improvements in standards of health and sanitation which reduced the incidence of epidemics and lowered the mortality rate in the 1860s to 19 per thousand. In the next thirty years, however, the Island was to enjoy boom conditions as the Steam Packet Company's growing fleet conveyed large numbers of tourists to what rapidly became known as a holiday Isle.

The Steam Packet and the Growth of the Visiting Trade

In 1801 the facilities of Douglas harbour were considerably improved when the Red Pier, which had taken eight years to construct, was formally opened. The pier, described as being 'the chief beauty and attraction of Douglas ... the promenade of the town, and in fine weather crowded with genteel company',[24] made Douglas more accessible to seaborne passenger traffic, though it did not protect the harbour from easterly gales. Moreover, until 1872 passengers had to be taken to and from their ships by rowing boat, an operation that could prove dangerous and uncomfortable in bad weather.

The first British steamer, the *Comet*, was built in 1812, and seven years later the businessman James Little established a steamship service between Liverpool and Glasgow, using Douglas as a port of call. In 1822 the St George Steam Packet Company of Liverpool opened a similar service using the *St George*, an outstanding steam vessel, and in

23] Birch, *The Isle of Man*, 176.
24] George Woods, *An Account of the Past and Present State of the Isle of Man*, etc (London, 1811), 105.

The RNLI *Fort Anne, the white crenellated building on the left, was the home of Sir William Hillary, who founded the Royal National Lifeboat Institution in 1824 and had himself been recognised for his role in helping to save five hundred lives. This splendid view of Douglas harbour shows on the slipway one of the last pulling/sailing lifeboats, the* Civil Service No 6, *stationed in Douglas between 1890 and 1924. (MNHL)*

1826 a small steamer, the *Triton*, made a weekly journey between Douglas and Whitehaven. In 1829 a group of Manx businessmen, presided over by James Quirk, the High Bailiff of Douglas, met to discuss the formation of a Manx steamship company, and in June 1830 the new company launched its first steamer, *Mona's Isle*, and at first called itself the Mona's Isle Company.[25] Competition between the new company and the St George Steam Packet led to spectacular races between the rival ships, which both started from Liverpool at the same time. Unfortunately, in November 1830 the *St George* was wrecked on Conister rock in Douglas Bay after breaking its cable while at anchor in the Bay during a south-easterly gale. Sir William Hillary, who lived at Fort Anne, a mansion on Douglas Head, saw the ship's plight and rowed out with volunteers to save the crew.[26] He subsequently raised money to build a miniature castle on Conister rock, partly as a hazard warning to vessels, and also as a sanctuary for anyone unfortunate enough to be wrecked there. This 'Tower of Refuge' was finished in 1832, the same year that a lighthouse was built on Douglas Head, making navigation after dark much safer.

The wreck of the *St George* was a serious blow to its owners, who withdrew from the Douglas run in June 1831, leaving the Mona's Isle Company to pick up the valuable mail contract, worth £1,000 a year, in return for which the company was required to deliver the mail twice weekly in summer, and once in the winter.[27] The company commissioned a second ship, the *Mona*, in 1832, the year in which it renamed itself the Isle of Man Steam Packet Company, and a third ship, the *Queen of the Isle*, was added to the fleet in 1834. Competition from companies in Ramsey and Castletown was successfully beaten off, and the Steam Packet conveyed twenty thousand passengers annually in its earliest years, in wooden and iron paddle-steamers with the resounding names *King Orry* (1842–58), *Ben-my-Chree* (1845–60) and *Tynwald* (1846–86). The *Douglas*, acquired in 1858, was claimed to be the fastest steamer then afloat and made the crossing from Liverpool to Douglas in four hours and twenty minutes.[28] With ships such as these the Steam Packet dominated the ferry routes just at the time when demand for travel to the Isle of Man was rapidly increasing.

George IV's patronage of Brighton had led fashionable society to take an interest in seaside pursuits, not only in the south of England but also in the north, where Scarborough on the east coast and Blackpool on the west began to receive visitors in the early years of the nineteenth century. Even in the 1820s Douglas witnessed a 'general and uninterrupted influx of numerous and respectable visitors', according

25] Connery Chappell, *Island Lifeline* (Prescot, 1980), 4.
26] Robert Kelly, *For those in Peril* (Douglas, 1979), 63–76.
27] Chappell, *Island Lifeline*, 7.
28] Chappell, *Island Lifeline*, 21.

to the *Manks Advertiser*.[29] In 1830 the steam railway from Manchester to Liverpool was opened, and the prospect of a crossing to the Isle of Man in one of the new steam paddle-steamers proved very attractive to those who could afford the time and the money for such an adventure aboard the machines of the new technological age. Estimates of the number of annual visitors to the Island between 1830 and 1850 have been put as high as twenty to thirty thousand, with an increase between 1852 and 1866 to between fifty and sixty thousand. As there was a poor inland transport system during these years, the great majority of visitors stayed in Douglas, where the population had risen to 12,500 by 1861.[30] However, Douglas was, even in the 1860s, far from being an ideal holiday resort. A.W. Moore has described how 'the steamers lay rocking in the bay, and passengers, who were taken off in boats to the Red Pier, were often wet to the skin by both sea and rain, and then had to scramble across the slippery cobble stones at the foot of the pier as best they could'.[31] Hotel accommodation was limited and tended to cater for the more prosperous classes, who at that time composed the majority of visitors.

By the early 1860s, therefore, the Isle of Man's economic future lay in the balance. A considerable number of visitors, growing each year, was brought to the Island by the ships of the Steam Packet Company. Should the mass tourist trade become the chief economic concern, thus giving a much-needed boost to the faltering agricultural and fishing industries, and creating a profitable market for local manufactures? If so, a dynamic approach to the development of the Island's infrastructure was urgently needed. Alternatively, should the Isle of Man continue with its outdated constitution and customs and remain a quaint outpost attractive to only a limited number of genteel visitors and 'stranger-residents'?

1863-1914

Governor Loch and the Development of the Island as a Holiday Resort
The last true 'Governor' of the Isle of Man was the fourth Duke of Atholl, who died in 1830. Since then a Lieutenant-Governor, the direct representative of the British monarch, has been the head of the Manx government until recent times. Lieutenant-Governors Smelt, Ready and Hope all lived in Castletown, but Francis Pigott, appointed in 1860,

---

29] Quoted in Birch, *The Isle of Man*, 32.
30] Birch, *The Isle of Man*, 34.
31] Quoted in Birch, *The Isle of Man*, 35.

leased from Samuel Harris of Douglas a charming seaside house named Villa Marina, located on Douglas Bay. Pigott died prematurely in January 1863, whereupon the youthful Henry Loch, aged 36, was appointed to succeed him. The eighth son of James Loch of Drylaw, Henry Loch was trained for a naval career but preferred the army and saw service in the Crimean War.[32] He then became secretary to Lord Elgin, who had been Governor-General of Canada, and who was entrusted with establishing political and trading links with China and Japan. Loch accompanied Elgin to both countries and was treacherously captured, imprisoned and tortured by the Chinese in 1860.[33] By a lucky chance he managed to escape, and later worked in the office of the Home Secretary, Sir George Grey, and it was Grey who arranged for Loch to go to the Isle of Man in Pigott's place in 1863.[34]

Still in his mid-30s, Loch was an enthusiastic and skilled administrator, determined, but also diplomatic, and he had learned a great deal from his former mentor Lord Elgin, one of Britain's most humane and progressive colonial statesmen. Moreover his newly married wife, formerly Elizabeth Villiers, was an aristocrat whose charm and talents as a hostess won her many admirers on the Island. Within days of taking up his post, Loch received a deputation from the Town Commissioners of Douglas, asking him to move the centre of government from Castletown to Douglas. He wisely made no hasty decision, though, like his predecessor, he decided to reside in the Douglas area, choosing as his home Bemahague in Onchan, which has served as Government House ever since. Loch also called meetings of Tynwald in Douglas as well as Castletown, but it was not until 1879, towards the end of his period of office, that a permanent home for Tynwald was purchased when the former Bank of Mona's building, on Prospect Hill, came up for sale.

The gradual move of government further emphasised the predominance of Douglas and confirmed the decline of Castletown, especially as the town authorities there were not anxious to see either it or the neighbouring Derbyhaven develop into a holiday resort. Meanwhile Loch realised that the limited harbour facilities in Douglas would prevent the Island fulfilling its true potential as a holiday location, and it became one of his main aims to build a deep-water pier at Douglas.[35]

32] Gordon Loch, *The Family of Loch* (Edinburgh, 1934), 296–315.

33] Henry Brougham Loch, *Personal Narrative of Occurrences during Lord Elgin's Second Embassy to China, 1860* (London, 1869).

34] Loch to Deemster Drinkwater, 3 Feb 1863, SRO: Loch Papers, GD268/116/7.

35] W.B. Kinley, 'The development of Douglas harbour: a mariner's view', *Proceedings*, X (1994), 79.

As the Constitution stood, however, the House of Keys – which was still a self-electing body – did not have the power to raise large sums of money of the size needed for harbour projects. The twin (and highly controversial) issues of reform of the House of Keys and financial control were so carefully handled by Loch in the first three years of his administration that in 1866 the Isle of Man Customs and Harbours Act was passed in Parliament, and the House of Keys Election Act was passed by Tynwald.[36]

These two reforms radically altered the way the Island was governed. From 1867 the House of Keys would be elected by adult males who owned real estate worth at least £8 a year, or tenants paying at least £12 a year. The power of this reformed house to control the Island's financial affairs was also considerably increased. In addition to the one-ninth of the Manx Customs revenue already set aside for harbour improvements and other public works, Tynwald would also have the right to decide, subject to the Governor's veto, how to spend any surplus Customs revenue, once the expenses of the Island's government, judicial courts and police force had been met. In addition the Island would pay £10,000 a year to the British Treasury.[37]

After the first Manx general election in 1867 Loch sat with a Committee of Tynwald appointed to direct the work on Douglas harbour. A breakwater begun in 1862 had collapsed three years later after several storms. Tynwald authorised the construction of the 'Battery Pier' on the site of the collapsed breakwater, and an entirely new pier, built of concrete blocks, to run from the Pollock rocks out into deep water. This was ceremoniously opened by Loch in 1872 and subsequently known as the Queen Victoria Pier. The increase in traffic permitted by the new pier was such that by 1879 as many as five steamers had to berth outside one another on some occasions. Work began on an extension to this pier in 1886 and it was completed in 1891, after which four steamers were able to berth alongside.[38]

With the completion of the Queen Victoria pier in 1872 another problem arose because access to the town lay through a warren of narrow, cobbled streets. In the 1860s Samuel Harris of Douglas had raised money by public subscription to build a promenade near the centre of Douglas Bay, and it was now suggested that land should be reclaimed from the sea so that a new promenade could be built to

36] D.G. Kermode, *Devolution at Work A Case Study of the Isle of Man* (Farnborough, 1979), 31–2.
37] R.H. Kinvig, *The Isle of Man* (3rd ed, Liverpool, 1975), 170.
38] Kinley, 'Development', 80.

connect the existing one with the Victoria Pier. This was a major project, involving considerable demolition and heavy expenses. It caused a great deal of controversy which went on for five years before work began on the new sea wall in 1874. By the end of 1877 a splendid new promenade, named after Loch, together with a fine new thoroughfare named Victoria Street, had transformed the heart of Old Douglas.

A Stockport architect, W.J. Rennison, managed to establish himself as the creator of the new promenade's range of hotels, starting with the Villiers (Mrs Loch's maiden name), which was open by 1878. A grand affair with two hundred bedrooms and twenty sitting-rooms, it soon expanded to three hundred bedrooms, and in 1889 charged three guineas a week for full board. Rennison designed most of the other hotels on Loch Promenade, though they were much smaller than the Villiers. The Belvedere, opened in 1878, was typical: a handsome, six-storey building, it had 47 letting bedrooms, a dining-room, coffee-room, drawing-room and sitting-room, but only five lavatories in the entire hotel – and, of course, no hot and cold running water. The hotels were equipped with gas lighting, fittings for which were often provided by local firms.[39] One of Rennison's last major projects was the Sefton Hotel, completed in 1895 and featuring gothic turrets, a hallmark of his. A detailed examination of the 1881 census enumerator's book for Douglas has shown that the skilled labour force which constructed the growing holiday resort was predominantly of Manx origin. Many of the new hotels displayed fine examples of the plasterer's art, and in 1881 64 men and boys earned their living in this trade, 83 per cent of them Manx. The fastest growing trade was that of plumbers, 73 per cent of whom were Manx in 1881. The largest overall group of tradesmen were the joiners and carpenters, with 195 listed: most of the internal fittings of the new buildings were made of timber. Of this group of workers 88 per cent were Manxmen, as were 92 per cent of stonemasons. In Douglas, as elsewhere on the Island, native Manx craftsmen profited greatly from the building boom.[40]

During the 1880s and 1890s, helped by the Douglas harbour improvements, the growth of the Steam Packet's fleet and the building of many new hotels, more and more visitors began to pour into the

39] Garrad *et al*, *Industrial Archaeology*, 103–11.
40] Alan Lawton, 'An examination into the origins of the skilled workforce of the Douglas/Onchan construction industry of 1881', unpublished ms, 1996.

Island, reaching 347,968 between May and September in 1887.[41] The vast majority of them were working-class folk from the industrial north-west of England, where the traditions and operating policies of the factories, together with the development of the railway network, had created the institution of the seaside summer holiday. By the second half of the century the traditional 'wakes' (originally a day's holiday to celebrate the consecration of the local parish church) had developed into an institutionalised holiday when whole communities would decamp for a week at the seaside.[42] Oldham, Darwen, Chorley, Nelson, Burnley and Blackburn all developed a 'wakes week' holiday in the 1890s. All these towns were close to Manchester, which, with a population of over half a million, was one of the chief starting points of the potential working-class holiday-maker. Their demands led to the creation of Rhyl, New Brighton and, above all, Blackpool: but Douglas – despite the sea voyage or, perhaps, because of it – was a major rival to these mainland resorts, and the 1880s and 1890s saw the development of many attractions in the town designed to lure the holiday-maker across the Irish Sea, and keep him and his family happy for their precious week away from work.

Thomas Lightfoot, a civil engineer from the Midlands who had retired to live on Douglas Bay, persuaded both the Douglas Town Commissioners and Tynwald to authorise the construction of a horse tramway along part of the Douglas sea front. This opened in August 1876 and proved an immediate success with visitors. In 1882 Lightfoot sold the network to a consortium called Isle of Man Tramways Ltd, who co-operated with the Derby Castle Company, formed in 1884, to extend the tramway. They also persuaded the Town Commissioners to construct the Queen's Promenade, opened in 1890 to the accompaniment of many festivities, including a guest appearance from the world-famous acrobat Blondin. By the 1890s the horse trams were handling over half a million passengers a year, and they served both as a tourist attraction and as a means of transport from one end of Douglas Bay to the other.[43]

In the scramble to capitalise on the opportunities open to developers

41] *Reports of the Board of Advertising for 1896 and 1897* (MNHL, Government papers, D151 15x). See also J.M. Cally, *Isle of Man Summer Passenger Arrivals 1887 to the Present* (Economic Affairs Division, The Treasury, Douglas, 1986), 6.

42] J.K. Walton, 'The demand for working-class seaside holidays in Victorian England', *Economic History Review*, 2nd series, XXXIV (1981), 249–65. See also Walton's *The English Seaside Resort* (Leicester, 1983) and his *The Blackpool Landlady* (Manchester, 1978).

43] Gordon N. Kniveton *et al*, *Douglas Centenary, 1896–1996* (Douglas, 1996), 21.

in Douglas, there were both winners and losers. Some entrepreneurs managed to avoid over-reaching their financial resources – for example, Alexander Gill, who owned about 150 boarding-houses and hotels, and was responsible for much of the development of the sea front and its adjoining side-roads. Others, like Lightfoot, who had to sell his tramway to meet the expense of constructing the Grand Theatre and Grand Hotel, were less fortunate. Many ambitious schemes, such as the construction of a tower to rival the one in Blackpool, never came to fruition – largely because by the end of the century there were so many amenities in Douglas that competition was crippling. There were four large dance halls at Derby Castle, Falcon Cliff, the Marina Pavilion and the Palace Pavilion, and in 1898 these were all merged into one company. The Falcon Cliff dance hall was closed down and the Marina Pavilion was converted into the Gaiety Theatre, designed by the celebrated Frank Matcham to great effect at considerable expense. In 1902 the Palace was destroyed by fire and the company replaced it with one of the largest and best dance halls in Europe, in which three thousand couples could dance on 16,000 square feet of parquet flooring to the music of famous orchestras. When the Palace Company opened the Coliseum Theatre in 1913, with seating for 3,500 people, and Douglas Corporation opened the Villa Marina 'Kursaal' in the same year, Douglas could truly claim to be one of the top resorts in the British Isles. This success had been achieved because both the Manx government and Douglas Corporation had played vigorous roles in directing the course of development, providing through Acts of Tynwald and local by-laws 'a framework of controls and regulations for the [tourist industry] which were designed to ensure the maintenance of basic standards in accommodation and an acceptable code of behaviour from the ever-increasing numbers of exuberant visitors'.[44]

The development of other towns as holiday resorts was dependent upon the internal transport system, which consisted, at first, of a few very badly surfaced roads unsuitable for tourist traffic. The railway mania that transformed Britain during the 1840s and 1850s was not mirrored in the Isle of Man, largely because the capital investment required was beyond the resources of Manx investors. However, the Isle of Man Steam Railway Company was registered late in 1870 and

44] C.P. Cooper and S. Jackson, 'The Isle of Man case study', *Annals of Tourism Research*, 16 (1989), 387. See also the same authors' 'Tourism in the Isle of Man: historical perspectives and contemporary problems', *Manchester Geographer*, new series, 3, (1982), 2, 18–30.

attracted some wealthy and influential British investors, including the Duke of Sutherland, who had close links with Governor Loch's family. The company appointed Henry Vignoles as engineer, and it was he who decided to adopt the narrow three-feet gauge. The contract for the construction of the first line, from Douglas to Peel, was won by Watson and Smith of London, and work began in the summer of 1872. An army of navvies was required for the construction, and many local men deserted their traditional occupations for the better pay of the railway company.[45] The Duke of Sutherland opened the Douglas to Peel railway on 1 July 1873, with large crowds lining the route and bands playing at each stop.

The railway route from Douglas to Peel, through the central valley, was comparatively easy to build compared with the railway company's next project, a line just under 16 miles long via Castletown to Port Erin. Steep gradients, tight bends and cuttings were necessary on the new line, which cost nearly £10,000 a mile to construct, and employed over four hundred men. It was opened on 1 August 1874, this time with little ceremony.[46] The Isle of Man Railway Company (IMR) needed to recoup its expenses and was not anxious to extend its network for the time being. This left Ramsey isolated, so a group of influential northerners formed the Manx Northern Railway Company (MNR) to construct a line from St John's via the north-west coast to Ramsey. With help from the Manx government, and despite initial opposition from the IMR, the line was opened in August 1879.[47] The IMR quickly saw the advantages of co-operation with the new company, and passengers were able to travel on the 26-mile route from Douglas to Ramsey without changing trains.

So within the space of a decade the Isle of Man witnessed a transport revolution which had vital economic repercussions. The towns of Ramsey and Peel, together with the fishing villages of Port St Mary and Port Erin, could all now join in the tourist boom, and developers moved in to build new hotels and boarding-houses in all these resorts. In 1872 Loch visited Ramsey to preside over discussions concerning the improvements to the harbour facilities, and a new south pier was constructed in 1876. However, it was still not possible to disembark passengers from vessels at low water until the construction of the Queen's Pier in 1886, designed by Sir John Coode and reaching 2,248

45] James I.C. Boyd, *The Isle of Man Railways* (Oakwood, 1993), i, 27–37.
46] Boyd, *Railways*, i, 71–81.
47] Boyd, *Railways* i, 95–125.

feet into the sea.[48] This meant that passenger steamers could now tie up at all states of the tide. With tourists coming to Ramsey by rail and by sea, the town saw a building boom in the 1880s, and a growth in the resident population from 2,891 in 1861 to 4,866 in 1891. Much of the new building took place on the Mooragh, previously an area of waste land to the north of the town. In 1886 work began on a new promenade and sea wall, and 1887 saw the official opening of the Mooragh Park and Lake, an attractive amenity for visitors and residents alike.[49]

The 1880s also saw a building boom in Peel, where a range of new boarding-houses and small hotels was built on a new promenade to the north of the existing town. A handsome new parish church with an impressive spire (taken down in 1907) was completed in 1884 to dominate the expanding resort and fishing harbour which had a population of 3,829 in 1881.[50] Loch's plans for a stone breakwater, and the consequent dredging of the harbour, led to the construction of a lighthouse and a breakwater 400 feet long, between 1891 and 1896. With these improvements Peel became a refuge for steamers when contrary winds made the Victoria Pier at Douglas hazardous.

In 1869 the first Ordnance Survey of the Island showed Port Erin to be a small fishing village with one hotel. When Loch arrived in 1863, plans were already being prepared for the construction of a breakwater which would provide a much-needed haven for fishing vessels on the west coast. Loch was enthusiastic about the scheme, not only for fishing purposes, but because he envisaged Port Erin becoming a harbour for steamers as well.[51] Accordingly, he suggested that the projected breakwater should be 800 feet long instead of 600 feet. Two hundred workmen were involved in the building operations, and large quantities of gunpowder were used to blast stone from local cliffs. Unfortunately, a series of vicious storms struck the unfinished breakwater in 1868, causing severe damage. It was eventually completed in 1876, but the cost had been very great and the whole enterprise had aroused the jealousy of fishermen in Peel and Port St Mary who objected to Port Erin being favoured in this way.

To make matters worse, Loch was faced with a serious financial crisis when the British government, which had contributed £58,200 to the Port Erin project, declared this to have been a loan, and charged £2,600 annual interest. In 1879 Loch travelled to London with a Manx

48] Radcliffe, *Shining by the Sea*, 84–6.
49] *The Isle of Man Examiner*, 13 Aug 1887.
50] Moore, *History*, ii, 646.
51] Moore, *History*, ii, 631–2.

deputation and managed to persuade the Treasury to accept a total payment of £20,000. Another storm damaged the breakwater in 1882, and two years later it was destroyed beyond repair.[52] The Port Erin breakwater was a costly failure, but the arrival of the railway in this scenic location brought the port a new role as a holiday resort, and during the 1880s a range of hotels was built around the bay, looking across the sandy beach to Bradda Head. Port St Mary also grew at this time, with hotels and boarding-houses being constructed on Chapel Bay, to the north of the main village. Port St Mary, however, never achieved the popularity with holiday-makers of Port Erin. In Castletown the leading citizens continued to oppose the development of tourist accommodation in the area despite the scenic attractions of Derbyhaven as a potential resort. While others towns were growing in population, Castletown's numbers declined steadily from 1851 onwards.

Sir Henry Loch, knighted in 1880, left the Isle of Man in 1882 after nineteen years as Lieutenant-Governor. His decision to abandon the Island's lower Customs duties in return for greater control over revenue resulted in the demise of the 'genteel' pensioner-residents from England, but he succeeded in increasing greatly the prosperity of both the Isle of Man and the Manx people, achievements that were readily acknowledged on his departure in an illuminated address presented to him by the town of Douglas. Loch was thanked for the constitutional and financial reforms of 1866, the harbour works in Douglas, Port Erin and Peel, the development of Douglas as a major resort, and important social reforms in the sphere of law, poor relief and education.[53]

Under Loch's successor Spencer Walpole (who had been secretary to his father, the Home Secretary of the same name), it became clear that the economic changes agreed as part of the 1866 reforms made by Parliament were not working satisfactorily, in particular the rules concerning Customs duties. It was difficult to ensure that commodities consumed in the Island paid duty there and not in the United Kingdom. The situation was made worse by the British government's reduction of its duty on tea which encouraged merchants to pay the duty in Britain before exporting tea to the Isle of Man, with a consequent loss to the Manx revenue. Before Walpole left the Island in 1893 he negotiated an agreement with Britain, on the basis of which Island duties would

---

52] Kermode, *Devolution*, 34–5.
53] Illuminated address presented on behalf of the inhabitants of Douglas to Sir Henry Loch, 22 Mar 1882, MNHL.

initially be paid into the British Treasury, which would repay a proportion based on actual consumption in the Island, taking into account the number of annual visitors. Despite its complexities, this 'Common Purse' system has survived in principle to the present day. At first (1890) the arrangement was confined to tea, but it was expanded rapidly after 1895, accounting for 41 per cent of total Customs revenue by 1900, and over 90 per cent by 1939.[54]

In the 1870s the steam railways established themselves as the backbone of internal transport, but in the 1890s they were challenged by the development of a new technology, electricity. Alexander Bruce, general manager of the respected Dumbell's Bank, was an enthusiast for electric transport. Between 1892 and 1894 he was one of the leading figures in the new Isle of Man Tramways and Electric Power Company which constructed an electric tramway from the north end of Douglas Bay to Groudle, and then to Laxey, following the coastline.[55] From 1894 to 1896 Bruce turned his energies towards the building of another line to the top of Snaefell as well as a cable railway, based on the San Francisco model, which ran up the sharp incline of Prospect Hill and along the upper streets of Douglas. Another company financed an ingenious tramway system which ran from Douglas Head south along the Marine Drive reaching Port Soderick in 1897, and the next year the northern tramway's extension from Laxey to Ramsey was completed. An electric tramway of such length and following so scenic a route was considered a marvel at the time and proved a big attraction to tourists, as well as providing electricity for domestic purposes. It also became a serious rival to the steam railway from Douglas to Ramsey via St John's.

The Collapse of Dumbell's Bank

Alexander Bruce's success as a builder of tramways was not mirrored in his career as general manager of Dumbell's Bank. The first effective banking venture on the Island seems to have been the Isle of Man Bank that carried on business in Castletown between 1802 and 1817. In 1817 Tynwald passed the Banker's Notes Act which prohibited the printing of notes of less than £1 value, and required all who wished to issue notes to apply for a licence from the Lieutenant-Governor. Among the first to be granted such a licence were John, Henry and James Holmes, sons of Henry Holmes senior, who had founded the Douglas and Isle of

54] Kinvig, The Isle of Man, 170; and Kermode, Devolution, 117–20.
55] For the development of the tramway network see Keith Pearson, One Hundred Years of the Manx Electric Railway (Hawes, 1992).

Man Bank in 1815. In 1840 Tynwald declared that the Isle of Man currency would in future work on the principle of twelve pennies to a shilling (instead of fourteen) to bring it into line with Britain, and Holmes' Bank assisted with the necessary changes. In the 1840s the bank lost money over the handling of shares in British railway companies, and on the deaths of John and James Holmes in 1853 the bank closed with debts of nearly £100,000.[56] Many depositors were ruined, including the lifeboat hero Sir William Hillary, who had to move out of Fort Anne, his palatial home on Douglas Head.

A second Isle of Man Bank was established in Douglas in 1836 but it soon encountered problems and was taken over by the Isle of Man Joint Stock Banking Company, which in turn was declared insolvent, with heavy debts, in 1843. This disaster was blamed on the directors, all of whom were members of the House of Keys, and it contributed significantly to the momentum behind the reform movement in the next few years. Another venture, the Isle of Man Commercial Banking Company, started in 1838, was forced to suspend payments in 1848 and was rescued by the City of Glasgow Bank, which took it over and began trading in Douglas, Castletown, Ramsey and Peel, as the Bank of Mona. The new bank occupied handsome premises on Prospect Hill from 1855, and survived a crisis faced by its parent company the City of Glasgow Bank in 1857 to become banker to the Isle of Man government and many of its officials. But in the summer of 1878 its chief cashier was found guilty of stealing over £9,000 from the bank, and in the autumn its parent, the City of Glasgow Bank, failed when charges of theft and fraud were brought against the directors, managers and secretary. Isle of Man depositors were paid in full, but the Bank of Mona came to an end and its Douglas premises became the government offices.

The Bank of Mona's closure left four banks trading on the Island. Two of them, the Isle of Man Savings Bank and the Manx Bank, were relatively small; the other two were rival giants. The Isle of Man Banking Company Limited was the first to be registered after Tynwald passed the Companies Act (1865) which permitted the establishment of companies with limited liability. Its leading lights included Henry Bloom Noble, a businessman who made a fortune from wise investment in the Island during these boom years. The other main bank was founded by George Dumbell, who came to the Island from the north of England as a young man and was called to the Manx Bar in 1826. He soon branched out into business ventures and became a prominent member of the House of Keys, and chairman of the Laxey Mining

---

56] Mark Solly, *Banks in the Isle of Man* (Castletown, 1995), 1–11.

Company. Within a few days of the failure of Holmes' Bank in 1853, Dumbell founded his own bank, officially the Douglas and Isle of Man Bank, but generally known as Dumbell's Bank.[57]

The new bank at first traded from St George's Street in Douglas and soon opened branches in Castletown and Ramsey, where its main competitor was the Bank of Mona. For three months during 1857 Dumbell was forced to close, but he was able to survive this crisis, and in 1861 he moved the bank's headquarters to an impressive new building in Prospect Hill. In 1874 the bank was reformed as a limited liability company in accordance with the Companies Act 1865, and shares offered to the public were heavily oversubscribed. At the first meeting of shareholders in 1874 Dumbell promised that he would personally scrutinise the bank's business. 'We keep a perfect tally by weekly and by monthly accounts', he said, 'showing every shilling that has been advanced and the names of the individuals, and a check is kept showing every man's balance as debtor or creditor, and what security there is for every advance.' Dumbell was a respected figure in Manx business and political life, and his bank flourished, especially after the closure of the Bank of Mona in 1878, when Dumbell's customers came to include the Isle of Man government, the Highway Board, the Harbour Board, the Great Laxey Mining Company, the Foxdale Mining Company and almost all the leading Douglas hotels.[58]

In 1878 Alexander Bruce, then manager of the Bank of Mona's Ramsey branch, lost his job when the bank closed, but he was appointed instead to be general manager of Dumbell's Bank. George Dumbell died in 1887, in his mid-80s, and Bruce became the controlling influence in the bank. Between 1893 and 1898 Bruce threw his energies into electric transport and through Dumbell's Bank financed many of the new tramlines. In 1898 he successfully acquired a number of tourist facilities in Douglas, and went on to launch a brewery syndicate scheme which took over three breweries and forty-six licensed premises, hoping to pay for them by a public share issue. However, of the £300,000 share capital on offer, only £51,665 was taken up: the rest had to be underwritten by Dumbell's Bank. In November 1899 the bank's head cashier, John Curphey, resigned, alleging that the bank's affairs were in 'a most dangerous and critical state ... brought about by years of gross neglect on the part of the managers'.[59] Bruce sweet-talked his way through a directors' meeting, but saw that the only solution was to sell

57] Solly, *Banks*, 11–16.
58] Solly, *Banks*, 19.
59] Solly, *Banks*, 22.

the bank. Parr's Bank, of London, showed interest in the purchase but their accountants discovered serious discrepancies in the Dumbell's records. On Saturday 3 February 1900 – 'Black Saturday', as it became known – the doors of Dumbell's Bank on Prospect Hill did not open for business.

After investigations had been made, Alexander Bruce, together with Charles Nelson, a director of the bank, John Shimmin, the manager, and Joseph Rogers, the secretary, together with two English auditors, William and Harold Aldred, were all arrested and charged with fraud. Bruce died in July 1900 and never stood trial. All the rest were found guilty and served prison sentences, except for William Aldred, who was 77 years of age, and seriously ill. Meanwhile, the liquidators worked steadily to sort out the bank's affairs, but it was not until 1922 that the final settlements were made to creditors, who received back about 63 per cent of their money. There were eight thousand depositors with Dumbell's at the time of its closure, and many of them were ruined – either because they lost a proportion of their savings or because they were required to pay back their borrowings. Several public companies collapsed, most notably the Isle of Man Tramways and Electrical Power Company, Bruce's brainchild, the assets of which were sold by the liquidators at half their value. According to the journalist and politician Samuel Norris: 'Everybody in the Isle of Man was affected, and every financial value was depreciated. Depression like a black, cloudy night was the dominant atmosphere and overpowering influence.' Norris was not impressed with the Manx government, which 'stood placidly by, indifferent and helpless', led by Governor Henniker, an 'affable, tottering old gentleman with no political opinions and no understanding of the principles of political economy'.[60] There were many in the Island in 1900 who remembered wistfully the great days of Sir Henry Loch.

Nevertheless, the ill-effects of the Dumbell Bank crash on the Manx economy should not be overestimated. It is true that personal hardship was suffered by many individuals, and that several companies went out of business. It is also true that there was, for a time, a general suspicion of all banks and a lack of confidence in investment and expansion. But these were short-term effects: the tourist trade continued to boom, and the ever-growing fleet of the Steam Packet Company continued to disgorge hundreds of thousands of passengers every season on to Douglas's Victoria Pier. In 1873, the year in which the pier opened, there were a reported 90,000 visitors: in 1884, the first year for which

60] Samuel Norris, *Manx Memories and Movements* (1938: rpt, Douglas, 1994), 70.

official passenger figures are available, the number had risen to 182,669, with 90 per cent sailing from the Lancashire coast, mostly from Liverpool.[61] In 1887, the year of Queen Victoria's Golden Jubilee, the Steam Packet reduced its fares dramatically, ostensibly in honour of the Jubilee, but chiefly to destroy competition from two new Liverpool shipping companies. The result of this price war was a record 347,968 passengers travelling to Douglas during the Jubilee Year, and from 1895 to 1913 the trend continued ever upward, helped by the publicity efforts of the Isle of Man Advertising Committee, set up in 1894.[62] The crash of Dumbell's Bank did not mean that Edwardian Douglas fell on hard times. On the contrary: these were boom years for holiday businesses, with the beaches thick with visitors in the summer months, the hundreds of hotels bustling with trade, and dense crowds moving to and from the Victoria Pier. In 1913, 634,512 passengers arrived on the Island between 1 May and 30 September.[63] The most distinguished holiday-makers of all were King Edward VII and Queen Alexandra, who, while cruising in the royal yacht in August 1902, made a two-day visit to the Island, landing at Ramsey and driving on to an enthusiastic welcome in Douglas. This was the first time a reigning British monarch had set foot on the Isle of Man.

Agriculture, Fishing and Mining

The growth of the holiday trade was the Island's great economic success story between 1863 and 1914, and it was much needed, because towards the end of this period the traditional industries fell upon hard times. In the 1870s British agriculture was badly hit by the mass importation of North American wheat, which led to an agricultural depression on the mainland. The Island, however, avoided this fate, owing partly to an increase in the total population to 55,608 in 1891 – a figure not exceeded until the 1970s. Also, the healthy tourist trade created a continuing demand for agricultural produce. Between 1885 and 1890 the acreages of both arable land and improved farmland rose to their highest recorded levels. The Commission on Local Industries, reporting in 1899, noted that 'owing to the excellent demand here for all sorts of agricultural produce in the summer, the position of our

---

61] Birch, *The Isle of Man*, 35.
62] See John Beckerson, *Advertising the Island: The Isle of Man Official Board of Advertising, 1894–1914*, unpublished MA thesis, University of East Anglia, 1996.
63] *Isle of Man Summer Passenger Arrivals 1887 to the Present* (Isle of Man Government, Economic Affairs Division, The Treasury, 1995). All subsequent details of summer passenger arrivals (1 May–30 Sept) come from this source.

farmers, except those in the remote districts, is an exceptionally favourable one'. The dark side of this picture was that 'the remote districts', or upland crofts, had been abandoned between 1885 and 1900 to the extent of 8,000 acres.[64]

Between 1863 and 1914 the Manx fishing industry experienced a thirty-year boom followed by a rapid slump. The peak of the boom was reached in the 1880s, and it was asserted at the National Fisheries Exhibition in 1883 that 'In the Isle of Man one person out of every five depends on fishing for his daily bread, and one person out of every four is directly or indirectly dependent on fishing for a livelihood'.[65] In 1880 there were 393 Manx vessels involved in fishing, crewed by 2,194 men and 402 boys. Robert Corrin, of Peel, had pioneered mackerel fishing off Kinsale in 1861, and Manx boats set out from Peel and Port St Mary in early March, returning at the end of June. They then changed to the different type of net used for catching herring, which they proceeded to fish as usual in home waters. Between seventy and eighty Manx boats also made the 500-mile voyage to Lerwick in July, and continued to fish for herring off the Shetlands until September. From September to December small open yawls fished for cod about five miles from the Island, and in the following spring larger boats searched for cod 15 to 20 miles offshore. The Manx fishing boats at this period were among the finest afloat. They were based on the west Cornish lugger, and known as 'nickeys', 48 to 55 feet long, fast enough for long runs to Kinsale and the Shetlands, and strong enough to withstand the Atlantic swells. Their disadvantage was that they carried three sets of sails for different weather conditions, and good seamanship as well as physical strength was needed to handle them. In 1883 more than forty of the nickeys had been fitted with steam engines which could haul in a two-mile train of mackerel nets in two hours instead of the four hours needed for manual toil.

Peel was undoubtedly the centre of the Island's fishing. The 1871 census showed that 95 boats left for Kinsale in March, with aggregate crews of 788: of these, 420 were Peel men and the majority of the rest hailed from nearby German and Patrick. In December 1886 the *Peel City Guardian*, writing about Peel and Port St Mary, observed:

> The fishermen of the two ports represent two entirely different classes of person. Those of Port St. Mary are for the most part crofters, as so many of the fishermen used to be also in this part of

64] *Report of the Commission on Local Industries* (1899).
65] From the Isle of Man's entry in the catalogue of the *Great International Fisheries Exhibition* (London, 1883), 216.

the Island, going to the sea part of the year, and working on their plots of land during the winter and early spring. Thus it comes to pass that there are probably not more than forty or fifty men in Port St. Mary wholly dependent on the 'harvest of the sea' for a living. But the case of the Peel men is utterly different. Not many years ago quite half of those who followed the herring in Peel belonged also to the crofter class, who have, however, disappeared from among them, having left the country for the town and, in this way, been the cause of Peel having doubled its population in the last fifteen years.[66]

The increased activity in Peel led to serious overcrowding in the harbour, and a thousand fishermen protested at the 1880 Tynwald ceremony about the inadequate harbour facilities.[67]

Yet all this activity quite unexpectedly quietened down between 1884 and 1898, mainly because the great shoals of herring, sometimes up to 10 miles long and 4 miles wide, could no longer be found. A Fisheries Inquiry in 1898 attempted to determine why, and considered in particular the effects of over-fishing, though Professor Herdman of the newly established Marine Laboratory at Port Erin attributed the herring failure to purely local decreases.[68] Because the increasingly specialist fishermen no longer had their crofting to fall back on, they were hard hit by the failure of the fisheries, and many young men emigrated altogether, or looked for employment in the Island's holiday resorts. There was little incentive to invest in new boats and equipment, just at the time when steam drifters from other countries began to operate in Kinsale and the Shetlands, rendering sailing vessels obsolete. Steam drifters could operate 60 to 80 miles offshore and travel at 9 mph in all weathers, but they cost between £3,000 and £4,000 to buy. The herring shoals did return to Manx waters between 1899 and 1914, but by then the Manx fishing fleet had become out-of-date: moreover, it was operated by elderly men, on the whole, and its numbers had fallen in 1913 to 185 vessels, crewed by 677 men and boys.[69]

Mining, like fishing, experienced a boom period after 1863, followed by a slump. Though there were lesser mines, such as Snaefell, Bradda and Ballacorkish, the two main centres were Foxdale and Laxey, which together were employing as many as a thousand men and boys in the

66] *Peel City Guardian*, 18 Dec 1886.

67] Moore, *History*, ii, 719.

68] W.A. Herdman, 'The cultivation of our sea shores', a lecture reported in the *Manx Sun*, 4 Sept 1897 (MNHL: B.356 1x).

69] *Isle of Man Statistical Abstracts* (1916), 21.

1870s and 1880s.[70] The two Laxey mines chiefly produced zinc ore and silver, while the five mines at Foxdale specialised in lead ore. In 1877 186,019 ounces of silver were mined, and in 1878 11,898 tons of zinc ore, with 6,868 tons of lead ore in 1885. But the prosperity did not last, partly because the mines were not inexhaustible and also because it was difficult to export the ore, even after the building of a railway link between Foxdale and Ramsey. The most serious problem of all was the development of mines in South Africa, Australia, the United States and Canada, which began to produce vast quantities of ore at lower prices. In due course many Manx miners emigrated to work in the mines of these countries, establishing small Manx colonies there. By 1900 only three mines were still working. One of them, the Snaefell mine, was the scene of a disaster in May 1897, when 20 men were killed by carbon monoxide poisoning.[71] This mine closed in 1905, to be followed by the last Foxdale mine in 1911 and the last Laxey mine in 1929. It was therefore more than fortunate for the Island, faced with the drastic decline of its fishing and mining industries, that it had adapted itself so successfully as a destination for holiday-makers and that they continued to cross the Irish Sea in increasing numbers throughout the first decade of the new century. Confidence and permanence were the keynotes of those Edwardian days, when the Isle of Man was a favoured part of a British world empire, when the King-Emperor himself had walked the streets of Douglas and Ramsey, and when the sun reputedly shone brightly over the Island in the summer months. Even when news filtered through to the Island's beaches in August 1914 that war had broken out in the faraway Balkans, few suspected how fragile this comfortable way of life would prove to be.

1914–45

The 1914–18 War and the Internment Camps
When Britain declared war on Germany on 4 August 1914, the Isle of Man was enjoying a bumper holiday season, expected to break the previous year's record of 634,512 visitors. The popular belief tended to be that the war would be over in a few months, but the Governor, Lord Raglan, advised holiday-makers to go home as soon as possible, and also suggested that hotel and boarding-house keepers should sell up and seek work elsewhere. This advice might have seemed harsh, but it was

70] Birch, *The Isle of Man*, 154.
71] R.F.M.Grant, 'The Snaefell Mine', *Mining Magazine*, XCII, 2 (1955), 79–86.

realistic. In committing itself to a European war, Britain became locked in a long struggle with a group of determined allies, headed by Imperial Germany, a rich and militaristic industrial state with a powerful standing army and a modern navy which included numerous submarines. Tynwald immediately voted funds to the British government, the naval reserve was called up, and recruiting offices were opened in Douglas. During the four years of the war the Island sent 8,261 men to fight, being 82.3 per cent of the male population of military age. Of these, 770 were killed and 395 died of wounds or disease, or were reported missing. A further 182 were made prisoners of war and 987 were wounded – a total of 2,334 casualties.[72]

The directors of the Steam Packet Company met on 10 August to discuss future plans, because the slump in business over the previous week-end had made clear the likely effects of war. Three of the company's fifteen operational ships were put in dock, and the service to Whitehaven was discontinued. By the end of October 1914 the paddle-steamers *King Orry*, *Peel Castle* and *Ramsey* were requisitioned by the Admiralty, soon to be followed by *Snaefell*, *Ben-my-Chree*, *Queen Victoria*, *Prince of Wales*, *Empress Queen* and *Viking*. Eventually, the Steam Packet's working fleet was reduced to three ships, *Tynwald*, *Fenella* and *Douglas*, all of them employed on the Douglas to Liverpool run.[73] The main fear was that they would be easy prey for a prowling U-boat, though in fact they were never attacked.

The limitations of 'Home Rule' status were made quite clear during the years of war: decisions that concerned the Island were frequently taken by the British government with scant reference to Tynwald. The first example of this was the decision to use the Island as a location for the internment of enemy aliens resident in Britain at the outbreak of war. It seems that Sir William Byrne, the permanent Principal Secretary at the Home Office, had previously visited Douglas and seen the famous Cunningham's Holiday Camp for young men, established in the town in 1904 and consisting eventually of 1,500 bell-shaped tents with eight men to a tent.[74] This prompted the Home Office to send over the first group of two hundred internees as early as 22 September 1914, and the former Cunningham's Camp was rapidly cordoned off with barbed-wire fences. Within two months three thousand internees had been deposited there, and on 19 November there was a serious riot during which five internees died. An inquest

72] Norris, *Manx Memories*, 148.
73] Chappell, *Island Lifeline*, 80.
74] Norris, *Manx Memories*, 150.

blamed the trouble on bad weather, poor food and, in particular, the overcrowded conditions.[75]

It was clear that another camp was needed, and the site chosen was a farm called Knockaloe Moar, near Peel, which had formerly been used as a camping ground for up to sixteen thousand Territorial Reserves. To begin with, the camp accommodated five thousand men, but after the sinking of the Cunard liner *Lusitania* by a German U-boat in May 1915, and the subsequent wave of hostile feeling in Britain towards remaining aliens, many more were shipped across to the Island. When American Embassy officials visited Knockaloe in 1916, they found 20,563 men, of whom 16,936 were German, 3,382 Austrian, 101 Turks, and 144 other nationalities. The same officials recorded 2,744 internees at the Douglas camp in 1916, of whom 1,968 were Germans, 759 Austrians, 14 Turks and three other nationalities. By the end of the war the numbers at Knockaloe had risen to 24,450. The camp, which was nearly 3 miles in circumference, was built and staffed by Manx people, about 250 of whom acted as censors, pursers, clerks, storekeepers, hospital dispensers and engineers, while a military guard was provided by two thousand men of the Royal Defence Corps.[76] Knockaloe was, in fact, a camp town with a population greater than that of Douglas, and this had important economic implications for the Island.

Samuel Norris calculated that the central stores which supplied Knockaloe camp carried stocks worth more than £100,000 and had a turnover of £12,000 a month; and, as far as possible, the goods were bought in the Isle of Man. 'What this meant to tradesmen will never be fully known', he wrote, 'but that policy saved tradesmen generally from absolute stagnation and bankruptcy, and, in many instances, meant wealth beyond their wildest dreams.'[77] Some twenty thousand contracts were made, the terms of which enabled many of the contractors to become rich by the end of the war, especially as there was no income tax on the Island at this time. Also many Manx farmers were able to benefit from the constant demand for agricultural produce at the camp throughout the war years. Though they lived a monotonous life, with only sport, educational and artistic recreations to divert them, the internees were looked after well and their general health was remarkably good.

75] For the internment camps see B.E. Sergeaunt, *The Isle of Man and the Great War* (Douglas, 1920), 58–87; Margery West, *Island at War* (Laxey, 1986) and Y.M. Cresswell (ed), *Living with the Wire* (Douglas, 1994), 81–107.

76] Cresswell, *Living*, 9–13.

77] Norris, *Manx Memories*, 151.

Bitte die Bücher mit Schonung zu benutzen. Die Bücher müssen an die für sie bestimmten Plätze zurückgestellt werden.

DIE·WOCHE

German prisoners-of-war *On 22 September 1914 the first consignment of two hundred German prisoners arrived at Cunningham's Camp, Douglas. To begin with, they lived in the tented holiday accommodation, but this was later replaced by huts, which housed additional areas for workshops, recreation and entertainment. (MNHL)*

Meanwhile Douglas had become a ghost town. 'I walked along the Douglas promenade from end to end – two miles – on August Bank Holiday Monday, 1915', Samuel Norris recorded: 'En route I passed eight people.'[78] Later that afternoon the small steamer *Douglas* berthed at the Victoria Pier and disgorged some 415 passengers, most of them soldiers, or their friends and relatives, and the wives of internees. Throughout the length of Douglas Bay hotels and boarding-houses

78] Norris, *Manx Memories*, 181.

were the hardest hit of all because they owed rents, but were earning little or no income. Those lucky enough to be a tenant of one of the 160 properties of Alexander Gill had their rent reduced by a third or more from 1915 onwards, but many others faced ruin, and began to agitate for government help.

The Governor, appointed in 1902, was Lord Raglan, a grandson of the commander of the British forces in the Crimean War. His main strength was an amiable social manner, which, when times were good, made him a popular figure. But he was an arch-conservative in politics and outlook, and he resolutely opposed any constitutional reform within the Island which might have resulted in the reduction of his own powers, or the authority of the British government. His manner was aristocratic and his methods paternalistic, but he was enough of a politician to build up a strong coterie of allies on the Island, the chief of whom was the Attorney-General, George Ring. During the years of peace and prosperity between 1902 and 1914 Raglan's rule, though offensive to liberals and reformers, caused little general opposition. But in the very different circumstances of wartime the Governor's apparent lack of concern for the hardships endured by certain sections of the Manx people created unrest which eventually resulted in popular demonstrations against him.

It was a remarkable fact that in 1915 the Manx government received an income higher than at any time in its previous history, largely because of the presence of the internee camps at Douglas and Knockaloe. The British government paid duties on all the excisable articles consumed by the internees and soldiers in the camps, and it also paid all the expenses of the war – such as soldiers' pay, family allowances, pensions and grants for certain losses. In the financial year 1914–15 Manx government revenue was £93,000, and expenditure £82,000, leaving a surplus of £10,900, which was added to an existing surplus fund to make a total of £74,665.[79] The Manx government should therefore, its critics argued, have been in a strong position to assist those who faced ruin because the holiday trade had ceased.

In response to pressure, the Loan Scheme to Distressed Boarding-House Keepers was introduced by Tynwald in June 1915, enabling boarding-house, lodging-house and hotel keepers to obtain loans from the Manx government upon certain rather harsh terms, which included the borrower having to pledge his furniture and personal assets as security for the loan. Most boarding-house and hotel keepers thought the terms far too severe, and wanted a reduction of the rates instead. But in September 1915 Raglan returned to England on sick leave, repeating his advice that those badly affected should sell up and leave the Island, in the anticipation of a long war. 'Never, so long as I am Governor', he was reported to have said, 'will I give any relief of rates.'[80]

In December 1915 Samuel Norris founded the War Rights Union, the aim of which was to persuade the Manx government to reduce local business rates to a third of their prewar value. To this demand the constant reply of Raglan was that the British government would not allow Manx government surpluses to be spent on reducing the local rates in Douglas and elsewhere; so deadlock ensued. The War Rights Union appealed to the Home Secretary, who, in a letter to the Manx government in March 1916, summed up the situation well:

79] Norris, *Manx Memories*, 163.
80] Norris, *Manx Memories*, 170.

It is to be remembered that taxation in the Isle of Man is still lighter than the ordinary standard prevailing in the United Kingdom, and the essential point is that while certain sections of the public are hard hit in the towns, the country people are admittedly prosperous, owing in part to agricultural conditions, and in part to the expenditure of Imperial funds in connection with the camps. The solution clearly indicated is that the latter should assist the former, that is, that taxation not bearing too hardly upon the towns should be imposed to replenish the Accumulated Fund, advances being made from that fund to the towns.[81]

The division between those to whom the war had brought prosperity and those to whom it had brought ruin was highlighted by the Mayor of Douglas in May 1916, in a speech to the Town Council. He was, he said

filled with anxiety for the town. Douglas was simply dwindling away, and he felt the disaster might, with courage and effort, have been avoided. There was more wealth in the Isle of Man that day than there was in the year before the war. Nearly one half of the population was doing better than they had ever done; the other half of the population was drifting into bankruptcy.[82]

Feeling was further inflamed in June 1916, when the Manx government's accounts for 1915–16 showed that, far from the deficit of £26,000 which Raglan had warned Tynwald to expect, there was a surplus of £18,000, mostly from taxes on food – such as sugar, tea, beer and tobacco consumed by the 26,000 internees, among others. The War Rights Union gave way to a more militant Redress, Retrenchment and Reform campaign (RRR), and an open-air meeting called at Broadway, in Douglas, resolved that 'it would be in the interests of good government that Lord Raglan should resign the Governorship, and that a strong Governor, of financial ability and sympathy with representative government, should be appointed forthwith'.[83] It was also demanded that Raglan should return part of his salary, as he had been off the Island, officially on sick leave, for the last nine months – another cause of popular discontent.

Raglan returned to the Island just in time for Tynwald Day, 5 July 1916, when the RRR party determined to present him with a petition of grievances, just as the Peel fishermen had petitioned Loch in 1880. On a

81] Norris, *Manx Memories*, 181.
82] Norris, *Manx Memories*, 184.
83] Norris, *Manx Memories*, 188.

sunny day at St John's placards were displayed which read 'We want a new Governor, Taxation of Wealth, No Food Taxes, Revenue from the Camps, For War Distress Redress, Retrenchment and Reform!' As the formal procession moved down from Tynwald Hill, a sod of grass was thrown at the Governor, grazing his hand harmlessly. The culprit was probably a mischievous ten-year-old boy, but his action did nothing to improve relations between Raglan and his critics.[84]

In August 1916 C.P. Scott, the influential editor of the *Manchester Guardian*, published a spirited defence of the Manx reform movement, asserting that 'on the mainland, direct taxation is established beyond criticism, but the Manx still have to suffer their finances to be raised by levies on foodstuffs, while the incomes of the Island's rich go free of imposts'.[85] Petitions were sent to the Home Secretary and the House of Commons, but they achieved little. Meanwhile, in October 1916 the Manx government sent in the coroner to seize and auction the furniture of some of those, including Samuel Norris, who had not paid their rates. Norris and the RRR party urged people not to bid at the auction, and as a result Norris was charged with 'wilfully and maliciously hindering and interrupting the coroner'.[86] Norris refused to apologise, and he was committed to prison, where he remained for 28 days.

In 1917 a further crisis arose over the price of bread, which had reached such a high price in Britain that Parliament introduced a subsidy on flour, reducing the price of a four-pound loaf to 9*d*. The Manx government, under local pressure, followed this lead, financing the subsidy in the first year with £20,000 taken from the surplus fund. The Treasury accepted this, but instructed that in the second year the subsidy must be funded by ordinary revenue, not from surplus. Accordingly, Raglan put before the House of Keys a bill to introduce income tax at a very modest rate, but the House was reluctant to pass it. Critics said this was because income tax would affect the pockets of all members of the House: MHKs argued that such a Bill would strengthen the British Treasury's control over the Island's internal affairs. On Wednesday 3 July 1918 trade union leaders in the Island called a general strike because the subsidy on bread had come to an end, and on Thursday 4 July all transport stopped, including the steamer to Liverpool. Electric power and light were switched off, and most shops stayed shut.[87] Captain Moughtin, an MHK who was also a

84] Norris, *Manx Memories*, 203.

85] *Manchester Guardian*, 12 Aug 1916, quoted in Norris, *Manx Memories*, 215.

86] Norris, *Manx Memories*, 237.

87] 'The Great Strike', *Manx Quarterly*, IV, 2 (Apr 1919), 237–57.

coal merchant in Douglas, attempted to open his business on the North Quay, but was assaulted by a mob, many of whom were women. Faced with the lack of transport, Raglan postponed the Tynwald ceremony scheduled for Friday 5 July, and restored the 9*d* loaf on his own authority. By the following Monday he was in London, explaining the awkwardness of the situation to the Home Office.

A new Home Secretary (Sir George Cave) gave Raglan firm instructions to return and inform the House of Keys that, if it failed within one week to pass a Bill introducing income tax, starting at 2*s* in the pound for incomes over £500 a year, such a bill would be imposed on the Island by Parliament. With ten minutes to spare, an acceptable bill was passed by Tynwald on 18 July 1918, and income tax became a fact of life in the Isle of Man.[88] In its first year of operation (1918–19) it raised £66,011, more than three times the sum needed to meet the expenses of the bread subsidy – so the rate of taxation was subsequently reduced. In any case, within four months of the passing of the bill, the war had ended.

The war seriously disrupted life in the Island and destroyed the holiday trade upon which it had come to depend for prosperity. Those most connected with that trade, in particular hotel keepers, were the worst hit section of the community, and the Manx government's failure to deal sympathetically with their plight led to a popular movement opposed to the government, and, in particular, the Governor. The Tynwald ceremony was disrupted for two years; a prominent citizen, Samuel Norris, had been imprisoned for his part in the opposition movement, and British newspapers carried articles criticising the 'Ruritanian' or 'Gilbert and Sullivan' nature of the Manx constitution.[89]

On the other hand the British government's decision to intern more than 23,000 enemy aliens in an Island whose population was only just over 52,000 brought great prosperity to certain sections of the community, especially farmers and landowners, and increased very substantially the revenues of the Manx government. The internment camps provided many job opportunities, while several hundred women and girls were employed on War Office contracts, making socks and clothing for soldiers, and the Palace and Derby Castle ballrooms were turned into factories which produced clothing and fabric for balloons.

88] 'The Income Tax Bill', *Manx Quarterly*, IV, 2 (Apr 1919), 260–71.
89] See, for example, the article by Spencer Leigh Hughes MP, 'The funniest Second Chamber on Earth', *Reynolds's Newspaper*, 1916, quoted in Norris, *Manx Memories*, 183.

The Isle of Man Banking Company paid a 30 per cent dividend in 1917, the Steam Packet received £350,000 in profits and as compensation for ships requisitioned or lost in the war, and the Isle of Man Railway Company paid an increased dividend of 5 per cent in 1917. Even the Laxey mine paid a 10 per cent dividend, its first for many years.[90]

For the poor, life was, as always, hard. By the end of the war the retail price of food had risen to 60 per cent above the prewar price, which was good news for suppliers, but not for the poorer classes. Farm labourers asked for higher wages and were given 16s a week. The Highway Board and the Harbour Board raised wages to 23s 4d a week for 56 hours' work, while the railway increased its wage to 25s a week. Many unskilled labourers worked a 70-hour week for between 22s and 25s, and over three hundred men and women received poor relief every week from the Boards of Guardians. But those who were damaged most of all by four years of war were, of course, the families of the 1,165 Island men who died as a result of the fighting.[91]

Between Two Wars, 1918–39

On 17 December 1918 Raglan resigned his position as Governor, after a tenure of sixteen years. He was replaced by Major-General William Fry, with a brief to inaugurate reforms – successive Home Secretaries had promised that constitutional reform, recommended in 1911 by a Departmental Committee headed by Lord MacDonnell, would be a major priority after the war. Some had hoped for a diplomat as Governor, and the novelist Sir Hall Caine had advanced his own claims for the post. Fry, however, proved a good choice. Born in Dublin, he chose the army as a career, and, while posted in the Isle of Man as a young officer, he fell in love with the eldest daughter of Sir John Goldie-Taubman of the Nunnery, Douglas. As a Major-General he had commanded a division in 1915, after which he was in charge of the administrative staff of the Irish command based in Dublin. Fry was appointed for seven years only, which itself was something of a reform, and within a few weeks he had introduced a Bill reforming the Legislative Council. In the winter of 1919 a general election returned a House of Keys with 17 new members, one of whom was Samuel Norris. He lost no time in moving that old-age pensions should be paid to those over 70 years of age, a proposal unanimously approved. The scheme was operating within six months – though ten years behind the United Kingdom.[92]

90] Norris, *Manx Memories*, 285.
91] Norris, *Manx Memories*, 286.
92] Norris, *Manx Memories*, 335–9.

With the war over and the internment camps closing down, it was essential that the holiday trade should be restored as quickly as possible. The first problem was the position of the Steam Packet Company. The Admiralty returned the three vessels that had survived the war – *Mona's Queen*, *Peel Castle* and the *King Orry*, which had proudly accompanied the captured German fleet to its final rendezvous at Scapa Flow. Moreover, the company received compensation for its many ships which had been destroyed. Even with the three small steamers *Douglas*, *Tynwald* and *Fenella*, which had served the Island during the war, the Steam Packet Company's carrying capacity was well under half what it had been formerly. However, by chartering additional vessels and purchasing or commissioning new ones over the next few years, the company was able to cope with the demand.[93] The number of summer arrivals in 1919 was 343,332, rising to a healthy 561,124 in 1920 – a figure that was not exceeded until the 585,508 of 1937. In one August day of that year 68,372 passengers were embarked and disembarked at Douglas, and about fifty separate steamer sailings were needed to transport them all.[94]

As might be expected, the number of visitors decreased when economic conditions in Britain were unfavourable. Hence there were only 427,923 summer visitors in 1921, the beginning of the postwar depression, and there was a record low for the interwar period in 1926, the year of the general strike in Britain. However, the seaside summer holiday remained popular among the employed between the wars, and the Isle of Man was still seen as an attractive resort, especially among young people.

The Island continued to appeal to its prewar clientele among the predominantly working-class population of north-western England – there was no obvious alternative holiday available during these years. The hoteliers and boarding-house keepers of Douglas and other resorts were anxious, for their part, to recover the losses and repay the debts incurred during the inactive years of the war. The return of holiday-makers in healthy numbers restored the prosperity of the hotel trade, though there is evidence that, in the 1920s, Douglas was considered somewhat expensive. By the 1930s this notion had been dispelled, with Promenade hotels offering full board for around 6s a day, and boarding-houses for 5s. Facilities offered by hotels gradually improved with the installation of electric light, hot and cold running water, and

93] Chappell, *Island Lifeline*, 93.
94] Chappell, *Island Lifeline*, 94, and *Isle of Man Summer Passenger Arrivals*, 6.

MORE JAM, PLEASE !

'**More jam please!**' *Holiday-makers occasionally felt they had been short-changed, as this cartoon depicting Cunningham's Camp shows. Notice the Rushen Abbey label on the strawberry jam container. With the success of Britain's first holiday camp, Joseph Cunningham moved from the Howstrake site to Victoria Road, where large numbers of eight-bed bell tents offered cheap and healthy holidays to young men. After being used as a prisoner-of-war camp, it was reopened in 1919, supported by its own farm at Ellerslie, as well as a butchery and a bakery. (MNHL)*

more comfortable furnishings. Bathrooms and lavatories, however, still remained a rarity.[95]

The last internees left Cunningham's Holiday Camp in March 1919, and the first of the postwar holiday campers arrived in May: within a few years the camp was accommodating up to four thousand young men in tents, chalet tents, bungalows and dormitories. The camp's new dining-hall was advertised as being the world's largest, with seats for over three thousand diners at a time, and the management was quick to

95] Kniveton *et al*, *Douglas Centenary*, 103.

make the most of the latest fashions in dancing, cinema-viewing and sport. The years between the wars were a boom period for the camp, where over a million young men had spent a holiday by 1939.[96]

The 1920s and 1930s saw some important additions and improvements to the amenities of Douglas as a resort, but there was nothing like the mass investment and development that had characterised prewar years. The new Villa Marina, opened in 1913, now came into its own as a multi-purpose hall with seats for three thousand, a suitable setting for concerts featuring international celebrities. The Villa's sea front colonnade was added in 1930, and the Arcade in 1931, mainly to provide shelter in bad weather. An ambitious scheme to widen the Loch Promenade and build a series of sunken gardens began in 1929 and took six years to complete, inconveniencing the Loch hotels with noise and dirt, but providing much-needed winter employment to local men, and eventually providing a most impressive amenity. A second cinema, The Picture House, opened in Strand Street in 1921, and a Palais de Danse in 1927. Two theatres were redeveloped as the Royalty and Regal cinemas, while a marble marvel, the two-thousand-seat Crescent 'Super' Cinema was built in 1930. The horse trams continued to be a major attraction, and in 1934 they made nearly two and a half million passenger journeys along the Promenade. 'I hesitate to have to confess it', wrote a journalist in the *Blackpool Gazette* in 1931, 'but compared with the liveliness on the Douglas Promenade on a sunny afternoon, even a Blackpool Bank Holiday crowd seems the height of respectability.'[97] Douglas Head, however, declined in popularity, especially after the destruction of the Port Skillion swimming-baths in bad weather in the early 1930s.

The return of the holiday trade and the prosperity that accompanied it made it easier for the British government to ask the Isle of Man for a substantial contribution to the expenses of the war. Though Raglan might have had his critics among liberals and reformers, there is no doubt that he left the Island's government in a very healthy economic position. As early as April 1918 the Home Secretary suggested that Jersey, Guernsey and the Isle of Man should make a contribution to the war expenses. Jersey and Guernsey each voted gifts of £100,000, and in May 1921 Tynwald assumed liability for £250,000 of War Stock, to be paid off in twenty annual instalments, effectively making a payment of £20,000 a year to Britain, in addition to the £10,000 a year agreed in

---

96] Kniveton *et al*, *Douglas Centenary*, 105. See also J. Drower, *Good Clean Fun: The Story of Britain's First Holiday Camp*, (London, 1982).
97] Quoted in Kniveton *et al*, *Douglas Centenary*, 109

1866.[98] Parliament was not satisfied with this offer, and a Committee
on National Expenditure reported in 1922 that the total revenue of the
Isle of Man had risen from £85,000 before the war to £369,000 in 1921,
with a surplus fund of £333,000. Income tax was low and there was no
National Debt, so the Committee recommended an annual contribution
of £150,000 with an initial single payment of £100,000. In 1923
Tynwald offered instead a lump sum of £200,000, but this was refused,
and a Committee of the Privy Council was appointed to look into the
dispute. Its eventual report recorded that the revenue and economic
structure of the Island was mainly dependent on the visiting industry,
because three-eighths of the Island's Customs revenue came from duties
on commodities consumed by visitors. The Committee recommended
that the Island should pay £100,000 a year for fifty years, and £50,000 a
year thereafter in perpetuity. The Committee also thought that
Guernsey and Jersey should pay £75,000 and £120,000 a year
respectively for a hundred years.[99]

These proposals were received in all three islands with a sense of
outrage. As it happened, the deadlock was broken by Britain's general
strike in 1926, which caused a drastic fall in the number of visitors to
the Island – from 540,628 in 1925 to 384,705 in 1926. This, in turn, led
to a loss in trading profits and a deficit of £10,000 for the first time in
the Island's history. Aware that the Island's economy was vulnerable in
this way, the British government eventually settled for an immediate
payment of £100,000, with £400,000 paid over twenty-five years.
Effectively this raised the 1866 payment of £10,000 a year to £60,000 a
year.[100] The whole dispute, moreover, highlighted the increasingly
thorny issue of the extent to which the Island was subject to the
financial control of Westminster.

Despite the resurgence of the tourist industry, serious social
problems affected the Island after 1918. One of the difficulties with
the hotel trade was that it operated at best only for a four-month
season, leaving many people unemployed during the winter months. In
the towns, especially Douglas, there were problems of poverty, bad
sanitation and inadequate housing. 'Houses fit for heroes' had been one
of the post-armistice slogans, and in 1922 Tynwald authorised the
demolition of slums between the pier and railway station in Douglas,
and the construction of wider roads in the town, such as Lord Street. In
1926 the Universal Housing Company was contracted to erect 150

98] Kermode, *Devolution*, 41.
99] Norris, *Manx Memories*, 355.
100] Norris, *Manx Memories*, 351–5.

modern houses, using its rapid construction methods, on the Pulrose farm estate, purchased in 1915, while further Council estates were established at Hills Estate and Olympia, with new apartment blocks being occupied in Lord Street in the early 1930s. But many people could not afford even Council rents, and during the 1920s there was serious discontent among the unemployed, many of whom turned to emigration as a solution. The Island's population, which had been 52,016 in 1911, rose to 60,284 in 1921 but had fallen back to 49,308 ten years later: after this there was a gradual rise back to 52,029 in 1939.[101]

The dependence upon the tourist trade was emphasised by the serious decline of other industries between 1918 and 1939. The last Laxey mine closed in 1929, ending the Island's career as a producer of extracted ores. Fishing continued to decline, with the 57 vessels in operation in 1914 falling to 47 in 1937, crewed by only 128 men and boys.[102] This was not the result of a lack of fish: 80 per cent of the herring offered for sale in the Island in 1937 was caught by boats registered elsewhere. The Douglas 'back fishing' came to an end in the 1930s when Manx vessels were generally motor 'nobbies', using traditional drift nets. Most fish in the area were caught by steam drifters from Lowestoft, Yarmouth or the Moray Firth. The year 1937 was a crucial one, because Manx vessels then abandoned drift nets for ring nets, which they used to catch herring until the 1960s. It was in 1937, too, that dredging for scallops began on a commercial scale at Port Erin, so beginning what would prove to be a growth industry.

Although Manx agriculture had profited from the presence of the internees during the war years, the growing of grain after the war became unprofitable. The Island's Agricultural Organiser noted in 1929 that 'Foreign competition with cheaper costs of production, greater uniformity in the product, and organised marketing, allied with the increased cost and scarcity of labour at home ... is largely responsible for the depressed state of arable farming'.[103] Between 1913 and 1939 the acreage of arable land under cultivation fell by 18,500 acres, or 25 per cent, while the acreage under cereals fell by 32 per cent, though, with the consequent increase of rough pasturage, the number of sheep in the Island increased to a record level. There was little activity in the area of manufacturing industries during these years, though the establishment

101] *Isle of Man Government Digest of Economic and Social Statistics* (1994), Topic 2, p. 1.
102] Birch, *The Isle of Man*, 139. See also articles on the decline of Manx fishing in MNHL scrapbook *Fisheries* (B306 1x), 11–13.
103] Birch, *The Isle of Man*, 86.

Mechanising agriculture *The hard graft of sheep-shearing was made easier with the introduction of mechanised clippers, which gradually replaced the traditional* joushers, or *hand shears. The Young Farmers' Clubs were quick to introduce competitions, among them shearing, ploughing and public speaking. (MNHL)*

of the Isle of Man Electricity Board and the development by Douglas Corporation of a high-capacity power station at Pulrose during the 1930s made possible the growth of light industries in the future.

The years between the wars did not, in general, see a great deal of new investment or technological development except for the important area of transport. The first motor cars had made their appearance on Manx roads in the closing years of the nineteenth century, and in 1904 Tynwald agreed to a request from Britain's Royal Automobile Club that certain roads should be closed to enable cars to practise for international races. Seven such events took place between 1904 and 1922, and the manufacturers of British cars profited greatly from the experience of racing their machines over several laps of a 50-mile course on still primitive roads. In 1907 the Auto-Cycle Union was given permission by Tynwald to hold motor-cycle races on the same principle, and in 1911 the famous motor-car Tourist Trophy course was adopted, starting in Douglas and leading through Ballacraine, Kirk Michael, Ramsey and the Snaefell mountain road back to Douglas.[104] The First World War stopped these competitions, but from 1919 the motor-cycle TT races became established as a part of Manx life, increasingly bringing the Island fame among motor-cycle enthusiasts. In 1926, aware of the publicity value of the races, Douglas Corporation invested £2,000 in the construction of a grandstand on Glencrutchery Road, and in 1935 the success of George Formby's film *No Limit*, a story about the TT races, brought cult status to its star and to the event.

Along with the growth of motorised transport went the gradual improvement of roads, the result of massive investment by the Manx government. Indeed, during the interwar period, highways were the biggest single call on public funds. Douglas Corporation acquired its first two motor buses in 1914 and operated them at first on the route from Douglas to Peel, and later as a replacement for some of the horse trams, many of whose horses had been sent over to the Western Front. After the war the Douglas bus fleet increased to 12 by 1925, and 31 by 1929. From 1926 buses operated along the promenade in winter, instead of the horse trams, and in 1929 the cable cars in the upper streets of Douglas were finally scrapped.[105] In 1927 Manxland Bus Services, promoted by an English bus company, began operations in direct competition with the Isle of Man Railway. Thus challenged, the

---

104] L.R. Higgins, *Tourist Trophy Races* (London, 1954), 5–10. See also Robert Kelly, *T.T. Pioneers* (Douglas, 1996).
105] William Lambden, *The Manx Transport Systems* (London, 1965), 25–32.

Gordon Bennett races *The writer of the Ward Lock Guide of 1935–6 noted that the 'Mannin Beg' and 'Mannin Moar' races (popularly known as 'Round the Houses') organised annually in late spring by the RAC were supported by 'the cream of British car-racing talent'. Before the introduction of car ferries, vehicles had to be craned on and off the boats, often a nerve-racking experience, and securely lashed to the hand-rails along the open deck. (MNHL)*

Railway eventually bought all the developing bus companies to create Isle of Man Road Services, providing an integrated rail and road service throughout the Island. There were, in addition, private operators such as Blair's coach tours, which by 1928 carried holiday-makers to all the Island's main resorts.[106] Douglas Corporation, Isle of Man Road Services and private tour operators controlled the Island's bus transport system for the next 50 years.

Claude Graham-White, wearing a smart blazer and white flannels, took the first flying-machine into Manx skies as part of the great carnival held in Douglas during the summer of 1911 to celebrate the coronation of King George V. Thereafter, pleasure flights became popular, with light aircraft operating from the Douglas foreshore. Seaplanes were used during the 1914–18 war to provide material for the factories in Douglas which were making airship ballonets, but it was not until 1925 that the first commercial flight was made to the Island – a small aircraft landing on Douglas Head, with copies of *The Motor Cycle* for TT enthusiasts. In 1928 a three-engined aircraft was chartered to carry a ton of these magazines, and a 68-acre field belonging to Ronaldsway farm, near Castletown, was chosen as a landing-place. In 1932 British Amphibious Airlines Ltd started the first passenger service, in a twin-engined amphibious flying-boat which flew from the shores of Blackpool to Douglas in 40 minutes. The aircraft could take four passengers at a time, and 348 were carried that season. In 1933 Blackpool and West Coast Air Services began operating from Ronaldsway, using larger de Havilland aircraft capable of carrying seven passengers, with luggage. This company used the Ronaldsway airfield and carried 5,095 passengers and 52 tons of cargo in 1934.[107]

Sir Hall Caine, the Manx novelist, died in 1931, and his two sons established in his memory an airfield named after him, at Closelake, 3 miles out of Ramsey on the Jurby road. Between 1935 and 1937 Hall Caine airport flourished as the centre of operations for United Airways and Northern Scottish Airways (NSA), linking the Island to Manchester and Glasgow: 1,957 passengers and 19.9 tons of freight were carried by NSA to Glasgow during 1935.[108] However, this company ceased operating from Hall Caine in 1937, perhaps because of the 20-mile journey to Douglas, and the brief career of the Island's northern airfield came to an end. Meanwhile, after heated deliberations, Tynwald decided in 1935 not to develop Ronaldsway as a

106] Lambden, *Transport Systems*, 34–51.
107] Gordon N. Kniveton, *Manx Aviation in War and Peace* (Douglas, 1985), 13.
108] Kniveton, *Manx Aviation*, 17.

national airport, leaving the task to be undertaken privately by Captain Gordon Olley's Isle of Man Air Services. This company levelled out the field, constructed a hangar and workshops, and acquired the landing rights to 150 acres. By the summer of 1939 Isle of Man Air Services were flying from Ronaldsway to Manchester, Liverpool, Blackpool, Belfast, Carlisle, Leeds/Bradford and Glasgow, and 21,200 passengers were carried that season, before the outbreak of war curtailed operations.[109] Though never a serious competitor with the Steam Packet in numerical terms, air transport did at least break the monopoly of sea travel during the 1930s, and it was to benefit the Island greatly when the Second World War brought the Manx tourist industry once again to a sudden halt.

The Second World War, 1939–45

When Neville Chamberlain announced that Britain was at war with Germany and Italy from 3 September 1939, prospects for the Isle of Man seemed bleak. The holiday trade would be ruined, and the Island itself might be vulnerable to enemy air attacks, or even invasion. As things turned out, the economy unexpectedly benefited from heavy investment by the British government in the development of three major aerodromes, and from its use of the Island once more as a convenient place to intern German and Italian nationals living in Britain at the outbreak of war. This time it was decided not to create one large internment camp, such as Knockaloe had been, but to make use of the hotels and boarding-houses in all the Island's resorts, thus avoiding the problems encountered by this section of the community in the 1914–18 war.

In 1931 there were about 75,000 Germans and Austrians living in Britain, many of them Jewish refugees from Nazi persecution.[110] The British government decided to regard all aliens as potentially dangerous, and arranged for them to be taken to internment centres, of which the Isle of Man was one among many. The first Island camp opened on the Mooragh Promenade in Ramsey in May 1940 and did not close until August 1945. It held Germans, Finns and Italians in the hotels on the sea front, which were surrounded by barbed wire enclosures. Six camps were in operation at various times in Douglas. Granville, based on the Loch Promenade hotel of that name, lasted one year, from October 1940, and held 750 internees. Sefton, based on the hotel and the Gaiety Theatre, lasted from October 1940 to March 1941

109] Kniveton, *Manx Aviation*, 26.
110] Connery Chappell, *Island of Barbed Wire* (London, 1984), 20.

and held 600 men, while Metropole, which opened in July 1940 and closed in October 1944, was the centre for up to 750 Italians. The largest camp was Palace, with 2,900 men in the 28 hotels surrounding the Palace itself, and it was open from June 1940 to November 1942. Central Camp detained about 2,000 men in 34 hotels on Central Promenade between June 1940 and the middle of 1941. Hutchinson Square, in the upper part of the town, was cordoned off between July 1940 and the end of 1944, first as a home for German and Austrian internees, and later as a camp for prisoners of war. In Onchan 60 houses in Royal Avenue held German and, later, Italian internees from June 1940 until November 1944.[111]

A camp opened in 1940 in several hotels at the northern end of Peel's promenade, and this accommodated at first enemy aliens, then British fascists, and finally Norwegian and Dutch refugees. In the south of the Island an extended camp for women and children was established at Port Erin and Port St Mary by the expedient of erecting a barbed wire fence from Fleshwick to Gansey, thus cutting off the whole of the southern peninsula. This arrangement operated from May 1940 until September 1945, under the control of the Home Office rather than the military authorities. Internees were billeted on families in Port St Mary and Port Erin, and their hosts were paid a guinea a week for each 'guest'. In due course a camp for married couples and families was established at Bradda Head. The busiest years for the internment camps were 1940 and 1941, and not all remained open for the duration of the war. Nevertheless, the presence of many thousands of internees brought profitable trading to the Island's suppliers and income to many hotel owners and boarding-house keepers, even if only by way of compensation for the use of their properties.[112]

When, in 1936, it became clear that Nazi Germany was rearming on a threatening scale, the British government inaugurated a scheme to modernise and expand the Royal Air Force. The Air Ministry approached the Manx government in 1937 with a view to establishing a training camp for aircrew at Jurby, a site chosen because of the surrounding flat land and sparse population, as well as its close proximity to Northern Ireland, Scotland and north-west England. The chosen area consisted of 307 acres, over half of them from the Ballamoar estate. There was opposition from 60 local farmers, but Tynwald approved the Defence Bill put forward by the new Governor, Admiral Leveson-Gower, later Earl Granville, a brother-in-law of

111] Cresswell, *Living*, 44–50.
112] Cresswell, *Living*, 50–2.

George VI's Queen, Elizabeth. The Island agreed to pay the British government £100,000 a year towards the cost of rearmament, and the Air Ministry undertook to finance the construction of the Jurby airfield, which would bring a population of three to four hundred to the area, thus benefiting Manx service industries such as agriculture, construction and transport. The building contract was awarded to a Manchester firm, and the *Ramsey Courier* reported in January 1939 that 340 men were hard at work at Jurby, many of them local labourers.[113] RAF Jurby opened on 18 September 1939, just after the beginning of hostilities, as No. 5 Air Observers School, a name soon changed in November to No. 5 Bombing and Gunnery School. It operated at first as a grass airfield, though in 1942 work began on the construction of tarmac runways. Towards the end of 1940 Jurby was used by fighter squadrons for defensive purposes, and in July 1941 the Air Ministry decided that navigation, bomb-aiming and air-gunnery training should all be concentrated at Jurby, which reverted to its original name of No. 5 Air Observers School, and became central to Bomber Command's policy of retaliation against German cities. By 1944 the training of navigators and bomb-aimers became the main priority of Jurby, and up to eighty Avro Anson trainers were based there. The accident rate among training aircraft throughout the war was very high. Both on and around the Island a total of 250 crashes during the war years were recorded, with total loss of life exceeding two hundred aircrew. On the other hand, thousands received vital training in navigation and bombing skills, which proved to be a major factor in the defeat of the enemy.[114]

In October 1940 the Luftwaffe began night attacks on British cities, using airfields in northern France. This meant that the industrial centres and ports of Belfast, Glasgow and Liverpool were well within range. The Air Ministry decided that it needed a fighter station on the Isle of Man, in addition to the bomber training school at Jurby, and in September landowners and farmers round Andreas were served with requisition notices for 500 acres of land. Much of the construction was undertaken again by local firms, using local labour and Irish navvies. The new airfield was built to the full specification of an operational fighter station, with a triangle of three intersecting runways, joined by a perimeter track. Much of the Laxey waste was used up, and the lorries then moved on to the Foxdale tips. In October 1941 457 Squadron's Spitfires were transferred from Jurby, and the airfield was thoroughly

113] Kniveton, *Manx Aviation*, 34.
114] Kniveton, *Manx Aviation*, 34–50.

The RAF at Andreas *During the Second World War the RAF's two airfields at Jurby and Andreas dominated the service and social life of Ramsey and the north of the Island. As this photograph shows, the fine tower on Andreas Church presented a hazard to low-flying aircraft before it was reduced to about half its height. (MNHL)*

operational six months later. It was necessary to reduce the height of
the tower of Andreas church, which lay close to the runway, and the
historic Andreas rectory found a new role as officers' quarters. In May
1943 Andreas changed its role to that of an Air Gunnery School,
teaching an intensive ten weeks' course, and in 1944 it was also used as
an emergency landing ground for the Atlantic Ferry route.[115]

Early in 1943 the Admiralty informed the Manx government that it
intended to develop the existing Ronaldsway airfield into a Royal Navy
Station, 850 acres in extent, as a training centre for the new Fairey
Barracuda torpedo/dive-bombers, expected to be a vital weapon in the
struggle against the Japanese in the Pacific. Under the authority of the
UK's Defence of the Realm Act, the Governor, Lord Granville,
authorised the requisitioning of the necessary land surrounding the
airfield, as well as the demolition of many buildings, including the
historic Ronaldsway farmhouse. The Admiralty also took over some of
the grounds of the nearby King William's College. Over five hundred
men were involved in the construction of the four runways, the control
tower and the main buildings, while local hauliers and construction
firms enjoyed boom conditions. The new station, named *HMS Urley*
(Manx for 'Eagle'), was commissioned in June 1944, and aircrew were
put through a three-month training course with the Barracuda aircraft.
By January 1945 there were three squadrons stationed at *HMS Urley*,
putting between sixty and seventy aircraft into the air each day.[116]

The Admiralty also made good use of Cunningham's Holiday Camp
by setting up there *HMS St George*, a safe location for their three
seaman boys' training ships *HMS Ganges*, *St Vincent* and *Exmouth*.
With the camp as their residential quarters, and the classrooms of the
newly built Ballakermeen High School for academic instruction, the
boys were trained for a naval career and lived under rigorous naval
discipline.[117] More than 8,677 of them served in *HMS St George*
between its opening in September 1939 and closure at the end of 1945.
Indeed, very few of Douglas's facilities were not put to good use one
way or another. Hotels that had not been requisitioned for internment
purposes were seldom left empty. The War Office took over the Villiers
and adjoining hotels, for an Officer Cadet Training Unit which
prepared four thousand men for army commissions, while the Majestic,
on Onchan Head, became a hospital run by the Royal Army Medical
Corps. The Empress Hotel was at first the headquarters of No. 1

115] Kniveton, *Manx Aviation*, 51–60.
116] Kniveton, *Manx Aviation*, 61–71.
117] Tom Robson, *Boy Seaman R.N.: The True Story* (Darlington, 1996), 49–74.

HMS St George *Seamen boys from* HMS St George *marching along Douglas promenade on Trafalgar Day, 1942. (MNHL)*

Ground Defence Gunnery School, and then of the RAF regiment, while the Douglas Head Hotel became the home of *HMS Valkyrie*, a radar training school which trained some thirty thousand radar operators before the end of the war.[118] Because of the emphasis on secrecy, many people were unaware of the variety of work that the forces were engaged in on the Island, and some of those who did have information were reluctant to talk about it decades later.

118] Kniveton *et al*, *Douglas Centenary*, 123.

With all this activity in Douglas, the atmosphere in the town was quite different from the gloom and neglect of the previous war. Thousands of off-duty servicemen and women, some of them arriving by train and bus from camps round the Island, were able to enjoy a night out at one of the four cinemas, or at the Palais de Danse in Strand Street, or in one of the many public houses. Though many servicemen lost their lives on the Island during the war, this was regrettably the result of training accidents, especially of aircraft crashing in poor visibility, rather than of enemy action. Air raid sirens sounded 43 alerts, 32 of them during 1942, when the bombing of Liverpool and Manchester could be heard and even seen from the Island. A few bombs fell on the Island itself, mostly jettisoned by enemy bombers lost or in retreat. They caused little damage and no casualties.[119]

As in the previous war, many of the Steam Packet Company's ships were commandeered. During the 1939 summer season the company was operating 16 vessels, ten of which were requisitioned by the Admiralty within days of the outbreak of the war. Six small ships were left, the *Rushen Castle*, *Snaefell* and *Victoria* operating for passengers, and the *Peveril*, *Conister* and *Cushag* carrying freight. The holiday trade dwindled to a small trickle, and most of the passengers were internees, prisoners-of-war and servicemen with their families. The bombing of Liverpool docks made the daily service hazardous, and after the *Victoria* was damaged by a mine in December 1940 the Douglas–Fleetwood route was used without further incident. Of the ten company ships on war service, eight took part in the evacuation of Dunkirk in 1940, bringing out 24,669 troops between them: for the rest of the war they acted as transport ships, and four were lost – including the *King Orry*, veteran of the first war, which went down at Dunkirk.[120]

The Island sent thousands of conscripted men to fight in the war, 490 of whom lost their lives. Three major airfields were constructed, thousands of internees were held in many locations, and Douglas became the centre of a wide variety of military training establishments for the Armed Services. For the Isle of Man the war years were hectic and inconvenient, but safe – and in economic terms far from disastrous. Holiday-makers were replaced by a different kind of visitor, whether internee or service personnel, and the Island's service industries and agriculture prospered accordingly.

119] Kniveton *et al*, *Douglas Centenary*, 124.
120] Chappell, *Island Lifeline*, 108–22.

Palais de Danse
STRAND STREET

TO - NIGHT
— IS —
CARNIVAL
═ NIGHT ! ═

DANCING
7-30 until Midnight. Admission 2/6

BILLY PAGE'S
Wonderful London Dance Band !

Beautiful Surroundings.
Gorgeous Lighting Effects.
Perfectly Sprung Floor.
Professional Dance Partners.

'Phone 891 and Reserve your Table !

Manxland's Gayest Rendezvous !

Printed at The Victoria Press.

Entertaining the visitors Holiday-makers were often spoilt for choice when it came to evening *entertainment. The 16,000 square feet of the Palace Ballroom could accommodate a thousand couples, with seating for five thousand, and an audience of 3500 could enjoy variety shows at the neighbouring Coliseum. Smaller dance halls such as the Palais de Danse offered special attractions, including telephones at each table enabling assignations to be made with the least of effort. (MNHL)*

Postwar Problems, 1945–70

Victory in Europe came on 8 May 1945, and in July King George VI and
Queen Elizabeth presided over Tynwald Day on their first journey
together outside the UK since the beginning of the war. On 14 August
Japan surrendered, and at the end of the month Lord Granville left to be
Governor of Northern Ireland. He was replaced as Lieutenant-Governor
by Air Vice-Marshal Sir Geoffrey Bromet, the first member of the RAF to
hold the post, and a relevant choice, given the vital importance of aircraft
and airfields to the Island in wartime. The barbed-wire fences came down
at last on Douglas promenade, and hotel furniture stored for the duration
of the war in Derby Castle and elsewhere was mostly recovered and put
back in place. Shortages and rationing imposed limits on what could be
done, but hoteliers and boarding-house keepers looked forward to a
return of the holiday trade in 1946. The Steam Packet had lost four ships,
three of them at Dunkirk, but had ordered replacements for the *King
Orry* and *Mona's Queen* from Cammell Lairds as early as 1944. The
Liverpool–Douglas route, closed since 1940, was reopened in April 1946
with the company operating its new ships as well as those returned by the
Admiralty. Compensation, plus the proceeds of a thriving trade after the
war, enabled the company to invest in several more new ships – *Tynwald*
(1947), *Snaefell* (1948), *Mona's Isle* (1951) and *Manxman* (1955).[121]

The visiting trade was no longer entirely dependent on the Steam
Packet. In 1948 the Admiralty agreed to sell Ronaldsway airport's land
and buildings to the Manx government for £200,000, a bargain price
considering that the construction costs had been well over £1
million.[122] Tynwald then set up the Isle of Man Airports Board as
the governing body of Ronaldsway and the other airports on the Island.
Britain's new Labour government nationalised air transport, and from
1947 British European Airways (BEA) operated the routes from
Ronaldsway to Blackpool, Liverpool, Carlisle, Newcastle, Glasgow
and Belfast. However, despite the demand for business, BEA made
heavy losses and cut back services, so that a number of independent
companies were able to take over the vacant routes under licence. The
Airports Board recorded that the number of arrivals during 1949 passed
the 100,000 mark for the first time. Between May and September 1949
there were 570,261 arrivals by sea and 41,025 by air.[123]

121] Chappell, *Island Lifeline*, 59–62.
122] Kniveton, *Manx Aviation*, 73.
123] Kniveton, *Manx Aviation*, 79.

Exporting milk to Liverpool *After the Second World War, surplus milk during the periods on either side of the 'season' was shipped from the Island to Liverpool, which was suffering a severe shortage, as dairy herds had been run down. On occasion milk was also flown to Liverpool, shown here in this 1949 photograph of an Isle of Man Dairies Bedford lorry loading churns on to an Aerovan IV belonging to North West Airlines (IOM) Ltd. (A.M. Goodwin)*

In holiday terms, business boomed in the years immediately following the war. Sea and air transport was available, and the traditional clientele from the north-west of England had money to spend, because there were few luxuries available to buy under the British government's continuing policy of imposed economies. Moreover, there was little alternative to a holiday in the British Isles at this time: travel to Europe or beyond was difficult, inconvenient and expensive. The Island was not slow to make the most of this advantageous situation. Hotels and centres of amusement swung rapidly back into action, the TT and Grand Prix races were reinstated, and the Villa Marina signed on Joe Loss and his orchestra for the 1947 season. Over the next decade his BBC broadcasts from the Villa Marina made Douglas familiar to millions of British listeners. In the three years 1947, 1948 and 1949 the number of summer visitors to the Island averaged 613,000, a figure which compared favourably with the most hectic years of the Island's Edwardian heyday.[124]

Unfortunately, this healthy state of affairs did not last long. The 1950s proved to be a disappointing period for the Island's economy, featuring a significant decline in the number of visitors, a recession in the fishing industry, a growth in unemployment and a drastic reduction in population. The decline in summer visitors to an average of 520,000 a year between 1950 and 1960 was unexpected, given that in this period the number of holidays taken in Britain rose 50 per cent: yet the number of Island visitors fell by 17 per cent.[125] The reasons for this may have included the antiquated nature of hotel and boarding-house accommodation, as well as a failure to invest in modern amenities, and the expense of travel to the Island. The war had benefited the Island's fishermen by removing foreign competition, and in 1948 local fishermen were responsible for 48 per cent of the value of fish landed on the Island. However, as the British fishing industry recovered after the war, Manx fishermen lost the initiative, and by the 1960s there were only 70 local fishermen and 24 boats, with only nine boats and 24 crew fishing all the year round.[126] This meant that fishing provided full-time employment for less than 1 per cent of the working male population.[127] A considerable house-building programme employed many workers in the immediate postwar years, but, when this came to an end in the 1950s, as many as two thousand people were registering as unemployed during the winter months, always the difficult period for a community which depended so much on a seasonal tourist industry. The response of many Manx people to these difficulties was to leave the Island in search of work, and the population accordingly fell from 55,253 in 1951 to 48,135 ten years later – a drop of nearly 13 per cent.

The only major growth area of the 1950s was manufacturing industry. The Manx government took active measures to stimulate existing industries such as knitting and cloth-garment factories established between the wars at St John's and Laxey. New enterprises were

124] Kinvig, *The Isle of Man*, 150.
125] *An Economic Appreciation for the Government of the Isle of Man* (PA International Consultants Ltd, 1971), 81.
126] Birch, *The Isle of Man*, 140.
127] Birch, *The Isle of Man*, 188.

Laxey Glen Flour Mills *The history of Laxey Glen Flour Mills has been dramatic. In 1913 a disastrous fire forced the mill to close for some years. Because the horse-drawn fire-engines had to come from Douglas, the mill was almost gutted by the time the brigade arrived, the horses were exhausted and there was insufficient water in the river to deal effectively with the fire. This event led to the formation of the Laxey Fire Brigade, which managed to avert another disaster in the 1940s. (MNHL)*

encouraged – such as the Ronaldsway Aircraft Company, which began manufacturing ejector seats in 1951; a textiles factory was set up in Ramsey in 1956 and a carpet factory near Douglas. By 1961 new factories established in the 1950s were employing well over a thousand workers.[128] Despite this fact, a commissioned survey of Manx industrial

128] Kinvig, *The Isle of Man*, 153.

development, published in 1960, was critical of government policy, and this led to the setting up, in 1961, of an Industrial Advisory Council and an Industrial Officer to formulate future industrial policies, including the awarding of loans and grants to new businesses.[129]

In 1964 Dr J.W. Birch of Bristol University published an illuminating appraisal of the Island's economy. Birch found that, despite relative decline, tourism was still responsible for 75 per cent of the Island's income from external sources other than investments, and for as much as 60 per cent of the gross value of the production of the major forms of industry: moreover, 21 per cent of the working population found employment in some branch of the tourist industry. Farming, which had enjoyed prosperity during the war and afterwards because it was able to cater for the needs of a large visiting population, employed 11 per cent of the working population in the early 1960s, and contributed almost 20 per cent of the income from all industries. Fishing and mining, however, each accounted for less than 1 per cent of the working male population. Birch's survey showed that the main growth area was manufacturing, which employed 14 per cent of the workforce, with 8 per cent of the Island's gross income from external sources other than investments deriving from textiles and light engineering factories established since the war. Though the contribution of manufacturing was healthy, Birch could not foresee a major increase in the development of this sector. With fishing and mining by now insignificant, and even agriculture dependent upon the visiting trade, it seemed to Birch that tourism was still the Island's lifeline, and that every measure should be taken to improve its viability:

> Seasonal employment may well be regarded as a comparatively small price to pay for the level of economic development, and the associated economic and social benefits, that the tourist industry has made possible. No other industry could have achieved or could maintain this level, because none can claim a comparable endowment of natural and man-made resources, or the outstanding attribute of serving a market which is brought to the Island and pays for its own transport. The scale of the tourist industry is the Isle of Man's greatest asset in earning its living in a fiercely competitive world: it is believed that all possible steps should be taken to rebuild and extend this industry and to give it every assistance available from modern techniques of publicity.[130]

129] B.A. Williams, *Report of the Isle of Man Industrial Survey* (Douglas, 1960).
130] Birch, *The Isle of Man*, 187.

During the 1950s a number of important constitutional changes were made which affected the Manx government's ability to handle economic affairs. In 1956 the Isle of Man Contribution Act specified that the Island should pay to the United Kingdom each year a contribution towards defence and other common services, amounting to 5 per cent of the net Isle of Man receipts from the Common Purse. In 1957 Tynwald also agreed that Manx Customs duties would generally be kept on the same level as Britain. These understandings made possible Parliament's Isle of Man Act of 1958, which, together with enactments of Tynwald, effectively removed the British Treasury's control of the Island's finances, and empowered Tynwald, with the Governor's approval, to control revenue and expenditure.[131] Armed with these powers, and persuaded by the recently installed Lieutenant-Governor, Sir Ronald Garvey, of the need for action to revive the economy, Tynwald passed the Income Tax Act of 1960, which provided that, from 6 April 1961, no surtax on personal incomes would be levied in the Isle of Man. The following year the standard rate of income tax was reduced from 22.50 per cent to 21.25 per cent. It remained at this level until further reductions from 1978 onwards brought the level down in 1980 to 20 per cent, where it has effectively remained.[132] The passing of these historic acts in the early 1960s was also accompanied by a vigorous campaign to advertise the Island's new tax advantages, and encourage new residents. With British income tax rising to 98 per cent under Labour governments in the 1960s, and the introduction of Capital Gains Tax in 1964, together with unavoidable Capital Transfer Tax, the Isle of Man became an attractive proposition for those wishing to pay less tax – especially as the Channel Islands imposed quite severe entry restrictions. The number of new residents each year, which had been 471 in 1960 and 516 in 1961, shot up to 812 in 1962 and reached a peak for the decade of 1,375 in 1966. Between 1961 and 1970 inclusive the Island welcomed 9,366 new residents, and the overall population – which had fallen to 48,133 in 1961 – reached 54,581 in 1971.[133]

This influx of new residents in the 1960s, together with the stimulus it gave to the construction and service industries, was a great help to the economy at a time when the tourist trade continued to run into difficulties. The number of summer visitors averaged fifty thousand a year less than in the previous decade, and hotels and guest-houses were under financial strain as many mergers and rationalisations took place,

131] Kinvig, *The Isle of Man*, 166.
132] Solly, *Banks*, 58.
133] *Economic Appreciation*, 127.

reducing the total number of such establishments from 1,593 in 1964 to 1,142 in 1970. Nevertheless Douglas, at least, remained a thriving tourist resort, and a number of modern amenities made substantial changes to its appearance. In 1964 the architecturally distinctive new Sea Terminal was opened by Princess Margaret, and in the same year the Palace Coliseum was demolished, to be replaced by the geometric structure of the new Palace Casino and hotel. At the Onchan end of the promenade Derby Castle was pulled down in 1964 and replaced by Summerland, a 3.5-acre sports and leisure complex finished in 1970, and proudly advertised as being one of the most innovative facilities of its kind.

1970–1996

The Rise of the Financial Sector since 1970

In 1970 the Manx government commissioned a firm of management consultants to produce a detailed inquiry into the economy, and this was published in 1971. On the key issue of the importance of tourism, the researchers challenged the official government view that profits from tourism produced £14.1 million, or 50 per cent of the Gross National Income in the year 1969/70. They argued that tourism produced – through accommodation, power, transport and communications, retail distribution, miscellaneous services and government duties – only 31.4 per cent of the national income, with manufacturing close behind with a contribution of 26.8 per cent. Income from abroad produced 20 per cent, and the construction industry 17 per cent. Agriculture, fishing and forestry together produced only 4.8 per cent of the national income. The biggest growth area within manufacturing in the 1960s was engineering, which employed 447 additional people, whereas the important contribution of the construction industry derived, in the words of the report, from 'private housebuilding which is stimulated overwhelmingly by the continuing inflow of residents to the Island'.[134] The importance of new residents was further emphasised by one of the main findings of the report: 'The Island benefits from a net gain on capital account, associated in large part with the movement of new residents to the Island.'[135] The message of the report was clear: tourism must not be allowed to dwindle further, manufacturing should be encouraged and the Island should continue its policy of attracting new residents.

The disaster that befell the Summerland complex on the night of

134] *Economic Appreciation*, 20 and 68.
135] *Economic Appreciation*, 3.

2 August 1973, when fire swept through the building, killing 50 people and causing many other casualties, might have seemed a deadly blow to the tourist industry. Front-page headlines carried the news throughout Britain, a major facility was put out of action for five years, and confidence had been shaken. Moreover, Tynwald's Fire Precautions Act of 1975 required hotels, boarding-houses and places of public entertainment to improve their fire precautions at what often amounted to a formidable expense, and sometimes proved too much for businesses on the financial borderline. Between 1970 and 1980 the number of hotels and guest-houses halved, from 1,142 to 620, and the number of bedrooms available in them fell from 15,062 to 11,093.[136] Yet, against all predictions, more summer visitors came to the Island in the 1970s than in the previous decade – an average of 527,000 a year, compared with 474,000 – and the attractions of Millennium Year in 1979 proved so successful that the official figure for summer visitors reached 634,616. This was 104 more than the previous record of 634,512 in 1913, but in the early years of the century children were counted as only one-half of an adult. In addition to the effects of a modernisation programme inside many hotels, and an aggressive advertising policy by the Tourist Board, one reason for the buoyant tourist figures was probably the devaluation of sterling between 1972 and 1974, and the major company collapses experienced in the overseas tourist package business. There was also a sharp increase in the cost of international air travel because of increased fuel costs.[137]

In fact the 1970s were years of great prosperity, reflected in the startling increase of population from 54,581 in 1971 to 66,101 in 1981. The chief reason for this prosperity was the unexpectedly rapid development of the financial sector, especially banking. A second economic report, commissioned from management consultants and published in 1975, found that the financial sector's contribution to the Manx economy increased from 8.5 per cent in 1969/70 to 18.4 per cent in 1973/4, and that bank deposits in the Island increased threefold between 1970 and 1975. The researchers also found that growth, particularly in banking, had been faster in the Island during these years than in both Britain and Jersey.[138] The development of the Isle of Man as a financial centre must be seen against the background of a massive extension of banking and financial services throughout the world during the 1960s and 1970s, stimulated by rapid growth in world trade and economic

136] *Tourist Board Statistics*, 1983.
137] *Economic Survey of the Isle of Man* (PA International, 1975), 29.
138] *Economic Survey*, 75.

development. In Britain the increase in money supply generated a property boom which lasted from 1969 to 1973. This was brought to a sudden halt by a global shortage of raw materials, commodities and energy fuels, which, in Britain, caused cost inflation followed by wage inflation, ruining many companies and leading to sharp falls on the stock market. To escape all these uncertainties, as well as personal taxation scales which many people regarded as punitive, those who had made money and who wished to hold on to it increasingly turned to 'offshore tax havens', usually small independent or semi-independent states such as Monaco, Liechtenstein, Luxembourg, Singapore, the Caribbean Islands, the Channel Islands or the Isle of Man – all of which enjoyed stable political conditions and a low rate of taxation. As we have seen, the Isle of Man lowered its rates of taxation in 1961 in order to attract new residents, not specifically to establish itself as a tax haven: but in the 1970s, because of international developments beyond the Island's control, a tax haven is what, increasingly, it became.[139]

In 1972 the sterling area was limited to Britain, the Channel Isles, Eire and the Isle of Man, with Gibraltar added the following year. In 1979 exchange controls in Britain were suspended, ending the Bank of England's control over offshore financial centres in the British Isles, and permitting British and Island residents to invest anywhere in the world. These two measures, it has been argued, 'were the turning points in the financial transformation of the British Isles tax havens of Jersey, Guernsey and the Isle of Man into centres for offshore banking, investment and international commerce'.[140] The rescheduling of the sterling area and the repeal of the Usury Acts made the Island attractive to merchant and commercial banks. Singer & Friedlander, the Bank of Bermuda, Julian S. Hodge Bank, the Royal Bank of Scotland, Tyndall's Bank, the Royal Bank of Wales, Rea Bros, the Royal Bank of Canada, Celtic Bank, the Anglo-Irish Bank and Northern Bank were among the major financial concerns that established offices on the Island during the 1970s. This brought an influx of banking staff and led to a rapid growth in associated services such as accounting, and to employment in the construction industry, which provided new offices and housing.

Tourism remained buoyant in the 1970s and nicely balanced the growing financial sector, but in the 1980s it lost its momentum, and an apparently irreversible decline set in. The easy availability of cheap package holidays to sunny foreign destinations, the high cost of the sea

139] *Economic Survey*, 77.
140] R.A. Johns and C.M. le Marchant, *Financial Centres: British Isles Offshore Development since 1979* (London, 1993).

crossing for the family and the family car, and the out-of-date accommodation offered by many hotels built a century before were all factors that diverted potential holiday-makers from the Isle of Man. The number of long-stay visitors in paid accommodation fell steadily from 243,327 in 1985 to a low point of 100,960 in 1992, and in Douglas major hotels such as the Villiers, Douglas Bay and Majestic were demolished or ceased to trade.[141] After 1992, however, there was a modest improvement, with 127,837 period visitors staying in paid accommodation in 1993, about 134,000 in 1994 and 1995, and 140,784 in 1996.

The proportion of the national income generated by tourism fell from 11 per cent in 1982/3 to 6 per cent in 1994/5, and income from manufacturing also declined, from 15 per cent in 1983/4 to 11 per cent in 1994/5, while agriculture and fishing together produced only between 2 per cent and 3 per cent of the national income during this period. The Industrial Advisory Council, set up in 1961, encouraged new industries: Dowty's opened a new aircraft component factory in Onchan in 1965 with a workforce of 187, one of the largest on the Island.[142] In 1969/70 manufacturing made an important contribution of 22 per cent to the national income, and in 1971 it gave employment to 3,111 people. During the 1970s the government continued to encourage the establishment of small businesses that would be friendly to the environment, but the international industrial recession of the late 1970s reduced the sector's contribution to 12.3 per cent by 1978. Continued government financial support increased manufacturing income to as much as 15 per cent during most of the 1980s, though after 1988 there was a decline to 11 per cent. In the 1990s most industry was concentrated in Douglas and the nearby Snugborough, Spring Valley and Hills Meadow trading estates; or the Balthane and Ronaldsway trading estates near Castletown, with fish-processing factories centred on Peel and Port St Mary, and some engineering and electronics at Ramsey.[143]

After prosperity during the war years, agriculture suffered from the general recession of the 1950s, prompting the Manx government to give financial support, in particular, to struggling upland farms. In the 1960s the Isle of Man Agricultural Marketing Association was set up to promote the sale of potatoes, poultry, milk and wool, and from 1966

141] *Digest of Economic and Social Statistics* (Douglas, 1994), Topic 7, p. 4.
142] Vaughan Robinson and Danny McCarroll (eds), *The Isle of Man: Celebrating a Sense of Place* (Liverpool, 1990), 232.
143] Robinson and McCarroll (eds), *The Isle of Man*, 236.

the local and export markets for meat were controlled by the Fatstock Association, which also operated an abattoir at Tromode, where a creamery opened in 1974 under the control of the Isle of Man Milk Marketing Association. In the late 1980s 86 per cent of the total area of the Island was farmland, divided between about eight hundred farms, and in 1986 the Manx government announced that 'the Island's only raw material is grass and the backbone of our industry is milk, beef, and lamb produced from the grain'.[144] However, agriculture and fishing together produced only 5 per cent of the national income in 1970, falling to 3 per cent in the 1980s, and 2 per cent in the 1990s.[145] Meanwhile the number of agricultural workers fell from 1,596 in the 1940s to 510 in 1971, partly as a result of increased mechanisation.[146] Fishing did well during the war years: there was an increased market on the Island, provided by the internees and service personnel. Moreover, there was no competition from vessels from other countries. In 1947 there were ten Manx fishing boats on the herring shoals, with crews numbering 52 in total: and eight of these were motor vessels of the new type. However, the fishing fleets of other nations soon recovered from the disruption of the war and proved to be severe competition. Many fishermen were attracted by the wages and less arduous lifestyle of employment in the tourist industry, and by 1971 only three Manx vessels continued to fish for herring. In the 1970s and 1980s over-fishing in the North Sea led to international agreements which imposed fishing quotas: these effectively reduced the Island's potential for catching herring to a very low level. In these circumstances Manx fishermen increasingly dredged for the scallops and queenies which could be found in the sandy, inshore areas round Port Erin, Peel and Douglas. This shellfish industry, which exported most of its produce to the United States and France, remained steadily profitable in the 1980s and 1990s, though the numbers employed remained comparatively small, as did the contribution of the whole fishing industry to the Island's income.[147]

The dramatic decline in the tourist industry in the 1980s, together with the dwindling contribution of the manufacturing, agriculture and fishing sectors, would have meant economic disaster if the financial sector had not come to the rescue. In 1982/3 this sector provided 21 per cent of the national income, rising to 27 per cent in 1987/8, 35 per cent

144] Robinson and McCarroll (eds), The Isle of Man, 214.
145] Digest of Economic and Social Statistics (1994), Topic 15, p. 3.
146] Kinvig, The Isle of Man, 143.
147] Robinson and McCarroll (eds), The Isle of Man, 215–17.

Splitting scallop shells, Peel, 1996 *Following the decline of the herring stocks in the Irish Sea, fishing for scallops and the smaller 'queenies' became a major source of income for the greatly reduced fishing fleet. The research work at the University of Liverpool's Marine Laboratory at Port Erin plays an important part in understanding the effects of human activities on the waters surrounding the Island. (Yvonne Cresswell)*

in 1992/3, and 36 per cent in 1994/5.[148] Even so, there was a difficult period between 1980 and 1986, reflected in the fact that between April 1981 and April 1986 the population – always a good indicator of the performance of the economy – remained static, and unemployment rose to 2,500. The main cause of this slowdown was the deep recession that hit Britain during these years, but the situation was made even worse by the collapse of the Island-based Savings and Investment Bank in June 1982, with debts of £42 million. Many investors both on and off the Island lost heavily, and the affair raised serious questions about both the safety and the regulation of 'offshore' banking. Alarmed by the adverse publicity, the Manx government dealt with this threat promptly by establishing a Financial Supervision Commission in July 1983, charged with providing stringent regulations concerning the licensing and operation of banks, and with rooting out abuses such as 'money laundering'.[149]

The Manx government also took steps in the 1980s to widen the base of the finance sector beyond banking. Acts of 1981 and 1986 attracted insurance companies to the Island by offering tax exemption incentives: any revenue lost through direct taxation would be compensated for by the payment of income tax by staff, as well as the increased profits from service industries. By 1994 there were ten international life insurance companies established on the Island – such as Royal Life International, Clerical Medical International, Eagle Star and Equity and Law International – employing a thousand people. Between 1986 and 1991 there was also a rapid growth of 'captive' insurance companies, which were subsidiaries of British companies, and whose specific role was to insure the risks of their parent companies. British Gas, British Telecom and Eastern Electricity are examples of three of the 130 captives established on the Island by 1994. The funds held by captive companies, estimated at over £2 billion in 1994, in turn stimulated the growth of investment management companies such as Warburg Asset Management, Robert Fleming Ltd and Rothschild Asset Management.[150] In 1986 Britain's Building Societies Act removed many restrictions from the operation of building societies, and permitted them, among other things, to make advances secured on land overseas. This made business in the Isle of Man attractive to them for both mortgages and deposits.

148] *Digest of Economic and Social Statistics* (1996), Topic 15, p. 3.
149] Colin F. Youde, *The Recent Development of the Isle of Man Economy and the Establishment of an Offshore Base in the Isle of Man by U.K. Building Societies*, unpublished MSc thesis, University of Salford, 1994, 73.
150] Youde, *Recent Development*, 84–6.

The first society to establish itself on the Island was the Leeds Permanent, which opened in April 1988 and exceeded its first-year target for attracting deposits in the first week of business. Five other major names were established in Douglas by 1990, and at the end of 1993 societies employed well over a hundred people and held deposits of about £2 billion, representing about 20 per cent of the total deposits held on the Island. Most deposits consisted of new business from British residents and people resident outside the British Isles: hence the customer base of the Island and awareness of it throughout the world as an offshore centre was significantly increased.[151]

Other growth areas encouraged by the Manx government were ship management and a free port. The Merchant Shipping Act of 1984, together with the extension of international shipping conventions to the Isle of Man, enabled ship management companies to establish themselves in the tax-exempt category on the Island, so that their number increased from eight in 1986 to 23 by 1994, with 678 ships registered on the Island by 1996.[152] In 1986 work began on the development of a free port site near Ronaldsway airport, designed to provide a duty-free zone where VAT and other duties do not have to be paid until the product enters the appropriate market.

As a result of all this activity in the financial sector, the economy strengthened, and between April 1986 and April 1996 the resident population moved upwards in number from 64,679 to 71,714, and of these just under half were Manx-born. Between 1961 and 1991 the population of the four original towns rose steadily, with Douglas reaching 22,214 in 1991. The most dramatic population increase was in Onchan, where the population grew from 3,618 in 1961 to 8,656 in 1996 so that by 1996 Onchan 'village' was considerably larger than Ramsey, which had a population of only 6,874 in that year.[153] The large numbers of post-1980 'luxury' houses and apartments on and around Onchan Head were visible proof of the success of the new residents policy and the buoyancy of the financial sector, and so was the extensive rebuilding of Douglas that took place in the 1980s and 1990s, with new office blocks rising on the sites of former hotels, defunct churches and derelict housing terraces.

Critics of the new residents policy argued that immigrants were mostly retired people, and therefore a burden on health and welfare

151] Youde, *Recent Development*, 90–112.
152] Youde, *Recent Development*, 88; *Digest of Economic and Social Statistics* (1996), Topic 13, p. 6.
153] *Digest of Economic and Social Statistics* (1996), Topic 2, p. 5.

services, and that they contributed nothing to the workforce, created an imbalance in the age structure of the population and by their sheer numbers were a threat to the Island's Celtic culture and heritage.[154] However, the 1971 census demonstrated that the largest percentage of new arrivals were aged between 20 and 24 years, and that they had done a great deal to correct the existing imbalance in the age structure of the population. A Select Committee of Tynwald appointed to study the new residents issue reported in 1980 that criticisms of the policy were ill-founded, and considered that a population of 75,000 would be a not undesirable target.[155] A drive to attract more new residents has remained government policy since then.

The decline of tourism and the rise of the financial sector has affected the Island's external transport services. There were 518,515 passenger arrivals on the Island in 1996, but of those only 140,784 were holiday-makers staying in paid accommodation. The largest single group (219,367) were Island residents, and a rapidly growing number (71,452) were business people.[156] Moreover, since 1988 most arrivals in the Isle of Man have been by air rather than by sea, a fact which emphasises the difficulties that faced the Steam Packet Company from the 1950s, when the declining number of visitors and the short duration of the holiday season meant that many of the company's ships were laid up at Barrow or Birkenhead for as long as nine months each year. In 1961 the Fleetwood to Douglas summer service – which had transported a hundred thousand passengers a year in its heyday – was closed because the Fleetwood wharf was in poor condition. In 1962 the company took delivery of its first purpose-built car ferry, the *Manx Maid*, which featured a spiral loading ramp suitable for loading and unloading cars at Liverpool and Douglas. Three similar vessels, the *Ben-my-Chree*, *Mona's Queen* and *Lady of Mann* followed in 1966, 1972 and 1976.[157] In the ten years from 1962 to 1972 the number of cars transported annually rose from 15,149 to 49,710. In the 1970s it became clear that 'roll-on roll-off' ferries had major advantages over side-loading vessels, and in 1978 a rival company, Manx Line, constructed a linkspan in Douglas harbour, and operated a 'ro-ro' service to Heysham. In 1985 Manx Line and the Steam Packet merged under the latter's name, and

154] The view of the Manx nationalist party, Mec Vannin, quoted in *Interim Report of the Commission on the Imbalance of Population* (Douglas, 1968), 74.
155] *Report of the Select Committee of Tynwald on Population Growth and Immigration* (Douglas, 1980).
156] *Digest of Economic and Social Statistics* (1996), Topic 7, p. 4.
157] Chappell, *Island Lifeline*, 64–7.

switched all passenger operations from Liverpool to Heysham, though the Liverpool service was later reopened on a seasonal basis. By the mid-1990s the company was operating the *King Orry*, a former Sealink Channel ferry, as well as the *Lady of Mann* on the passenger routes to Heysham and Liverpool respectively, while the *Peveril* carried cargo to and from Heysham. By 1993 the number of cars transported to the Island annually had risen to 76,767.[158] However, in the same year only 233,633 passengers arrived on the Island by sea, compared with 257,357 by air.[159]

Andreas airfield closed in 1946, and Jurby in 1963, but Ronaldsway was progressively developed by the Airports Board. A new terminal building was finished in 1953, and up to 1966 there was a steady increase in the volume of passenger traffic, with arrivals and departures together numbering 408,000 in that year, falling back in subsequent years before climbing to an all-time record in 1973 of 480,000. After this, airlines were hit by both the international oil crisis and the decline in tourism on the Island, and numbers slumped to 283,000 in 1982. In that year Manx Airlines came into being as the result of a merger, and the company was able to profit from the boom in the financial sector, so that 425,000 passengers used Ronaldsway in 1987.[160] In the 1990s new buildings dramatically increased the airport's size and amenities, while the development of the nearby free port gave the area the appearance of a growing town. By 1996 Ronaldsway was used by over six hundred thousand passengers a year.

The continuing prosperity of the financial sector in the 1990s has undoubtedly made the Island's economy buoyant, and government revenue exceeded expenditure to the extent that the market value of the government's reserve fund in 1993 was £81.4 million.[161] Critics have argued that not enough has been done to preserve tourism, and that some holiday resorts – Blackpool in particular – continued to thrive in the 1990s. Some of the Island's attractions still retained a wide appeal, however, especially the motor-cycle TT and Manx Grand Prix races. The Steam Packet's ferries carried 19,179 motor-cycles to the Island in 1984 and 28,688 in 1993.[162]

An issue that is most relevant to the Island's economic future is its relationship with the European Union. A Protocol annexed to the

158] Isle of Man Steam Packet Company minutes, 1962–93.
159] *Digest of Economic and Social Statistics* (1994), Topic 7, p. 3.
160] Kniveton, *Manx Aviation*, 81–104.
161] *Isle of Man Budget*, 1993-94.
162] Isle of Man Steam Packet Company minutes, 1984–93.

United Kingdom's Treaty of Accession to the European Economic Community in 1972 put the Isle of Man into a special relationship with the EEC and its successor the European Union, though the Island has not been a member or an associate member of either.[163] The Manx government has developed further its traditions of independence in recent years, and its response to possible resolutions of the European Union on such issues as – for instance – offshore financial centres, will be crucial. Many on the Island will hope that, like its three-legged symbol, the Isle of Man will continue to stand on its feet economically whichever way it is thrown.

163] Youde, *Recent Development*, 52–9.

Labour History

ROBERT FYSON

T he history of labour movements is a hitherto neglected area
of Manx historiography. Little has been written on this
subject, except for memoirs by a few participants. Samuel
Norris's major work, focusing on the reform movements of
1903 to 1919, is a substantial contribution to Manx history, but refers
to labour movements only peripherally: Norris made common cause
with labour leaders on issues of constitutional reform, but was himself
an independent Liberal.[1] Less well-known voices, from within the
Manx Labour Party, are to be found in the illuminating but sketchy
accounts by Alfred Teare and Cecil McFee.[2] This chapter will explore
this area of Manx history more fully, if necessarily selectively, and
demonstrate that, especially during the last hundred years, Manx trade
unionists and socialists have played a larger part in the Island's history
than is now generally recognised.

1830–80

The Manx common people expressed their grievances for much of this
period primarily through riot or direct action: the bread riots of 1821
and the potato or tithe riots of 1825 were followed within our period by
the copper currency riots of 1840, and direct action against enclosure of
common lands in Lezayre in the 1850s and in Rushen in the 1860s.[3]
These popular 'pre-industrial' protests merit further research, but
cannot be analysed here. 'Labour history' as usually understood is

---

1] Samuel Norris, *Manx Memories and Movements* (Douglas, 1938, rept 1994).
2] Alfred J. Teare, *Reminiscences of the Manx Labour Party* (Douglas, 1962/3); C.C.
McFee, Notes on Rushen Labour Party, 1979, MNHL: MD15081/4.
3] A.W. Moore, *A History of the Isle of Man* (2 vols, London, 1900), i, 417; ii, 560–2,
661–2; David Craine, 'The potato riots, 1825', *Manannan's Isle* (Douglas, 1955), 197–
209; Anon, 'The copper riots of 1840', *JMM*, II, 38 (Mar 1934), 180–1; Mona Douglas,
'Sulby Cossacks ...' *This is Ellan Vannin* (Douglas, nd, *c.*1964), 126–8. Unrest in
Rushen in the 1860s is documented in the Governor's Letter Books, MNHL: I owe this
information to John Belchem.

concerned with the development of the characteristic modern forms of articulation of popular demands, through trade union activity and political organisation, usually embodying an element of working-class consciousness, and radical or socialist ideology. Such movements are the subject of this chapter.

The years from 1830 to 1850 saw widespread social and political turmoil and large popular movements in Britain, but not in the Isle of Man. The 'early trade union episode' at Ramsey which attracted the attention of the authorities in 1829/30 involved delegate meetings of cotton spinners from England, Ireland and Scotland, with no Manx participation.[4] The middle-class agitation in the 1830s and 1840s for reform of the House of Keys did not embrace universal suffrage, and, as the Chartist Bronterre O'Brien observed, 'the great mass of the Manx people take little or no interest in the struggle'.[5] The 1840s influx of Chartist journalists, wishing to exploit Manx postal privileges to produce newspapers aimed primarily at the British public, initially made no greater impact.[6] However, in the spring of 1846 there was a wave of strikes and industrial unrest in Douglas, which included cabinet-makers, painters and glaziers, sailcloth weavers, printers and tailors.[7] This was followed in the autumn of 1847 by a series of public meetings throughout the Island, addressed by emissaries of the London-based National Association of United Trades, whose journal was about to be printed in Douglas. Three hundred working men attended the initial Douglas meeting, and a fortnight later between seventy and eighty had joined the newly formed NAUT branch, which planned to hold weekly meetings in the Old Assembly Room, Fort Street, now 'Mr. Moffatt's schoolroom'.[8] Meetings were also held in Ramsey, Laxey and Castletown, but the brief upsurge of interest from August to November was not related to any particular dispute, and seems to have rapidly faded.[9] There may,

4] W.R. Serjeant, 'An early Trade Union episode at Ramsey', *JMM* VII 1971, 177–81; R.G. Kirby and A.E. Musson, *The Voice of the People: John Doherty, 1798–1854, Trade Unionist, Radical and Factory Reformer*, (Manchester, 1975), 87–100.

5] Extract from O'Brien's *National Reformer* in *Manx Sun*, 27 Sept 1845. For O'Brien see R. Fyson, 'Bronterre O'Brien: a Chartist in the Isle of Man 1844–1847', *Proceedings*, X, 4 (1998), 393–400.

6] For the 'alternative' Manx journalism of the 1840s see John Belchem, 'Radical entrepreneur: William Shirrefs and the Manx free press of the 1840s', *Proceedings*, X, 1 (1992), 33–47.

7] *Mona's Herald*, 18 Mar 1846; *Manx Sun*, 11 Apr 1846; *Manx Liberal*, 7 Nov 1846.

8] *Mona's Herald*, 25 Aug 1847; *Manx Sun*, 18 Sept 1847.

9] *Manx Liberal*, 9 Oct 1847; *Mona's Herald*, 6 Oct, 10 Nov 1847.

however, have been some continuity of craft trade unionism in Douglas from the 1840s onwards.[10]

In the mid-Victorian period the main potential threat to social order was perceived as likely to come from the Island's miners, as appears from an 1866 Head Constable's report to the Lieutenant-Governor, listing their numbers and locations: there were then over a thousand miners in the Island, almost all about equally divided between the Foxdale and Laxey mines.[11] In the highly profitable decade of the 1870s the Laxey mines erupted into conflict: the miners sustained an unsuccessful strike for higher wages for four months in 1872, and further disputes culminated in another major conflict in 1879.[12] The history of these disputes has yet to be written. It appears that severe struggles were organised by ad hoc strike committees, rather than a permanent union, and were largely isolated from the rest of the Island's labouring population. By the time trade unionism became an established force in Manx life, the mining industry was already in decline.

Trade Unionism and Socialism in the 1890s

The development of Douglas as a leisure town, with the resulting diversification of trades and seasonal demand for labour, combined with developments in the British world of labour to stimulate the emergence of the Manx labour movement during the 1890s. In September 1894 painters, joiners, labourers, coachbuilders and typographers decided to form a 'council of trade union societies', to be known as the Douglas Trade and Labour Council.[13] The Council's first year saw a great deal of union activity. In March 1895 the *Examiner* observed that 'nearly all sections of skilled artisans in Douglas have associated themselves in trade unions'.[14] The Douglas house painters struck for five weeks from 1 March for higher wages and a better distribution of work throughout the year, but were forced back to work on the old terms by the introduction of Scottish blacklegs and the exhaustion of their funds. As a result, in November they agreed to

10] Teare, *Reminiscences*, 5: ' "Craft" trade unions were in being in the Island in the latter half of last century.'
11] George Turnbull, *The Isle of Man Constabulary* (np, 1984), 83.
12] Helen J. Wilson, 'The Great Laxey Strike', *Manxman*, summer 1978, 20–3. Thanks to Frank Cowin for this reference.
13] *Examiner*, 30 Nov 1895. For several years 'Trade' and 'Trades' were used interchangeably in the council's title. 'Labourers' appear to have been plasterers' labourers.
14] *Examiner*, 23 Mar 1895.

abandon their own union and join the high-benefit Manchester-based National Amalgamated Society of Painters and Decorators.[15] The Douglas tailors, whose local union already existed in the early 1880s, were more successful: the threat of strike action over pay and hours brought a speedy capitulation by nine out of ten local employers, and union membership rose within a year from twelve to seventy, though here too there was concern about rumours of imported labour.[16] Plasterers and their labourers won half their wage demand without striking in February, affiliated to the Trades Council later in the year and were able to sustain a year-long strike two years later, in 1897.[17] Carpenters and joiners opened a Douglas branch of their Amalgamated Society in March. The shop assistants' early closing association affiliated to the Trades Council at the end of the year, and the Council took the initiative in calling a meeting to set up a branch of the Amalgamated Masons' Society.[18]

Thus during 1894–5, as the secretary reported at the first annual meeting, trade unionism in Douglas was significantly strengthened. The Council campaigned for a fair wage clause in local government contracts, to which Douglas Town Council agreed in 1897, and the Douglas School Board in 1905;[19] they pressed for legislation to give Manx trade unions the same legal status as in England, for Manx government work, including printing and the manufacture of uniforms, to be done in the Island, and for cheap non-Manx labour to be excluded.[20] Trade union branches listed in Douglas increased from seven to twelve in the years 1896–9 with engineers, plumbers, stone-masons, shop assistants, even a Retail News Agents' and Booksellers' Union, joining the movement.[21] Printers were prominent in the Council's leadership: J.C. Quine, a compositor in the *Examiner* printing office, described as the John Burns of the Isle of Man, doubled as secretary of the Trades Council and also of the Typographical Association branch from 1894 until 1922, while his colleague J.D. Fell, an overseer at the same workplace, was President of both bodies for most of that time.[22]

15] *Examiner*, Mar *passim*; 6 Apr; 9, 23, 30 Nov 1895.
16] *Examiner Annual*, 1902, 31. *Examiner*, 16, 23, 30 Mar, 6 Apr, 4 May, 15 June, 30 Nov 1895.
17] *Examiner*, 19, 26 Jan, 2, 23 Feb 1895; 6 Nov 1897.
18] *Examiner*, 23, 30 Mar, 28 Sept, 30 Nov, 21 Dec 1895.
19] *Examiner*, 12 Jan, 1 June, 30 Nov 1895; *Examiner Annual*, 1906.
20] *Examiner*, 15 June, 31 Aug, 30 Nov 1895.
21] *Examiner Annuals*, 1897–1900.
22] *Examiner Annuals*, 1895, 73; 1896, 81; 1901, 17; 1904, 77; 1918, 55; 1923, 103.

During 1895 the *Examiner*, the Island's most progressive paper, ran a series of articles by Ben Cormode of Port Soderick, a young man who enthusiastically propounded the ethical socialism of Robert Blatchford, editor of the *Clarion*.[23] After six months' sustained newspaper polemic and controversy, in October 'at a largely attended meeting in Finch Road ... it was decided to form a Manx Socialist Society for the study of Socialistic literature and to provide lectures for the benefit of all working men'. The first open meeting was attended by 25 to 30 young men, described as 'intelligent, well-dressed and from the better class of workmen', including four or five printers, besides a local preacher, a student, an 'intellectual barber', a school teacher or two, and two or three employers. They unanimously agreed that the objects of their society were

> the common or collective ownership of the means of production, distribution and exchange, to be controlled by a democratic state in the interests of the whole community; and the complete emancipation of labour from the domination of capital and landlordism, with the establishment of social and economic equality between the sexes.

These earnest enthusiasts, presided over by the appropriately named Robert Owen, decided that they would not hold a social tea and smoking concert as their next function, but instead the first of a series of discussion meetings, on land, capital and labour.[24]

Such ambitious objectives might appear distant from the practical concerns of Manx trade unionists, but in fact the 'immediate programme' of the Socialist Society was much closer to the current concerns of organised labour. Comprising demands for an employers' liability act, income tax and death duties, vote by ballot in all elections, a 'free breakfast table' (that is, no taxes on food), payment of members of the Keys, reduction of government expenses, manhood suffrage and the taxation of land values, it differed little from the 'Newcastle programme' of advanced liberalism, and was to be achieved by 'constitutional persuasion'.[25] Within two years the Socialist Society achieved its greatest publicity coup by bringing Tom Mann, at that time general secretary of the Independent Labour Party, to speak to a crowded meeting in the Douglas Gymnasium in November 1897. Chaired by a sympathetic Congregational minister, the platform

23] *Examiner*, 30 Mar 1895 on, *passim*. Ben Cormode died in February 1903, aged 28: *Manx Reformer*, Mar 1903.
24] *Examiner*, 5, 19 Oct 1895.
25] *Examiner*, 23, 30 Nov, 7 Dec 1895.

included J.C. Quine as secretary of the Trades Council, and the vote of thanks was given by Tom Cormode, 'the radical blacksmith of Quine's Hill', brother of Ben and soon to be the first working-class member of the House of Keys.[26]

Socialist ideas were widely disseminated to many people who did not attend Socialist Society meetings. As the *Examiner* remarked:

> Socialism is, as the saying goes, in the air. Take up the syllabuses of debating and mutual improvement classes, and you generally find this subject on the list. Last year it was well thrashed out at St. Matthew's; this year it is on the programmes for Finch Hill, the Wesleyan, the Primitive, St. Thomas's, and how many more?[27]

The Island's organised network of debating societies and mutual improvement societies, which held their second annual conference in April 1895, were often linked to particular churches, but generally progressive in tone. The secretary to the conference was S.K. Broadbent, editor and publisher of the *Examiner*, whose role was clearly crucial both as a tolerant employer of labour and as an editor who allowed space to socialist views. Those present included Egbert Rydings, manager of the Ruskin-inspired St George's Mills at Laxey; John Wrangham, a journalist; George Preston, land reformer; James Cowley, later secretary of the Manx Labour Party; and J.D. Fell. The societies often debated socialism, household suffrage, constitutional reform, the position of women, and other social and political topics, sometimes in joint debates with the Socialist Society.[28]

This activity was not restricted to Douglas, though the subject matter of Douglas meetings might be more 'advanced'. The Rushen Mutual Improvement Society or Young Men's Class was based at the Rechabite Hall at the Level, Colby, where in 1895 members gave papers on such topics as 'Ignorance', 'Heredity', 'Failure' and 'Ancient Egypt'. These were ardent Methodists and teetotallers who founded a Rushen Political Progressive Association. Among the most active was J.R. Corrin, a carpenter and Primitive Methodist lay preacher who was threatened with removal from the Castletown circuit for preaching Christian Socialism. He and others later founded the Rushen Labour Party. The fishermen, craftsmen and farm labourers of Port St Mary, Port Erin, Colby and the surrounding villages and countryside,

26] *Examiner*, 6 Nov 1897.
27] *Examiner*, 9 Nov 1895.
28] *Examiner*, 27 Apr 1895.

predominantly Methodists, were the basis of what became an area of Labour strength.[29]

Manx Labour and Reform, 1900–14

The Manx labour movement in its early years was able to achieve very little to alleviate the poverty, unemployment and poor living and working conditions of the working classes.[30] But the Trades Council was persistent, focusing its energies on pressure for an employers' liability act, organising a well-supported public petition in the spring of 1901, discussing their demands with Douglas members of the Keys, and returning to the issue with a leafleting campaign in 1903. They also pressed for a factories and workshops act, but on both issues the Keys were recalcitrant.[31]

As J.C. Quine had realised in 1895, it was essential to elect supporters of the claims of labour to public office.[32] In 1901 some hopes were raised when Hall Caine, styling himself 'the People's Man', was elected as MHK for Ramsey, but his inconsistency and absenteeism soon disillusioned the Island's radicals and socialists.[33] In 1902 the Trades Council put up candidates in the School Board elections. Seven new members were elected to the Douglas Board, and four members of the Clarion Club won seats: George Thornley in Douglas, Alfred Cormode and W.S. Weigh in Onchan, a Dr Davies in Ramsey.[34] Then

29] *Examiner*, 2 Feb, 2 Mar, 6 Apr 1895; McFee, Notes on Rushen Labour Party, 1–2. See also McFee, 'Methodism and social/political reform', paper delivered to Isle of Man Methodist History Society, 1987, MNHL: MD1061, 2–3.

James Robinson Corrin, 1878-1972. Fisherman's son. Carpenter and joiner, mineral water manufacturer, boat-builder, MHK 1919–28, MLC 1928–55. Methodist lay preacher 1898–1971. Pacifist until 1940, then member of War Cabinet. Lived in the same house on Colby Level all his life. The grand old man of Rushen Labour Party. Thanks to his daughter, Mrs Marjorie Woodworth, for an interview at Port St Mary, 30 Dec 1997.

30] For a thumbnail sketch see Norris, *Manx Memories*, 14.

31] *Examiner Annuals*, 1902 and 1903; *Manx Reformer*, Nov 1902, Jan 1903. The Trades Council Leaflet is in MNHL: Early Election Material, D155/1x.

32] *Examiner*, 30 Nov 1895.

33] *Manx Reformer*, Feb, Nov, Dec 1903. However, despite the paper's criticism, Hall Caine was voted equal first as the most popular Manxman of his day in a 'prize competition' for readers in Feb 1903.

34] *Examiner Annual*, 1903; *Manx Reformer*, Nov 1902.

George Thornley, bookseller and newsagent, Douglas town councillor 1899–1908: G.N. Kniveton *et al*, *Douglas Centenary 1896–1996* (Douglas, 1996), 190.

Alfred Cormode: another Cormode brother: Teare, *Reminiscences*, 3.

W.S. Weigh, New Connexion Methodist, emigrated to USA in 1895, returned by

in the 1903 general election Tom Cormode, despite not being a Peel man, defeated the town's unpopular High Bailiff and was elected to the Keys. Not adopting a party label, but standing as a progressive independent, Cormode was nevertheless recognised as the solitary voice of labour in the Keys from 1903 until 1919, and his election was secured with the vigorous support of Fell and Quine and other Douglas Trades Council members who campaigned for him.[35]

Meanwhile, in November 1902 the Island's socialists launched a vigorous free monthly journal which survived until October 1904, financed by advertising and the free services of its editor and contributors, and claiming a circulation of two thousand copies. In its first number it announced itself as 'the official organ of the Manx Branch of the Clarion Fellowship in particular and the cause of Socialism in general'. It gave eclectic support to 'the Socialism of Blatchford and Fay, of Prince Kropotkin, A.R. Wallace, Henry George, Morrison Davidson and William Morris' and carried a letter of good wishes from Keir Hardie. Articles on socialist principles and policies abounded, but, as Ben Cormode wrote in February 1903, 'while our main object is to forward the formation of a Manx Party, based on the principle of state control of the means of production and distribution, at the same time we are willing to help forward every reform'. Called the *Manx Reformer*, not the Manx Socialist, the paper gave much space to immediate issues like the campaign for an employers' liability act, the need for municipal dwellings, work for the unemployed in winter, and other issues seen within the perspective of a programme of municipal socialism for Douglas, including a campaign for public baths which was endorsed by three leading School Board members and five headmasters.[36]

1902 and secretary of the Clarion Fellowship and Socialist Society, teacher of shorthand and typewriting, in 1908 lawyer's clerk, emigrated to Australia in 1911. *Examiner*, 24 Aug 1895; *Manx Reformer*, 1902–4, *passim*; Teare, *Reminiscences*, 7; information from Ann Harrison.

35] Teare, *Reminiscences*, 5–6. For Cormode's election publicity see *City Star*, 11–16 Nov 1903, MNHL. After his long service in the Keys Cormode was admitted to 'the Asylum' and, after absconding, was found dead in a field: CCD, MNHL: MG/MC/3/ 1–11, 29 Jan, 13, 14 Oct 1920.

36] *Manx Reformer*, Apr 1904. Among the less well known socialists admired by the *Manx Reformer*: E.F. Fay, 1853–96, friend and collaborator of Blatchford on the *Clarion*; Alfred Russel Wallace, 1823–1913, better known as a Darwinian biologist; J. Morrison Davidson, journalist, author of *Annals of Toil*, 1899, a series of booklets outlining labour history.

At the same time the paper continued to publicise the meetings of the Clarion Fellowship and the Manx Socialist Society, which were evidently virtually synonymous with each other. The socialists often felt they were a beleaguered minority: J.D. Fell grumbled in November 1902 that the visiting season 'threw all out of joint' and that 'it is indeed difficult to keep a spark of life in social, political and labour organisations in the Isle of Man'. Nevertheless the Socialist Society, though small, was active in spreading the word, and its members were reminded in April 1904 that a few years ago they had issued six thousand of a series of leaflets written by their own members, in addition to sustaining a programme of public meetings and debates and launching their own journal. As the paper's last issue in October remarked, an Employers' Liability Act had now at last been put on the Manx statute book, the duration of Parliaments had been reduced from seven to five years, the ballot and household suffrage now operated in all Manx elections, national and local. Reform and progress were possible, despite the stultifying weight of Insular conservatism.

The *Manx Reformer* was founded a year earlier than the Manx Reform League of October 1903, of which Samuel Norris was secretary. As Norris acknowledged, three of the League's six founder-members, Fell, Weigh and R.C. Callister, were socialists, although they were not prominent in the League's campaign.[37] The League drew on a wider cross-section of public support than the socialists alone could achieve, but the idea of a broad coalition for reform owed more to the socialists and their journal, perhaps, than Norris's memoirs suggest. A few years later, Norris's own journal, the *Manx Patriot*, imitated the *Reformer* by issuing two thousand free copies monthly.[38]

In April 1908 a Manx socialist party at last emerged with the foundation of the Manx branch of the Independent Labour Party. The new party immediately succeeded in electing Walter Craine as a Douglas Poor Law Guardian. Later in the year, however, Weigh failed to be elected to Douglas Town Council, and Craine, standing as first official Labour candidate for the Keys in South Douglas, 'doing a good deal of outdoor speaking', won 282 votes and split the reform vote.[39] The

37] Norris, *Manx Memories*, 103–4. For a critical study see Jeffrey Vaukins, *The Manx Struggle for Reform*, unpublished M Phil thesis, Lancaster University, 1984, copy in MNHL: MD12548.

38] *Manx Patriot*, Oct 1906 to Dec 1909, from Oct 1908 cost 1*d*.

39] *Examiner Annual*, 1909; Teare, *Reminiscences*, 7. *Manx Patriot*, Nov 1908, June 1909.

Walter Craine, 1877–1961. Clarion Club treasurer 1903, Douglas Poor Law Guardian 1908–11. Baker, commercial traveller and commission agent, served in

foundation of the Manx ILP did not result in any political breakthrough, though the party began to play a part in the Island's political life, for example in 1909 giving a platform to Samuel Norris to air his views about the purchase of the Villa Marina.[40]

Socialists and reformers alike, especially in the wake of the British Liberal government's welfare reforms, carried through with Labour support, wanted to see old-age pensions, national insurance, workmen's compensation, adult suffrage and Manx constitutional reform, but none of these was achieved before the war. By 1909, however, a Factories and Workshops Act was at last in place, based on legislation which had been in force in England for many years, and the first successful prosecution under the Act occurred in March 1911. Agitation on the pensions issue was at its height in 1909–11, culminating in a petition with eight thousand signatures organised by the Island's Joint Labour Associations, and sent to Winston Churchill as Home Secretary.[41]

The British labour unrest of 1910–14 affected the Island: in the summer of 1911 there were strikes by Steam Packet firemen and Douglas Corporation tram drivers, and during the British railway strike a cruiser was anchored in Douglas harbour to act as transport in case of a seamen's strike, a move which produced a panic exodus of holidaymakers.[42] In the autumn of 1913 Charlie Gill, a Ballaugh farm labourer, made a determined attempt to start a Manx farm labourers' union, and an emissary from Manchester tried to unionise Isle of Man Railway workers, but neither initiative was successful.[43]

The Douglas Trades Council held its own; bakers were unionised by 1908, and postmen and postal clerks by 1912.[44] But the Manx Socialist Society collapsed in 1911, and some of its members were involved in founding a short-lived Manx Liberal Association.[45] The ILP failed to produce a slate of candidates for the Keys election of 1913. Parliamentary socialism was apparently a hopeless cause. But the

---

France and Salonika in the army 1914–20. MHK for South Douglas 1924–46, 1950–6; Douglas Town Council 1926–59 and Mayor of Douglas 1937–9. Secretary of Isle of Man Licensed Victuallers' Association, and Isle of Man Football Association, for many years.

40] *Manx Patriot*, Nov 1909.
41] *Examiner Annual*, 1912; Teare, *Reminiscences*, 13–15.
42] *Examiner Annual*, 1912.
43] *Examiner Annual*, 1914; Teare, *Reminiscences*, 9; CCD, 13 Oct 1913.
44] *Examiner Annual*, 1909 and 1913.
45] I owe this information to Ann Harrison.

privations experienced during the war of 1914–18 were to alter the public mood substantially. The achievement of the small but persistent interlinked trade unionist and socialist movements of the twenty years before 1914 was to educate a generation who were to provide effective leadership to the Manx labour movement for many years to come.

The War Years: the Breakthrough

The hardships of wartime life in the Isle of Man, and the protests that they provoked, have been vividly chronicled by Samuel Norris.[46] Working-class unrest, however, was at first muted and passive. Norris's War Rights Union of 1915 was primarily concerned with the grievances of seaside landladies, hoteliers and boarding-house keepers, and labour leaders did not feature prominently in public protests until 1916. At Peel in January, William P. Clucas, addressing an open-air meeting of five hundred people, blended familiar prewar demands for income tax, pensions, national insurance and workmen's compensation with an element of anti-war sentiment and Manx nationalism, opposing conscription unless approved by Tynwald and deploring the draining of youth from the Island.[47] In the summer labour leaders appeared at Norris's meetings on the shore at Douglas, notably J.D. Fell, who, with a different emphasis from Clucas, said 'rather than that the present state of affairs should continue, the working man would prefer annexation to England'.[48] At the famous Tynwald Day demonstration against Lord Raglan, Clucas and Christopher Shimmin, also from Peel, spoke stirringly against the poverty and inequality of the Governor's regime.[49] Norris's petition to remove Raglan and introduce income tax, circulated in July and August, was well supported in Douglas, Peel and Port Erin, all centres of labour activity, but not in Ramsey or the country districts.[50]

46] Norris, *Manx Memories*, 147–331.

47] CCD, 22, 24, 25 Jan 1916.

William Philip Clucas, 1856–1933. Born Peel, Liverpool Police 1882–1908, retired as Sergeant. Chairman of Peel Commissioners and first Chairman of the Manx Labour Party 1918. MHK for Glenfaba 1924–33. The oldest Manx Labour leader.

48] Norris, *Manx Memories*, 194–5.

49] Norris, *Manx Memories*, 200–1, 204.

Christopher R. Shimmin, 1870–1933. Born Peel. Apprentice sailmaker in grandfather's business. Worked in England. Emigrated to USA and unemployed there *c.*1895–6. Several years as a seaman before returning to Peel and starting own business as a monumental stonemason. MHK for Peel 1919–33. President of the Manx Labour Party and President of the Manx Society 1924–5. Author of eight Manx dialect plays and an outline of Manx history. Visited Iceland in 1929. Left £3,000.

50] CCD, 2 Aug 1916.

Political unrest *On 14 September 1916 a crowd gathered to watch Henry Ainley leading the fishermen to Tynwald Hill in a re-enactment in a play by Hall Caine about the 1880 fishermen's protest. (MNHL)*

During 1916 Norris's popular front for reform reached its peak but thereafter declined, especially when his month in prison for contempt of court at the end of the year cooled his ardour and discouraged some of his supporters.

The popular mood during 1917 and 1918 was dominated by concern with the price and availability of food. The cost of living early in 1917 was nearly 80 per cent above the 1914 level, while wages had risen scarcely at all.[51] There was an acute shortage of potatoes, a staple food, partly because of the large quantity consumed in the internment camps: in March 1917 the Governor came into line with English practice by banning exports and introducing rationing. This was the first of a series of measures aimed at improving the food supply and allaying popular discontent and suspicion of profiteering. By early 1918 bread and tea had to be sold by weight; the export of milk, eggs, pickled herring and margarine was forbidden; there were penalties for wasting or hoarding food, and a Food Controller had been appointed.[52] None of this prevented the development of a rebellious, resentful popular mood, compounded of fear of shortages, suspicion and hostility directed against German prisoners, English soldiers, rich farmers and the Island's government alike. Echoes of a premodern 'crisis of subsistence' combined with Nonconformist anti-militarism and anti-alcoholism to produce an indiscriminate anger articulated at large prohibition meetings and from the pulpit. One minister said that British troops would have more success in winning the war if they were teetotal; another, the superintendent of the Peel Wesleyan Methodist circuit, preached at Castletown that 'he would rather go to Hell with conscientious objectors than to Heaven with the drunken, whoremongering, blaspheming scoundrels of soldiers in France and Flanders', which earned him three months' prison with hard labour for using language likely to discourage recruitment. Probably more common was the alleged view of a Laxey man that 'if the Germans came we'd be no worse off', though, with 17,000 Manxmen at war, pro-Allied patriotism remained predominant, even if complicated by contradictory cross-currents of opinion.[53]

This was the context in which, in March 1917, a small group of men approached Alf Teare, an experienced trade unionist,[54] for advice

51] Teare, *Reminiscences* 16; Norris, *Manx Memories*, 286, says food prices had risen by 60 per cent.
52] CCD, 14 Feb, 27 Apr, 9 Oct 1917; 25 Jan, 6 Feb 1918.
53] CCD, 2, 22 Aug 1917; 26 Jan – 2 Feb 1918.
54] Alfred J. Teare, 1879–1969. Born Barrow-in-Furness of Manx parents. Linotype operator, *Isle of Man Times*. Member, Isle of Man Volunteers 1899–1902. Active trade

about forming, or joining, a union for unskilled workers. Teare then called a meeting in Douglas, attended by about fifty Douglas Corporation employees, coalyard and gas workers and railwaymen. A second meeting agreed to join the Workers' Union, which appeared most suitable as a union not confined to any particular industry, and catering for all grades of workers: 'The speakers emphasised the need for organisation, in view of the high costs of living. Reference was made to the exportation of foodstuffs, thereby causing inflated prices, and they asked for restrictions to be imposed, if not prohibition of exports.'[55]

Alf Teare, first as Douglas branch secretary and then as union secretary for the whole Island, became the key figure in a rapid and massive expansion of general unionism. Teare, Quine, Shimmin, Clucas and others spread the unionist message widely, sometimes 'tramping the mountains for ten or sixteen miles in wind and rain' to address meetings and enrol members.[56] Douglas Corporation employees, gas workers, coalmen, carters, foundry labourers, harbour and highway workers, dockers, railwaymen, farm labourers, lead miners, quarrymen, brickmakers, and women brushmakers, glovemakers and sock knitters were all enrolled in the Workers' Union. Isle of Man Railway employees, organised by the station masters, under Teare's guidance, achieved a hundred per cent union membership.[57] Other unions were inspired to campaign anew, such as the Shop Assistants' Union initiative on working hours and early closing.[58] The Workers' Union Manchester district organiser, George Titt, became a familiar visitor to the Island, accompanying a deputation to Tynwald to resist a reduction in the wages of government-employed women sock knitters, meeting the Governor and employers to discuss setting up a Whitley Council as a permanent framework for industrial relations.[59]

---

unionist from *c.*1902. ILP member from *c.*1908. Douglas secretary 1917–20, then paid Isle of Man organiser, Workers' Union/TGWU 1920–35. Chair, 1918 strike committee and member, 1935 strike committee. First working-class JP 1919. Main founder of Manx Labour Party and Treasurer for many years. President 1932–3. MHK, South Douglas 1919–51. MLC 1951–62. Douglas Town Council 1933–65. Published *Reminiscences of the Manx Labour Party* 1963. MBE, 1946. The most influential Manx labour leader.

55] Unidentified press report quoted in Norris, *Manx Memories*, 291.

56] *WU Record*, Dec 1917, 'Isle of Man notes', 9.

57] Teare, *Reminiscences*, 12.

58] Teare, *Reminiscences*, 7–9; *The Shop Assistant*, 4 July 1925, 'Our Manx movement', 552, photocopy in MNHL.

59] *WU Record*, Dec 1917, 9; June 1919, 9.

The first Labour representatives in the Keys *Four out of the eleven Labour candidates met with success in the general election of 1919. From left to right they are Christopher Shimmin (Peel), J.R. Corrin (Rushen), Gerald Bridson (Middle) and Alf Teare (South Douglas). (MNHL)*

This activity achieved results. Many, perhaps most, Manx manual workers were, until 1917, expected to work 60 hours a week or more, with no overtime, for £1 or 21s a week. By 1918 the Workers' Union had made considerable headway in establishing a 56-hour maximum working week, and a weekly wage of 28s as the norm.[60] By the end of 1917 the Douglas WU Branch had nearly five hundred members. There were also branches at Peel, Ramsey, Laxey, Rushen and Castletown and separate women's branches in Douglas and Ramsey. Total membership in the Island by the end of 1917 was over one thousand and growing.[61] The Workers' Union had rapidly become a power in the land.[62]

The union continued to campaign, in line with the concern expressed at its very first meeting, on the issue of food prices. The Workers' Union organised public meetings and deputations to the Governor and

60] Teare, *Reminiscences*, 10–11; *WU Record*, Feb 1918, 3.
61] *WU Record*, Dec 1917, 9. The women's branches were short-lived, in Ramsey recorded only in 1918, in Douglas surviving until 1922; see *Workers' Union Annual Reports* with branch balance sheets, at Warwick University Modern Records Centre.
62] See also Warwick University Modern Records Centre, Mss 51/3/1/50, letter from Alf Teare to Richard Hyman, 21 June 1965; Richard Hyman, *The Workers' Union* (Oxford, 1971), 106; *WU Record*, Aug 1924.

pressed for a subsidy, as in England, to bring the cost of a four-pound loaf down from 1s to 9d. The Governor agreed to a commission of inquiry, which heard evidence from, among others, Norris, Teare, Fell and C.A. Cormode.[63] Tynwald finally agreed in October 1917 to make a grant of £20,000 to cover a bread subsidy for six months, while income tax legislation was prepared.[64] The expiry of this subsidy in the summer of 1918, before the legislation which would provide an alternative method of financing it had been agreed, led directly to the crisis in which the Workers' Union demonstrated its strength by organising a general strike which rapidly achieved an astonishing victory.

Raglan's announcement at the end of June 1918 that the bread subsidy would be discontinued provoked protest meetings throughout the Island and resolutions in favour of a general strike for the 9d loaf. The strike committee, chaired by Teare, included John Holden of the Seamen's Union, J.D. Fell of the Douglas Trades Council, Harry Emery of the Shop Assistants' Union and John Coole of the Tailors' Union. Although the Workers' Union was numerically predominant, this was a genuine common front of organised labour. The outcome on 4–5 July was impressive: seamen, dockers, railway workers, gas workers, Douglas Corporation workmen, including bus and tram drivers, shop assistants, factory workers and some schoolchildren joined the strike. Factories, businesses and shops were forced to close. The strike committee, meeting in permanent session at the Salisbury Hall, Douglas, issued permits for journeys to be made and for some shops to open, ordered cargoes of fish landed at Douglas to be sold to the poor at a low price and pacified militant crowds, notably at the siege of the coalyard and offices of the provocatively anti-strike Captain Moughtin MHK. Outside Douglas, Castletown unionists, women knitters at Port St Mary and, on the second day, workers at Ramsey – where the Workers' Union branch claimed three hundred members, including one hundred farm labourers – all joined the strike. Superintendent Quilliam, acting Chief Constable, refused to guarantee protection for public transport or shops remaining open, or to apply for Army assistance; he was subsequently criticised by property owners, but may have played a crucial role in maintaining the public peace and

63] C. Arthur Cormode, 1868–1948. Blacksmith at St Mark's for many years. Brother of Ben, Alfred and Tom Cormode. One of the founders of the Manx Socialist Society. President of the Manx Labour Party 1921–2. Unsuccessful candidate for the Keys in Rushen 1919 and 1924. Widely respected figure.
64] Teare, *Reminiscences*, 16–20; Norris, *Manx Memories*, 285–91.

averting violence. At 3 p.m. on 5 July Raglan announced that the 9*d* loaf would continue and the strike ended with total victory.[65]

Samuel Norris later described the strike as 'not merely a general strike of labour' but 'a public demonstration of discontent against the Government of the Island'. However, during the strike Norris's constitutionalism was sidelined and it was the power of organised labour which fundamentally altered the balance of forces on the Island. The *Examiner*'s assessment was that 'practical protest from the Manx proletariat ... took the form of the most complete ... dislocation of trade and industry ever experienced in the Island' due to the

> neglect – contempt were the better word – with which the aspirations of the Manx proletariat have been treated for many years past ... For two days the Isle of Man underwent the most stirring experience in the Island's history and the memory of democracy's determined and successful effort to obtain concession of what they deemed their just demand will remain for years to come.[66]

After the strike the logjam of government inertia was broken. The 9*d* loaf was guaranteed for as long as the subsidy continued in England; strikers were not to be victimised; the Income Tax Act, to take effect from April 1919, was passed into law and a promise was made of no further increases in indirect taxation.[67]

The Manx Labour Party, founded in 1918, very largely owing to the initiative and judgment of Alf Teare, now effectively replaced the Manx branch of the ILP. Modelled closely on the British Labour Party constitution of 1918, including Sidney Webb's famous Clause Four, this was nevertheless an independent Manx political party, seeing itself as the political wing of the trade union movement and aiming at winning electoral power. The new constitution was formally adopted at the Manx Labour Party's first annual conference in September 1918, where Clucas was elected as the first chairman and Teare as Treasurer. With thirteen others they formed the first Executive, consisting of eight Workers' Union members and seven from other unions, including two teachers, two shop assistants, a tailor, a carpenter and a printer.[68] Two of these – Annie Watterson, a teacher, and Nellie Taylor, a

65] This account of the strike is based on 'The great strike', *Manx Quarterly*, XX (Apr 1919), 237–57 (an article based on *Examiner* coverage of the strike); Teare, *Reminiscences*, 20–5; Norris, *Manx Memories*, 305–11; CCD, 30 June, 3–5, 8–9 July 1918.

66] Norris, *Manx Memories*, 307; *Manx Quarterly*, XX (Apr 1919), 237, 241, 253.

67] *Examiner Annual*, 1919.

68] Teare, *Reminiscences*, 26–7; MNHL: D155, Manx Labour Party Constitution, 1918.

shop assistant – were women.[69] The crucial breakthrough for the Manx labour movement occurred in 1918, and its two wings, industrial and political, now prepared for the postwar struggles which lay ahead.

Labour's Heyday, 1919–29

Even before the election of a new House of Keys in November 1919 Tynwald showed a new sensitivity to the claims of labour and reformers, allocating £20,000 for unemployment relief in the winter of 1918–19, pressing ahead with legislation on national insurance, adult suffrage, workmen's compensation and constitutional reform. Lord Raglan's resignation in December 1918 made little difference: Raglan in defeat had become an irrelevance.

Writing in 1941, Samuel Norris characterised the Governorship of Major-General Fry from 1919 to 1926 as

> a period of great activity and marked development in social betterment and applied ideas of popular Government. Old Age Pensions, National Insurance, employment on Government works, housing schemes, educational advancement and judicial, financial and legislative reforms were dealt with.[70]

These changes, however, were not solely the product of enlightened paternalism in Government House, or consensual reformism in Tynwald, but came about during a period of labour militancy and unprecedented 'establishment' uncertainty. This was a period of tension and strife, rather than social harmony.

Labour's advance did not automatically translate into overwhelming popular support at the polls, but the general election of November 1919 saw the first Labour successes, with four out of eleven Labour candidates elected to the Keys, Shimmin at Peel with 64 per cent of the vote in a straight fight, Teare in South Douglas and Corrin in Rushen both heading the poll in multi-member constituencies and Gerald Bridson squeezing in by a narrow margin as the third-placed member for Middle.[71] The four new members were pledged to support old-age

69] Annie Watterson, later Bridson, 1893–1985. Schoolteacher. Manx Labour Party Executive 1918, representing Douglas Class Teachers' Association. Secretary 1921–3, President 1924–5, MLP Women's Branch. First woman President, Manx Labour Party 1922–3. Married Gerald Bridson. MHK for Garff 1951–6.

70] *Norris Modern Press Year Book* (1942), xvii.

71] See MNHL: D155, Sherratt Collection, for a tabulated list of Manx parliamentary election results since 1919.

  T. Gerald Bridson, 1893–1967. Poultry farmer. MHK for Middle 1919–24. Persistent

pensions, national health insurance and hospital care, abolition of the
poor law, a Manx national housing scheme, industrial joint councils of
employers and workers and a single education authority for the Island.
In 1924 Labour representation rose to six, a quarter of the membership
of the Keys, with a programme which now included widows' pensions,
rent restriction, an unemployment board, a 48-hour week, a national
minimum wage, redistribution of seats in the Keys, security of tenure for
tenant farmers, fixed food prices and the nationalisation of banks,
railways, steamships and land. The loss of Bridson's seat was more than
compensated for by the election of Clucas in the rural constituency of
Glenfaba at his fourth attempt, Walter Cowin, top of the poll in Garff,
and Walter Craine, Teare's running-mate in South Douglas. In 1929
Labour reached its highest point with seven elected members, with
Richard Kneen replacing J.R. Corrin, promoted by the Governor to the
Legislative Council, in Rushen and John Kelly elected by four votes over
Samuel Norris in North Douglas. Labour, as the only party political
group, however loosely organised, in the Keys, were an influential
minority who had an important role to play in supporting, sometimes
initiating, progressive legislation. That all Labour MHKs were also
members of the Workers' Union reflected the continuing importance of
the labour movement's extra-parliamentary strength, which enhanced
the status and influence of its representatives in the Keys.[72]

   Industrial conflict was especially prevalent in the immediate postwar
years. The foundation in 1918 of the Isle of Man Employers' Federation
as a counterbalance to the Workers' Union provided a basic framework

---

campaigner who stood for the Keys nine times in general elections and by-elections, but
was re-elected only once, as Independent Labour MHK for Garff 1942–6. Later
rejoined the Manx Labour Party. Well known as a long-distance walker. Married
Annie Watterson.

72] Walter K. Cowin, 1871–1942. MHK for Garff 1924–42. Born Lonan. Shoemaker,
latterly own business at Laxey. Munitions worker, Barrow, in First World War.
Secretary of Laxey Unemployed Committee *c.*1920. Chairman of Laxey Commissioners
1923. Manx delegate to Workers' Union's last conference 1929. 'A rough diamond with
a generous heart' (*Examiner Annual*, 1930).

   Richard Kneen, 1880–1959. MHK for Rushen 1929–50, MLC 1950–4. Baker, then
fisherman at Port St Mary. Workers' Union secretary, Rushen, 1917 on. Manx Labour
Party Executive 1918. Port St Mary Commissioner. Lifeboat coxswain. Methodist lay
preacher and Sunday School superintendent. President of Manx Labour Party 1929–30.

   John Kelly, MHK, North Douglas 1929–34, 1943–6. Wesleyan local preacher from
*c.*1900. Renowned orator. Douglas Workers' Union committee 1918 and negotiator
1921. Appointed to various government committees in 1920s. TGWU strike committee
1935. Treasurer, Manx Labour Party 1946.

for industrial relations, but with the 1918 strike and its outcome very much in the minds of employers and unionists, the threat of a repetition was always latent and sometimes explicit. In February 1919 the Government Secretary asked the Chief Constable to provide a list of 'dangerous persons on the Island' and the new Governor, Fry, asked the police in June to provide him with weekly intelligence reports from all the main police stations on a variety of topics, including 'labour troubles'.[73] The Laxey miners, now enrolled in the Workers' Union, were a case in point. In June 1919 they struck against their wages being reduced by the employer's refusal to continue the wartime bonus and stayed out, supported by union strike pay, until late November when they won their claim. The mines, however, were barely economically viable and closed in May 1920, throwing 120 people out of work. They reopened under new ownership in 1922 and limped along for several years, providing work for about eighty men before they closed for good in 1929.[74]

More central to the Island's economy was the building trade, to which the wage levels of general labourers were closely related. An arbitration award in January 1919 met the workers' demands, but early in 1920 there was a further dispute, a general strike was threatened and in the autumn all the Douglas building trade workers – including joiners, bricklayers, plasterers, painters and plumbers – struck for 12 weeks from October 1920 to January 1921. They returned to work on terms which went some way towards their claim, but, according to Teare, were not consistently sustained thereafter.[75]

Labour unrest reached its height in 1919–20 with inflated prices fuelling demands for wage increases. Gas, harbour and highway workers were all involved in disputes, and a teachers' strike was narrowly averted in the autumn of 1920. From 1921 on, the Workers' Union succeeded in establishing the principle that annual wage agreements should incorporate a cost of living element according to a comparison with 1914.[76] Disputes also involved the older unions –

73] CCD, 21 Feb 1919; MNHL: Government Office Papers, 9310, Police Intelligence Reports, June 1919–Dec 1920.
74] *Examiner Annual*, 1920, 1923 (lists of events of previous year); Teare, *Reminiscences*, 11; CCD, 30 June, 31 July, 1, 11, 25 Aug, 3, 11 Sept, 25 Nov 1919, 19 Jan, 31 May 1920, 26 June, 21, 22 Nov 1922; Police Intelligence Reports, 28 June, 12 July, 9, 23 Nov 1919, 22 Feb, 14 Mar, 1, 22, 30 May 1920.
75] *Examiner Annuals*, 1920–2; Teare, *Reminiscences*, 48–9; CCD, 31 Jan, 2, 3, 7, 12, 14 Feb 1920; Police Intelligence Reports, 1920, *passim*.
76] See CCD and Police Intelligence Reports 1919–20; *Examiner Annual*, 1922; Teare, *Reminiscences*, 56–7. For shop assistants' unionism see also Teare, 7-9; *The Shop Assistant*, 4 July 1925, 552–5, photocopy in MNHL.

printers, shop assistants, sailors, tailors. On the whole, led by the Workers' Union, the unions were remarkably successful in raising traditionally low Manx wages to the English level, keeping up with postwar inflation and then sustaining their gains against employers' attempts to reduce wages in a worsening economic climate.

Food prices remained a pressing issue, especially in 1920, when the Manx Labour Party denounced all increases, and a mass meeting of five hundred Workers' Union members in Douglas market place supported a proposal to set up a new co-operative society and buy the redundant bakers' ovens from the Knockaloe internment camp, now being dismantled: thus the Manx Co-operative Society was begun, as a union initiative.[77] In 1922 the union initiated a further scheme, buying farm produce and vegetables direct from farmers and selling them to customers at a low price, undercutting shopkeepers' profiteering. Soap was also sold cheaply by the union in 1920.[78]

Unemployment loomed large every winter. Every year from October 1920 onwards, there were mass meetings of unemployed ex-servicemen, deputations and demonstrations for more generous poor relief and more extensive publicly funded winter work schemes. In a hard winter local Poor Law Boards of Guardians sometimes exhausted their funds and had no more to give. Eventually, after much Labour pressure and Teare's participation in a commission of inquiry, in 1928 Governor Hill announced that the Manx government would assume responsibility for 75 per cent of the wages on unemployed work schemes and 50 per cent of the dole payments for those who remained without work, according to uniform scales of relief, which was a great improvement on the hitherto patchy and inadequate provision of the local authorities.[79]

Housing was also vital. When Tynwald moved in 1924 to end the wartime Rent Restrictions Act, huge protest meetings were held at the Villa Marina. Gerald Bridson and Walter Craine even went to England to lobby Arthur Henderson, Home Secretary in the new Labour government, and a general strike was threatened. The courts backed off, delaying repossession orders on tenants. A union member sent to prison was rapidly released and found new accommodation in public housing. In 1925 a new Rent Restrictions Act was passed and rent controls remained in force until the 1950s, a notable victory for popular

77] In addition to sources cited above, *WU Record*, Apr–July 1920.
78] *WU Record*, Sept 1922.
79] *Examiner Annuals*; Teare, *Reminiscences*, 46–7; CCD, to 31 May 1924. Unfortunately the diaries are missing between this date and 8 July 1930.

pressure and direct action by the labour movement.[80] Labour councillors on local authorities also played an important part in pressing for public housing schemes, like the Pulrose estate outside Douglas.[81]

The various campaigns and activities of the 1920s produced a vigorous, enthusiastic labour movement subculture in the Island. The 1919 election in Rushen, for example, involved concerts and teas, leading to a 'Labour Party Annual Eisteddfod' in the south of the Island, meetings in barns where 'the seats were bundles of straw and light provided by hurricane lamps and cups of tea for all', and lively discussions in workshops and sheds even at a remote location such as Cregneish.[82] Annual hiring fairs for farm labourers were another venue for socialist entertainment and propaganda.[83] In Douglas the Salisbury Hall in Fort Street, the market place and, for really big events, the Villa Marina, were familiar meeting places. In Peel and also in Ramsey large meetings were held. Recruiting was assisted by 'an excellent concert party', including a family of 'expert performers on their concertinas' who provided free entertainment to lure people to meetings, and by 1925/6 there was a Workers' Union choir and troupe of entertainers which raised money, by performing at Christmas carol concerts and socials, for charabanc trips into the countryside, which, like the Clarion vans, combined enjoyment with rural socialist mission work.[84] Meetings usually confined themselves to Manx political issues, though in August 1920 in Peel William Clucas announced that he supported a revolution and a general strike in the UK on the issue of miners' pay and the meeting resolved, as recommended by the *Daily Herald*, to support peace with Russia.[85] However, when Wilfred Chandler, 'a communist from Liverpool' according to the police, spoke in Peel market place in September 1923, 'there was so much opposition that the meeting had to close'.[86] Manx socialism might sometimes be militant, but remained more Methodist than Marxist.

By 1926 the most militant period was over. The Island was exempted from the British general strike, but felt the adverse effects of the dispute, especially through the effect on coal supplies of the seven-

---

80] *Examiner Annuals*; Teare, *Reminiscences*, 54; CCD, 1924; *WU Record*, Jan 1925.
81] *WU Record*, Apr 1927.
82] McFee, Notes on Rushen Labour Party, MNHL: MD/5081/4.
83] Teare, *Reminiscences*, 32–3; *WU Record*, Dec 1921.
84] Teare, *Reminiscences*, 41–2; *WU Record*, Apr 1926, Jan 1927.
85] Police Intelligence Report, 22 Aug 1920.
86] CCD, 1 Sept 1923.

month miners' strike until December. This probably modified attitudes to industrial action and contributed to the popularity of large meetings deploring the general strike, addressed by the Archbishop of York in June and by Havelock Wilson, seamen's leader, on behalf of his 'Industrial Peace Union' in November.[87] Certainly, not all unionists were militant: John Holden, the Manx seamen's branch secretary, had quiet chats with the Island's police chief, and Alf Teare himself, an astute negotiator, always regarded strikes as a weapon of last resort.[88]

A significant turning-point was reached in 1929 when the Workers' Union, the focus of labour activity since 1917, was absorbed into the much larger, more centralised and bureaucratic, Transport and General Workers' Union. The historian of the Workers' Union is in no doubt that the Isle of Man was one of its success stories. By 1920 the union had between three and four thousand members in the Island. Then, as the union as a whole went into decline during the 1920s, in the Lancashire region 'the best record of any district was achieved in the Isle of Man, where membership was still 2000 in 1929'.[89] Nowhere in Britain did the union's original ideal of 'One Big Union' for all kinds of workers come closer to fulfilment than in the Isle of Man in the 1920s.

Through Depression and War, 1930–45
In the Isle of Man the labour movement was now an established part of the social and political scene. In the 1930s, Labour everywhere was thrown on to the defensive by the world slump. The Manx Labour Party in general held its own, though with some loss of representation, largely reflecting the strength of personal allegiances in Manx politics. When Christopher Shimmin and William Clucas both died in 1933, Shimmin was replaced as MHK for Peel by his widow Marion, twice elected unopposed and the first woman in the Keys, but Clucas's seat, held in a rural area owing to his personal popularity and persistence, was not contested by Labour. In the general election of 1934, with John Kelly losing his toehold in North Douglas, Labour held five seats, breaking no new ground and electing no new MHKs.[90]

87] *Examiner*, 7 May, 19 Nov 1926; *Examiner Annual*, 1927; *WU Record*, Jan 1927.
88] CCD, 3, 12 Feb, 8 Oct 1920, 9 Apr 1921, 10 May 1924; Teare, *Reminiscences*, 48–50. For the Seamen's Union see also Isle of Man NUS Branch Minute Book, 1927–49, Warwick University Modern Records Centre, Mss. 175, 1992 supplement.
89] Hyman, *Workers' Union*, 151.
90] Marion Shimmin, 1878–1942. Born Manchester, schoolteacher, LRAM. President, Peel branch, Women's Temperance Society, 1919–31, MHK for Peel 1933–42, and from 1934 a Peel Licensing Magistrate. Manx Museum Trustee and member of Council of Education.

Labour's MHKs were especially concerned about unemployment. The 1931 census showed 10 per cent male unemployment in the Island; in November 1932 there were over two thousand registered unemployed men in Douglas, under 40 per cent of whom found work in the government schemes.[91] Labour members made an important contribution to social welfare issues, but, in the context of a parliament otherwise composed entirely of independent members, with no 'Government' and 'Opposition', found it difficult to operate as a cohesive group and rarely spoke with a united voice. In May 1930, for example, three days after founding a new formal Parliamentary Labour group 'in an effort to secure unanimity of working', they split their votes four to three on the desirability of a new electricity scheme for the Island.[92] Despite pressure from their party outside Tynwald, notably in 1933, the culture of 'independence' in the Keys was dominant and Labour members made their contribution to Manx politics very largely as individuals, as, for example, when Walter Craine successfully piloted through Tynwald, in 1938, the Manx Divorce Act.

Outside Parliament the Labour Party continued at its annual conferences to put forward a series of proposals for improved social welfare and the redistribution of wealth, in 1930 demanding death duties and pensions of £1 a week for all at the age of 65, in 1931 a 44-hour maximum working week.[93] The presidential speech of Cecil McFee in 1936 waxed eloquent on 'the age of potential abundance', prophesying a golden future for humanity when capitalism was overthrown and replaced by socialism, when it would be impossible for a ruling class to exist. McFee's rhetoric was consistent with the pristine optimism of the Manx Socialist Society in the 1890s.[94]

Everyday perspectives for trade unionists were more limited and practical. A regular pattern of annual wage negotiations between the Employers' Federation and the Transport and General Workers' Union was now the main feature of industrial relations. The large exception to this 'normalization' was the general strike of 1935.[95] This was the result of a breakdown in negotiations over the TGWU's initial claim for 48s

---

91] *Examiner Annual*, 1932 and 1933.
92] *Examiner Annual*, 1931.
93] *Examiner Annual*, 1931 and 1932.
94] Attached as an appendix to McFee, Notes on Rushen Labour Party.
95] *Examiner*, Mar–May 1935 *passim*, 7 June 1935; Teare, *Reminiscences*, 49–50; Isle of Man Employers' Federation (IOMEF) minutes, 1935, MNHL: 9192; *Examiner Annual*, 1936.

for a 48-hour week for general labourers throughout the Island, involving a rise of 8s for workers in Douglas and 10s in the rest of the Island. The Federation refused to negotiate, but were outflanked by Douglas Town Council Finance Committee, chaired by Walter Craine. In May Harry Pugh, Liverpool district organiser of the TGWU, assumed leadership of the union side. The union came down to 46s and the employers offered 42s, but the gap was not bridged and a general strike of Douglas workers on 3–4 June was the result. As in 1918, trade and business were paralysed; electricity and gas were cut off; factories, workshops, newspapers, public transport, shops, pubs and cinemas were closed down, as three thousand men came out on strike. Hastily convened negotiations, chaired by the Government Secretary, resulted in an agreement of 46s for 48 hours. Large-scale direct action, this time over wages, not the price of bread, had again won a substantial victory.

This time, only the TGWU went on strike, but so widespread was its membership that the practical effects were much the same as in 1918. The dispute seems to have been rooted, essentially, in a determination to improve workers' standard of living, in line with rising expectations. As an unsympathetic Douglas councillor noted, 'pictures and wireless were mentioned as apparently now being considered necessaries'.[96] A union negotiator two years later said: 'There is today a keen desire to get more out of life than they have had before. They want wireless in their houses and are not satisfied to live in two rooms.'[97] Other factors were also influential. Alf Teare, now a 55-year-old MHK and magistrate, still district secretary of the TGWU, was a reluctant strike leader on this occasion, resigned his post in July and later claimed the same outcome could have been achieved by arbitration; he also maintained that, whereas the Isle of Man unionists had enjoyed considerable freedom of action within the Manchester-based Workers' Union regional structure, that was not so within the Liverpool-based docks-oriented TGWU district.[98] In other words 'Liverpool militancy' was to blame. It also seems likely that the imminence of the TGWU biennial conference, held in Douglas in July, may have had something to do with the Liverpool office's pressure for strike action, which was backed by Ernest Bevin and the National Executive.[99]

96] IOMEF minutes of meeting at Douglas Town Hall, 18 Mar 1935.
97] IOMEF minutes of meeting with TGWU, 7 May 1937.
98] Teare, *Reminiscences*, 50.
99] Alan Bullock, *Ernest Bevin, Vol. I 1881–1940* (London, 1960), has nothing to say on this. The TGWU archives at Warwick University Modern Records Centre may contain relevant material which I have not succeeded in locating.

The outcome, in any event, was that a second general strike, called by the Island's leading union, had succeeded in its aims, and, like its predecessor in 1918, would long loom large in popular memory and expectation of workers, employers and government. 'Anti-strike' legislation, brought into effect early in 1936, set up conciliation machinery, penalised intimidation and conferred on the Governor emergency powers to meet any future threat to essential public services. This legislation, however, does not seem to have hampered trade union activity significantly. Employers' previous intransigence was moderated and in 1937 the Federation agreed to the union's demand for 50s for a 48-hour week.

Vigorous negotiations, with further wage rises to meet the increased cost of living, continued during the war years 1939–45. Building workers were especially in demand for the construction of military aerodromes, where English wages were paid by English contractors, with a significant 'knock-on' effect on Manx wage levels. Joint Industrial Councils for general labourers and building workers, agreed in principle before the war, were at last set up in 1943 and by the end of the war wages for both groups were around £4 per week. Occasional brief unofficial strikes did not seriously dent the mood of wartime unity, in which Labour politicians sometimes assumed unfamiliar roles; for example, Alf Teare in 1939 became an employers' representative from Douglas Council and J.R. Corrin, who had a small joiner's business in Port Erin and had been a pacifist until 1940, became chairman of the Employers' Federation 1941–5. The hardships of 1914–18 were avoided and a War Conditions Committee of Tynwald, on which Teare served, closely monitored social conditions. As in Britain, Labour was well represented in government: the Governor's War Cabinet included Corrin, Craine and Teare. Labour polled well in eight by-elections for the Keys in 1942 and 1943, losing Peel on Marion Shimmin's death in 1942, but John Kelly regained his North Douglas seat and Gerald Bridson returned as an 'Independent Labour' MHK for Garff.

In 1945, especially after the huge Labour victory in Britain, hopes were high of a Labour majority in the forthcoming general election, the first since 1934.[100]

The Labour Movement since 1945

The British general election swept Labour to power in July 1945, but the Manx general election was not held until May 1946. Labour fielded

100] IOMEF minutes, 1939–45; *Examiner Annuals*, 1940–6.

eighteen candidates, but the result was a disaster: only two were elected, the veterans Alf Teare in South Douglas and Richard Kneen in Rushen. The Manx People's Political Association, a new anti-socialist party backed by the Employers' Federation, won four seats in Douglas and retained three of them at the next election in 1951. Much was made by Labour's opponents of their programme of nationalisation, not that this was new. Wartime radicalism had receded; in fighting on such a broad front, Labour over-stretched its resources; and the electorate, wary of the Labour government in Britain, took fright at the possibility of a Labour majority in the Keys.[101]

The outcome, however, did not entail a period of true blue reaction. The Manx government, as usually since 1919, was at pains not to diverge too far from British practice. In 1948 a new National Insurance Act covered industrial injuries; a National Health Service Act, closely following the British model, was passed; and a new Education Act was followed by the opening of Castle Rushen comprehensive school, by the British Home Secretary, Chuter Ede, in May 1949. In 1951 the National Assistance Act at last abolished the local poor law boards and set up a Board of Social Services to cover all aspects of social security. Dockers and bus drivers were strike-prone, but in June 1949 the threat of another all-out strike by the TGWU was narrowly averted and the union's claim was settled by negotiation. Workers' pay and conditions steadily improved, in line with British advances, and Labour's strength in the Keys rose to four through by-elections.[102]

In the Keys election of 1951 Labour won six seats, in addition to its three members of the Legislative Council, Corrin, Kneen and Teare. The year 1956 saw five victories, and in the delayed election of January/February 1962 Labour was back up to seven MHKs, equal to its best previous result in 1929. The 1950s were hard years in the Island, which may explain the revival in Labour's fortunes: from 1951 on winter unemployment, work schemes, demonstrations and migration of labour to Britain in search of work characterised a decade of declining population and economic difficulty, in contrast to the new affluence of 1950s Britain.

The revival of Labour enthusiasm can be seen in the Manx Labour Party's policy pamphlet of 1960 and its publication *Manx Labour Party Review* which ran to over twenty issues, published irregularly from

101] *Examiner*, 27 Sept 1946; *Manx Labour Party News and Views*, 1–4 (Feb–May 1946); IOMEF minutes, 24 Nov 1945, 25 Apr 1946, and Northern Branch minutes, 28 Dec 1945.
102] *Examiner Annuals*, 1949–52; IOMEF minutes, 1947–50.

1960 to 1965.[103] Trade unionism also flourished. The Douglas Trades
Council had faded out during the 1930s, but in 1951 the TGWU district
secretary, Thomas Moughtin, took the lead in founding a new Isle of
Man Trades Council. In 1953, affiliating the Council to the TUC,
Moughtin said that it included twelve unions, had 35 delegates of
whom 24 usually attended and approximately four thousand affiliated
members, including three thousand from the TGWU.[104] The Trades
Council's minute book from 1962 to 1974 reveals a record of diligent
activity during the secretaryship of Arthur Quinney, TGWU full-time
official and later an MHK, carefully monitoring, discussing and making
representations on industrial and welfare issues. Sometimes the Council
took a cautious or conservative line, for example opposing the
government taking over the Isle of Man Railway, which might be a
burden on taxpayers, in 1966, and refusing to accept the Claimants'
Union into membership in 1971.[105]

The strike which made the greatest postwar impact was a dispute of
non-Manx origin, the 1966 British seamen's strike, which for seven
weeks at the beginning of the holiday season halted all ships to and
from the Island. The loyalties of the Trades Council were divided
between union solidarity, leading them to affirm that no Manx trade
unionists should act as blacklegs, and concern for the impact of the
strike on the Manx economy: two weeks into the strike, at the request
of the Manx government, they approached the TUC in a vain attempt
to ensure the Island's exclusion from the strike.[106]

The seamen's action may have contributed to a downturn in
Labour's fortunes. It came close on the heels of the election with a large
majority of a British Labour government, which annoyed many Manx
people by towing away the 'pirate' ship, Radio Caroline, which had
based itself off the Manx coast near Ramsey. Longer-term trends,
notably the beginnings of a Manx economic upturn, were also
influential. The Manx Labour Party by the 1960s was also, perhaps,

103] *Manx Labour Policy* (nd, *c*.1960); *Manx Labour Party Review*, incomplete run,
Dec 1960 to Apr 1965 in MNHL.

104] TUC Isle of Man Trades Council file 1953–60, Warwick University Modern
Records Centre, Mss. 292/79I/8: 1953 annual return, 1952–3 statement of accounts.
There is also a second file, Mss. 292/9428/2, most of which concerns unemployment in
1954 and a threatened Emergency Powers Bill.

105] Isle of Man Trades Council minutes, 1962–74, MNHL: MD15139. This file
appears to be the sole survivor of a regrettable holocaust of archives which occurred
when the Isle of Man TGWU moved to new offices *c*.1982.

106] Isle of Man Trades Council minutes, 1966; *Report of the Strike Emergency
Committee* (of the Island government) (Douglas, 1966), MNHL: D102.

in some respects a rather traditional institution, set in its ways. The founding fathers of the party, many of them very long-lived and tenacious politicians who had given a lifetime of public service, were dying or ceasing to be active, but even some of their successors, like Cecil McFee, a prominent figure in Tynwald in the 1950s and 1960s, were old enough to remember the 1919 election and steeped in Manx Labour tradition.[107] Younger recruits to Labour politics with similar idealism, determination and durability were hard to find, though a few such emerged. The party maintained its emphasis on social welfare, but was less at ease with the new single-issue politics of the 1960s and 1970s and was cautious in its approach to controversial human rights issues. Between 1969 and 1977 three women, two of them Labour Party members, campaigned successfully to end birching, but without official Manx Labour Party support.[108] Similarly, in 1988 the party conference voted down a motion supporting liberalisation of the law on homosexuality.[109] From the 1960s on, the revival of Manx nationalism offered an alternative politics which attracted some radically minded young people. Whatever the reasons, the Manx Labour Party since the 1960s has operated on a more restricted basis than previously. In no election since 1962 has Labour won more than two or three seats. With the exception of Eddie Lowey's victories in Rushen from 1975 to 1981, Labour representation in the Keys has been confined to the Douglas–Onchan conurbation.

During the 1980s and 1990s the Labour Party has been less closely associated with the TGWU than previously. The union, and the Trades Council, have been involved in controversy. Following a relatively low-key 'non-political' moderate TGWU leadership from 1978 to 1986, the appointment of Bernard Moffatt in 1986 signalled the adoption of a more militant high-profile strategy and coincided with a series of bitter disputes in the 1980s, some of which may be seen as a response to the impact of 'Thatcherism' and reflecting deeply felt

107] Cecil C. McFee, 1905–92. Plumber, latterly with own business advertised as 'the Island's largest plumbing and heating contractors'. MHK, Rushen 1951–62, MLC 1962–70. Chairman of Local Government Board 1962–6, Health Services Board 1966–70. Methodist local preacher; musician and composer of hymn tunes; author of various unpublished manuscripts in MNHL.

108] Millicent Faragher, 1916–87. President, Manx Labour Party, 1958–9, and secretary, Isle of Man Fabian Society; Angela Kneale, 1926–97. Belgian anti-Nazi resister, Quaker, MLP member; Valerie Roach, b 1942, journalist.

109] *Manx Independent*, 18 Oct 1991. Thanks to Alistair Ramsay for supplying me with a copy of his review of Manx politics 1986–91, in *Manx Independent* 11 Oct–8 Nov 1991.

grievances about social injustice, inequality and unacceptable demands by employers. These problems surfaced among plumbers, electricians, gas workers, brewery workers, printers and journalists. In 1987 the TGWU organised a general workers' 'day of action' in July and an all-out one-day strike, with secondary picketing, over a victimisation issue in the Palace Group, in December: the picketing was ended by a High Court decision enforced by the police. At the same time the Steam Packet Company imposed new contracts with shorter holidays on its crews and demanded redundancies to reduce alleged overstaffing, thus provoking a strike which spread to include all British passenger ferries. A deal was brokered by ACAS (Advisory Conciliation and Arbitration Service) in February and, in the opinion of the historians of the Seamen's Union, 'the Isle of Man members did not emerge without some advantage ... The strike may well have compelled the company to settle on terms more favourable to the union than it originally intended.'[110]

The rights and wrongs of the Manx 'winter of discontent' of 1987/8 remain hotly disputed, as does the extent of social division and inequality in the prosperous Island of the 1990s, cushioned by the success of the finance sector and enjoying virtual full employment. TGWU publications, like *The Betrayal of the Manx Working Class* (1990) have emphasised the persistence of low pay, poverty, poor housing and exploitation. In December 1989, almost twenty-five years after the UK, the Keys accepted the principle of redundancy payments. In December 1988 a new Emergency Powers Act was passed and in February 1991 a Trade Union Act and Employment Act, which provided a new legal framework for trade unionism on the Island.[111]

Whatever view is taken of trade union strategies, it is undeniable that the TGWU, still very much the dominant union, shows no sign of diminishing in strength, rather the reverse, since, contrary to the general trend in Britain, membership increased from about 1,500 members in 1979 to about 2,500 in 1996.[112] The Manx Labour Party is the only political party to have survived as a permanent presence in Manx politics, with elected members in the Keys ever since 1919. Union

---

110] *Manx Independent*, 18 Oct 1991; *Manx Worker*, newsletter of Isle of Man District TGWU, published irregularly July 1986 to early 1988; Arthur Marsh and Victoria Ryan, *The Seamen: A History of the National Union of Seamen, 1887–1987* (Oxford, 1989), 231–2.

111] *Manx Independent*, 25 Oct–8 Nov 1991.

112] Thanks to Bernard Moffatt for an interview at his office in Douglas, 26 March 1997, during which he showed me printed membership figures.

and party in their different ways remain committed to the cause of the poorest members of society, at the turn of the century.

Some Characteristics of the Manx Labour Movement

Manx labour history has distinctive features: its major landmarks and lines of development, as the preceding narrative has shown, differ from developments in Britain: for example no Chartism; no general strike in 1926 but instead in 1918 and 1935; no great Labour victory in 1945. Nevertheless, this history is not the story of 'socialism in one island' and cannot be divorced from developments in Britain. For example, the London-based National Association of United Trades in 1847, Robert Blatchford's Manchester-based *Clarion* in the 1890s, the British Labour Party constitution of 1918 and the Liverpool office of the TGWU in 1935 were all major influences. Manx socialism and trade unionism were also part of a general Western European phenomenon.[113]

Manx trade unions discovered in the 1890s, if not before, that, in order to ensure strike pay, union benefits and protection from British blacklegs, it was to their advantage to become branches of British unions, rather than remain autonomous small groups. In practice one British union, the Workers' Union from 1917 to 1929 and the Transport and General Workers' Union since then, has dominated the world of organised labour on the Island. In a largely rural environment, devoid of large towns and heavy industry (with the exception of lead mining until the 1920s), trade unionism, strongest in Douglas, has some notable achievements to its credit and has been able to make its influence felt within the confines of a small island more strongly than in most rural or small-town areas in Britain. At key moments organised labour has achieved a decisive, briefly hegemonic, position, asserting its power most crucially in 1918 to undermine the old order and usher in a period of wide-reaching social and political change. Unions since 1918 have succeeded in achieving, then maintaining, wages and conditions for their members broadly equivalent to those obtaining in Britain.

To assess the achievement of the political wing of the labour movement may appear more problematic. From the 1890s on the Manx Socialist Society, Clarion Fellowship and ILP branch made socialist propaganda for twenty years, making converts but achieving only a toehold in Manx politics. The Manx Labour Party which succeeded them has remained an autonomous Manx institution, maintaining friendly contact with its British counterpart. A modern study of Manx

---

113] See Donald Sassoon, *One Hundred Years of Socialism: The West European Left in the Twentieth Century* (London, 1997).

politics has described the MLP as 'a relatively minor political force'.[114] Certainly it has never come near to winning a majority in the Keys, but through its representatives in Tynwald it has remained a persistent influence, especially on questions of social welfare. Within the Manx political system, characterised by horse-trading and a state of 'permanent coalition', Labour members holding socialist views have served as ministers and chairmen of boards as a matter of normal practice, some of them, like Teare and Corrin, among the most respected and influential of Manx politicians.[115] It is unlikely that, without the Labour presence in Manx politics for the past eighty years, the Manx welfare state would today be, as it is, more generous in some areas of social provision than its British counterpart. Between 1918 and 1997 British Labour has held or shared in power for only twenty-five years; Manx Labour has never won power, but has had constant influence.

The rapid transition of Manx labour leaders from protest to respectability has sometimes been remarked. When J.D. Fell became President of the Douglas Trades Council in about 1900, he was also 'by virtue of his office ... a member of the Chamber of Commerce'.[116] After the 1918 general strike, when Alf Teare was seen by many as 'the most powerful figure in the Isle of Man', an attempt to victimise him failed, and instead, even before he had been elected to the Keys, he was appointed as the Island's first working-class magistrate.[117] J.R. Corrin, socialist and recent pacifist, was chairman of the Employers' Federation and a member of the War Cabinet during the Second World War. Class conflict has been softened by conciliation, co-option, compromise in a small island community. At most times this has been the way in which Manx political and social life has worked.[118]

114] D.G. Kermode, *Devolution at Work* (Farnborough, 1979), 87.
115] Thanks to Eddie Lowey MLC for an interview at Ballasalla, 7 Dec 1997, which added to my understanding of Manx Labour politics.
116] *Examiner Annual*, 1904, 77.
117] Teare, *Reminiscences*, 25; *Examiner Annual*, 1920, 33.
118] After the completion of this chapter a small collection of Workers' Union/TGWU material was deposited in the Manx National Heritage Library in April 1998, including the Peel Workers' Union secretary's letter book 1922–3, and the Peel Workers' Union/ TGWU minute book 1921–35. Unfortunately it was not possible to incorporate this material in this chapter.

Cultural History

Introduction

JOHN BELCHEM

This chapter of the *New History*, co-ordinated with considerable skill and diligence by Fenella Bazin and Martin Faragher,[1] not only addresses the gamut of cultural behaviour on the Island but also stresses the interactive flow between various forms of cultural expression – cosmopolitan, popular, indigenous and ethnic. Taken together, the individual expert contributions add much to our understanding of the complex cultural and social history of the Island, as embodied not only in art and learning but also in attitudes, beliefs, associations and ordinary behaviour – the ways of being, speaking, thinking and acting that guide and shape life. In accordance with the major theme of the volume, particular attention is accorded to the representational: forms of consciousness, images, myths and conceptual schemes – the cultural idioms through which Manxness was constructed, expressed and contested. As this chapter attests, there were bewildering cultural choices and trajectories for the Manx, particularly when confronted with the tourist influx at its height. Without abandoning 'high' and polite cosmopolitan norms, the gentlemanly antiquarians of the 'Manx renaissance' of the late nineteenth and early twentieth centuries girded themselves against cultural anglicisation through assertion of ethnic Celticism, a project which tended to downgrade Norse contributions to the Island's past. Others retreated into an indigenous culture of frugality and abstinence, the Manx 'way of life' sustained through Methodist fellowship and rural self-sufficiency. Some, however, openly joined the visitors from 'across' in common enjoyment of the latest delights of commercial popular culture.

1] We would like to express our thanks to Vivien Allen and others who attended seminars and submitted papers in the planning stages of this chapter.

The Manx Language

R.L. THOMSON

The major period of literary activity in Manx took place during the second half of the eighteenth century and thus belongs to Volume 4 of the *New History*. This may be regarded as the 'classical' period of the language, and is also the period in which the first descriptions of it in grammar and lexicography were written, though the first published dictionary appeared in 1835.[2]

Already under threat from the pressure of English, the language was still widely spoken in the first half of the nineteenth century, appearing in newspaper advertisements and articles, in use in the courts[3] and in the churches (there were editions of the Book of Common Prayer in 1840 and 1842, and a collection of hymns in 1830 and 1846). Publication tailed off and nothing of great importance appeared; church services in Manx Gaelic became fewer, down to once a month or even once a quarter by 1875 (and an increasing proportion of the Anglican clergy come from off the Island). Although 1848 there were some sixty Wesleyan Methodist local preachers who preached only in Manx,[4] it seems that Cregeen's expectation in the preface to his dictionary dated 1834, that the book would be 'an important acquisition' to 'the students of Divinity and the students of Law' for whom the language was 'so essentially necessary within the precincts of Mona', was not to be fulfilled, true as it may have been earlier in his own lifetime.[5] His dictionary was the only one to be published as a commercial venture (apart from the abortive attempt of Kelly's *Triglott*, which in any case was aimed at a different public); Kelly's own Manx dictionary appeared only in edited form in the series of *The Manx Society for Publication of National Documents*, vol. XIII in 1866, a series which, apart from the dictionary, Kelly's *Grammar*, the abridgment of *Paradise Lost* and some short pieces in its Miscellany volumes, contains nothing else in Manx until the very end (see below). Cregeen's 'Introduction' defended his enterprise: 'Some will be disposed to deride the endeavour to restore vigour to a decaying

2] A. Cregeen, *A Dictionary of the Manks Language* (Douglas, 1835).

3] Although Manx Gaelic was still spoken by some witnesses in court, from 1819 fluency in Manx was not regarded as essential for appointment as Deemster.

4] J. Rooser, *History of Wesleyan Methodism in the Isle of Man* (Douglas and London, 1849).

5] Cregeen, *Dictionary*.

language ... But those will think otherwise who consider that there are thousands of natives of the Island that can at present receive no useful knowledge whatever, except through the medium of the Manks language.' But just as the translation of the Bible could hardly have been undertaken at any later date than it was, so Cregeen's *Dictionary* marked the end of the period when Manx speakers were in the majority.

Toward the end of the century, however, there was some revival of interest in the language, a recognition perhaps that its decline was nearly complete in the sense that it was no longer being passed on to the younger generation and would vanish with the death of their elders. The major work of this period is A.W. Moore's collection and publication in 1891 of some of the Manx carvals,[6] of which many manuscripts exist but which had never been printed, followed up by his other verse collection of 'ballads' in 1896.[7] Further work along similar lines was undertaken in the first half of the twentieth century by P.W. Caine and C. Paton for the carvals, and more recently by G. Broderick for traditional songs and secular verse from manuscript sources, published with notes in various periodicals.[8] The Manx Society also undertook the publication in 1893–4, again under Moore's editorship, of the manuscript of Bishop Phillips's early seventeenth-century translation of the Book of Common Prayer in parallel with the 1765 version, thus making available the text of the earliest substantial piece of Manx prose.[9]

With the second volume of this work was included Professor Sir John Rhys's *Outlines of the Phonology of Manx Gaelic*, based on visits to the Island between 1886 and 1893, recording in a phonetic alphabet of his own the pronunciation of Manx speakers in all parts of the Island, from conversation and from their reading aloud.[10] Rhys had a predecessor in Edward Lluyd, the 'father of Celtic philology', who

---

6] A.W. Moore, *Carvallyn Gailckagh* (Douglas, 1891). Carvals are religious songs that were popular in the Isle of Man from at least the eighteenth century (see under MUSIC).

7] A.W. Moore, *Manx Ballads and Music* (London, 1896).

8] C.I. Paton, 'Manx carvals and carval books with notes on some of the manuscripts' *Proceedings*, II, 4 (1926); P.W. Caine, 'Manx carols and their writers' *Proceedings*, II, 4 (1926), and 'Manx carvals and their writers' *Mannin* 2 (1913); G. Broderick, *Some Manx Traditional Songs* (Douglas, 1991). See also Broderick's series of papers on 'Manx traditional songs and song fragments' *Béaloideas: Journal of the Folklore of Ireland Society*, 48–50 (1980–2).

9] *Manx Society*, XXXII (1893).

10] *Manx Society*, XXXIII (1894).

travelled through the Celtic-speaking lands collecting material for his *Archaeologia Britannica* (1707). He collected material in Man also, probably by the agency of one of his assistants, and a few words from this collection appear in his book, again in a modified alphabet. Rhys in his preface expressed the hope that some phonetician with a Gaelic background would follow where he had led, but the next major worker in the field was the Norwegian comparatist and Celticist Carl Marstrander, at work on the Island in the 1920s, who left his notebooks to the Museum and also made wax cylinder recordings and contributed to the study of Manx place-names in the light of his knowledge of the language and as part of his national interest in the history of the Vikings and their settlements overseas. In the postwar period both the Irish Folklore Commission and the School of Scottish Studies (University of Edinburgh) have undertaken fieldwork and recording in the Island, and this is also the time at which local enthusiasts for the language were active in making recordings of the last generation of native speakers, a source upon which Dr Broderick has drawn, together with Marstrander's notes, for his work on Late Spoken Manx.[11] Professor K.H. Jackson also produced in 1955 an outline of Manx historical phonetics based on a trial run of the questionnaire devised for the Gaelic side of the Linguistic Survey of Scotland.[12]

An enduring product of the late-nineteenth-century revival of interest and concern for Manx was the foundation in 1899 of Yn Cheshaght Ghailckagh (The Manx Language Society). It would be too much to say that it succeeded in its declared primary aim of preserving Manx as the national language, or indeed in its attempt at the cultivation of a modern literature in Manx, but it has been successful in promoting the study and publication of existing Gaelic literature. It made a modest start on this part of its programme in its early days, and a notable product of its activity was Edmund Goodwin's *First Lessons in Manx*,[13] but it was not until the middle of the century, with the society set on a sounder financial footing and the development of facsimile reprints, that substantial progress was made. Out-of-print works were reissued, new or revised editions of texts or aids for learners were produced, thanks to a more active society and the existence of the newer grant-aiding bodies such as the Isle of Man Arts Council and the Manx Heritage Foundation. They were useful alike to the members of classes

---

11] G. Broderick, *Handbook of Late Spoken Manx* (3 vols, Tübingen, 1984–6).
12] K.H. Jackson, *Contributions to the Study of Manx Phonology* (Edinburgh, 1955).
13] This was jointly published in 1901 by the Manx Society and the Dublin-based Celtic Association.

and to the private student of the language, and members of the society were active in teaching both in freelance classes and in those under the adult education and evening classes supported by the Department of Education and in some cases by the University of Liverpool. The society now has a substantial list of publications, reproductions, new works and adaptations or translations to its credit, to keep the language before the public and facilitate its acquisition, or satisfy curiosity about it. In 1979, with financial assistance from Tynwald, a comprehensive new Manx Dictionary was published.[14] It claimed to provide 'a basis for the expansion of the language into everyday life and a possible language revival'; to this end it coined new words (eg *co-earrooder* for 'computer'). In the same year the *Bible Casherick yn Lught Thie*,[15] which had been out of print for some 160 years, was republished, and in the late 1990s the eighteenth-century reworking in Manx Gaelic of *Paradise Lost*[16] and a translation of a well-known detective novel became available.

In the 1901 census some 4,500 declared themselves to be Manx speakers (which could mean no more than a knowledge of a few phrases and expressions) but by 1921 this number was down to 900. By 1950 there were only ten known native speakers, and the last of them died in 1974 aged 97 (see preface to Fargher's *English–Manx Dictionary*). During this period some elderly informants stated to the Manx Museum's Folk-Life Survey that their bilingual parents had reserved Manx to themselves to discuss matters not for children's ears. At the 1991 census, in response to a question about knowledge of Manx, a total of 643 people claimed to be able to speak Manx, 343 to write it, and 479 to read it; this, of course, is based on self-assessment. When the figures are broken down into towns, villages and parishes, the extremely low figures for some of the more rural parishes – Bride, German, Jurby, Lezayre, Maughold and Santon – suggest that, in contrast to the situation at the beginning of our period, knowledge of and interest in the language is now an urban rather than a rural phenomenon.

The teaching of the language existed in a few schools as an extracurricular activity in the postwar period beside other signs of a revival of interest in Manx, but no official steps to provide for the language in the school system were made until the 1990s, when the

14] D.C. Fargher, *Fargher's English–Manx Dictionary* (Douglas, 1979).
15] *Bible Chasherick yn Lught Thie* (Onchan, 1979).
16] R.L. Thomson (ed), *Pargys Caillit: An Abridgement of John Milton's Paradise Lost by Thomas Christian with the Anonymous Translation of Thomas Parnell's The Hermit* (Douglas, Centre for Manx Studies, 1995).

appointments were made of a Manx language officer (supported for the first two years by the Manx Heritage Foundation) and two other peripatetic teachers, and parents who wished their children to be introduced to the language were invited to register the fact. The numbers were to some surprisingly large, but the provision for teaching fell far short of that for modern languages and the subject was largely confined to the primary schools, the pressure of the national curriculum making it difficult to find space for it among the secondary schools. The last year of the century saw the first course for the GCSE-equivalent examination in secondary schools. The desire to acquire some Manx Gaelic is not confined to those with native roots, and 'new residents' are numbered among its exponents at every level of accomplishment. In the late 1990s a Manx-speaking play-school was established, again supported by the Manx Heritage Foundation. These new developments have been the spur to the production by the teachers of materials in a contemporary form and suited to the needs of children to supplement the more traditional approach aimed at adult learners.

The local media have also played their part in the revival. Currently there is a weekly language-teaching article in a local newspaper, while Manx Radio provides a regular programme in Manx. Active manifestations of a growing use of the Manx language as a symbol of cultural identity are on the stationery of government departments, in the naming of new schools and in phrases used on local airlines and radio, while the old custom is maintained of announcing new legislation in Manx at the annual public Tynwald ceremony. However, the bilingual use on street and road names has occasionally misfired when the new English translation has been used in preference to the long-standing Manx name.

The Use of Englishes

JENNIFER KEWLEY DRASKAU

Although several young local families are currently being raised bilingually in Manx Gaelic and (Standard) English, the linguistic profile of the present population of the Isle of Man is exclusively English-speaking. Until well into the eighteenth century, however, Manx Gaelic was not only the vernacular but the general medium of communication: although the upper classes and some traders knew English, most of the Island's inhabitants spoke only Manx. Over two centuries there were successive bilingual and 'diglossic' stages, leading to a situation where monolingual English speakers used either Manx English or Standard English according to circumstance and context. For purposes of definition, 'Manx English' is that variety of English which is distinct from both Standard English and from other varieties, is encountered among native Manx people, usually resident in the Island, and which may reflect influences from Manx Gaelic in its word order, sound and vocabulary

The socio-economic pressures urging the acquisition of English, the language of power, authority and opportunity, are not far to seek: a command of English facilitated advancement, both social and professional, employment, travel and commerce. The absence of native rulers, meanwhile, and of any attendant aristocracy or scholarly caste to champion the cause of Manx Gaelic, hastened the advancement of English: already in 1611, Speed notes that the wealthy inhabitants of Man imitated the Lancashire gentry, whereas the common folk followed the Irish language and customs.[17] Notwithstanding, a century later Bishop Wilson (1698–1755) would remark that 'one third of the best of the natives' could not understand English, this perception spurring the urgent endeavour of translating the Bible into Manx Gaelic. However, by 1740, compulsory English teaching in schools was reputedly bringing Manx Gaelic into 'disuse'. By 1764, although most of the population still had little English, the impetus towards English intensified. Certainly more English was heard in towns than elsewhere, although no definite barrier existed. These townships were then, after all, little more than villages, one of whose principal official *raisons d'être* was to function as market centres for agricultural produce from the outlying districts, ensuring regular interaction between town and country dwellers. Neither was there any *Gaeltacht* proper – the northern parishes and the relatively isolated southern hamlet of Cregneash constituting the closest approximation thereto. However, there can be little doubt that considerable differences existed between the speech habits of rural and urban communities, a disparity which persists in many respects today. Just as it was in rural areas that Manx Gaelic lingered longest as a general medium of communication, outlying districts promise to furnish the most fruitful source for contemporary research into Manx English in the quest for survivals of varieties of English peculiar to the Island, especially those reflecting the syntactic and phonetic features of Manx Gaelic.

It is difficult to date unequivocally the onset of bilingualism in Man, or to ascertain precisely when bilingualism with a bias towards English

17] J. Speed, *Theatre of the Empire of Great Britain* (London, 1611).

led eventually to the abandonment of Manx Gaelic in the towns. At the dawn of the twentieth century three speech communities may be assumed to have coexisted: a rapidly declining minority of Manx speakers (8.51 per cent in 1901 as against 25 per cent in 1871); numerous bilinguals and/or speakers of a distinctive Manx English displaying strong Gaelic influences; and an ever-growing number of monoglot English immigrants. Whatever the term used, the language 'death', 'decay' or 'suicide' at that period should be recognised as an ideological choice on the part of speakers. Probably the Manx themselves, even while still in the majority in their homeland, demonstrated little hesitation in relinquishing their grasp on their native language, perceiving it to be unlikely to enhance power or status. Manx appeared to have a low market value, and was therefore not passed on to the next generation. A monograph manuscript in the Manx National Heritage Library dating from around 1878, noting this 'decay' of Manx Gaelic, predicts that within 60 years Manx Gaelic will cease to exist as a spoken language – being currently 'seldom or never used in churches, with the exception of two or three northerly parishes such as Jerby and Belaf [sic]'. It would be tempting to offer a parallel forecast for Manx English today.

Even the detractors of Manx English admit the variety's unique character. According to the folklorist Killip, writing in 1975:

> The Anglo-Manx dialect, a hybrid tongue made up of expressions and idioms translated straight out of the Gaelic mixed up with imported elements, is an entirely different kind of speech, and though by now characteristic of the people and entirely Manx in feeling it is still something that has been grafted on, not the original growth.[18]

For most speakers of non-standard dialects the standard variety forms a point of reference. When speaking to strangers they will shift their speech towards the standard. The term 'dialect of English' as used in this way cannot be applied to the most distinctive types of Manx English, since these are uniquely characterised in terms of a separate, non-English underlying system.

The founders of Yn Cheshaght Ghailckagh also took an interest in the English dialect of the Island, the fruit of which appeared in the *Vocabulary of the Anglo-Manx Dialect* in 1924,[19] but this was not a field

18] M. Killip, *The Folklore of the Isle of Man* (London, 1975), 58.
19] A.W. Moore, S. Morrison and E. Goodwin, *A Vocabulary of the Anglo-Manx Dialect* (London, 1924).

in which the society's interest was maintained, the recording of the last native speakers of Manx taking precedence as more urgent. The Island was however included in Professor H. Orton's *Survey of English Dialects*, in the first part, which covered the six northern counties of England and the Isle of Man, and two localities were chosen as representative.[20] Nothing further was attempted until the late 1990s, when the Manx Heritage Foundation, through the Centre for Manx Studies, set on foot a four-year project in this area, entailing the recording and analysis of a considerable body of Manx English material.

Dialect in Written Sources

In the early days of English in Man, Manx Gaelic having little surviving literary tradition, official reports and documents were written in either English or Latin. Schooling was generally carried out by the clergy – and by several licensed schoolmasters – and in English, with the aim of improving the religious knowledge and strengthening the moral fibre of the Manx peasantry. By the standards of the day these clergymen were relatively well-educated. Small wonder, then, that Alexander Ellis should remark that Manx English appeared closer to Standard English than the neighbouring dialects in Britain, or that his comments should ignore the influence of Manx Gaelic on Manx English.[21] It is only when sustained regular contact approaches a bilingual state that each language will influence the other in a systematic way by the exchange of lexical items, the creation of calques (exemplified below), the disintegration of morphophonological rules and the adaptation of linguistic structures. In the earlier stages of second language acquisition, where a lack of security in the new language inhibits language users' creativity and innovation, the merging of first and second languages occurs haphazardly and idiosyncratically rather than systematically. Regular recodification takes place, as with creoles, at a later stage (creoles develop when pidgins, simplified blends of two languages which develop for specific purposes such as trading, become the primary socialising language of the next generation of speakers).[22] It is systemisation at this level which produces a recognisable variety with its own characteristic features capable of being recorded, in the case of Manx English, in the 'vernacular' texts of T.E. Brown and others which

20] H. Orton (ed), *Survey of English Dialects: Vol i: The Six Northern Counties and the Isle of Man* (Leeds, 1962).
21] A. Ellis, 'Early English pronunciation', *Philological Society* (1889), 351–63.
22] D. Hymes (ed), *Pidginization and Creolization of Languages* (Cambridge, Mass, 1971).

constitute part of the Manx English corpus ('vernacular' here, of course, denoting Manx English rather than Manx Gaelic).

The vernacular was not the natural speech of authors such as Brown. Hence, although their vernacular compositions merit attention as indicative of the degree to which a linguistic variety has been systemised, codified and accepted, there is a caveat. Authors consciously exploiting vernaculars assume *faux-naif* literary *personae*; such works must always be regarded as constructs drawing upon an extensive, somewhat amorphous body of material assimilated from anonymous first-hand informants. These vernacular linguistic elements have undergone some measure of informal analysis and synthesis in the creative process. However, comparison with unscripted spontaneous utterances of Manx English speakers allows the linguist to check the authenticity of these authors' attempts at the vernacular.

Several scholars and enthusiastic amateur linguists, including Sophia Morrison, William Gill and John Clague, have recorded Manx Gaelic elements – words and phrases – formerly frequently encountered in Manx English. The currency and number of these idioms has declined sharply since the early part of the century, although some have proved tenacious: *traa dy liooar*, time enough – frequently misunderstood, as Killip points out, as a version of the Spanish *mañana*, implying shift-lessness rather than, more appropriately, unworldliness;[23] the *qualtagh*, greeter, or first foot; the *haggard*, stackyard or home paddock, and so on, remain current and understood.

Manx English idioms having the greatest linguistic interest reflect Gaelic patterns. What are called 'calque' compounds abound, for example: 'to take rest, to take ease' = to rest; 'take joy' = rejoice, be glad; 'to be on foot' = to be up and about. Distinctive prepositional idioms include: 'there's no money at me'; 'there's plenty of them in' (that is, in existence), 'come in on the door'. Predictably, for a Gaelic-influenced variety, the most distinctive syntactic phenomena are verbal or prepositional – among the salient linguistic features of Manx Gaelic, the Gaelic verbal noun and the pronoun-preposition paradigms must be accounted the most dominant. The verbal noun combines with an auxiliary (the verb 'to be' in present, 'to do' in past, although Manx Gaelic also possesses an alternative one-word past tense) to create the functional equivalent one-word tenses. Prepositions such as *er*, 'on', combine with personal pronouns to produce a paradigm *orrym*, 'on me'; *ort*, 'on thee', *urree*, 'on her', and so on. These features differ radically from the systems of most Englishes, but create in Manx English echoes

23] Killip, *Folklore*, 157.

GOLD?
Where? On Cushags!
CUSHAGS!
Where from?
PURT IERNE!
Where at?
THE GAIETY!

The "PURT IERNE CUSHAGS" Manx Dramatic Company will present the very funny Play "GOOL ON CUSHAGS" (J. J. Kneen) at the GAIETY THEATRE, on THURSDAY, 16th Dec., 1926. You had better book your Seat! Popular Prices!

Proceeds in aid of The Manx Society Publication Fund.

Printed at "Herald" Office, Douglas.

Gold on Cushags *Now largely neglected, the Manx dialect plays of the early part of the twentieth century were usually presented in village halls throughout the Island. This performance of* Gold on Cushags *by Manx scholar J.J. Kneen was one of a series given at the Gaiety Theatre to raise funds for the Manx Society which published important works like Kneen's own* Place-names of the Isle of Man *in 1925. (MNHL)*

which are typical of the Gaelic Englishes. Thus Manx English is characterised by a high incidence of complex verbal clusters, frequently comprising catenatives,[24] for example 'Do not be going tormenting the creature!', as well as aspectual, modal and tense-forming auxiliaries. The imperfective aspect expressed in Manx English by an -*ing* form, as in 'It's himself I'm wanting to spake to', reflects the underlying Gaelic construction comprising substantive verb and verbal noun. Passive notions in Manx English may be expressed with an active present participle rather than the past participle demanded by the Standard English passive construction, for example 'Of course the case will be going a-trying', that is will be tried (T.E. Brown, *Tommy Big Eyes*).

In more recent times, predictably, the influence of the media, the growth of the finance sector, the explosive increase of off-Island travel, for purposes of study, work and leisure, immigration, intermarriage with non-natives have all contributed to the diversification of the Manx Englishes and to the decline of the 'typical' intonational patterns and other characteristic phonetic features. Manx English, as Orton recognised, shares many of the characteristics of the dialects of northern English. Since the 1930s a new northern English influence, that of Liverpool, has been detected in the speech patterns of towns, Douglas especially. Typical accent features include the pronunciation of wh-words, for example 'white', 'wheel' (Manx Gaelic *queeyl*) with initial kw-, and words such as 'hard' being sounded more like 'haird'. Occasionally the intrusive 'b' is still heard in vowels such as 'Tom' (Tobm), and some speakers still use distinctive Manx English intonational patterns.

It is gratifying that Manx English has at last prompted the implementation of a major research project, complementing the revival of Manx Gaelic; it is a matter of some urgency, since, in many respects, because of fuzzy boundaries, the recording and analysis of a given variety of language may exceed in complexity that of investigating a recognisably distinct linguistic system. Manx English, not least by virtue of its 'hybrid' character, merits study as the manifestation of a unique taxonomy of the concepts and perceptual linguistic habits of a language community translated into and expressed through an alternative code. This renders research into Manx English potentially of considerable interest beyond the narrowly linguistic.

24] The term 'catenative' denotes verbs such as 'appear to', 'come to', 'fail to', as used in constructions like 'appeared to recognise', 'failed to recognise', etc. See R. Quirk, S. Greenbaum, G. Leech and J. Svartvik, *A Comprehensive Grammar of the English Language* (London and New York, 1985), section 3.49, 146–7.

Nineteenth-century Literature in English Relating to the Isle of Man

ULLA CORKILL

The Romantic movement gained momentum in Europe during the second part of the eighteenth century and coloured much of the artistic and literary trends during the nineteenth century. Its search for the original and the soulful led to a deepened interest in folklore and ancient poetry; James MacPherson's controversial but influential *Fingal, an Ancient Epic Poem, in Six Books*, published in 1762, purporting to be the translated work of the Celtic bard Ossian, made the Celtic world fashionable.

Well-read Manx people and the discerning visitor discovered to their delight that they were living in a treasure-house of folklore. The legends quoted by George Waldron in *A Description of the Isle of Man* (1731) were recounted and enlarged upon by the Scottish antiquarian Joseph Train (1779–1852) in his monumental *An Historical and Statistical Account of the Isle of Man*, published in 1845, and new myths or variations of old ones were tracked down and displayed in learned journals and popular magazines (see under FOLKLORE). No respectable guide book of the Isle of Man was complete without a chapter on folklore. Usually the stories were told unadorned, but it was inevitable that such fascinating material should lend itself to literary embellishment. Typical of this treatment are, for instance, the beautifully produced *The Phynodderree and Other Legends of the Isle of Man* (1882) by Edward Callow and the novelistic *Shadowland in Ellan Vannin; or Folk Tales of the Isle of Man*, published in 1890 by I.H. Leney (Mrs J.W. Russell). The folklore also provided useful padding in novels. This trend is particularly marked in Hugh Coleman Davidson's *The Green Hills by the Sea* (1887), and the wealth of folkloristic details contributed to the enthusiastic reception of Hall Caine's first Manx novel, *The Deemster* (see below).

The popularity of all things Celtic led to the smallest fragment being used. The most startling example is perhaps the 249-page poem *Blanid*, published in Boston, USA, in 1879 by Robert Joyce, about a Manx princess who meets a untimely death in an epic of love, jealousy and treachery. But better-known Manx legends inspired many poets. Some of these versified versions were sufficiently interesting to be included in *Mona Miscellany*, volumes XVI and XXI of *Manx Society* (1869 and 1873). The most famous is the dark and haunting *The Carrasdoo Men* by Esther Nelson (see below) (volume XVI). Also included in volume XVI are two colourful poems by William Kennish (see below), *Customs of Old May Eve* and *The Manx Oiele Verree*.

The volumes also contained English translations of the Manx ballads. The popular ones often appeared in more than one version (see MUSIC). The most famous translator was George Borrow (1803–81), whose fascination with the Celtic world led him to visit the Isle of Man in 1855.[25] Many accurate translations and additions were provided by John Quirk (1800–85), a self-contained Manxman of little education but considerable talent and a deep love of the old ballads. He was said to be the last of the genuine carval composers.[26] Particularly popular was Elizabeth Cookson's ballad version of *Cutlar MacCulloch* (volume XXI), which had first appeared in her *Legends from Manx Land* (1859).

Both Nelson's and Cookson's collections of poems reflected the period's interest in the ancient Isle of Man. In Cookson's 'Introduction' to her *Poems from Manxland*, published in 1868, she stated the Romantic movement's beliefs:

> What fossils are to the geologist, customs and creeds are to the historian. Popular tales, songs, and superstitions are not altogether profitless; like the fingers of a clock, they point to the time of day. Turns and modes of thought, that else had set in darkness, are by them preserved.

The tales by Esther Nelson (1810–43), were taken from her collected poems *Island Minstrelsy* (1839), which contains *The Rival Minstrels*, a cycle prefixed by a quote from Ossian. In the guise of Isadore she sings the praises of the Isle of Man, its beauty and its eventful past. Esther Nelson was held in high esteem by her contemporaries. Poems were dedicated to her by other poets, often under her pen-name *The Island Minstrel* or *Hadassah*, the Hebrew name given to her by G.H. Wood, a gentleman poet and scholar. Nelson died from tuberculosis, and death is never far away in her intensely personal poems. T.E. Brown referred to her as a woman of genius.[27]

A genius of a different kind was the remarkable inventor William Kennish (1799–1862). The poems about his childhood possess such a great interest to folklorists that his poetic talent and originality have often been overlooked. His slightly old-fashioned style was frequently referred to as 'rough'. However, his capacity for sharply observed and remembered details gives to many of his poems the richness of a Dutch

25] See *Manx Society*, XVI (1869), 54.
26] A.W. Moore, *Manx Worthies* (Douglas, 1901), 105–6.
27] *Letters of T.E. Brown* (London 1900) i, 110–11.

genre painting and he is rarely trite. Kennish wrote some delightful love-poems to his wife, but equal to his love of Mary is his love of Mona and, as he avows in Canto II of his *Mona's Isle and Other Poems*, published by subscription in 1844, the purpose of his verse-making is 'To sing my long neglected Island's fame – to bring the customs of her sons to light'.

This expressed love of homeland was another result of the Romantic movement, which had heightened the awareness of national character-istics. The patriotic fervour had been further fanned by the Napoleonic Wars. An early exponent of this love was the Reverend Robert Brown (1792–1846), father of T.E. Brown. In 1826 he published a volume of *Poems; Principally on Sacred Subjects*. Among these pious outpourings are poems dealing with Manx subjects: the most famous of these, *My Native Land*,[28] tells of Brown's deep love of the Island in spite of its being poor and insignificant. This pride in and love of the Isle of Man finds an increasingly strong voice. By the end of the century the 'Island of mountains so steep and bare' has become a 'gem of God's earth', its apotheosis being written by 'The Manx Poet' T.E. Brown in Part III of 'Epistola Ad Dakyns' (1869; *The Collected Poems*, 1901).

Thomas Edward Brown (1830–97) was the Island's greatest poet. His fame rests on his dialect poems, but he wrote a considerable amount of poetry in standard English. Some deals with Manx subjects, as in 'Mary Quayle', 'The Curate's Story' and 'Bella Gorry: The Pazon's Story', and most famously 'Catherine Kinrade', a poem about the simple-minded woman ill-treated by Bishop Wilson. He used standard English for his childhood reminiscences of 'Braddan Vicarage' and 'Old John'. Unex-pectedly, he did the same in his 'Dedication' to the Manx people of the two series of *Fo'c's'le Yarns* (1881, 1887) and in his invocation 'Spes Altera, To the Future Manx Poet', urging him to write 'With Keltic force, with Keltic fire, With Keltic tears'. Brown's vivid *Letters*, pub-lished in 1900, reveal a brilliant, humorous and generous-minded man.

Inspired by philosophical ideas, the Romantics 'discovered' nature and their search for emotionally satisfying landscapes led to the development of tourism, although the rogues travelling to the Isle of Man portrayed by the Reverend Samuel Burdy (1760–1820) in *Ardglass, or The Ruined Castles* (1802) would hardly have been interested in purchasing the volume entitled *The Pier and Bay of Douglas; or Forget Me Not from the Isle of Man, In a Series of Marine Poems*, published in 1825 by Trevor Ashe (1770–1836). Perhaps William Wordsworth

---

28] The poem is possibly inspired by Walter Scott's lines in *The Lay of the Last Minstrel* (1805): 'Breathes there a man, with soul so dead, / Who never to himself hath said, / This is my own, my native land!'

(1770–1850) would have been a better customer. He visited the Isle of Man in 1833 and wrote poems about the newly constructed Tower of Refuge ('On entering Douglas Bay') and about Tynwald Hill. His most quoted lines refer to Peel Castle – 'Elegiac Stanzas' – but, as the full title spells out, his inspiration was a painting by Sir George Beaumont, not the actual building.[29] Peel Castle was otherwise the place which more than any other inspired Manx poets. As for Ashe, the titles are the most Manx part of his poems. He started a trend of 'topographical' poems, describing various houses with the owner's name thrown in as a selling-point. The poems themselves are on the whole conventional in imagery and content but reveal a genuine fascination with the sea. However, the stanzas 'Meditation on the Ocean from the elegant Marine Villa' have been pirated from 'Canto IV' of Byron's *Child Harold*, published in 1818, a fact which casts doubt on the originality of his other poems. But no such doubt is attached to the last poem in the collection. It was written by Miss E.S. Craven and entitled 'A Dream of Glenmay'.

Eliza Craven Green (1803–66) and her sister Jenny had come to the Isle of Man as members of a touring theatre company in 1824. In spite of Eliza Craven's profession, she was well regarded and became friendly with many of the leading writers on the Island. The Misses Craven left again in 1825 and in that same year Eliza published her poetic work *A Legend of Mona*. She continued her poetical association with the Isle of Man through regular contributions to the 'Poets' Corner' in the *Manx Sun*. On 19 August 1854 an advertisement appeared stating that her poem *Ellan Vannin*, 'a New and Elegant Song', with music by J. Townsend and illustrated with 25 views of Douglas, Ramsey, Peel and Castletown, would be on sale. The popularity of the song was immediate and is still strong. Many Manx people, particularly those in exile, regard *Ellan Vannin* almost as a national anthem. In 1858 Craven's volume of collected poems, *Sea Weeds and Heath Flowers, or Memories of Mona*, appeared. In the preface she mentioned that the poems about the Isle of Man had been written in her early youth and stated boldly that they were

> the first poetical tributes of admiration for the beautiful and romantic Scenery of the Isle of Man, ever published. Possibly they were the remoter causes of the harmonies and hues, with which Poet and Painter have since lavishly imbued glen, mountain, and streamlet of the lovely Island, as I trust they may be the pioneers, of its prosperous and enduring celebrity.

29] 'Elegiac Stanzas suggested by a picture of Peel Castle in a Storm, painted by Sir George Beaumont'.

Perhaps she wanted to stake her claim. In 1853 Thomas John Ouseley (1805–74), who was highly regarded as a poet – he was compared to Keats and Shelley – had published a volume of verse, *Mona's Isle and Other Poems*, dedicated to the Prime Minister, Benjamin Disraeli. Ouseley came from a distinguished family and he and Disraeli had become friends when they were both young men of letters in London. Owing to Ouseley's reputation his poems had a wide circulation, and it was said that they did much towards making the scenery of the Island known to the English.[30] Much of Ouseley's Manx poetry reads like a versified guide book. On the other hand real guide books included poems by all the above poets to stress the beauty or interest of a place. However, tourists flocking to the Isle of Man were drawn there not by poetry but by the novels of Thomas Henry Hall Caine (1853–1931).

'The readers of novels don't care one straw about the Isle of Man', claimed T.E. Brown's brother Hugh, the famous Baptist minister in Liverpool, when asked by Hall Caine about the possibility of making literary use of the Isle of Man.[31] Hall Caine proved him wrong. He wrote a series of novels set wholly or partly in the Island: *The Deemster* (1887), *The Bondman* (1890), the lighthearted novella *Capt'n Davy's Honeymoon* (1892), *The Manxman* (1894), *The Christian* (1897), *The Master of Man* (1921) and *The Woman of Knockaloe* (1923). Translated into every European language and some others besides, they made him known all over the world as 'The Manx Novelist'. To many of his readers the Isle of Man became simply 'Hall Caine's Island' and droves of tourists came to see for themselves the places that he had described. But the Manx felt uneasy about his novels. They were regarded as coarse because of their presentation of sexual desire as a powerful force shaping human lives. Manx booksellers, being prudent, simply did not stock his books.[32] In 1891 Hall Caine gave a series of lectures about the Isle of Man to the Royal Institution in London which were published under the title *The Little Manx Nation* and dedicated to his close friend T.E. Brown. Always ready to promote the Isle of Man, Hall Caine also provided the Isle of Man Steam Packet Company with a guide book, *The Little Man Island* (1894), of high literary quality. He wrote other novels beside the Manx series, and these proved equally popular. The strong dramatic quality of his books permitted them readily to be transformed into stage and screen adaptations. Hall Caine was actively engaged in issues of British or international importance which added to

30] See Trevor Kneale, 'A love affair with Mona's Isle', *Manx Life*, Jan–Feb 1982, 9–13.
31] H. Caine, *My Story* (London, 1908), 308.
32] A. Moore, *Manx Scene* (Douglas, 1973), 93.

Hall Caine *Hall Caine's internationally popular novels, many with a Manx theme, lent themselves to stage adaptations. This poster advertising* The Eternal City *in 1901 includes the note 'the object of the present performance is to protect the novel from unauthorized dramatisation in the United Kingdom, and in every country with which a copyright treaty or understanding exists, while securing as far as practicable to the English public the first fruits of English dramatic art'.* (MNHL)

his status. He was knighted for his journalistic and literary contributions to the war effort in 1918. King Albert of Belgium made him an Officer of the Order of Leopold for his humanitarian aid to the Belgian refugees. In 1922 Hall Caine was made a Companion of Honour for his contribution to English literature. Finally in 1929 the Isle of Man recognised his value to the Island by making him a Freeman of Douglas. None the less, the Manx continued to have mixed feelings about him, and he never gained the same undivided love and admiration as T.E. Brown.

Hall Caine was by no means the first to write novels about the Isle of Man. The entrepreneurial Thomas, also known has Trevor, Ashe (see above) wrote the first known novel with a Manx setting in 1792. It was called *The Manks Monastery: or, Loves of Belville & Julia*, and was allegedly based on historical documents given to the author. He dedicated his book to Mr John Taubman of the Nunnery, where the medieval action is set. The focal point of the book consists of the long-drawn-out seduction of Julia, a young nun, accompanied by much weeping by the two lovers. However, genuine Manx historical figures and events attracted Walter Scott (1771–1832) to set part of the action in *Peveril of the Peak* (1823) in the Isle of Man. The book is a romance set in the aftermath of the Civil War, but Scott took great liberties with Manx history. He never visited the Isle of Man and the Manx scenery is stagy but Scott's brother Thomas, who worked in the Island for some years, furnished him with sufficient material to make a reasonable success of it. The popularity of the novel turned fiction into fact, and many visitors to Peel Castle have been shown by the custodian the place where Fenella made her daring leap.

It was the Isle of Man itself, 'the one inaccessible place left in the world',[33] that attracted Wilkie Collins (1824–89). He visited the Island in August 1863 and found Douglas rough and Castletown dull but the Sound and the Calf of Man ideal for his literary scheme. It is in the Sound that he places the pivotal scene in *Armadale* (1866) where the two cousins Armadale spend the night together on the wreck of the *La Grace de Dieu*. Collins may have amused his British readers by describing how intolerably dull Castletown was, but to Hugh Coleman Davidson (1852–?) Castletown, with its garrison and government offices, was full of interest. Davidson gave a lively account of Castletown life in *The Green Hills by the Sea* (1887). The south was also the setting for a melodramatic love-story, *Feet of Clay* (1889), by the popular

33] K. Robinson, *Wilkie Collins* (London, 1951), 182.

Lancashire-born novelist Amelia Edith Barr (1831–1919), who lived and worked in America.[34]

However, the Manx themselves, many of them staunch Methodists, had a puritanical dislike of fiction unless it was educational or morally uplifting. Particularly popular as a prize for Sunday School attendance or good exam results was Frederic W. Farrar's (1831–1903) *Eric, or Little by Little, a Tale of Roslyn School* (1858), a story about a bright and engaging boy corrupted by school life but finally redeemed in death by a new-found religious faith. Although Dean Farrar publicly denied that Roslyn School was identical with King William's College and in spite of an evident lack of Manxness in the setting, Eric had enough biographical details in common with the author for it to be generally accepted that King William's College was the model, and it caused a good deal of gossip. Even more popular as a school prize was *The Fishers of Derby Haven*, published by the Religious Tract Society in 1867. The novelist Sarah Smith, known as Hesba Stretton (1832–1911), visited the Isle of Man in July 1865,[35] and she gave a vivid account of life in a Manx fishing community. The thrills and tribulations of the book's young hero Peter are on the whole realistic and the religious message is skilfully worked in. A strong religious message had also been sent out by Bellanne Stowell (1814–89) in her novel *Manxland: A Tale* (1863), which aimed at showing the importance of the Manx Home Mission. In the process she drew detailed pictures of life among farm labourers and clergymen.[36] Held in high regard by the Manx as a good account of Manx life and character was *The Captain of the Parish*

34] More important as a propagandist in the United States for the Isle of Man and its culture was the Manx-born writer and poet Henry Hanby Hay (1848-1940). Aged 16 he emigrated to North America, where he had a distinguished academic career. In 1876 he joined the staff of Girard College, Philadelphia. He taught English literature at the college for forty years. He championed Hall Caine and T.E. Brown. His poems *Trumpets and Shawms*, published in Philadelphia in 1896, had a preface by Hall Caine and a special section, 'The Ramsey Lanes', dedicated to Brown. He returned for good in 1925 to the Isle of Man, where he continued to have a highly regarded literary career. He was a fellow of the Royal Society of Literature and founded the T.E. Brown Fellowship.

35] See V. Boland, 'Who wrote "The Fishers of Derby Haven"', *Manx Life*, Jan–Feb 1984, 49–51.

36] Another facet of the Evangelical movement was represented in the highly charged religiosity of *Gilbert Vince, Curate and His Struggle to Attain the Ideal*. Published in the same year (1897) as Hall Caine's controversial *The Christian*, the novel received favourable reviews. The author, Richard Nicklin Hall (1853–1914), was Manx-born and went on to have a distinguished career in Rhodesia. Several scenes are set in the Isle of Man, which is described as having restorative powers. The noble-minded Cambridge-educated Vince feels his calling to the priesthood confirmed while meditating in Peel Castle.

(1897) by the Reverend John Quine (1857–1940). He was an Oxford-educated mill-owner's son from Malew, and the novel is set within the farming community. It has added interest as an account of different religious attitudes and of the Mormons' missionary work on the Island.

At the beginning of the nineteenth century the majority of Manx people were Gaelic-speaking with a rich oral tradition. By the end of the century the Isle of Man had a well-developed English literature. Manx writers were well aware of reigning literary fashions. Some very good poetry had been written describing mainly the Island's natural beauty and its historical past. Its history has been documented in various forms. In this context it should be mentioned that the Manx perception of the esteemed eighteenth-century cleric, Bishop Wilson, was strongly influenced by the Reverend Hugh Stowell's (1768–1835) *The Life of the Right Reverend Thomas Wilson DD*, published in 1819. An increasing number of novels had been produced, describing various strata of Manx society. The majority aimed at giving realistic accounts of contemporary Manx life. Two names stood out among the rest, those of T.E. Brown and Hall Caine. By the end of the century Brown had died, leaving a vacuum, but Hall Caine's fame was still growing.

Literature in English since 1900

MARTIN FARAGHER

Within a decade or so of the death of T.E. Brown his poetry and personality had inspired a strong cult. *Betsy Lee* had been dramatised and performed locally, and some of his poems had been set to music by eminent composers. The first of many memorials to him had appeared, and the World Manx Association had established an annual gathering in his honour. A newspaper established a 'Tom Brown' column and club for children, while every school was provided, by public subscription, with his portrait and collected poems. In 1930 the centenary of his birth was celebrated by the publication of a prestigious but hagiographical symposium[37] and was followed by a T.E. Brown Memorial Room in the Manx Museum. Since then there have been further scholarly publications.[38] Quotations from Brown

---

37] Sir A. Quiller-Couch, *T.E. Brown, a Memorial Volume* (Cambridge, 1930).
38] R.C. Tobias, *T.E. Brown* (Boston, Mass, 1978); M.K. Sutton, *The Drama of Storytelling in T.E. Brown's Manx Yarns*, (Newark, Delaware, 1991); D. Winterbottom, *T.E. Brown: His Life and Legacy* (Douglas, 1997).

T.E. Brown and 'Tom Baines' *The World Manx Association's Annual Luncheon honours the memory of Manx poet T.E. Brown, whose narrative poems in Manx dialect include such favourites as 'Tommy Big Eyes' and 'Betsy Lee', here brought to life in a 90-minute dramatisation performed in the early 1990s by Dollin Kelly on the Island and at the Edinburgh Festival Fringe. The narrator, Tom Baines, is often thought to be T.E. Brown's alter ego. (Tony Lakin)*

have joined the Manx literary vocabulary and there has been a succession of virtuoso performers of his poems, the most notable in recent years being Geoffrey Crellin and Dollin Kelly. The latter's *Betsy*

Lee has appeared at the Edinburgh Festival and been marketed on audiotape.[39] He has also published an anthology with explanatory annotations intended for use in schools.[40] In 1997 the centenary of Brown's death was observed in many ways, and, since the 'Future Manx Poet' of whom he conjectured has not materialised, he remains the unchallenged literary icon of Manx cultural patriotism.

In 1947 Hall Caine's Manx biographer conceded that the works of Hall Caine 'even if not immortal, were of inestimable service to his country in helping to bring its amenities to the notice of the English reading public' and drew attention to the statement in the *Cambridge History of English Literature* that Caine's 'novelistic melodramas must be dismissed unnamed'.[41] However, the 1985 *Oxford Companion to English Literature* described his novels as having been 'of wide popularity and a somewhat sensational reputation', and since then a definitive biography has been published.[42]

In Arnold Bennett's *Anna of the Five Towns* (1902) there is a substantial episode in the Isle of Man, but it is only an interlude from life in the Potteries. In the first half of the twentieth century a few ephemeral works of popular romance were set in the Isle of Man, but so superficially that they could have been anywhere. An exception of no serious literary significance was *Mirry Anne* by Norma Lorrimer, who had lived on the Island for a while and became a popular writer of circulating-library romances in the 1920s.[43] In contrast, the works of Catherine Dodd, a Manx woman who had a distinguished teaching career in England, do merit consideration.[44] With thirteen novels published by Jarrolds, she was regarded as a leader in the field of historical romance, and *The Farthing Spinster* (1926), *Clad in Purple Mist* (1926) and *Three Silences* (1928) are set in the Isle of Man. The latter follows an Anglo-Manx family through the eighteenth and nineteenth centuries and, notwithstanding a didactic strain, has charm and originality.

Since then there have been other novels set in the Island which have achieved substantial national circulation, notably those of Harold Blundell, who, writing under the pen-name of George Bellairs, was a successful writer of numerous detective stories in Gifford's Thriller

39] Produced by Studio 13, Douglas, 1992.
40] D. Kelly, *T.E. Brown – an Anthology* (Douglas, 1997).
41] S. Norris, *Two Men of Manxland* (Douglas, 1947).
42] V. Allen, *Hall Caine: Portrait of a Victorian Romancer* (Sheffield, 1997).
43] *Isle of Man Times*, 30 Oct 1920.
44] *Mona's Herald*, 22 July 1969, 8, and *Manx Star*, 7 Oct 1974, 10.

Book Club series.[45] In *Half Mast for the Deemster* (1953), *Corpse at the Carnival* (1958), *The Cursing Stones Murder* and *Death Treads Softly*, murders on Manx shores are solved with the aid of an indigenous amateur sleuth, one Archdeacon Caesar Kinrade. The author, who had formative Manx influences in his life, makes credible use of folklore and vernacular speech, and gives perceptive portrayals of contemporary life.

In Jonathan Gash's *Gold from Gemini* (Collins, 1978) a picaresque antiques dealer comes to the Isle of Man in pursuit of buried Roman treasure. The book became an episode, with Manx location shots, in the 'Lovejoy' television series. In the 1990s *Echoing Yesterday*, *Karen Kinrade* and *The Red Bird* by Alexandra Manners were published by Corgi. They have sufficient Manx detail to meet the needs of the genre of historical romance. Sue Dyson's *Across the Water* (Headline, 1995) is the story of a Manx girl who becomes a nurse in London during the period 1939–45, and gives insights into the culture-shock of such a transition. A *Far Tomorrow* (1996) is set in the women's internment camp in the Island in the same period. The author has a Manx parent, and the local background has been well researched.

Over the years there have been children's books with a Manx setting. *Orry Son of Gorry* (1903) by Manxman Clucas Joughin was published in London (Jarrolds) and in America. A Victorian example of a boys' adventure tale, its plot involves the suppression of smuggling by the Redcoats and conveys a Manx nationalistic sentiment, the more so as the boy hero is descended from Orry, the legendary Viking King of Mann. *The Stallion from the Sea* (Lutterworth, 1953) is the only Manx story in the successful output of children's historical stories by Kathleen Fidler, and is of appeal to girls.[46] Its plot involves some tension between native Manx and English in-comers in the mid eighteenth century.

Throughout the twentieth century Manx folk-tales have been perpetuated as children's stories. Sophia Morrison's *Manx Fairy Tales* was published in 1911 as a collection of folk-tales told to her by adults.[47]

45] *Manx Star*, 30 Apr 1982, 10 (obituary).

46] The author's dedication of the book to the Douglas Town Librarian, suggests her source of research.

47] As Secretary of the Manx Language Society and Founder Editor of the journal *Mannin* (which ran from 1913 until her death in 1917) and by other means, Sophia Morrison brought Manx literature and drama to the public.

The Celtic revival *One of the most active figures in the cultural revival was Sophia Morrison, who collected folklore, promoted the Manx language and produced plays. She collaborated with A.W. Moore and Edmund Goodwin in the fascinating* Vocabulary of the Anglo-Manx Dialect, *and her collection of Manx folk-tales (1929) was delightfully illustrated by Manx artist Archibald Knox. (MNHL)*

SOPHIA MORRISON

CLOSE TO THE HEART OF HER LOVED PEEL SHE RESTS,
ALL PAIN FORGETTING, WHILE AROVND HER STILL
THE WINDS, THE WATERS AND THE CVRLEWS CRY,—
  THAT ANCIENT CALL THAT ERST ST PATRICK HEARD
AND WITH HER QVIET PRESENCE PASSED AWAY
BRIGHT, BVRNING BRANDS THAT FIRED OVR ISLAND HEARTS,
AND SHOWED THE SWEETNESS IN OVR HOMELY WAYS,
FINDING THE GOLD AMID THE RVGGED QVARTZ.
'ALAS' AN OLD FRIEND MOVRNED 'A LIGHT GOES OVT
WITH HER THAT NEVER WILL BE LIT AGAIN.'
NAY, FRIEND, THE BEARER PASSES, BVT HER LAMP
BVRNS ON VNDYING ; SELF-EFFACING LOVE,
VNSELFISH AIMS AND SINGLE-HEARTED TOIL
LIGHTED AND KEPT IT CLEAR, WHILE LIVING SPARKS
HAVE FOVND RESPONSIVE GLOW IN KINDRED MINDS
THAT THROVGH THE DAILY GRINDING OF THE MILL,
AND THROVGH THE CLANGING TVRMOIL OF OVR LIVES,
WILL BRING VS BACK TO NATVRE'S OLDEST CALL,
THE WINDS', THE WATERS' AND THE CVRLEWS CRY.

·CVSHAG·

With the 1929 edition, illustrated by Archibald Knox, it came to be regarded as a children's book. *Fairy Tales from the Isle of Man* (Penguin, 1951) was a mixture of fictitious and recycled folk-tales by Dora Broome, the author of the Matilda Mouse stories on BBC Children's Hour. Recently some folk-tales have been produced by students at Queen Elizabeth Secondary School, Peel, for Tara Television in Ireland, and marketed on video.[48]

In 1949 Collins published a collection of short stories for adults called *Tomato Cain and Other Stories*. It won Nigel Kneale, its young Manx author, a Somerset Maugham Travelling Scholarship, and in its preface Elizabeth Bowen wrote that 'not all his work has an Isle of Man setting but he has drawn strength from it ... he turns for his inspiration to creeks in which life runs deep ... In his universe, passions stalk like those Island monsters.' Subsequently Kneale scripted the television production of Orwell's *Nineteen Eighty Four*, which so shocked the nation that questions were asked in the House of Commons. He then proceeded to unleash his own monsters by writing the 'Quatermass' television series. More television dramas were to follow, mostly with an occult or science fiction theme.[49]

When *Tomato Cain* was published there were neither local outlets nor guidance for aspiring creative writers. Since then, in the wake of the post-1960s population and economic changes, there have been opportunities for publication in coffee-table magazines like *Manx Life*, while some successful authors have settled in the Island and encouraged others by running workshops and competitions. In 1994 the Isle of Man Arts Council arranged poetry workshops in schools and published a resultant anthology called *Kangaroos and Monday Morning*, while in 1997 it published the winning entries of the two previous years in the long-running Olive Lamming Memorial Literary Competition.

Throughout the century much poetry about the Island, both in standard English and dialect and ranging from the sentimental to the satirical, has appeared, mostly in author-financed publications, in newspapers, or as performance in the largely unpublished repertoire of village entertainers.[50] The most influential poet has been Mona Douglas (1898–1987). Her early literary hero was W.B. Yeats, and in

48] *Manx Myths and Fairy Tales* (Isle of Man, Beckman Home Video, 1996).
49] M. Faragher, 'The road to 1984', *Manx Life*, May–June 1984.
50] The most enduring of such poets is Cushag (Josephine Kermode), whose first book of collected poems appeared in 1907; amongst many others worth consideration there are P.W. Caine, R.J. Fell and Kathleen Faragher.

1915 her first collection of poems, *Manx Song and Maiden Song*, was published by William Morris Press. She was only 17 when her published work earned her admission to the Order of Gorsedds at the Royal National Eisteddfod of Wales. Her novels *Song of Mannin* (1976) and *Rallying Song* (1981), both embodying Manx legend and Celtic mysticism, were published locally.[51]

The Media

ROBERT KELLY

Newspapers

The first Manx newspaper, the *Manks Mercury*, published on 27 November 1792, was not targeted specifically at Manx people. Nor was its immediate successor, the *Manks Advertiser*, which was launched on 8 August 1801. Produced by English journalists in English, they catered principally for the few hundred non-Manx residents who wanted a cheap source of international news. Imported newspapers bore UK stamp duty and taxes. A Manx newspaper did not. Thus one which copied imported 'intelligence' had a ready sale. So was established the precedent, when most Manx could speak and read only Gaelic, that English was the language for news. Cover prices were also in British currency, not Manx.

As sales were only several hundred at most, viability depended on getting government notices and jobbing work.[52] When the boats which brought UK newspapers arrived late, meanwhile, or changed sailing schedules, Manx newspapers were also late or changed their publication dates.[53] Editor-printers were the principal writers, aided by contributors. The poet John Stowell of Peel Grammar School was one. Eventually the *Manks Advertiser* emerged as an 'instrument of war'[54] between the Manx who resented the presence on the Island of non-Manx and the latter who claimed that they were its source of prosperity.

Some reporting became so maliciously libellous that Tynwald, on 21

51] *Manx Life*, Nov 1987, 11, and Mar–Apr 1983, 34.

52] Appeal by *Isle of Man Weekly Gazette* for government advertising. Atholl Papers, MNHL, 1 Dec 1812.

53] *The Manks Advertiser* on 16 February 1802 attributed publication delays to awaiting the arrival of the Packet.

54] H.A. Bullock, *History of the Isle of Man* (London, 1816), 358–9.

May 1817, made the spreading of false news and malicious libelling criminal offences.[55] Editorials still remained vicious for many years, but material of a higher literary standard was gradually attracted to new publications. T.E. Brown's early verse, for example, was published in the *Isle of Man Times* from 1871. *Betsy Lee* was also serialised by the *Times* as were Hall Caine's novels *She's All the World to Me* and *The Bondman*.[56]

Politically, newspapers served as propaganda vehicles for rival factions. The *Advertiser* supported the disliked Duke of Atholl.[57] The *Manx Sun*, launched on 24 April 1821 as the *Rising Sun*, allied itself with the self-elected House of Keys to defend Manx constitutional rights which it believed to be threatened by the Duke. When this was resolved, the *Sun* supported the Keys against reformers who wanted public elections. It believed that a transfer of control from land-owners to 'trade' through elections would lead to instability. This led to reformers launching the *Mona's Herald* as their mouthpiece on 3 August 1833. Bitter exchanges between it and the *Sun* followed.

In 1840 a UK Act of 1834, which enabled newspapers printed in a British colony to be posted free to Britain or any other colony, was extended to the Channel Islands and the Isle of Man. The result was the production locally, for distribution by the Post Office, of non-Manx publications for temperance, socialist and communist movements.[58] A Newspapers Act, introduced into the House of Keys on 22 April 1845, required publishers to register their names and titles within 14 days of the Act's promulgation by Tynwald on 1 December 1846, but failed to curb the abuse. The UK, therefore, passed an Act on 3 September 1848 which empowered the Post Office to reimpose mail charges. When it did so in April 1849, it tried to retain the postal concession for truly Manx newspapers by defining eligible ones as those published in the local language. As that was Gaelic, however, none qualified. The Inland Revenue Commissioners then said in a letter of 22 May that if copies of Manx newspapers were lodged with the Treasury, they would be subjected only to the 1*d* letter rate instead of the 4*d* pre-paid newspaper rate.[59]

Most entrepreneurs left the Island. The principal group, Shirrefs and

55] Sections 41 and 45 in a new Criminal Law Act.
56] *Isle of Man Times*, 9 May 1936.
57] Atholl Papers, MNHL: 106 (2nd)–44; 36 (A) 12.
58] See John Belchem, 'The neglected "unstamped": the Manx pauper press of the 1840s', *Albion*, XXIV (1992), 605–16.
59] *Manx Sun*, 18 Apr, 2 May, 30 May and 13 June 1849.

Russell, became insolvent after having attempted since January 1847 to acquire local legitimacy by publishing the *Isle of Man Times*. One who stayed was James Brown of Liverpool. He established his own printing business and eventually launched a new *Isle of Man Times* on 4 May 1861. This campaigned, as did *Mona's Herald*, for public elections to the House of Keys. When both newspapers were deemed by the House on 15 March 1864 to have libelled and held the House in contempt, their editors were brought before the House next day. Robert Christian Fargher of the *Mona's Herald* apologised, but Brown claimed justification. The House regarded this as an aggravation of his contempt and sentenced him to six months' imprisonment at Castle Rushen. The Court of Queen's Bench granted a writ of *habeas corpus*, however. Brown was released after seven weeks and three days and won damages for wrongful imprisonment. He claimed that this broke the grip of the land-owning class on Manx politics.[60] In two years there were public elections.

Development of tourism prompted the *Sun* to launch a seasonal daily on 3 July 1876.[61] National news and sports results, received by telegram, beat UK newspapers by up to half a day. The *Sun* did not repeat the idea the following year. Nor did the *Times*, which experimented with a one-sheet *Daily Telegraph* from 25 June 1878 but also abandoned it. As tourist arrivals rose further, however, the *Sun* relaunched its daily from 14 May 1888 and it continued on a seasonal basis until a brief receivership in 1900. Whilst the *Times* reckoned that it thrived by not representing sectional interests, the *Isle of Man Examiner*, launched on 10 July 1880, demonstrated that factionism still existed. It succeeded by representing Nonconformists and trade unionists.

All newspapers specialised in shorthand reports of meetings, but it was the *Times* which was contracted to provide official coverage of the legislature. This commenced with the Legislative Council sitting of 24 November 1887. The contract required publication of the reports in the *Times*. Because of typesetting problems, weeks could pass before publication. When prompter, short reports in rival newspapers appealed more to readers in the 1930s and 1940s, the *Times* dropped verbatim reports but maintained a contract for private publication until tape recorders replaced shorthand writers in the autumn of 1964.

The emergence of large circulation newspapers reflected the growth in literacy, a rise in demand by tourists for news, an expansion in advertising aimed at the new readers and a growth of the industry's

60] *The Jubilee of the Isle of Man Times*, 6 May 1911.
61] Copies at Douglas Borough Library.

productive capacity. For much of the nineteenth century type was hand-set, and individual or pairs of pages had to be printed on each side separately. The sheets then had to be folded, guillotined and collated. On press days printers often worked all day and night. Although the replacement of hand-operated presses by steam-powered belt drives reduced labour, the printing process remained a multi-stage one until the property and tourism boom of the 1890s. In 1892 the *Times* installed the first press which could produce a newspaper in one process. Five years later it launched a successful two-year campaign to treble sales of its weekly edition and started the first all-year-round Manx daily newspaper, the *Daily Times*. At a time when compositors were demanding big pay rises, the *Times* mechanised typesetting by the phased installation, from the spring of 1897, of four Linotype machines, each one reckoned to be the equal of four compositors. The machines had been introduced into Britain from America in 1889. The new daily was launched on 4 May and provided national news hours before the Liverpool steamer arrived with UK newspapers. Encouraged by large wage settlements, the *Sun* and *Mona's Herald* installed Linotypes within the year. The *Sun* was compelled also to halve its cover price after the *Times* did so in January 1899. By then, however, the *Sun* was in financial difficulties. It went into receivership after the Dumbell's Bank crash in 1900 and, after a short spell in other ownership, was merged with the *Weekly Times* from 27 October 1906. The *Daily Times*, meanwhile, continued to be important until UK newspapers were flown to the Island in the 1930s. For example, the *Times* gave the first news to an assembled Tynwald of the First World War peace settlement.

The *Weekly Times* so dominated the market between 1900 and 1920 that its circulation was claimed to equal the combined sales of other Manx newspapers.[62] That advantage was lost by slowness to adopt new technology. Installation of its own process department so that it could make its own photographic blocks, thereby providing weekly pictorial coverage, was anticipated in 1921[63] but not acted upon until 13 years later. In 1932 photographic coverage of a royal visit yielded record sales. Photographs, however, had to be sent to Blackpool by private plane. The blocks were made by the *Blackpool Gazette* and flown to the Island the same day. It was the *Examiner* which was first to install its own process department. A weekly page of pictures from 9 February 1934 captured such a significant percentage of the *Weekly*

62] Typical advertisement, 6 May 1911, booklet *The Jubilee of The Isle of Man Times*.
63] John Brown at *The Isle of Man Times* staff dinner, 4 May 1921.

Times circulation that the *Times* quickly imitated the *Examiner*,[64] but an unstoppable shift of reader support had started. The *Examiner* doubled its circulation that year[65] and became the top-selling newspaper by 1938. In 1958 its new owner bought the *Times*. The daily edition was closed by him from 26 October 1966 because its profit was not as great as the pay cuts that could be achieved by a reduction from a daily to weekly newspaper wage rate.

Computerised typesetting was introduced by the *Examiner* Group between November and December 1972 when its supremacy was challenged by the former *Ramsey Courier*, now renamed *Isle of Man Courier* and publisher also of the *Mona's Herald*. The latter was closed in late March 1975 by an industrial dispute; then in January 1987 disputes linked to the operation of a new generation of computers closed the *Examiner* Group. Former *Examiner* and *Times* staff launched the *Manx Independent*. The *Courier*, a free-sheet since 15 January 1982, acquired the *Examiner*'s assets in May, relaunched the *Examiner* on 28 July and later acquired the *Independent* title.

Radio

Radio services via weak BBC transmissions from Manchester became receivable in November 1922. This led to radio receivers being marketed by demonstrations known as 'Wireless Concerts' in March 1923. The Manx writer Mona Douglas claimed later that 'Radio English' was the most significant factor in the loss of the Anglo-Manx dialect.[66] Many early receivers were made locally, principally by rivals Harold Colebourn and Sidney Hinton. To do so, they had to buy shares in the BBC.[67] To encourage the expansion of local radio coverage Tynwald let the UK control broadcasting on the Island. In the mid-1930s, however, the idea developed that a Manx commercial station could promote the Island as a holiday resort throughout Europe. For 30 years UK governments which were opposed to commercial radio prevented it; then, in 1964, said that the Island could have its own station provided the signal did not reach the UK. Hoping to achieve overspill into the UK later, Tynwald accepted the licensing by the UK Postmaster-General of a low-power Manx Radio and granted an operating concession to a private syndicate. Experimental VHF trans-

---

64] Reminiscence of former *Times* process engraver and later Speaker of the House of Keys, Victor Kneale MHK.
65] *Isle of Man Examiner*, 8 July 1955.
66] M. Douglas, *We Call it Ellan Vannin* (Douglas, 1970).
67] Roy Colebourn, Harold Colebourn's son, 1996.

missions started for the TT races from a caravan on 7 June 1964 but the Isle of Man Broadcasting Company Limited was not registered until 8 July 1964. Because the ultimate aim was a UK audience, the use by announcers of Manx dialect was discouraged. An Oxford accent was considered inappropriate also, however. The management preferred a 'mid-Atlantic sound'. Failure to get high transmission power led to Manx support for a ship-based pirate radio station, Radio Caroline, which operated between 5 July 1964 and 3 March 1968 just outside territorial waters in Ramsey Bay. Extension to the Island on 1 September 1967 of the UK's Marine Broadcasting Offences Act, which prevented British citizens aiding pirate stations, led to a constitutional crisis and a decision by Tynwald that the Island should have greater independence from the UK.

Manx Radio, meanwhile, was nationalised by Tynwald in January 1968. The aim was to free it from UK licensing controls by making it an 'Agency of the Crown'. As the Isle of Man was not a sovereign state, however, the legality of this was disputed and the plan was never acted upon. Tynwald realised then that, while waiting to serve its intended role, Manx Radio had become a community station. It was accepted thereafter as a subsidised arm of government. 'Access' radio, as phone-in shows were called, was started experimentally in 1976 with a short late-night programme. It was expanded on Sunday nights, and eventually the phone-in programmes were introduced at peak periods during the day. Initially Manx Radio failed to broadcast national and international news. Listeners had to retune to the BBC on the hour. To lure them back, Manx Radio broadcast local news 15 minutes later. From December 1977, however, it subscribed to the Independent Radio News service and transmitted this, with Manx news, at the same time as the BBC. At first the service was supplied by a dedicated landline but later by satellite. Live coverage of Tynwald debates started in April 1992. Until then only the Budget speech could be broadcast. The emergence of the Alternative Policy Group suggested that impartiality in broadcasting could be guaranteed in future only by full coverage.[68] Live coverage of Question Time in the House of Keys started in October 1992, and in Tynwald three years later.

The first voluntarily operated station began transmitting on 1 April 1995 as Community Radio Laxey: it provided a service for the Laxey Valley area for two-and-a-half hours on Sunday afternoons. The rapid increase in popularity in 1995–6 of the Internet led to the first dissemination of Manx news via this medium. The Manx government

68] Information supplied by Stewart Watterson, Managing Director, Manx Radio.

downloaded its verbatim reports of legislative debates from the autumn of 1996.

Magazines

There have been at least fifty Manx magazines. The first was *The Douglas Reflector* in 1821, but this merely copied non-Manx material from UK publications. Subsequent magazines concerned themselves with the Island's history and customs. There were two attempts (in 1867 and 1885) to produce a satirical *Manx Punch*, with some of the humour based on Manx dialect, but they both failed. The *Manx Quarterly*, launched in February 1907 by the *Examiner*, was to be a storehouse of historic and biographic articles previously printed in Manx newspapers. It lasted until the *Examiner* had financial problems in 1922. The *Manxman*, launched in 1911 to promote the Isle of Man Steam Packet Company, included an exclusive Three-Legged Club. National cartoonists who contributed to it were made honorary 'Three-Leggers'. The longest-lived magazine was *Manx Life*. This was launched at the Tynwald Day ceremony at St John's in July 1971. *Manx Life* became monthly and inspired the production locally for a short time of *Wight Life* (for the Isle of Wight), *City Life* (for London) and *Jersey Life* (for the Channel Islands).[69] Publication became irregular when it had to share production facilities with local newspapers. Viability for magazines depended on advertising support, and this was not readily forthcoming for a readership perceived to be interested primarily in Manx history and traditions. This led to the rise in the 1980s of specialist magazines for the newly emerging financial community: for example *Money Media* and *Manx Tails*, given to travellers aboard Manx Airlines flights, tapping a market which generated high-value image-creating advertisements. Eventually *Manx Life* was transformed under new ownership in 1997 to cater for this market. It became known then as *Manx Life Style*.

Folklore

STEPHEN HARRISON and YVONNE CRESSWELL

A subtle product of the community's interaction with its landscape and environment, folklore provides an unparalleled insight into how the Manx people perceived the world around them and how it affected their attitudes, behaviour and beliefs. It is an important layer

69] Robert Kelly.

of community analysis which 'histories' such as this often ignore in preference to the more tangible records of law, politics and formal religion. Folklore and traditional folk beliefs are not just about witches and fairies, irrational superstitions, or about protection against bad luck or natural catastrophes. Rather they are the material evidence of a complex and highly structured belief system which has evolved through time to make sense of and assist life in a pre-scientific pre-literate culture and society. The currency of this folklore within areas of society is simultaneously communal and also essentially a private selection of duties, allegiances, confidence and uncertainty. The process of transmission and continuance is similarly public and yet also at times secret, and occasionally mischievous.

Folklore and folk beliefs also provided a form of 'etiquette and manners' for a community whose everyday life experience was far removed from that small sector of society that made 'the rules'. In this respect they were a cohesive social 'glue' which provided the community with a group of commonly held and observed social responses which could transcend and often conflict with the laws of church and state. In many ways Manx folklore beliefs provided a parallel system of daily control and compliance which was more closely related to daily domestic and working life than those which were created by more formal laws. The operation of this alternative system frequently led to censure and the ostracising or punishment of an individual. The Manx ecclesiastical court records of 'presentments' contain several references to cases of women being tried on the grounds of ill-wishing their neighbours and casting the 'evil eye'.[70]

The Collectors

Manx folklore contains elements which can be viewed as a mixture of unique or atypical Manx specific beliefs and customs, and Manx variations of more universal customs. The folklore-collectors varied in their concerns and interests. Some seemed content with recording evidence of Manx folklore and making little attempt to place the material discovered within a wider Celtic, British or European context. Discovering 'pre-Christian' and even 'prehistoric' roots to contemporary folk traditions seemed a common desire in the early collectors. One of the earliest folklore collectors was George Waldron. In his book *A Description of the Isle of Man* (1731)[71] he recorded stories about giants

---

70] Presentment, 1659 (*JMM*, III, 44 (1935), 58); Presentment, 1666 (*JMM*, III, 46 (1936), 98–100); Presentment, 1659 (*JMM*, IV, 55 (1938), 39).
71] A rare publication, reprinted in *Manx Society*, xi (1865).

and subterranean castles under Castle Rushen which acted as a portal to the underworld. These fantastic and imaginative legends were later expanded upon by the antiquarian Joseph Train in *An Historical and Statistical Account of the Isle of Man* (1845). However, as 'strangers' in the Isle of Man, these early chroniclers suffered from an understandable reluctance by the local people to trust them with their precious lore: 'The Manxman would not trust the foreigner with his secrets; his eyes twinkled suspiciously and his hand seemed unconsciously to grasp his mouth, as if to keep all fast.'[72] Indeed, some collectors may have accepted fictions invented for their benefit, or fragmentary tales developed for their consumption.

Although Manx myths and legends were a staple ingredient in nineteenth-century Manx tourist guides, the more systematic collection of evidence for popular vernacular belief systems was not begun until the late nineteenth century. Collectors such as Charles Roeder,[73] Dr John Clague,[74] William Cashen[75] and A.W. Moore,[76] together with their own network of local informants, collected and published a wealth of material on a wide variety of rituals and customs. Sophia Morrison[77] also collected the various versions of folk and fairy tales that were told from generation to generation around the hearth. In the twentieth century folklore-collecting was continued by Mona Douglas and by Walter Gill, who published 'scrapbooks' on a wide variety of aspects of folklife and the Manx language and dialect.[78] In addition to the collection of folk-tales and beliefs, many antiquarians also collected Manx proverbs and sayings, particularly in the original Manx Gaelic. These were felt to provide a most distinctive and illuminating insight into the character and habits of a community and its people.[79]

As literacy spread within the community, the Manx folk and fairy tales moved out of the oral folk tradition, where each family had its own version, and became 'standard' stories formalised in one of the

72] Campbell in A.W. Moore, *The Folklore of the Isle of Man* (Douglas, 1891, rpt Dyfed, 1994), i–ii.

73] Charles Roeder (*c*.1848–1911), 'Contributions to the folk-lore of the Isle of Man in *Yn Lioar Manninagh*, III, 4 (1897), 129–91; *Manx Notes and Queries* (Douglas, 1904).

74] Dr John Clague (1842–1908), *Manx Reminiscences* (Castletown, 1911).

75] William Cashen (1838–1912), *Manx Folklore* (Douglas, 1912, rpt 1993).

76] Moore, *Folklore*. See further notes on Manx folklore in *The Antiquary*, 31 (1895).

77] Sophia Morrison (1859–1917), *Manx Fairy Tales* (2nd ed, Douglas, 1929, rpt Douglas, 1991).

78] W. Gill (1879–1963), *A Manx Scrapbook* (London, 1929); *A Second Manx Scrapbook* (London, 1932); *A Third Manx Scrapbook* (London, 1963).

79] Moore, *Folklore*, 181–92.

many Manx fairy story books published in the late nineteenth and early twentieth centuries. However, the process and currency of other elements of the folklore tradition continued, and this has been a consistent element of the material collected by the Manx Folk Life Survey, initiated by the Manx Museum in the 1940s by William Cubbon, Basil Megaw and Eric Cregeen. This Survey was based on and encouraged by the Irish Folklore Commission in Dublin. Although much of the early work concentrated on collecting the Manx language from the last of the native speakers, it also revealed the rich supply of informants who were still able to impart a treasury of information concerning all aspects of the traditional folk-life of the Isle of Man. Systematic support groups of field workers and informants were established and the work of Mrs G.M. Quilliam, E. Flanagan, M. Stevenson, I.M. Killip,[80] Harry Rogers and Walter Clarke did much to prove the continuing currency of Manx folklore into the present day.

Calendar Customs

Folklore and folk beliefs permeated all aspects of Manx life and dictated specific behaviour both throughout the year, as determined by the season and date, and through an individual's life cycle. The passing of the seasons has always been of fundamental importance, especially for agricultural communities with the planting and harvesting of crops. Firmly established pre-Christian rituals and seasonal dates and events were rarely erased but rather assimilated within the new Christian culture. Festivals were established which superimposed Christian beliefs on earlier belief systems. Their observance was of paramount importance to guarantee the fertility and success of crops and livestock since failure would lead to famine and starvation.

The wide variety of customs and rituals was described in 1939 by C.I. Paton in his *Manx Calendar Customs* – 'most are now extinct', he concluded,[81] a common error of perception by folklore collectors throughout the ages. The calendar festivals of Easter, May Eve, Harvest, Hop Tu Naa (All Hallows Eve), Christmas and New Year each had its own distinct collection of customs to be performed, some of which were unique to the Isle of Man, whilst many were Manx variations of folk traditions found throughout Britain and many parts of Europe. Some customs with 'pagan origins' are subsequently provided with explicitly Christian explanations, such as the packing away of all iron objects in the home on Good Friday in deference to the

---

80] I.M. Killip, *The Folklore of the Isle of Man* (London, 1965).
81] C.I. Paton, *Manx Calendar Customs* (London, 1942), v–vii.

fact that Christ was nailed to the Cross.[82] Some customs are a combination of Christian and pre-Christian beliefs: *crosh cuirns* or rowan-twig crosses placed over the cottage door prevented evil spirits crossing the threshold, and crosses pinned over the entrances to cowsheds or tied to cows' tails on May Eve protected the cows from going dry.[83] Although the cross is an explicit and powerful Christian symbol, specific use of rowan is significant because it was considered a powerful defence against evil in pre-Christian tradition. It is interesting to note that if the wood was touched by iron it lost its potency against evil. Elsewhere in Britain and Europe, May Eve crosses were made of elder rather than rowan. Elder, or *tramman* as it is called in Manx, was a powerful symbol in Manx folklore against evil and bad luck and was traditionally grown outside the cottage door as a home for 'Themselves', or the fairies, and as such should never be cut down. Many ruined crofts in the Manx hills are still marked by a stand of *tramman* outside the cottage door.

A *babban mheillia* (corn dolly), made with the last sheaf cut in the harvest, was paraded around the field to celebrate the safe gathering in of the harvest.[84] There is also a song and a dance associated with the Mheilliah festivities and in the evening a communal meal would be staged to celebrate the harvest.[85] The festival became more explicitly Christian as the focal point became the church or chapel harvest festival service and the Mheilliah meal became a chapel 'social'. The ritual is still evolving in response to a changing society and, although the harvest festival is still an important part of the church calendar, the Mheilliah is now, in most Manx villages, an auction of produce held in

82] Manx Folk Life Survey (FLS), Informant S/38-B2 (Mr Stowell, Castletown, 1971): 'On the Thursday before it [Easter], the poker and the tongs, all the fire-irons and the fender were put out in the outhouse and locked away. His mother used to get all the aprons in the house and fold them and put them in a drawer and lock it the night before – this was because the women brought the nails for the Crucifixion in their aprons, so his mother and grandmother never wore aprons on Good Friday. The fire was cleared out with a bit of wood and a piece of cardboard; no fire-irons were used. Then at three o'clock on Good Friday afternoon everything was brought back and could be used again.'

83] Moore, *Folklore*, 110–11.

84] FLS Informant Q/48-2 (Mr Qualtrough, Port St Mary, 1963): 'The idea of doing it was that it procured a blessing on the corn and made sure that it would be got in safely.'

85] FLS Informant C/85-A8 (Mr Corlett, Kirk Michael, 1957): 'They had a big supper in the barn – plenty of meat, scones and soda cakes and a lot of sweet cakes. Then there was a bit of a randy – a singer and a fiddler and ones doing step dancing. They carried on until one or two o'clock in the morning.'

the local public house or village hall. In this modern version the participants are not restricted to the agricultural community and, along with the traditional harvest produce, novelty items may be auctioned for local charities.

Other festivals which have evolved and altered in response to external cultural influences include the original Manx festival of Hop Tu Naa held on All Hallows Eve.[86] In the twentieth century children made lanterns out of turnips and chanted the associated Hop Tu Naa song from door to door in their local community to collect money. With the increased anglicisation of Manx traditional culture, Hop Tu Naa became Hallowe'en and now under wider American cultural influences is developing into 'Trick or Treat'. Therefore turnip lanterns are sometimes replaced by carved pumpkins in the lantern competitions, and the latest development, following concern about Satanic influences, has been the staging of non-Hallowe'en children's parties on 31 October with Disney-character lantern competitions.[87]

The Kegeesh Ommidjagh (the Foolish Fortnight) encompassed both Christmas and New Year. It was a time for festivities and feasting and also a 'feast of Misrule' where the normal social conventions could be turned upside down. After the Christmas Eve service the congregation remained for the singing of carvals.[88] As the Oiell Verree (the Eve of the Nativity) celebrations wore on, the worshippers were joined by other revellers, whose behaviour often became out-of-hand; the younger members of the congregation might fire peas at each other.[89] The White

86] FLS Informant R/11-E2 (Mr Robinson, Maughold, 1972): 'Thump the Door night, and young fellows would be going and banging on people's doors with cabbages and turnips.'

T/23-1 (Mr Taylor, Ramsey, 1967): 'Hop Tu Naa night – the 31st October – they went round with turnip lanterns and sang Hop Tu Naa for a penny at people's doors.'

Q/48-1 (Mr Qualtrough, Port St Mary, 1963): 'We were going out singing on Hop Tu Naa night and I remember going to an old woman and she was very poor, and we had done rather well at the houses we'd called at and had been given apples and oranges and salt herring. When the old person came to the door and saw all the things we had, she asked us for a herring and you can tell how poor she was when she had to ask for that – most people had their own herring if they had nothing else.'

87] As seen at Trinity Methodist Church, Douglas, 1996.

88] See under MUSIC.

89] FLS Informant R/11-E1 (Mr Robinson, Maughold, 1972): 'They used to hold these [Oiell Verree services] around Christmas down in Maughold church. When the evening service was over some young men would come and sit at the back of the chapel, and the ordinary congregation would sit in their pews listening while these men sang half a dozen carols. No one thought of going home, they just sat there and listened.' See also Moore, *Folklore*, 127–8.

Boys' play and the Mollag Band's[90] bawdy and riotous songs were performed in the streets and in the homes of anyone who would let them enter. A degree of behaviourial licence that would not normally be tolerated was allowed and even encouraged amongst young men. As well as the White Boys' play, the ritual of 'Hunt the Wren' on St Stephen's Day also survived, one of many variations on the theme found throughout Europe. Past antiquarians have attempted to trace its roots and symbolic meanings back to prehistoric times.[91] An unbroken tradition is that of the *qualtagh* (first-footer); the first person to cross the threshold on New Year's morning must be a dark-haired man carrying a selection of gifts symbolising salt and fuel.

Some rituals and festivities were celebrated according to the new calendar dates whilst some, such as Christmas, maintained links with the old calendar before its change in 1753. Therefore until late in the nineteenth century there are references to people still celebrating the 'old Christmas' on 5 January. Sophia Morrison's book of Manx fairy tales contains a story with the tradition that old Christmas was the true date for the rituals of watching the flowering of the myrrh and the bowing down of the cattle in homage to the birth of Christ, a belief reflected by contributors to the Manx Museum's Folk Life Survey.[92]

Rites of Passage

The observation of rituals and folk beliefs was also important to ensure individual or family survival. High infant and maternal mortality rates ensured that this was a major consideration for the whole community. During pregnancy and birth it was important that the mother-to-be was

90] FLS Informant S/38-B1 (Mr Stowell, Castletown, 1971): 'As children they used to be terrified of the Mollag Band. There were six men dressed in outdoor clothes – blue jerseys and with evergreens around their shoulders. One carried a mollag – he was a kind of buffoon – carried a pig's bladder on a stick and he belaboured anyone who came too near. One member was dressed as a bear – the skin and head of a bear, made of pasteboard ... It had been done by good musicians at one time, with good dancers too, but it became vulgarised – they would be getting drunk and catching hold of the girls and turning the youngsters upside down and smacking them.'

91] Gill, *A Second Manx Scrapbook*, 357–430. Sylvie Muller, 'The Irish wren tales and ritual: to pay or not to pay the debt of nature', *Béaloideas, The Journal of the Folklore of Ireland Society*, 64–5 (1996–7), 131–69.

92] FLS Informant C/33-A1 (Mrs Clague, Dalby, 1949): 'Old Christmas Eve – she remembers three-year-old bullocks going down on their knees and bees coming out – Myrrh representing suffering.'

C/86-C2 (Mr and Mrs Comish, Grenaby, 1971): 'They used to watch the myrrh come up after the Oiell Verree'. See also Morrison, 'The Old Christmas', *Manx Fairy Tales*, 159–62.

A Manx wedding *The enactment of a Manx wedding is a tradition shared with Norway. Usually dressed in Victorian costume, the 'bride' and 'groom' are accompanied by actors playing the parts of the parson, the families, attendants, guests and musicians, before sitting down to a 'wedding breakfast' and suitable entertainments including recitations and games. In this photograph the progress of the happy couple is being halted by a rope across the path, which is removed only on payment of a ransom, a custom still practised at real weddings in the Island. (MNHL)*

not ill-wished by a jealous neighbour. Once a child was born, concern was for supernatural dangers. Vervain was sewn into their clothes to protect babies and young children against being 'took' by the fairies.[93] The iron hearth tongs or poker placed over the cradle would prevent

93] FLS Informant KJR-F1 (Mr and Mrs Kinvig, Ronague, 1949): 'And vervain is a cure if you were bewitched. You had to go and pick it yourself. If you thought anybody was doing you harm you carried a bit of it. You were supposed to be sewing it inside your corsets.'

the fairies from 'changing' the child for one of their own fairy changelings.[94] Although vervain and iron provided protection, natural preference was for an early infant baptism, which was believed to be still more powerful. It was seen as a good omen for future prosperity if coins offered to a baby were clasped tightly by the infant.

Wedding customs were (and still are) joyful and fun as horns were blown and guns were fired by friends and family from the early hours of the wedding morning, and a rope held across the road to obstruct the wedding party en route to the church was removed only on payment of a 'fine'.[95] The rituals associated with death were highly symbolic and illustrate almost universal folk beliefs in life and death. A plate of salt and a sod of earth would be placed by the corpse when it was laid out in the best room of the house to symbolise the everlasting eternal nature of the soul (salt) and the corruptibility of the body (earth).[96] A light was left lit through the night by the corpse[97] and the windows were opened after death to allow the spirit of the departed to leave. The practice of opening windows after death was still being mentioned to student nurses at Noble's Hospital, Douglas, in the 1960s.

Occupational Folk Beliefs

Specific occupations also have their own assemblages of associated folklore and ritual. The most superstitious occupational group, even surpassing the agricultural workers, appears to have been the fishing community, who practised and observed a wide variety of rituals and customs to ensure good luck for the catches and avert bad luck in the form of storms and poor catches.[98] The rituals began as fishermen left home. Good or bad luck was associated with the various people or animals they might meet en route to the boat. Whilst a woman or a church or chapel cleric were omens of bad luck, a Catholic priest was

94] FLS Informant C/86-C3 (Mr and Mrs Comish, Grenaby, 1971): 'Her mother said they wouldn't go out of the house without putting a pair of trousers or else the tongs cross the cradle that the fairies wouldn't come and take the child.'

W/11-A2 (Miss Wade, Rhendhoo, 1953): 'I remember hearing of them taking the babies down to the fields and leaving them in the corners of the fields while they worked and putting the tongs across them so that the fairies would leave them alone.'
95] FLS Informant KJR-C3 (Mr and Mrs Kinvig, Ronague, 1949): 'The cow's horn was blown the night before a wedding. Some were putting off a gun before we got married. The gun went off and we thought the house had fallen in.'
96] FLS Informant L/19-B1 (Mrs Lahmers, Bride, 1963).
97] FLS Informant L/19-B1 (Mrs Lahmers, Bride, 1963).
98] Cashen, *Manx Folklore*, 27–43; Roeder, *Manx Notes and Queries*, 38, 107–15; Killip, *Folklore*, 113–28.

considered a portent of good luck. On board a fishing boat there were a wide variety of words which were thought to bring bad luck and therefore were replaced with 'noa' or safe words.[99] Words such as 'rat' were prohibited and were replaced with 'long tail fellow',[100] 'ring-tailed gentleman' and others. If the inexperienced novice boy cook inadvertently used a prohibited word, then to 'burn' out the bad luck he would have to remove with his teeth a nut or bolt off the boat's iron boiler,[101] an experience that would ensure the mistake was not repeated, although normally to touch and to say 'cold iron' would suffice. Once luck was thought to be with a boat then all efforts would be made to ensure it stayed. Therefore nothing would be lent or given away from a boat which would allow the luck to leave with it, and equally the crew would be on the lookout for crew from other vessels trying to steal something as seemingly insignificant as a dish cloth. The boat itself was, of course, the major source of survival and therefore the prime object of protection. It was very bad luck to be the third boat out of harbour on the way to the fishing. To avoid this, the second and third boats were tied together so neither boat could be said to be the unlucky third in line.[102] Neither would the ballast of the boat be allowed to contain quartz stones, possibly because of their association with early Christian burial customs.[103]

There were a wide variety of domestic rites and rituals to observe around the home and in particular around the hearth. The earth floor of the *thie mooar* or large room of a cottage was never to be swept towards the door but always to the hearth, to ensure that the good luck was never swept out of the home but towards the spiritual heart of the home. For similar reasons all the lustre jugs on the dresser were to face towards the hearth and not the door. Sweeping the dust was seen as a potent force for the dispensation of luck, since anyone suspecting they had been ill-wished would go to the crossroads to sweep the dust and the ill-wisher would be identified as the next person to pass the crossing.[104]

99] Roeder, *Manx Notes and Queries*, 107–8.
100] FLS Informant GJB/S1 (Mr J.B. Gawne, Port St Mary, 1958).
101] FLS Informant KM-A4 (J. Callister, Laxey, 1950).
102] Cashen, *Manx Folklore*, 29.
103] Paton, *Manx Calendar Customs*, 187.
104] FLS Informant C/86-C4 (Mrs Clague, Dalby, 1949): 'At Grenaby there was a horse sick and the boss said "You'll have to go to the three roads and sweep the three roads at Grenaby". She had to go and take a brush and shovel and sweep and she carried the dust home with her in her brat [apron] and threw it on the horse and it got better.'

Folk Medicine

Although there were many rites and rituals to promote good luck and good health, once someone was ill there were a variety of folk remedies that could be called into use. The two most common forms of cures were the use of charms and herbal remedies. Therefore the local 'wise' man or woman, the practitioner of folk medicine, would possess a well-stocked herb garden and various written charms said to have been passed down from generation to generation.[105] The best-known and documented practitioners were Nan Wade of Poortown, German and Teare of Ballawhane, the 'Fairy Doctor'.[106] The most common ailments for which cures were sought were bleeding, bone setting, warts and toothache. Charms would either be a set of words known only to the practitioner or a verse taken from the Bible. As late as 1985 an Alderman of Douglas Corporation had a considerable reputation for being able to cure shingles by waving his hands over the affected areas and whispering the secret words.[107]

Supernatural creatures

Manx folk-tales were originally peopled with a wealth of heroes and deities from the early Irish myths and legends[108] but by the nineteenth century the main survivor was Manannan Mac Lir, who had changed from being the immortal god of the sea into a mortal early Manx ruler, magician and navigator. Although fishermen no longer give up prayers to Manannan at sea for their protection, his memory is still implicitly acknowledged every Tynwald Day by the strewing of rushes along the processional way between St John's Royal Chapel and Tynwald Hill (originally a tribute made to Manannan every midsummer),[109] and there is still a strong belief that his mantle of mist will protect the Island from foreign invaders. The bestiary and pantheon of Manx folklore contained a wide variety of creatures that were still acknowledged well into the nineteenth century, the best-known being the fairy-folk. Manx fairies portrayed strong similarities to the 'li'l folk' of the surrounding

105] FLS Informant P/3-A1 (Miss Creer, Douglas, 1951): 'got toothache and she went to the wise woman to get a charm. The old woman looked in the Bible, picked out a few verses and wrote them down and folded the paper up. She did not look at them but her toothache went and she had no more trouble with her teeth for the rest of her life.'
106] Killip, *Folklore*, 48–50 and 125; Joseph Train, *History of the Isle of Man* (Douglas, 1845), ii, 161–2; S. Morrison, 'The fairy doctor', *Manx Fairy Tales*, 40–4.
107] The words could have been specially composed.
108] Moore, *Folklore*, 52–75.
109] Moore, *Folklore of the Isle of Man*, 1–18; Killip: *Folklore*, 42–4; J. Kneen, 'Another version of the Manannan ballad', *JMM*, III, 49 (1936), 154–6.

isles as small creatures of supernatural origin, without wings and who could be called not by their real name but by euphemistic terms such as 'Themselves'. They displayed an ambiguous mixture of good and bad intentions towards humans which resulted in the fear of unprotected babies being stolen or of individuals walking the country lanes or mountain tops at night being 'took' by the fairies to return to the world of humans possibly only years later.[110] Besides the fearful respect for the power of fairies, they were also viewed as good-natured mischievous creatures. Therefore they would always receive the hospitality of the house.[111] A bowl of *cowree* (oat-meal in water) would be left by the *chiollagh* (open hearth) for the fairies to eat. The band would be removed from the spinning wheel at night as the fairies often tried to help with the spinning; this was a problem since it kept the family awake, as fairies were considered poor spinners.

Another creature of ambiguous intentions was the Phynnodderee (or Fynnoderee), defined by Cregeen as a satyr[112] but perhaps more accurately by Killip as a troll. He was a cantankerous but helpful being known for helping farmers as long as he was not intentionally, or unintentionally, offended by some slight. A folk-tale recalls how a grateful farmer from Gordon tried to repay the hairy and naked Phynnodderee for his work with the gift of clothes only to discover that this was received as a grave insult.[113] The Phynnodderee is depicted as highly conscientious, although not very bright, when it spends all night chasing the one remaining sheep from the flock around Snaefell (or South Barrule, depending on where the story is told), only to discover in the morning that it is not a 'li'l' *loaghtan* sheep but a mountain hare.

110] FLS Informant W/11-A2 (Miss Wade, Rhendhoo, 1953).
111] FLS Informant P/3-A1 (Mrs Corlett, Douglas, 1951): 'Always left the door on the latch at night for the fairies and a little fire on the hearth for them to warm themselves and a little food for them to eat.'
112] A. Cregeen, *A Dictionary of the Manks Language* (Douglas 1835, rpt Yn Cheshaght Ghailckagh, Ikley, 1984), 148.
113] Morrison, 'The Fynnoderee of Gordon' in *Manx Fairy Tales*, 52–7; Killip, 'The Fynnoderee and the L'il Loghtan, a consideration of a Manx folk-tale' *JMM*, VII, 8 (1967), 58–61.

Paying tribute to Manannan *The spreading of rushes on the processional way between The Royal Chapel of St John's and Tynwald Hill is believed to be a tribute to the Manx sea-god Manannan. It was traditional to cut them before daybreak, before donning best clothes for an 8 o'clock breakfast, then spreading the rushes in good time for the ceremony. For at least a hundred years the St John's village joiners have also been responsible for the maintenance and erection of the canopy on the hill. This photograph shows Robert Joseph Quine preparing to spread the rushes in the early 1960s. (Duncan Patrick)*

Other creatures appearing in Manx tales told around the *chiollagh* were the Tarroo Ushtey ('water bull') and the Glashtin (defined by Cregeen as 'a goblin, a sprite'),[114] who were considered dangers to both people and livestock. There was also the Tehi Tegi, a beautiful temptress who could lure men to their doom and then revert to being an evil old sorceress. The most evil and feared of the creatures, though, was the Buggane, who repeatedly tore down the roof of St Trinian's Church and was finally outwitted only by the guile and cunning of the local tailor, who for a wager stayed in the church. The folklore beast most frequently mentioned today is the Moddey Dhoo (black dog) said still to be roaming the ruins of Peel Castle on St Patrick's Isle.

Conclusion

It is a mistake to assume that in the late twentieth century traditional Manx folk beliefs were discarded as old-fashioned and unnecessary encumbrances to modern life. Instead some traditions have been maintained almost in their entirety. Most households would feel uneasy without a *qualtagh*, or 'first-footer'. The use of the term 'longtails' is a general custom observed frequently by new residents to the Island but, ironically, not as strongly now by older members of rural Manx communities. A feature of the cultural revival of Manx language, music and dance has been the resurrection and maintenance of customs such as putting up a *crosh cuirn* over the door and spreading primroses on the doorstep on May Eve. Also it is now increasingly popular for everyone, particularly coach drivers taking coaches of tourists around the Island, to say 'hello' to the fairies at the Fairy Bridge between Douglas and Castletown. However, there is a distinction to be drawn between the various strands of folklore in terms of its significance to the Manx community. A relatively weak folklore exists which people remember from their own family traditions and which they observe to keep custom alive or for a sense of national identity. But there are also stronger belief systems which people strictly adhere to and practise and which they firmly believe are effective. Folklore and folk beliefs are a constantly evolving and adapting feature of human existence. The increased belief and interest in complementary medicines such as homeopathic remedies and reflexology can be compared with the past belief in the effectiveness of charms and herbal potions. The deeply felt need for a supernatural world to fear and to intrigue can be perceived in the periodic media headlines about organised witchcraft and coven activity on the Island. The next task in the study of Manx folklore is to

---

114] Cregeen, *Dictionary*, 80J.

discover and record the new generation of Manx 'superstitions' and folk beliefs and to establish whether truly Manx folklore is still being developed and maintained within the rapidly changing community. As the old Manx saying has it: *Mannagh vow cliaghtey, nee cliaghtey coe* (If custom be not indulged with custom, custom will weep).[115]

Religion in the Nineteenth Century

ANN HARRISON

> A more loving simple-hearted people than this I never saw – and no wonder; for they have but six papists and no dissenters on the Island ... It is supposed to contain near thirty thousand people remarkably courteous and humane.

This well-known extract from the Journal of John Wesley's first visit to the Island in 1777[116] not only shows the Manx people in a favourable and often-quoted light but also marks the beginning of the end of the period when the religious life of the Island was ordered by one all-embracing, monolithic church. Even before Wesley's visit Richard Richmond, the Bishop of Sodor and Man, was beset with the presence of 'several weak persons' combined in a new Society, 'contrary to the divine government, Rites, and Ceremonies of the Established Church, and the civil and ecclesiastical laws of this Isle', in other words Methodists. Having been converted by John Crook, an earlier evangelist in 1775, their numbers were calculated by Rosser, the recorder of Wesleyan Methodism, at some five hundred.[117] In July 1776 the Bishop issued a pastoral letter to his clergy:

> We do therefore for the prevention of schism and the re-establishment of the uniformity in religious worship which so long has subsisted among us, hereby desire and require each and every of you to be vigilant and use your utmost endeavours to dissuade your respective flocks from following or being led and misguided by such incompetent teachers.[118]

115] Moore, *Folklore*, 191.
116] Wesley's Journal, 2 June 1777, quoted in James Rosser, *The History of Wesleyan Methodism in the Isle of Man* (Douglas, 1849), 94.
117] Rosser, *History*, 89.
118] Bishop Richmond's pastoral letter to his clergy, quoted in A.W. Moore, *History of the Isle of Man* (2 vols, London, 1900), ii, 675–6.

Richmond's successors, however, did not view Methodism as a
threat to the established church, possibly because of Wesley's insistence
that he was in communion with the Church of England; as Rex Kissack
has postulated, Manx Methodism was true to Wesley's ideal, an order
working within the Anglican Church for its renewal.[119] By the time of
Wesley's second visit in May 1781 the conversion of the Island was well
under way: in 1805 the Isle of Man became a District of the Methodist
Society. It was not long before a variant branch – John Butcher's
Primitive Methodism with its revivalism, women preachers and
concern for the poor – challenged the first group to be true to the
original values of Methodism. The mission came to the Island in 1823
and built its first chapel at Clougher (Clycur) in Malew, in the same
parish as Derbyhaven where the storm-struck John Butcher was
precipitately cast ashore.[120] Mirror images of Methodist organisation,
both societies were to experience remarkable growth in terms of
membership in the Island and of places of worship.

The position of the Anglicans was somewhat different.[121] The
functions of the Church of England, embodied in the post-Reformation
ecclesiastical constitution and the Spiritual Statutes of Tynwald, had
evolved naturally through the centuries. Age-old powers over the moral
behaviour of its members, the mechanism of parochial discipline by
penance and, in serious cases, physical punishment and imprisonment,
were a prime concern of the episcopate of Bishop Wilson. They had
begun to lapse by the succession of Bishop Hildesley – first in minor
offences such as absence from church, and use of profane language –
and fell into contempt after his death in 1773. Thenceforth the
disciplinary powers of the church courts went into material decline, but
still provoked censure in 1791 from Richard Townley, a cultivated in-
comer: 'My pen revolts ... with transcribing such nonsensical stuff, as
must draw a smile from every person of common sense; an indignant
one it must be; that within a Protestant country, in this enlightened age,
such absurdities should be tolerated.'[122] The Anglican Church was by
no means wealthy, and its parishioners were beset with ever-increasing
tithe demands, ruthlessly pressed by Bishop Murray (1814–27) in

119] Rex Kissack, *The Contribution of Methodism to the Culture of the Isle of Man*
(Manx Methodist History Society, Port Erin, nd, 1980s).
120] Rev. William Curry, *A Kingdom Won: The Story of Primitive Methodism in the
Isle of Man* (London, 1923).
121] Canon J. Gelling, *A History of the Manx Church 1698–1911* (Douglas, 1998) was
published by Manx Heritage Foundation after this section had been written.
122] Richard Townley, *A Journal kept in the Isle of Man* (2 vols, Whitehaven, 1791), ii,
47.

respect of the modern green crops of potatoes and turnips to the point of causing riots in a period of agricultural depression.[123] Bishop Ward, who succeeded Murray in 1827, criticised his predecessors for failure 'to find means for the building of churches equal to the extraordinary increase of the population' – from 27,913 in the Clergy Return of 1792 to 40,081 in 1821, the first official census. As 'local means' were 'wholly inadequate to furnish the necessary church accommodation', he was forced to resort to English charity: a vigorous campaign in England raised subscriptions amounting to almost £9,000.[124] However, there was still an urgent need for chapels, chaplains and parsonage houses in the remote parts of parishes where industrial mining had increased the population of poor people ignorant of the church. Bishop James Bowstead, Ward's Evangelical successor from Cambridge, described the problem in dramatic terms: 'the large population inhabiting the mountains dispersed among the glens and immured among the bowels of the earth at so great a distance from the churches as almost to preclude any attendance of the means of grace'; a new chapel was erected at Dalby, a small coastal hamlet with a 'large and overflowing population', but previously 'no services in connection with the Establishment had been held since the Reformation'.[125]

In 1838 Bishop Bowstead inherited not only the on-going, endemic financial problems but threats to the very existence of the bishopric itself, which had been briefly united to the Diocese of Carlisle by pre-emptive Act of Parliament in 1836. Aided by powerful allies in England, Manx clerics and laity rose 'as with one heart and voice to resist such an encroachment on their ancient privileges'. The Act was repealed, and the Isle of Man Diocesan Association (1839–67) was established to protect the diocese against further threat. The Association was formed 'with a view to promote the interests of the Island, by increasing the efficiency of the established church', an essential reform to avoid financial failure and further British intervention.[126]

Containment of the financial problems of the see allowed the pastoral side of its mission to take precedence and proceed alongside the work

123] David Craine, 'The potato riots' in his *Manannan's Isle* (Douglas, 1955), 197–209.

124] Edith Caroline Ward, *An Island Bishop, 1762–1838* (London, 1931); see also Moore, *History*, ii, 671.

125] Quoted in J.W. Bardsley, 'The founding of the Isle of Man Diocesan Association', *Manx Church Magazine*, I (1891), civ.

126] For further details of the Diocesan Association see the directory entry in Ann Harrison, *Associational History of the Isle of Man 1764–1914*, unpublished postgraduate thesis, submitted to University of Liverpool, 1998. Material relating to the Association can be found in MNHL: E205.

of the expanding Methodists. In 1829 Teignmouth noted that the
Methodists had not yet seceded from the established church: 'they
adhere ... to its services ... in the country parishes, the Methodists
generally attend more regularly than others on the public worship
of the Church'.[127] According to Moore, however, secession soon
occurred:

> in the towns, the line of demarcation had been for some time more
> strongly marked, and, from 1836, when the chapels began to be
> opened during the time of Church service, though many of the
> Wesleyans considered this 'a great evil', their separation may be
> dated. The process of separation was, however, even then a slow
> one, and, owing probably to the pronounced evangelical feeling
> which has gradually increased in the Manx Church, it has never
> extended to nearly the same extent as in England.[128]

The gap was widened by the Memorial of three Dissenting ministers
– William France, Methodist, Samuel Haining, Independent, and Peter
McGrath, Roman Catholic – presented to the Insular Legislature in
1843 on the advice of the Home Secretary, Lord John Russell. They
called for the introduction of clauses in the Registration legislation 'to
make the registration of baptisms by us valid in the Courts of Law, the
Marriages celebrated by our Ministers legal and to place us in an equal
footing with our brethren in the United Kingdom'. Weighted with the
membership of conservative churchmen, the House of Keys delivered
a curt response on Tynwald Day 1843: 'It is not necessary nor
expeditious to comply with the prayer of this memorial.'[129] The
Dissenters Marriage Act was passed six years later in 1849.

The pastoral work of the main Protestant congregations, Anglican,
Wesleyan and Primitive, was similar in aim but, as research on their
associational activities has shown, there were differences in cultural
style. For example the Wesleyans of Victoria Street, Douglas, and the
Anglicans of St Mary's, Castletown, both supported Dorcas societies 'to
administer relief to the poor and necessitous of plain and necessary
articles of Clothing'. However, the relaxed, democratic, female-
empowering atmosphere of the Victoria Street church differed markedly
from the hierarchical proceedings of the clergy and anglicised society of
the old capital.[130]

127] Lord Teignmouth, *Sketches of the Coasts and Islands of Scotland and the Isle of
Man* (2 vols, London, 1836), ii, 254–5.
128] Moore, *History*, ii, 679.
129] MNHL: Council Book, ii, f.351-62.
130] See the relevant directory entries in Harrison, *Associational History*.

Membership statistics are difficult to extract with accuracy.[131] Statistical research on Methodism undertaken by Frances Coakley has highlighted the impact of cholera on numbers of adherents. The Primitive Methodist District Report for 1835 noted the cholera effect:

> The state of our circuit is evidently satisfactory and has been ever since that extraordinary excitement the cholera which produced such astonishing effects in this Island abated. The principal cause of the lowering of the numbers since that period is the removal of the cause of excitement by the cholera. No sooner did that event cease than the new members began to leave and they have continued to do, more or less even unto today.

Indeed, the cholera years saw a rapid climb of around 50 per cent additional members, of whom some 75 per cent were lost by 1840. The 1833 and 1834 District Reports enlarged upon the point:

> The most common propensity in this Island is drunkenness which have (*sic*) overturned a many who in the late sudden influx only flew to the arms of the church for safety from the threatening pestilential storm which raged with such fury amongst us (so as to make the stoutest heart to bend for a while) ... it is to be feared at that time some hundreds rested short of an assured interest in Christ by pardon and adoption therefore in seasons of temptation they yielded to the intoxicating drought [*sic*] and renounced the irreligious proffession [*sic*] for want of root.[132]

Statistics on church provision are more reliable. The completed returns of the Ecclesiastical Census of 1851, a reliable bench mark of the number of places of worship by denomination, provide a solid gauge of growth. The Church of England possessed 32, Wesleyan Methodists 53, Primitive Methodists 23, Roman Catholics 4, Presbyterians 2, and Independents 2: an overall total of 116 buildings for a population of 52,387. Statistics for 1862 display a continued upward trend for the Nonconformists: 91 chapels with 35,000 sittings, 20 ministers and 200 local preachers jointly between Wesleyan and Primitive Methodists.[133] The Roman Catholics were also to progress, establishing a commanding

131] For Methodist statistics see Frances Coakley's web-page at www.ee.surrey.ac.uk/Contrib/manx/methodism/index/htm
132] F. Coakley, 'Primitive Methodism in the Isle of Man, 1835–40', *Manx Methodist History Society Newsletter*, 27 (1998).
133] Moore, *History*, ii, 680.

presence in Douglas though not without serious sectarian confrontation hitherto unknown in the Island.[134]

The background to the growth of anti-Catholic feeling was a reaction to a series of events which, in emancipating Catholics, appeared to undermine the rights of the dominant Low Church Protestants: increased numbers of Irish immigrants in the famine years of 1846–8; re-establishment of the Roman Catholic hierarchy in Britain in 1850 (when the Isle of Man was placed in the Diocese of Liverpool); and the acquisition of a prominent site in Douglas for a new church and presbytery. Completion in 1859 of Clutton's St Mary's of the Isle, 'one of the finest churches in the Island', brought many Protestants into active opposition. All this was set against the background of a constant press concentration on religious controversy, theological contention and sectarian dispute, fed by such groups as the Evangelical Alliance (a pan-Protestant body, established in 1847 to withstand the Roman Catholic threat: 'an organised army like the Popish one must prevail over a broken and disunited multitude').[135]

Alarmed by threats against the unfinished building in 1858 – and amid preparations for commemoration of the Gunpowder Plot and rumours of a 'Grand Protestant and No-Popery' demonstration – the Reverend James Carr, head of the Catholic Mission in Douglas, wrote to the High Bailiff warning him of the potential dangers of a serious sectarian clash, should the militant Protestants confront the members of the Catholic Young Men's Society, mainly Ulster men 'trained amidst the faction fights of the North of Ireland'. The night passed off peaceably with no demonstration beyond the customary bonfires and fireworks 'and a few party cries and songs opposite the Catholic Chapel, during the time of Religious service'. On 20 November, however, Carr's letter was published in the *Manx Sun* under the heading, 'Threatening Letter of a Romish Priest to the High Bailiff', together with the claim that the Young Men's Society, an Anti-Protestant Ribbon club, was ready to attack the lives and properties of Manx Protestants. Rumours of a death threat to the High Bailiff and the counter-moves of Orangemen from the active Manx lodges of the 1850s swelled the numbers at Hill Street, where the new Catholic church was under construction. The crowd proceeded to the house of the High Bailiff, who advised them to break up and go home, but he offered no protection to their Catholic quarry. Warming to the cause,

134] For a general history see Rev. W.S. Dempsey, *The Story of the Catholic Church in the Isle of Man* (np, 1958).

135] For details of the Alliance and similar bodies see Harrison, *Associational History*.

the crowd advanced on the Catholic chapel, broke all its windows and then proceeded to smash the windows of Catholic shopkeepers in the town, at which (belated) point the High Bailiff read the Riot Act, gave the mob sixty minutes to break up, took no names and made no arrests.

These events, a dangerous precedent for a town of growing pretensions to civilised attractions, were a shock to Manx public opinion, always wary of High Churchmen from 'across' but previously unconcerned by Roman Catholicism. The High Bailiff himself ended the affair with some propriety. Carr's account of the riots ends on a note of hope:

> December 7, 1858. It is but justice to add now, that his worship, since my return, has stationed a guard of police each evening at the Catholic Chapel, has issued a proclamation threatening punishment against those who insult the Catholic population, and, in conjunction with a few friends, has offered to repair all the damage done in the riots, and therefore to show their disapproval of those lawless proceedings.[136]

From this low point the relationship of the churches began to improve. Over the years the Catholic congregation grew in status and respectability under the able guidance of priests who, like Father Walsh, an astronomer, were part of the cultured society of Douglas. Relations never reverted to the hostility of the 1850s: indeed an ecumenical force drove them together on the big question that created the great Manx debate of the turn of the century, the struggle of temperance to prevail against the modern forces of drink. St Mary's League of the Cross was one of ten church societies which made up the Douglas Temperance Confederation inaugurated in February 1894 to combat the permissive licensing laws favoured by the powerful licensed victuallers' lobby as Douglas became an increasingly successful popular holiday resort.[137]

The last quarter of the nineteenth century brought more changes to the established church. The Ecclesiastical Judicature Transfer Act of 1884 removed all Probate jurisdiction from the church courts to government. In 1875 another attempt to merge and incorporate the see – this time with the proposed Liverpool diocese – was once more fought off with national vigour. Feeling ran so high in all Manx circles that Governor Loch, who approved the change on financial grounds, felt

136] Carr's letter to the editor of the *Liverpool Daily Post*, 1 Dec 1858, was reprinted in pamphlet form.
137] See the various temperance associations listed in Harrison, *Associational History*.

obliged to advise the British government to abandon the scheme.[138] The
League of St Germain, a forerunner of new attitudes in religious life for
the Island, added a distinct Manx identity to religious conviction.
Founded in 1896, at the height of the Manx renaissance, the League
sought 'the recovery of the religious houses on St Patrick's Isle':

> There are some churchmen in Douglas who desire that the very real,
> active blasphemy of the ruin and abandonment of those houses may
> be brought to an end; that the place where now blow blight, and
> deathly agony, may once more be the beautiful place in Man; that
> the Holy Spirit of their thousand years may once more be a power
> for life; that the lantern chancel of St. Germain may once more be a
> source of the light that shall guide the feet of Manx men into the way
> of peace ... Lieutenant Governors come and go; Lord Bishops come
> and go; Vicars of German come and go, and to the Manx spirits in
> prison comes no friendly minister. A body of opinion on the subject
> must be formed in the Island that it will be impossible for
> Englishmen or any who hold office in Man to resist.[139]

Inspired by Archibald Knox, the famous designer and an ardent High
Churchman, the League brought a sense of history and place to Manx
religion: it also added a spiritual dimension to Manx identity. Further
research is required to pursue these themes into the twentieth century.

Architecture, Photography and Sculpture

MARTIN FARAGHER

Architecture
In the Isle of Man as elsewhere in the nineteenth century the decorative
aspects of the dwellings of the affluent were cultural expressions of the
way in which their occupants saw themselves in the social order. In the
same manner, civic, ecclesiastical and institutional buildings conveyed
their position. The senatorial concept of the Georgian upper classes
was symbolised by the Greco-Roman style, to which came to be added
a Gothic element which evoked English ancestry and authority. By 1830

138] MNHL: Governor Loch's statement to Tynwald Court of approval in reference to
proposed amalgamation of the Diocese of Sodor and Man with part of Chester
Diocese, F22 1x.
139] See Archibald Knox's letter in *Examiner*, 26 Dec 1896.

there were two stately homes in the Isle of Man with such architectural elements: Castle Mona and the Nunnery.

As the Duke of Atholl's official residence from 1804, Castle Mona demonstrated both his power over the Manx people and his aristocratic superiority in British society. It was the work of George Steuart, who was the first architect of distinction known to practise in the Island, and who also built two courthouses and the Tuscan Tower, beloved of generations of Manx artists, on Douglas pier.[140] In 1823 the Nunnery mansion was built to the designs of John Pinch of Bath for the Taubmans, a family of great social and political influence and whose estates were exceeded only by the Duke's. Their family portraits by Romney are one indication that they displayed the same appurtenances of their position as similar families elsewhere.[141]

Throughout the first half of the nineteenth century an influx of newcomers was added to that stratum of Manx society which had long adopted the culture of the British gentry, and numerous substantial dwellings in fashionable styles were built for both newcomers and natives.[142] Contemporary newspaper advertisements give ample evidence that cosmopolitan goods and services were imported for their interiors, while the assimilation of building craft skills as practised elsewhere is illustrated in a number of cases. Menzie McKenzie was brought in to face Castle Mona with Arran stone. He married a Manx woman and founded a family building business, which also operated extensively in Liverpool.[143] Charles Swinnerton came from Stafford-shire to work as a mason on King William's College,[144] married a Manx woman, set up in business as a stone carver and subsequently built to his own designs. John Robinson was the son of an in-coming craftsman who had married a Manx woman and set up as a builder. Both John and his brother were apprenticed to their father. From 1835, in partnership with his brother who had worked on prestigious buildings in London and New York, John Robinson practised extensively as an architect. His most imposing houses (The Esplanade

140] M. Rix and W.R. Sergeant, 'George Steuart, architect, in the Isle of Man', *JMM*, VI no 79 (1962–3).
141] A.M. Cubbon, 'The Romney portraits of the Taubman family', *JMM*, VII, 88 (1976).
142] Examples survive in the Crofts in Castletown, Auckland Terrace in Ramsey, and in Finch Road, Derby Square, Windsor Terrace and sections of the Central Promenade, Douglas. Larger individual houses include Falcon Cliff, Marathon and Harold Towers in Douglas, Kentraugh near Port St Mary, Milntown near Ramsey and Greeba Castle.
143] Information from privately held manuscript written by McKenzie's grandson.
144] The architects of this public school (1830) were Hansom and Welch.

and Windsor Terrace) and public buildings were in the manner of Nash, and hence, although built for other purposes, the former Douglas Courthouse (1840) and the oldest part of Government Office (1855) are fortuitously in the classical pillared style which symbolised state power.[145]

During the 1830s several parish churches of vernacular appearance were rebuilt, using architects who had experience elsewhere. Thomas Brine designed St Mary's, Castletown, and St Paul's, Ramsey; his use of castellation may arise from his initial employment in 1810 to refurbish Castle Rushen. John Welch, in some cases with his partner Hansom, was responsible for others including Lezayre, Ballaugh and Kirk Michael.[146] As a result of religious norms and limited funds, these new churches were decoratively austere. However the ecclesiological style was soon to arise out of the religious reforms of the Oxford Movement. It led to Gothic spires and pointed arches, a layout which gave visibility to the Eucharist, and colourful adornment with iconography and religious symbolism. Such decorations did more than support the proposition that beauty aided spirituality; they illustrated the Catholic leanings of the religious reformers.

The first Manx church to embody ecclesiological principles, though the intended spire was never built and the remarkable murals by J.M. Nicholson were not planned for another half-century, was St Thomas's, Douglas (1849). Its London architect was Ewan Christian, who was of Manx descent. Many subsequent Manx churches were designed by him or others connected with his practice. The work of his cousin John Henry Christian included the building of Bride and alterations to Andreas, whilst J.L. Pearson was the architect of Braddan (1873) and St Matthew's (1897). Finally, St Ninian's was to the designs of W.D. Caroe. The Christian cousins were closely related to John Christian Moore, Archdeacon of Mann from 1843 to 1886, who devoted his wealth to church building and was in a position to influence the choice of architect. It was fortunate for Manx architecture that this group was pre-eminent in their field. Ewan Christian was a president of the Royal Institute of British Architects and consultant to the Ecclesiastical Commissioners. Caroe, architect of Truro Cathedral, also held the latter position and both he and J.H. Christian were presidents of the Architectural Association. However, the Manx churches of these and

145] P. Kelly, 'His loved name shall not perish', *Manx Life*, Sept–Oct 1983.
146] The Isle of Man Victorian Society Manchester Group Visit 1982 – Guide compiled by Peter Kelly, also gives information on churches from the Ewan Christian practice and from Giles Gilbert Scott.

other architects did not originally have much ecclesiological interior decoration; in a diocese with a long evangelical tradition embellishment which symbolised controversial High Church ritual[147] would not have found doctrinal or financial support.

From 1875 pulpits, choir stalls and screens with woodcarving of outstanding workmanship were executed for numerous churches of various denominations by J.D. Kelly, who also carried out such work for English churches. Before returning to the Island, Kelly had also worked on Manchester Town Hall and the college which was later to become the University.[148] Roman Catholic churches have benefited from the hand of Giles Gilbert Scott, architect of Liverpool Cathedral. He designed St Maughold's, Ramsey (1910), and later made interior additions to St Mary's, Douglas, and to St Anthony's, Onchan. Although some of the earlier Wesleyan chapels in remoter places were vernacular in the extreme, those in towns and villages were usually built (as elsewhere in Britain) in classical style for some time after the Anglican revival of Gothic. An example is the chapel (1860) in Glen Road, Laxey, now converted for domestic use and renamed Palladian House. Eventually Gothic began to be adopted for Nonconformist churches, notably in the case of Trinity (formerly Rosemount) Methodist, Douglas, which opened in 1886, and was of a size intended to meet the additional needs of holiday-makers.[149] However, the interior retained the Nonconformist layout which focuses attention on the performance of the preacher and the music without the worldly distraction of decoration.

In the late nineteenth and early twentieth centuries there was a significant growth of suburban dwellings,[150] much of it influenced by the Arts and Crafts movement, which looked to vernacular and pre-industrial styles and craftsmanship for its inspiration in accordance with the precepts of William Morris and John Ruskin; furnishing and decoration were regarded as the architect's domain. From 1880 this movement was disseminated by the Douglas School of Art. It was a local manifestation of the policy of the Department of Education and Science to improve industrial design: the school's headmasters,

---

147] K.A. Forrest, *Manx Recollections* (London, 1884). See also A.W. Moore, *Manx Worthies* (Douglas, 1901), 40, for Archdeacon Moore's evangelism.
148] MNHL (uncatalogued pending conservation): Scrapbook of J.D. Kelly & Sons, Builders.
149] R.B. Moore, *The Story of Rosemount* (Douglas, 1956).
150] For example architects R.F. Douglas and Armitage Rigby in Selborne Drive, Albany Road, Cronkbourne Road and Little Switzerland in Douglas. Also Port Lewaigue, near Ramsey.

Interpreting the Island's artistic past Archibald Knox (1864–1933) is one of the Island's most famous artists. Although his freely painted, unsigned watercolours of Manx landscapes are highly sought on the Island, he is best known internationally for his silver and pewter work for Liberty's of London, with designs derived from Manx Scandinavian and Celtic crosses. (MNHL)

including one with architectural experience, were trained at the Department's London institutions. In its first 24 years its vocational classes had been attended by 22 architects and 143 cabinet-makers or joiners, while numerous affluent ladies attended its leisure classes.[151] From 1888 to 1913 the Isle of Man Fine Arts and Industrial Guild sought to stimulate the arts and crafts, both in the workplace and as a

151] M. Faragher, 'The arts and industry in Victorian Isle of Man', *IOMNHAS Proceedings*, X (1998) 4.

leisure activity.[152] Its annual exhibitions introduced the public to the ongoing work of local designers and architects, including two who were to rise to international eminence:[153] Archibald Knox and H.M. Baillie Scott.

Archibald Knox (1864–1933) was a Manx-born artist who qualified and taught at the Douglas School of Art. Between 1897 and 1912 he was a prolific designer for Liberty in pewter, silver and other media: his distinctive Art Nouveau style was an adaptation of the interlace designs on Manx Celtic–Norse crosses. Owing to Liberty's policy, the loss of their records and his own reticence, little of this was attributed to him until the 1975 Liberty's Centenary Style Exhibition at the Victoria and Albert Museum, and the 1981 Liberty Style Exhibition in Tokyo. Since then he has been accorded international esteem.[154] His work has long held a pre-eminent place in Manx cultural consciousness. Since he had studied the crosses out of the antiquarian interest led by P.M.C. Kermode, he may be regarded as contributing to the upsurge of Manx cultural patriotism at that time. Later he entered the consciousness of the general public through his designs for Manx war memorials, gravestones, medallions and illuminated addresses. In the second half of the twentieth century some of his motifs were increasingly used as symbols of Manxness, almost as recognisable as the Three Legs of Man. Although he is a cult figure and an exemplar to some, others may be perplexed by his unidentifiable landscapes and unreadable calligraphy.

When Baillie Scott (1865–1945) arrived in the Isle of Man in 1889 he had served only a short period of articles: when he left in 1901, not only had he been the architect of some Manx buildings and interiors of great importance but his work for the Duke of Hess's Darmstadt Palace and for the Crown Princess of Romania had already placed him in the European *avant-garde* of the Arts and Crafts movement.[155] His initial employment on the Island was as a land surveyor, and it is stated that he studied under Knox and later employed him on some decorative

152] M. Faragher, 'The rise of a musical nation', *IOMNHAS Proceedings*, X, 1 (1992), 12–13.

153] *Catalogues of Annual Exhibitions of the Fine Arts and Industrial Guild* (Douglas, 1881–1913).

154] S.A. Martin *et al*, *Archibald Knox* (London, 1995). Also A.J. Tilbrook, *The Designs of Archibald Knox for Liberty* (London, 1976); S. Harrison (ed), *100 Years of Heritage* (Douglas, 1986), 106–10.

155] J.D. Kornwulf, *Baillie Scott and the Arts and Crafts Movement* (Baltimore and London, 1972), chs II, III. Also D. Haigh, *Baillie Scott: The Artistic House* (London, 1995).

aspects of houses. The exhibition catalogues of the Fine Arts and Industrial Guild show that many of Baillie Scott's designs for furniture and fittings, were made by local craftsmen, which must have provided them with innovative ideas. Most of his Manx houses displayed half-timbering, then a novelty which he later popularised in England, but in time so widespread as to evoke derision. However, the corpus of his work has led to favourable comparison, and even parity, with Voysey and Lutyens. Certainly Baillie Scott is the only architect of such stature to have worked on houses in the Isle of Man, but it is only recently that surviving buildings have been given statutory protection.

The suburban growth of Douglas took place in the wake of its redevelopment to meet the rapidly increasing needs of mass tourism. From 1876 terraces of boarding houses were built along Loch Promenade on land reclaimed from the sea. Since they were built of slate rubble and rendered, there was scope for a wealth of decorative mouldings. Although designed by several people, the elevations had to conform with an overall scheme and be approved by a Liverpool architect appointed by the New Streets Board which had devised the project. Thus, despite variations of detailing, the overall result was architectural unity, and their proprietors considered the result to be 'the finest marine promenade in the world'. The adjacent Victoria Street, although likewise subjected to architectural approval, provided premises which had a variety of purpose and hence of appearance.[156]

Much of the opulent architecture of the burgeoning tourist industry may be seen as an expression of business confidence and local pride. For the visitors it was an inducement to enter, and the ornately vulgar interior of the Gaiety Theatre, designed by Frank Matcham and opened in 1900,[157] and of the Palace Ballroom (1902) set the mood for frivolous pleasure. After 1914 there were few decorative additions to the built environment. They included the 1930s Villa Marina Arcade in Art Deco style, and the 1960s landmark tower on the Sea Terminal, quickly nicknamed the 'lemon squeezer'. Since then the piecemeal proliferation of finance sector offices has resulted in a variety of styles. Many of them have entailed demolition. In the mid-1990s the replacement of the Villiers section of Loch Promenade in an unrelated style aroused conservationist controversy, but since then there has been some

156] Victorian Society Manchester Group visit guide, 1982.
157] R. McMillan, *A full circle* (Douglas, 2000). Matcham was the leading theatre architect of the time. Since 1976 the Isle of Man government has owned the Gaiety Theatre.

worthwhile façade retention, notably in the case of the former Falcon Cliff Hotel.

Photography

Like many painters of his time, J.M. Nicholson used photography as another artistic medium, and in the 1890s he documented bustling street scenes in 'candid camera' fashion despite the limitations of technology.[158] In contrast, his contemporary G.B. Cowen, an accomplished art-photographer, produced posed and static scenes of romanticised country life. Hilda Newby came to the Island in 1924 having worked in London with society and advertising photographers. She spent the next 44 years as a leading portrait photographer, and extended her work to creative portraiture, including *The Laughing Flower Girl* which was exhibited internationally and won 40 awards.[159] In the 1970s Christopher Killip produced starkly revealing photographs of some of the Manx men and women from his own farming background which were published in book form by the Arts Council of Great Britain with an accompanying text which sought solace in 'local history, community feeling and rural peace', as the tax-haven Island adjusted to 'cosmopolitan culture, superficial, ubiquitous and synthetic'.[160]

Sculpture

Publicly accessible sculptures on local subjects have the potential to create a relationship between art and the community. The first whose work was so utilised in the Isle of Man was John Swynnerton (1849–1910). After apprenticeship to his father, Charles Swinnerton (*sic*), as a monumental mason, he trained in Rome as a sculptor. He produced busts of such notables as Garibaldi and the Nizam of Hyderabad, and was described in the *Encyclopaedia Britannica* as a 'leading English artist'[161] Some of his busts of Manx notables are displayed in the Manx Museum restaurant.

On Swynnerton's death it fell to Frank Mowbray Taubman to make a bust of Speaker A.W. Moore for display in the Legislative Buildings. Taubman was born and educated in London, where he was prominent in Edwardian artistic circles, but, although he was conscious of his descent from a distinguished Manx family, there was no Manx influence evident

158] V. Roach, *Douglas in the 1890s: The Photographs of John Millar [sic] Nicholson* (Douglas, nd).
159] *Diamond Jubilee Booklet of the Isle of Man Photographic Society 1988*.
160] C. Killip, *A Book About the Manx* (London, nd).
161] F. Swynnerton, 'A Manx Sculptor and His Work', *Mannin*, May 1914.

in his work. However, some of it portrayed the brutal side of nature, and this can be seen in the two examples in the Island. His group entitled *Saved* in Derby Square gardens was produced in Brussels in 1895 and was acclaimed as being in the manner of Rodin.[162] His 1924 bronze in the Manx Museum may have influenced both the theme and form of some of the work of Michael Sandle, who states that as a boy he was 'always being drawn to the mounted knight skewering the naked damsel on his lance'. Sandle, a professor in Germany, trained at Douglas School of Art and the Slade: much of his work is concerned with the brutality of war. This includes the Siege Bell in Malta and his *Monument to the Twentieth Century*, which portrays a decaying Mickey Mouse manning a machine gun. In 1997 his Viking sculpture, a door commissioned by the Isle of Man Arts Council, was installed in the Port Erin Arts Centre.[163]

Bryan Kneale, a professor at the Royal College of Art whose work is also known internationally, was trained at Douglas School of Art and the Royal Academy Schools. He attributes his inspiration to a deep feeling for his native island and a study of its rock formations and traditional farming artefacts. Two of his naturalistic bronzes are displayed in the Isle of Man: one of Hall Caine is in a small park on Strathallan Crescent, Douglas, the other, a Millennium of Tynwald monument interpreting the Three Legs of Man, is at the Island's airport. There are also two abstracts in welded metal. One, named *The Watcher*, is in the grounds of the Manx Museum, while the other is in the 1996 Courts of Justice and represents the backbone of the herring referred to in the Deemster's oath. Kneale's extensive study of skeletal structure has been utilised in his dinosaur designs for UK postage stamps.[164]

David Gilbert is the sculptor of the frieze on the outside of the Manx Museum extension of 1988. It represents aspects of Manx history and is 'a fusion of modern art with the Island's ancient sculptural tradition'. His favoured medium is wood, and when he came to the Island in 1971 some of his work had been acquired by national museums. He and his family lived off the land at an isolated Manx farmstead: 'this closeness to the land and its creatures are central to Dave's being and work, for it is the clue to his respect for materials and his reverence for the handling of them'.[165]

162] M. Faragher, 'Taubman of the Three Arts', *Victorian Society Newsletter*, Jan 1995 (from privately held papers).

163] *Michael Sandle Exhibition Guide*, Isle of Man Arts Council 1998. Also *Manx Tails*, May 1995, 26, and Jan 1998, 11–12.

164] Ingram *et al*, *Art of Mann*; also Harrison, *100 Years*, 114–15; *Bryan Kneale Exhibition Guide*, Manx National Heritage, 1992.

165] *David Gilbert Exhibition Guide*, Isle of Man Arts Council 1998.

In the 1990s the street sculpture of Amanda Barton, a Manx resident who trained at Goldsmith's, has become familiar to the public. In Douglas there is a naturalistic group showing Norman Wisdom and George Formby in their screen roles, the latter as a TT rider. More striking in its setting, however, is her Viking group in the forecourt of the House of Manannan in Peel.

The Isle of Man Arts Council was formed in 1965, but lack of a suitable place in which to exhibit contemporary art and lack of funds prevented it for some time from supporting the visual arts in the way it might have wished. As the finance sector has expanded, there has been growth in corporate patronage, sponsorship and support: Singer & Friedlander, for example, holds an annual competition allowing Manx artists to measure their work on a British scale. In recent years a number of talented artists have contributed to the artistic life of the Island by their actions as well as their art. These include Norman Sayle (watercolour landscape artist) and David Fletcher (abstract artist), consecutive Heads of Art at the Isle of Man College, who both served on the Arts Council and gave generously of their time. David Fletcher also instigated the Isle of Man Arts Council's Loan Collection of Contemporary Prints, which is displayed in schools and public buildings. David Fletcher, David Gilbert (sculptor, see above), Kate Shakespeare (abstract painter) and Paul Ford (sculptor) have all been involved, with others, in the activities of AIM (Arts in Mann, founded in 1982) which, with the help of the Arts Council, purchased a double-decker bus which was converted into a travelling gallery. Businessman Albert Gubay also provided them with a rent-free shop for a year, enabling them to mount static exhibitions. Reg Quayle (sculptor) created Artstratagem for the same purpose. Cheryl Cousins (painter), through the generosity of Bob Jeavons and support from the Arts Council, opened the Courtyard Gallery in St John's, mounting twelve or more exhibitions a year, and providing a forum for many local artists as well as an artist-in-residence. There is now a vibrant and energetic artistic community in the Island: at the 1998 Isle of Man Art Society Exhibition 137 artists entered 455 works.

Interpreting the Island's past *Until recent years there had been a dearth of good sculpture in the Island. This is now being addressed, and a number of statues have been commissioned. This splendid group of Viking figures stands at the entrance of the award-winning House of Manannan in Peel, one of the centres for the interpretation of the Island's history, opened by Manx National Heritage in 1997. (MNHL)*

Painting

SUSAN MORONEY

In the absence of aristocratic grand houses with large landed estates – neither the Nunnery nor the Castle Mona would be classified as such – the Island has lacked significant private collections of art. Furthermore, it was not until the 1930s that the art collection of the Manx Museum came into being. Both these factors contribute to a seemingly sparse Manx national artistic patrimony. However, the Manx Museum has gradually built up an interesting collection of works, many of which have been gifts or bequests. This has preserved and conferred status on deserving works which might otherwise have been dispersed, destroyed or ignored, 'regional' art for some time not being considered fashionable.

It is evident from surviving works that the beauty of the Manx countryside, its coastline and harbours has been a continual source of inspiration to artists. These were the subject matter of 26 watercolours by John Warwick Smith, now in the Museum's ownership, and described by Alan E. Kelly as 'the most important collection of eighteenth-century paintings depicting the Island'.[166] Early in the nineteenth century Jacob Strutt RA and John Martin RA both worked in the Isle of Man. One of the latter's awesome landscapes, entitled *The Plains of Heaven* (in the Tate Britain, London), was said to incorporate a Manx landscape.[167] Flaxney Stowell and John Miller Nicholson, two self-taught Manx artists, both born in the 1840s into family-run painting and decorating businesses, enjoyed considerable success. John Miller Nicholson (1840–1913), encouraged by Governor Loch's wife and Ruskin, made a trip to Italy, and some of his consequent work was acclaimed by art critics when exhibited in England. On his death a large collection of his works was purchased by a charitable trust and eventually became the nucleus of the Manx Museum Art Gallery. Nicholson and Lady Loch inaugurated the first art exhibition in Douglas in 1880. The interest this created led to the establishment there of an art school.[168]

166] M. Ingram *et al*, *Art of Mann* (Surby, 1996).
167] S. Harrison, *100 Years*, 100–1. Also M.L. Penderel, *John Martin – Painter* (London, 1923) which, on the testimony of Martin's family, denies this picture's scenic provenance.
168] Ingram *et al*, *Art of Mann*; see also Harrison, *100 Years*, 102–5; also A. Knox, *Mannin*, May 1913, 25–7.

The rise of the tourist industry provided a new demand for art depicting the Island's romantic scenery to adorn the interior of boarding-houses, hotels and public houses. These were supplied by both Manx and non-Manx artists. The best remembered is probably John Holland (1857–1920), who was already established as a Nottingham artist when he settled in the Island in 1883, while others like John Holden and J.H. Butterworth trained at the Douglas School of Art.[169] Holland's home was a popular venue for artists on Sunday afternoons when music would be played on instruments including an American organ, and the fun continued long into the night. The group also met in pubs and reading-rooms, and among those attending such meetings were E.C. Quayle (who was described as having painted more pictures of the Isle of Man than any other artist),[170] Archibald Knox, J.H. Butterworth, John Holland, Peter Chisolm and Frederick Leach,[171] all now counted amongst the foremost Manx artists of the past. William Hoggatt (1879–1961) settled in the Isle of Man in 1906, having studied art in Paris. He was a prolific painter who earned his place in patriotic cultural consciousness by designing the T.E. Brown Memorial Window (1934) in the Manx Museum, and through the presentation of two of his paintings to the King and Queen on the occasion of their 1945 visit.[172] James Aitken (1854-1935) moved to the Isle of Man in 1911 and he, and then his son John Ernest Aitken (1891–1957), continued to produce paintings of the Isle of Man, as did Knox's great friend A.J. Collister (1869–1964). John Hobson Nicholson (1911–88), grandson of John Miller Nicholson, not only was a popular watercolourist of the Manx landscape but also played a significant role in the dissemination of Manx imagery and identity through his designs for the Isle of Man government banknotes (instituted in 1961) and depictions of scenic landmarks and Manx crosses.[173] In 1973 he designed the first stamps issued by the Manx Post Office and continued to design many more.[174]

Apart from the war years and their aftermath, amateur art societies attracted considerable interest and support, attested to by a compilation of Manx exhibition and auction catalogues from 1880 to 1996

169] Ingram *et al*, *Art of Mann*.
170] Ingram *et al*, *Art of Mann*.
171] B. Quayle, 'Nostalgia column', *Manx Independent*, March 1966.
172] Ingram *et al*, *Art of Mann*; also Harrison, *100 Years*, 111–13.
173] Ingram *et al*, *Art of Mann*; also E. Quarmby, *Banknotes and Banking in the Isle of Man* (London, 1994).
174] Stanley Gibbons, *Collect Channel Islands and Isle of Man Stamps* (London and Ringwood, 1997).

which contain some seventeen thousand pictures by two thousand painters.[175] During the Second World War Kurl Schwitters was one of those interned on the Isle of Man. He managed to continue working, making collages from necessarily 'found' objects, statues out of porridge and paintings on lino stolen from the floors of the Manx houses in which he worked.[176]

Dramatic Entertainment

MARTIN FARAGHER

Although censorship and regulation by the Lord Chamberlain did not apply to the Isle of Man, visiting actors from 'across' performed their standard repertoire. A newspaper account in 1794 described performances which included Shakespeare, contemporary melodramas entitled *The Road to Ruin* and *The Haunted Tower*, *The Beggar's Opera*; and, only five years after its first production, *The Critics* by Sheridan. The three-month season ended with a concert, given with the aid of local amateurs, and a ball.[177] Such repertoires prevailed for the next forty years: sometimes alongside such acts as 'a lecture on heads and the Real Phantasmagoria'. The famous American dwarf named Rush appeared in 1805, admission being 6*d* for the gentry and 3*d* for servants.[178] Most performances were in Douglas, but occasionally they were held in the smaller towns.[179] The first known theatre was established by Captain Tenison circa 1788, and an account of an inept performance there to a disruptive audience by 'some gentlemen of the place' implies that it was by amateurs.[180]

Some of the players spent some years in the Island, including Eliza Craven Green (see NINETEENTH-CENTURY LITERATURE). Actor-manager Moss, who at the end of an unsuccessful season in 1810 was imprisoned for debt, was described on his death elsewhere in

175] A.E. Kelly, *Art Exhibitions 1880–1993* (Douglas, 1993); also A.E. Kelly, *Catalogue of Isle of Man Oil Paintings, Watercolours and Drawings sold by Chrystals Auctions 1969–1993* (IOM, Peel, 1993).

176] J. Elderfield, *Kurt Schwitters* (London, 1985).

177] *Manks Mercury*, 19 Apr 1794.

178] *Manks Advertiser*, 27 July 1805.

179] T.A. Bawden *et al*, *Industrial Archaeology of the Isle of Man* (Newton Abbot, 1972), 111–19, for some details of theatres etc up to the 1930s.

180] R. Townley, *A Journal Kept in the Isle of Man* (Whitehaven, 1791).

1817 as 'a comedian well known in this Island'. Around 1822 John Newton's company, presented *School for Scandal*, *Romeo and Juliet*, *Richard III*, *Macbeth*, *Rob Roy* and *The Miller and His Men*; his Manx-born daughter was one of the players. Occasionally some actor is announced as having claim to metropolitan fame, such as a Mr De Camp of Drury Lane, but the most notable was Edmund Kean, who played the roles of Richard III, Hamlet, Othello and Shylock.[181] In 1823 some 'Gentlemen Amateurs' set up a theatre, with shareholders and a committee. The proceeds were for charity and the 16 productions in 1824 included *Othello* and *The Rivals*. A pit seat cost 2*s*, and a box was 3*s*. Two years later its costumes and scenery were sold off to meet debts.

These amateur theatricals incurred the displeasure of local Nonconformists.[182] On an earlier occasion there appears to have been official intervention when a visiting company were 'prohibited from continuing their performances because the fishermen attributed the failure of the herring fishing to the holding of such vain amusements'.[183] A fight between three members of the audience led to their appearance before the Deemster, and their identities, Major-General Stapleton, Sir John Piers and Captain Edwards, give some insight into the social composition of audiences in this period.[184] By the time a letter to the editor attributed the rainy weather in 1838 to the current 'theatricals', the audiences were being supplemented by holiday-makers, and in due course entertainment responded to the tastes of the lower classes from manufacturing towns. In 1865 a company offered 'Operetta and Burlesque', including short versions of Greek tragedies, an opera called *Guy Mannering*, a ballet called *Daughters of the Regiment*, and *Ali Baba*. In the cast, but not yet knighted, was Henry Irving.[185]

The theatre in which Irving acted was advertised as open by permission of the High Bailiff (the town stipendiary magistrate), but it was not until 1888 that the Local Government (Theatres) Act systematically regulated all forms of entertainment. The Town Commissioners made building safety by-laws, while theatres were licensed by the High Bailiff. In addition every play was to be licensed either by the Lord Chamberlain or by the High Bailiff, who in any case could forbid any part which

181] *Manks Advertiser*, 8 and 29 Sept 1825; 4 and 11 Sept 1828. Also *Manx Sun* 4 and 10 Sept 1825.
182] *Manx Sun*, 3 Feb 1824.
183] *Manks Advertiser*, 6 Oct. 1804.
184] A.W. Moore, *Douglas a Hundred Years Ago (Douglas, 1904)*.
185] *Mona's Herald*, 21 June 1865 onwards.

threatened 'good manners, decorum, public peace or public morals' or was 'dangerous to life, e.g. wild beasts'. Performances other than of a religious nature were not permitted on Sundays. The courts refused to issue alcoholic drinks licences to places of entertainment, but the Derby Castle remained the historical exception. It had its origins in 1876 as a large-scale pleasure garden around a public house, and had incurred religious opposition by opening on Sunday, although it provided vocal recitals known as 'sacred concerts' and served no alcohol.[186]

In 1897, only a year after the first commercial cinematic screening in Britain, a film show took place in the Isle of Man. It was transferred from its success in London, and included specially commissioned Manx scenes. In 1904 newsreels of the first motor-races held in the Isle of Man were screened in Douglas and London. By 1910 one recently built small theatre had become a cinema, using live acts during reel-changes, while other places showed films as part of variety shows. In 1913 the Island's first purpose-built cinema opened.

Throughout the heyday of mass tourism Island residents had the opportunity to see stars of musical comedy and variety theatre. However, there was a dearth of classic drama: the occasional prestigious productions were farces or – as in the case of Hall Caine's plays in the early 1900s – melodrama. In 1935 the Gaiety Theatre was showing films for part of the tourist season and the Grand Theatre had been rebuilt as a cinema, but there was still sufficient opposition to entertainment on Sundays for a Castletown cinema to be refused a licence to open on that day. The stars of the screen were Gracie Fields and George Formby, and it was the year when the latter's TT comedy *No Limit* was filmed on the Island.

From the turn of the twentieth century there was a movement centred on the Manx Language Society to celebrate the traditional ways of life which were apparently being eroded by tourism. One manifestation was the proliferation of amateur plays, which were often one act long in Manx English dialect. They often drew on the traditions of farming and fishing, although some had historical or mythological themes. Although more notable for holding up a light-hearted mirror to Manx nature than for any dramatic profundity, a few won British Drama League awards. Through the first half of the twentieth century they were performed extensively in village halls and Douglas theatres alike. The most successful were written by Christopher Shimmin and performed by Sophia Morrison's Peel Players. Other authors included Josephine Kermode ('Cushag'), Mona Douglas, P.W. Caine and

186] R. Kelly, *The Summerland Story* (Douglas, 1972).

Film-making on the Isle of Man *The emergence of a film industry on the Isle of Man in the 1990s is not a new phenomenon. Earlier productions include George Formby starring as the hapless TT competitor in* No Limit *and adaptations of Hall Caine's novels such as Hitchcock's version of* The Manxman *and, shown here,* The Bondsman, *filmed around 1928. (MNHL)*

J. Kneen, all active in other areas of Manx literature or studies.[187] Their
plays were also taken up by expatriate Manx societies, and the London-
Manx Players performed them to large audiences for much of the
interwar period. From the mid-1920s the Chruinnaght (see MUSIC)
also stimulated the writing of such plays, as did the Manx Music
Festival from 1933 when, in partnership with the recently formed Manx
Amateur Drama Federation, it introduced one-act play performance
competitions.[188] In 1960 the Drama Federation began running the play
competition independently, and this has developed into a successful
annual festival of eight full-length plays presented by visiting amateur
societies. In recent years this federation has revived the one-act-play
festival.

The oldest amateur society to provide regular theatrical entertainment is the Douglas Choral Union. Founded in 1892 to perform
oratorios, it was soon found that staged musical forms of drama were
more attractive.[189] Amateur drama did not achieve comparable prestige
until 1932 when a group of ex-service personnel founded the Legion
Players and performed *Journey's End*.[190] Because of the seasonal nature
of work in tourism, most amateur entertainment took place in the
winter, but with the primacy of the finance-sector economy this is no
longer so. Other effects have been the availability of considerable
corporate sponsorship of productions, and an influx of experienced
amateur performers. However, growth and support is most evident in
the various forms of musical drama, and there are now four such
amateur production societies.

The increase in prosperity has enabled the Department of Education
to finance youth drama groups, and to the active promotion of drama
by the Arts Council. Furthermore, since 1976 the government has
owned and maintained the two-thousand-seat Gaiety Theatre, which
had survived from 1900 virtually as designed by Frank Matcham. It is
operated by the Department of Tourism and Leisure, while the
Friends of the Gaiety raise funds for its decorative restoration and
provide volunteer front-of-house staff. In contrast to its working
Victorian stage machinery, it has state-of-the-art lighting and sound
equipment.

187] M. Douglas, 'Christopher Shimmin: the Manx dialect dramatist', *Manx Life*,
March–April 1980; also 'The play's the thing', *Manx Life*, Jan–Feb 1983.
188] M. Faragher, *With Heart, Soul and Voice* (Burtersett, 1992), 44–58.
189] R. Kelly, *With a Song in their Hearts* (Douglas, 1995).
190] Legion Players Diamond Jubilee Programme, 1992.

The Peel Players *Sophia Morrison's ambition to create a theatrical tradition comparable to that of the Abbey Theatre in Dublin led to the creation of the Peel Players. Performances were usually in Manx dialect and, as this photograph shows, with elaborate stage sets representing the traditional ways of Manx country life. This farm kitchen is complete with a dresser laden with rosy-basins and lustre-ware, fine country-made Chippendale chairs, a three-legged table (which gave extra stability on rough stone floors) and tools and equipment necessary for everyday living. (MNHL)*

Music

FENELLA BAZIN

Introduction

There has always been a strong musical tradition in the Isle of Man, with a particular love for singing and dance music. The violin seems to have been extremely popular but harps and pipes had died out long before the 1800s if, indeed, they had been employed at all. The repertoire was affected by constant contact with musicians from other parts of the British Isles and further afield. Within the Island there are strong indications that music crossed language, social and religious divides, often with interesting results. Methodists, for example, introduced new words to a tune which was probably a medieval carol: 'In excelsis Deo' became 'For I Have a Sweet Hope of Glory in my Soul'. Melodies which began life as plainchant were recycled and adapted as ballads and dances.

Church Music
There were four distinct styles of church music in the Isle of Man in the 1830s.

First, surviving in the remoter country areas were remnants of the old-style Gaelic psalm-singing, wild and discordant to our ears, a reminder of the Byzantine origins of the Celtic church.

Second, in most of the parish churches clerks raised the hymns, 'lining-out' the metrical psalms for the congregation to echo, in the style widely practised throughout most of the British Isles.

Third, on special occasions 'West Gallery' musicians amazed the congregations, but often dismayed the clergy, by providing splendid anthems with instrumental accompaniments in the style of Purcell and Handel. Some of this music was locally composed, but most was copied painstakingly into precious manuscript books from numerous published collections. Some two dozen surviving manuscripts offer an insight into the social lives of 'West Gallery' musicians, many of whom were artisans who learned their musical skills through joining such bands and providing music for polkas, quadrilles and quicksteps as well as psalms and hymns.[191]

Fourth, the introduction of surpliced choirs accompanied by organ music was a novelty which attracted churchgoers but was often detrimental to the standard of congregational singing, although it generated printed collections of hymns specially designed for use in Manx churches. In 1799 came the first collection of hymns in Manx, based on 'Wesley and Watts, etc.', printed in Douglas and republished with

191] Among those in the Manx National Heritage Library are the 'Colby Manuscripts' (MNHL mss 2201/1–10A (J.66/7087–96) and 435–8A (J.66/6523 and 6525–7)), a collection of 14 part-books containing hymns, anthems and chants and dating from *c*.1810 to *c*.1860, and 'John Sayle's Serpent Book', MNHL 1234A (J.66/5596), which is a collection of instrumental parts for dance-tunes and hymns, and vocal part-settings of hymns and anthems.

additions in 1830 and 1846. Published in London about 1835 and dedicated to Bishop Ward was *A Selection of Psalms and Hymns Chiefly Designed for the Use of Congregations in the Isle of Man.* The volume contained 58 tunes, none of Manx origin, without accompanying texts. This was followed some five years later by 108 tunes (only ten of which duplicated the 1835 collection) in Isaac Dale's *Mona Melodist* published jointly by Quiggin's of Douglas and English companies from London, Liverpool and Whitehaven, and including the traditional Manx melody 'Molly Charane' (The Manx National Air), and featuring Island composers such as the Reverend R. Brown, I. Cretney and G.H. Wood as well as several Wesley hymns.

The language of the 'old-style' Gaelic psalms was predominantly Manx, and the hymn-raising parish clerks were more likely to use Manx, especially in country areas. An authorised selection of metrical psalms had been published in 1760, with a special dispensation 'to allow one psalm in English if the Minister so desires'. The language of West Gallery music was English, as anthems and hymns were generally copied from English-language collections. The music-loving Methodists clung to 'West Gallery' music, and remnants still survived in tiny country chapels into the 1950s; Nonconformists kept alive the tradition of instrumental music in worship, through the 'Hallelujah' and Teetotal bands, and the Salvation Army. In urban areas the use of organs and surpliced choirs became widespread, partly in a bid to attract visiting churchgoers, who filled the new churches and chapels which had sprung up to meet the needs of the developing towns and tourism. Open-air services attracted huge numbers of worshippers to Braddan, chapel and Sunday School anniversaries became more and more ambitious, Moody and Sankey evenings were popular in country districts, and the increasingly English-speaking congregations adopted the repertoire of hymnbooks printed in England. The decline of church music in the late twentieth century was such that few parish churches have regular choirs and many have difficulty in appointing organists, in spite of the activities of the Manx branch of the Royal School of Church Music.

Carvals

A still earlier form of non-liturgical church music was the carval (closely related to the medieval English carol). Hall Caine wrote that he was just in time to experience carval-singing at first hand, 'for I saw the last of it, nevertheless I saw it at its prime, for I saw it when it was so strong that it could not live any longer'.[192] This was in Maughold in

192] H. Caine, *The Little Manx Nation* (London, 1891), 119.

1866, and the occasion affected the 13-year-old boy profoundly, so that he was still able to recall details vividly 25 years later, when he wrote, 'I remember that it told the story of the Crucifixion in startling language, full of realism that must have been horribly ghastly, if it had not been so comic'.[193] The singers, mainly elderly men, began at the west end of the church, taking a step towards the communion rail at the beginning of each verse. Caine commented that the singers used 'a lofty key' and produced a 'wailing, woful [sic] sound',[194] suggesting a style similar to that of the Gaelic psalm-singers in western Scotland.

The texts were often specially written and could be 120 lines or longer. A collection of 86 carvals in Manx dating from about 1720–1819 was published by J.C. Fargher and A.W. Moore in 1891.[195] In 1920 P.W. Caine estimated that there were some twenty thousand lines of text still extant.[196] The texts dealt with topics which included judgment (22), salvation (16), Christian duty (10), Advent (5), and Christmas (9), as well as recounting stories from the Old and New Testaments. A particular favourite was the story of the Prodigal Son. None has refrains. Some texts quote, or refer to, literary works such as Milton's *Paradise Lost* and to hymns like Addison's 'The Spacious Firmament on High' and Nahum Tate's 'While Shepherds Watched their Flocks'. The words were usually sung to existing melodies. Some tunes, such as 'Yn Mac Stroialtagh' ('The Prodigal Son'), seem to have been popular and to have produced a number of local variants. One, collected from a Mr Shimmin of Ramsey by P.W. Caine in 1910, contains tuning characteristics found in Norwegian country music, suggesting that the idiom could have survived from medieval times and was still familiar in the early twentieth century. Generally, there are only a few examples of carval melodies that are shared with other regions: most seem to be exclusively Manx.

Carval singing usually took place at the Oiell Verrees, which were held in church after the Christmas Eve service. They were not popular with the clergy and some members of their congregations. In 1825 a correspondent deprecated the custom of holding 'Ill Verries' (*sic*) on Christmas Eve, particularly at Kirk Braddan.[197] In spite of this, the tradition still continues in country districts today, but takes the form of informal concerts, usually held in chapels, and no longer tied to Christmas. The survival of the carval in the Island has close parallels

193] H. Caine, *The Little Manx Nation*, 122–3.
194] H. Caine, *The Little Manx Nation*, 127.
195] J.C. Fargher and A.W. Moore, *Carvalyn Gailckagh* (Douglas, 1891).
196] P.W. Caine, 'Manx carols and their writers', *Proceedings*, II, 4 (1926).
197] *Manx Advertiser*, 22 Dec 1825.

with Yorkshire, Wales and Cornwall,[198] areas which had agricultural and mining industries, strong Methodist communities and thriving choral traditions.

Social music

Social music was greatly affected by the trading and immigration patterns during the eighteenth and early nineteenth centuries. The influx of half-pay officers, entrepreneurs and debtors fleeing imprisonment in England inevitably resulted in the importing of new styles of performance and repertoire. Professional and amateur musicians often seem to have worked alongside each other in bands, orchestras and choirs, taking part in concerts and festivals. Private teachers offered tuition in piano, singing, harp, guitar and cornet, as well as figured bass, a musical skill more often associated with the Baroque period than with the nineteenth century. Many singers and instrumentalists learned their skills by joining one of the many bands and choirs which flourished in villages and towns, often closely linked with churches, and the Friendly and Benevolent Societies, which played an important role in raising money to help individuals fallen on hard times or to assist the charitable societies which predated the welfare state. After playing anthems and psalms on Sundays, West Gallery musicians provided quadrilles and polkas during the week at a variety of functions ranging from country 'hops' in barns to formal balls at the Assembly Rooms in the towns. Traditional fiddle playing still had a part to play, and old Christmas and wedding customs (many similar to those in Scotland and Scandinavia) were still being observed in Douglas in the middle of the nineteenth century, and lingered later in the countryside. Concerts of sacred and secular music were popular, and often featured singers from Ireland and the north of England. String bands and formal orchestras began to be popular around the 1870s. A huge amount of sheet music was published on and off the Island, featuring songs, ballads and dance music, much of it aimed at the growing tourist industry. Some has lived on, including 'Ellan Vannin' (see NINETEENTH-CENTURY LITERATURE). Visitors from northern England and Scotland were richly entertained with indoor concerts, outdoor band music and, of course, the music hall.

The tourist industry had a far-ranging effect on popular music, with

198] H. Keyte and A. Parrott (eds), *The Shorter New Oxford Book of Carols* (Oxford, 1992), xix and xx; I. Russell, *A Festival of Village Carols* (Sheffield, 1994), 2–6; and R. Saer, 'The Christmas carol-singing tradition in the Tanad Valley', *Folk-Life: Journal of the Society for Folk-Life Studies*, VII (1969), 15–39; and J. Fisher, 'Two Welsh–Manx Christmas customs', *Archaeologia Cambrensis*, LXXXIV (1929), 313.

dance bands led by Joe Loss, Ivy Benson and Ronnie Aldrich entertaining holiday-makers and residents alike, and the growth of radio and
recorded music hastened the decline of vernacular music, which began
to be seen as old-fashioned. The music of the internment camps had
little effect on music generally, but did give birth to the Amadeus
Quartet, later to become one of the world's greatest string quartets. The
1960s and 1970s saw a proliferation of subscription concerts, events such
as the Manannan festival, and international competitions for viola, harp
and double bass, and major concerts during the TTs attracted some of
the best rock bands in the world. The standard of amateur music-
making is spurred on by the Manx Music Festival ('the Guild'), which
celebrated its centenary in 1992. This is still a highlight of the year,
particularly for singers, and competition for the Cleveland Medal
(donated by the members of the Cleveland Manx Society in North
America) is keenly fought and of a very high standard. Country
traditions such as Oiell Verrees and hymn-raising survived the advent of
'pop' music and were increasing in popularity in the 1990s. Miss M.L.
Wood, founder of the Guild and 'mother of Manx music', and her
musical successors would have been sad to see the decline in choral
singing, although they would probably have been impressed by the
professionally produced shows mounted at the Gaiety Theatre by the
amateur music societies. The choral tradition which was so strong at the
beginning of the twentieth century has declined, but several choirs still
flourish. The instrumental tradition has strengthened since the 1970s,
particularly as a result of educational policy, which has led to regular
foreign tours by the Manx Youth Orchestra and Choir, Saturday
schools, and the encouragement of music-making of all types in school
classrooms. Youth groups also flourish outside the educational system,
and the high standards of the Manx Youth Band have developed
alongside the resurgence of several town bands, and the popular brass
band festival. Like their nineteenth-century predecessors, all these
groups have a fine record of charitable fund-raising. The pop scene is
also well catered for, with many local groups performing to large and
appreciative audiences on and off the Island. In 1998 the Bee Gees drew
on their Manx heritage by releasing their version of 'Ellan Vannin'.

Vernacular Music and the Oral Tradition
The increasing international awareness of nationhood was reflected by
the interest in ethnic music, which began with *Mona Melodies*,[199] the

---

199] The publication was described as: 'The Manx Melodies, A Collection of Ancient
and Original Airs of the Isle of Man. Arranged for the Voice, with Pianoforte

Recording the Island's music *The second part of the nineteenth century saw a dramatic surge of interest in the Island's customs and traditions, and some great efforts were made to collect songs, stories and customs. A major effort by Dr John Clague, W.H. Gill, A.W. Moore and others resulted in the publication in 1896 of two major song collections. Gill's* Manx National Songs *proved to be the more popular and was still in print a century later. Mrs Lawson of Jurby East, pictured in 1897, was an important contributor. (MNHL)*

first publication of Manx tunes arranged for voice and piano in 1820, and peaked in 1896 with W.H. Gill's *Manx National Song Book*[200] and A.W. Moore's *Manx Ballads and Music.*[201] The remarkable work of the late-nineteenth-century collectors such as Gill, Moore and Dr John Clague rescued over three hundred popular songs, melodies, hymns and dance tunes which had lingered in the memories of country musicians and are today the basis of the folk revival. The music had survived in spite of the opposition of the established church, which had often 'presented' musicians to the ecclesiastical courts for breaking the Sabbath.

The men and women who collected and transcribed the music were all amateurs, unlike many of their contemporaries elsewhere. Little information was given about the singers themselves or their performance styles. W.H. Gill was perhaps the collector most influenced by the English folksong revival. He was happy to adapt tunes to conform to the conventions of the late nineteenth century, often completely changing the character and the context of the songs. However, he was highly successful in popularising the music and brought some of it to an international audience. His arrangement of 'The Manx Fishermen's Evening Hymn' is still included in *Hymns and Psalms*, the most recent edition of the Methodist hymnbook. Gill was intent on establishing the 'Manxness' of the collection, often discarding and adapting to reinforce his case, and romanticising the lives of the 'rough sons of the soil'. Moore and Clague were perhaps more intent on recording the songs and tunes as faithfully as possible, content to allow the material to speak for itself. The 'revival' was left in the hands of Sophia Morrison and her disciple, Mona Douglas, who perhaps did more than anyone else for Manx music in her untiring efforts over a period of seventy years.

In addition manuscripts such as the Andreas Flute Book,[202] Sayle's Serpent Book[203] and Kerruish's Cornet Book[204] contain many tunes

---

accompaniment. By an Amateur. The words by Mr JB ... By C St George. Price 8s. London.' 'C St George' was Mrs Catherine St George, author of *Edwardina* (1800) and *Maria, a Domestic Tale* (1817), novels both set mainly in the Isle of Man. 'The Amateur' was John Barrow, organist at St George's Church, Douglas, who was admitted to Gray's Inn in 1823. According to the authors, the words of the songs were entirely new.

200] W.H. Gill, *Manx National Songs* (London, 1896).

201] A.W. Moore, *Manx Ballads and Music* (London, 1896).

202] MNHL: microfilm only. The original manuscript belonged to J.C. Callister, West Craige, Andreas, but was destroyed some time after it was copied in 1957.

203] MNHL: ms 1234A.

204] MNHL: ms 5644A.

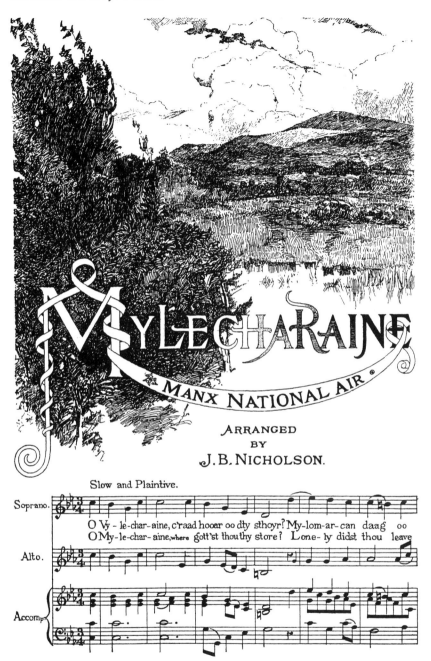

'The Manx national song' *The plaintive air 'Mylecharaine' (sometimes called 'Molly Charane') was such a long standing favourite with the Manx that it was regarded as the 'Manx National Air', and the major version by W.H. Gill was adopted as the National Anthem. This limited edition, published in 1901, was arranged by J.B. Nicholson and illustrated by his brother John Miller Nicholson, one of Island's greatest painters in oils. (MNHL)*

which have local titles and were almost certainly composed on the Island. Although the total number is relatively small, the tunes demonstrate great variety, with ballads that commemorate Manx events, work songs, lullabies, jigs, step-dances, prayers and invocations, children's songs and, of course, hymns and carvals. Favourites appear in a number of guises. 'Ny Kirree fo Niaghtey' ('The Sheep under the Snow') was first published in *Mona Melodies* in 1820 and tells the story of a Lonan farmer whose sheep were lost in a sudden, terrible snowstorm. But perhaps the most popular and versatile of all was 'Mylecharaine', which appears in major, minor and modal forms as a ballad, dance tune and hymn. Known from the 1840s as 'The Manx National Air', the major version was later arranged by Gill and adopted as the National Anthem. The text of 'The Wreck of the Herring Fleet' was sung to at least two different tunes, one of which closely resembles an Irish lament. Manx and English texts occur throughout the late-nineteenth-century collections; none of the thirteen songs in *Mona Melodies* had the original words but all retained their Manx titles and appear in later collections. As might be expected, there are clear links with the traditional music of surrounding countries, particularly the Western Isles, Ireland and northern England, with occasional Scandinavian accents. Manx musicians stamped their individuality on imported tunes: melodic lines were smoothed out, the range of intervals was frequently extended to span elevenths, twelfths and even more, and phrase lengths were less likely to conform to the classical norm of four bars.

The developments in popular music led to a change in the type of music contained in the oral tradition. Most musicians in the first 70 years of the twentieth century learned their Manx music from *The Manx National Song Book*, but, as Morrison, Douglas and later collectors were to discover, not all traditional music had died. Local *cruinnaghts* and eisteddfods were still held, even after the demise in the 1930s of Cruinnaght Ashoonagh Vannin (Manx National Chruin-naght). Choral and orchestral arrangements by composers such as Elgar, Vaughan Williams, Arnold Foster and Haydn Wood, as well as numerous local musicians such as J.E. Quayle, gave opportunities to amateur musicians to perform traditional music in contemporary styles. The successful revival in 1977 of the Manx Gaelic festival Yn Chruinnaght gave an astonishing new vitality to Manx music, and the festival's links with other major Celtic festivals in Ireland, Scotland, Wales, Cornwall and Brittany fuelled the vigorous growth of traditional music and dance among people of all ages. The movement was further stimulated and sustained by Colin Jerry's publications of long-forgotten tunes from the manuscripts of the early collectors, previously difficult of access to all but determined scholars. As sound recording became more available, Manx performers produced records, tapes and CDs, and it is fascinating to chart stylistic changes from the 1960s, through the performances and compositions of groups and individuals such as Phynodderee, the Mannin Folk, Charles Guard, Stuart Slack, Bernard Osborne/Peter Lumb, the Mollag Band, Mactullogh Vannin and Emma Christian. The first history of Manx music appeared in 1997; written by Fenella Bazin, it covers the period up to 1914 and was published by the Manx Heritage Foundation for use in schools.[205]

Associational Culture, 1830–1914

ANN HARRISON

D rawing upon nineteenth-century local newspapers (and other record bases), this section addresses a critical gap in Manx historical knowledge: the associational behaviour of the proverbially sociable Manx people. It serves as an introduction to a major on-going research project which has two central aims.[206] First, the creation of a chronologically arranged descriptive list and database of associations in the period 1764–1914. (This includes information about sources, structure, operation and origin, and the extent of divergence from British norms.) Second, assessment of the cultural impact of Manx associations in contributing to a distinct way of life or 'Manxness'. It is this second aspect which is highlighted here.

Habermas dates the origin of associations to the time when a community has developed the cultural infrastructure necessary to foster the development of free debate and discourse in the public sphere, typically a long-term, trade-driven transition from feudalism to capitalism, usually somewhere between the late Middle Ages and the eighteenth century.[207] Fitting neatly into this scheme, the first two Manx associations on record so far, the Society of Bucks of Douglas

205] F.C. Bazin, *'Much Inclin'd to Music': Manx Music before 1914* (Douglas, 1997).
206] Ann Harrison, 'Manx identity and associational culture *c*.1760–1914', in *Assocational History of the Isle of Man 1784–1914*, postgraduate dissertation for the University of Liverpool.
207] Jürgen Habermas, *The Structural Transformation of the Public Sphere: An Inquiry into a Category of Bourgeois Society* (Cambridge, 1989).

and the Manx Society, were founded at the climax of the Manx running trade, in June and July, 1764 respectively. The first was a branch of a quasi-Masonic society originating in London and spreading north to Liverpool; the second was a classic 'patriotic' society, dedicated to the promotion of the public good of the Island, modelled on the Royal Society for the Encouragement of Arts, Commerce and Manufactures in Great Britain, founded in London in 1754. Further analysis of these gentlemanly societies should shed important new light on the controversial process of revestment in 1765, a topic explored in volume 4 of the *New History*. By the early nineteenth century the starting-point of volume 5, Manx associations extended throughout the social scale to include artisans, labourers and working women.

Friendly Societies
By 1830 there were already at least 26 box-clubs or friendly societies in operation. The authorities, unconcerned by possible subversive tendencies, allowed their spread throughout the Island without any registration or monitoring processes (hence a frustrating lack of documentation for historians!). No fewer than 89 friendly societies have been recorded in operation between 1790 and 1914, and some who failed early have eluded entry altogether.

Operating against a patchy background of time-honoured charitable bequests, the friendly societies tackled the recurring problems of poverty by united self-help and collective mutuality, providing protection from loss of earnings by sickness and the death of a spouse; in many cases medical help was also provided. The Onchan Friendly Society was founded on 11 May 1810 to

> promote the advantage and happiness of each member ... considering that this life is liable to many accidents, by which numbers are reduced from flourishing and easy to necessitous circumstances; and as it is commendable to alleviate as much as possible the visitations of Providence, by relieving such as by some unhappy accident stand in need.

By rumour and repute the richest of the joint mutuality clubs (though its membership was not large), it held £1,500 in funds in 1838 to be lent out as speculative capital.[208]

The Manx societies were usually place-centred, as at Andreas, an ancient and prosperous parish: the Society, founded in 1812, is,

208] MNHL: Onchan Friendly Society, club records, 1810–85, MM Mss. 5179–5183C, Articles of Association.

remarkably, still in existence. At Abbeylands, an isolated hamlet of Braddan parish, still distinctive by its past history as part of the lands of the Abbey of Rushen, a society was founded in 1834; and, in 1822, the Strangford Union Society at Union Mills, a Braddan district with a flourishing modern textile factory. Some grew out of religious affiliations or specific trades – the Methodist Friendly Society of Douglas founded in 1798, and the Artificers' Friendly Society of Douglas and the Douglas Labourers Friendly Society, both founded in 1811. The 'classic' Manx friendly society of the early period, 1790–1840, was a local male group brought together by common sense and exemplary prudence into an association which offered financial security and a welcome sense of social solidarity and status. In the absence of poor law provision, Manx friendly societies provided an efficient welfare instrument, going with the grain of human nature, a blend of utility and the feel-good factor. Only the Sisterly Society of Douglas (1816) and Mrs Gawne's philanthropic Sisterly Society, otherwise known as the Rushen Female Benefit Society (1843), were concerned with the general welfare of working women. The former, in particular, merits further research as a pioneer exercise in female mutualism. An all-female committee of president, two stewardesses, one secretary salaried at £2 a year, a committee of seven members and two wardens, with one male officer, the surgeon, with an unspecified salary determined annually at the anniversary meeting, all resident in Douglas, offered Society membership to females from 15 to 30 years old residing within two miles of Douglas, of good character and 'free from any infirmity of body'. Once balloted for at the monthly meeting and approved, the new members paid a 5*s* admission fee and thereafter a monthly payment of 9*d*. After two years the fully paid up member, if 'rendered incapable of following her calling by sickness or accidental misfortune (not to be understood to extend to any incapacity arising from a state of pregnancy) was entitled to 5s. per week for the first 12 weeks, and afterwards 3s. per week till her health be restored'. A member 'visited by sickness, lameness, &c., so that she cannot follow her usual employment', a great problem in an age without public transport, would, on writing to the stewardesses, be visited, the necessary first step to receiving benefit, if agreed.[209]

The comprehensive network of collective mutuality was the subject of much Manx self-congratulation. A press review of 'The Friendly Societies of Mona' in December 1850 underlined their importance:

209] Sisterly Society entry in the Directory of Associations in Harrison, *Manx Identity and Associational Culture*.

These valuable institutions have a greater tendency to benefit the community than is generally imagined. It has been frequently remarked that the number of native paupers are very small in proportion to the population of the Island, and the obvious reason for this difference is, because the portion of our artisans and yeomen have exercised a sense of provident forethought in having seen the expediency of uniting themselves with benefit clubs; and so long as these societies are judicially regulated, poverty must be checked. Every town, parish, and district in this Island can boast of one or more of these benefit associations, and as they present a formidable barrier against pauperism and other social evils, they are justly entitled to the patronage of the Philanthropist.[210]

By this time some local societies were experiencing actuarial problems on account of their ageing membership, but three newer associations, the affiliated Oddfellows, Foresters and Rechabites, extended the range of options for collective mutuality. All three offered the financial security for benefit funds of uniform, closely-linked lodges in combined operation under efficient centralised control, and the option of interchange of membership and benefits from lodge to lodge, important for the movement of skilled itinerant workers. Although individually different in style and character, all three affiliated orders became firmly rooted in the life of the Island.

The Oddfellows (whose first lodge in the Island, the Loyal Mona Lodge, opened at the Saddle Inn, Douglas, in 1830) offered an exciting mixture of efficiency, prudence, opportunities to drink in company, and a certain worldly political sophistication from 'across' which was very stimulating – in 1844 William Shirrefs, a Scottish radical printer working in Douglas, took advantage of Manx free postage to publish the *Oddfellows Chronicle* for circulation throughout the entire Salford Unity.[211] The affiliated Order of Foresters offered the same mixture of prudent benefit and (bibulous) sociability, and the same facility for membership transfer, but they were never quite as successful on the Island, with only two major long-established Courts, both in Douglas: the Star of Mona Court, and Court 1356, founded in 1840 and 1841 respectively. They matched the Oddfellows in affiliated security, Christian values and convivial practices, and appeared to outshine them in ritual and pageantry. The affiliated Independent Order of Rechabites, Salford Unity, was started in 1835 to cater for the people

210] *Mona's Herald*, 28 Dec 1850.
211] John Belchem, 'Radical entrepreneur: William Shirrefs and the Manx free press of the 1840s', *Proceedings*, X, 1 (1992), 33–47.

Andreas Benevolent Society, 1906 *After the introduction of the NHS in 1948, the primary role of the numerous benevolent societies was lost. Many, however, have survived, including Andreas, which at the end of the twentieth century still had around seventy members. The AGM was traditionally held on the morning of Ascension Day, followed by the Andreas Sports in the afternoon and an entertainment in the evening. Although sick pay and funeral benefits are still available they are not claimed nowadays. Two hundred pieces survive from the original tea service inscribed 'St Andrew's', commissioned in the early 1800s and still in use.*

who required insurance but did not wish to face the temptations of a non-teetotal organisation. The fourteen Rechabite Tents founded between 1836 and 1898, each formed around the nucleus of a strong Methodist chapel, greatly strengthened the cause of temperance on the Island.

An audit of members and funds made in 1902 showed virtual parity between the Oddfellows and the Rechabites. The Oddfellows were slightly ahead, with an adult membership of 3,315, juvenile of 1,076, a total of 4,391, and capital of £51,701; the Rechabites had an adult membership of 3,184, juvenile of 1,140, a total of 4,324, and capital of nearly £45,871.[212] The two societies were equally esteemed, and the relationship between them – and, indeed, with the Foresters and the remaining local societies – was always close and cordial. Their work together continued well into the twentieth century, functioning as prototypes for the eventual National Health Service. Small groups of Rechabites in Ramsey and Peel and Oddfellows Lodges in Castletown, Douglas, St John's and Ramsey are still active, principally for social reasons and participation in much modified insurance schemes.

Towards the Half-pay Paradise

In the early nineteenth century polite Manx society embraced a culture of British, even English, manners. Strong bonds to the Crown were reinforced by the exploits of two Manxmen, icons of British Napoleonic Wars patriotism, Captain John Quilliam, Nelson's Flag Lieutenant at the battle of Trafalgar, and Mark Wilks, Governor of St Helena and custodian of the exiled Napoleon. After 1815 polite society was strengthened and intellectual and artistic standards raised by the influx of 'gentlemanly stranger residents', half-pay officers attracted to the Island by the comparative lowness of prices and freedom from taxation.[213] The associations of the period testify to the processes of gentrification and anglicisation, especially in Douglas.

The Finish Club, founded in 1821, invited suitably eminent Manxmen to dine at the York Hotel on the club's first anniversary, 30 September 1822. Guests were invited to celebrate allegiance to the Crown and the prosperity of the Isle of Man by drinking many jovial toasts 'interspersed with elegant speeches'. The president, John Tallan, himself a half-pay officer, served also as secretary of the Mona United Services Club (1822), which developed out of a social club opened in 1819 for retired British serving officers. A key amenity of the 'half-pay paradise', it continued to play a large part in the social life of the expatriate establishment: on 11 June 1863 it held a subscription ball at the Castle Mona in honour of the arrival of the new Lieutenant-Governor Loch and his family.[214]

212] *Examiner Annual* (1902), 65.

213] On the 'half-pay paradise' see John Belchem's chapter, 'The Onset of Modernity, 1830–80'.

214] MNHL: MM ms, 688A, Standing Rules, 1828–63; and MM ms, 689A, A/cs &c.of Loch's welcoming Ball.

The Royal Cameronians, presumably Scottish expatriates with some military connections, banded together in Ramsey in 1844 to 'promote good fellowship and conviviality and, to render aid in preserving the land and enforcing the observance of order and gentlemanly deportment'. This group, half social club, half private vigilantes, was engaged in struggle with juvenile poultry thieves and 'their depredations on the larders and poultry gardens of the gentry'.[215] In the absence of adequate police there were a number of peace-keeping associations – for example, the Protection of Property Association (or Douglas Association for the Prosecution of Felons), founded on 5 February 1841, and the Protection Society of Kirk Braddan, founded on 11 October 1845 – and various attempts at joint private and public funding of law enforcement.

The Visiting Industry
There was little recognition of the potential of the tourist industry until the formation of the Amusement and Recreation Committee of Douglas in May 1859. Neglect of basic amenities had been a feature of Douglas life, as attested in damning detail by Hugh Stowell Brown in his autobiography and lectures:

> In England and other places every attempt is made to make watering places attractive to strangers ... we have plenty of good water and pure air, but notwithstanding this, we have hitherto done everything in our power even to tamper with these blessings: our once beautiful bathing beach has been stripped of its sand and the abominable state of parts of the town is such as to render the atmosphere unfit to breathe in.[216]

Such problems did not deter Samuel Harris, the new Committee's Honorary Secretary and leading spirit. A Douglas lawyer and agent of the Goldie-Taubmans of the Nunnery, one of the principal families of the Island with estates on the southern fringe of Douglas, Harris was convinced of the economic benefits of tourist development: 'never before had he taken part in a movement which was likely to be the nucleus of more prosperity to the town'. Proposals for action were published in great and intriguing detail, followed by advertisements of professional and innovative amenities and amusements.[217] The Committee touched a popular chord, aroused a feeling of common

215] *Manx Sun*, 7 Sept 1844.
216] W.S. Caine (ed), *Hugh Stowell Brown, His Autobiography, His Common-place Book and Extracts from His Sermons and Addresses* (London, 1887), 3–15.
217] *Mona's Herald*, 18 May 1859.

citizenship in the town and laid the foundations for the subsequent success of Douglas as a holiday resort. Thus, the simple strategy of calling for support for a free association of men of diverse origin – two aristocratic sons of the Nunnery; the reforming radical journalist Robert Fargher; Douglas tradesmen and businessmen; and an astute, wealthy and apparently charismatic lawyer – was entirely justified by events. Though the committee itself did not stay formally in place for more than a couple of years, the inspired individual members stayed firmly with the cause, which was taken up by the newly elected Town Commissioners established by Act of Tynwald in 1864 and chaired by Harris, elected top of the poll. (Harris subsequently led the campaign to create a promenade in the centre of the bay, still known as the Harris Promenade, and concerned himself with Douglas affairs for the rest of his life, dying in 1905 at the age of 90, with mass tourism well established and supported at government level, and his home town, now a borough, at the height of its success.)

The Manx Enlightenment – the Culture of Learning

In the early nineteenth century the Island was poised for discovery in two main areas: its physical and its historical past. These were neatly incarnated by the appearance of a museum of miscellaneous specimens and marvels from all parts of the world, a popular and fashionable feature of the public sphere, brought to Douglas in 1825 by Thomas Ashe, an Irish entrepreneur in cultural services, an author and a surprisingly competent museum director. (There is much intriguing and/or contradictory personal information about him, or his *alter ego*, Trevor Ashe, the typical half-pay officer immigrant: 'Possessing now my half-pay ... I formed the resolution of retiring to some cheap place, and living independently on my own contracted means. I chose the Isle of Man; but so little did this project succeed, that I spent nearly all my ready money, and was considerably in debt in the course of two years.' After he left the Island in 1828, his past of adventure and crime was reported in the Manx papers.)[218] The museum's most interesting exhibits were those from the Island or with allegedly Manx connections. The 'Fossil remains of Manx Animals and Vegetables' had a special significance, directing attention to the fossil-bearing rocks and lignified organic remains of the bays south of Castletown, later the focus of serious academic debate as to their date – and of hopes of finding coal in the Island.[219]

218] Ann Harrison, 'Trevor Ashe and his Manx Museum, 1825', *JMM*, VI, 1 (1965), 237–40.
219] *Mona's Herald*, 10 Nov 1837.

Although accompanied by commercial interest, geological study promoted a wider antiquarian enthusiasm for all aspects of the Island's past. In the age of the gentlemanly polymath, geologists, archaeologists and historians all joined forces as antiquaries, sharing a new pride in their Manx heritage within the British Empire.[220] From its origins in the campaign to set up a records society in 1858, the Manx Society was emphatic about the 'most interesting and important nature' of the 'local peculiarities':

> Surely this Island has peculiar claims to have the light of catholic publicity at length cast upon all its documents and peculiarities. It was not in jest merely that Burke speaking to Doctor Johnson and Boswell about a visit to the Isle used the famous line of Pope – 'The proper study of mankind is Man' ... A society for the publication of all the valuable documents illustrating the past, and promotive of the Manx people, will have claims of no ordinary strength on the patronage of the Nobility, Commons and Churches of the British Empire and all who look to the United Kingdom as the leading model nation of mankind.[221]

By any standards the achievements of the Manx Society were considerable: the publication of 33 volumes between 1859 and 1882, indispensable sources for students of Manx history.

The Isle of Man Field Naturalists' and Antiquarian Society was established in 1868, probably by E.W. Binney, the renowned geologist, another scientist attracted to the Island by the quest for coal. Further research is required into this learned society, which predated by eleven years the founding of P.M.C. Kermode's renowned (and active) Isle of Man Natural History and Antiquarian Society. After a difficult start in 1879 the new society enjoyed sound development, boosted by the participation of leaders of the waning Manx Society, a generation which had fulfilled the greater part of its record-publishing aims by the 1890s.

Mutual Education Societies
The liberal ideas and imperial confidence of the late nineteenth century made it an outstanding period of high-minded endeavour in the task of educating the masses. The reformers, drawn from all denominations,

220] For discussion of these themes see John Belchem, 'The Little Manx Nation: antiquarianism, ethnic identity and home rule politics in the Isle of Man, 1880–1918', *Journal of British Studies*, 39 (2000), 217–40.
221] See the 'Prospectus' inserted in the MNHL copy of *Publications of the Manx Society*, I (Douglas, 1859).

were led by S.K. Broadbent, founding editor of the Liberal and highly political *Isle of Man Examiner*, a keen cyclist and key member of the Douglas Progressive Debating Club, and secretary and treasurer of the Conference (after 1897, Union) of Manx Debating Societies, 1894–1900. The constituent societies were a mixed bag, varying markedly in levels of intellectual sophistication: St Thomas's Church Guild led by the Reverend Ernest Savage, pioneer of the Manx Museum, member of the Manx Language Society and the Natural History and Antiquarian Society, was among the highest; others had simpler agendas and aims. One of the ten societies in attendance at the fourth conference at Peel exemplified the Manx talent for sociability, conviviality and mutuality, displaying a lively and humane understanding of the youthful needs of the less cerebral members:

> The Ramsey Wesleyan North Shore Road Young Men's Mutual was started in the winter of 1895. There are about 18 members. We have been fortunate in the past two sessions to have a lady president who really has been the mainstay of the association. A few of our topics have been 'Ancient Civilization', 'Cycling', 'Physical culture', 'A few things worth knowing' by the president. 'Mahomet', 'Temperance', 'Socialism', 'The evils of strife and contention', 'What benefits society most – the Spendthrift or the Miser', 'Books', 'Education', 'Can England feed herself?', 'The natural history of the Bible', 'The Duke of Wellington', 'President Garfield', and 'Duty'. We have had one or two social gatherings, and in the summer of last year we had a splendid drive to Laxey Glen Gardens, thus keeping the association together during the summer months. Perhaps unlike our kindred societies, we resolved to put 'Physical Culture' into practical shape, and have started a football club for the mutual benefit of our physical bodies.[222]

Broadbent's report of the conference was optimistic in tone: 'a wave of intellectual life seems to have passed over the Island, and left beneficial results in its wake, which it is hoped will be permanent'. The Manx 'enlightenment for the people' had started well.[223]

Aspects of Manx Nationality

Apart from the sophisticated and vitalising expatriate sector, the Manx community in the eighteenth century was unified by Manxness in birth, speech and culture – and by an almost uniform Protestantism.

222] *Examiner*, 10 Apr 1897.
223] *Examiner*, 10 Apr 1897.

Although under 'colonial' control, government of the Island was necessarily mediated through the employment of Manx-speaking officers. The Manx language, however, was soon under threat. English was attractive to aspiring business people or those whose ambition reached beyond their class or beyond the Island: indeed, a negative attitude to the Manx language was increasingly common amongst educated and upwardly mobile Manx people. By the early nineteenth century Manx was associated with ignorance and poverty.

The first of the recorded associations concerned with Manx language – the Manks Society for promoting the education of the inhabitants of the Isle of Man through the medium of their own language – set out to 'rescue' the Manx poor, not to revive the language. Launched in November 1821, it followed Irish precedent. Confronted by 'fifteen to twenty thousand of the inhabitants incapable of receiving religious instruction in any other language than the Manx, and with a large proportion of them unable to read', the Manx Church sought the advice of two Irish societies involved in religious instruction in vernacular Gaelic.[224] In following their example, the Manks Society averred that it was not its intention 'to perpetuate the Manks language or in the smallest degree to impede the progress of the English tongue amongst the inhabitants of the Island'.

In the late nineteenth century, as the prospect of language death began to loom, priorities were reversed. Scholars and native speakers, and those who simply enjoyed and valued the vanishing traditional way of life, coalesced into association to attempt a language revival. Under Sophia Morrison, an inspiring teacher and scholar, much loved in the west of the Island, the Peel Manx Language Association was the first in the field in the winter of 1897:

> A notice appeared in the *Peel City Guardian*, inviting all those interested in the Manx language to attend a meeting in the Primitive Old Chapel. The result was that one night, soon after, the little building was packed to the doors with Manx people – there was not one single English person present ... it was decided by the meeting that classes for the teaching of the Manx language should immediately be started in Peel ... the Manx language was taught, and Manx songs and history, and little Manx entertainments were given.

Interest spread quickly, aided by Broadbent, who published a weekly column in the *Examiner* in Manx. In 1899 the Manx Language Society

224] *Manx Advertiser*, 22 Nov 1821.

was founded in Douglas under the auspices of the committee of the Isle of Man Fine Arts Guild. With A.W. Moore, historian and Speaker of the House of Keys in the chair, the first resolution called attention to the revival of the language which had already begun:

> within the past few months considerable efforts have been made in many districts throughout the Island with a view to the revival of the language, and ... several classes have been formed. It was a matter of pride that the Manx Language Society was of PURELY MANX ORIGIN, a spontaneous growth from the people.

In his first presidential address Moore gave a carefully defined interpretation of the aims of the new society which crucially broadened its scope:

> Though called the Manx Language Society, it should, I think, by no means confine its energies to the promotion of an interest in the language, but extend them to the study of Manx history, the collection of Manx music, ballads, carols, folklore, proverbs, place-names, including the old field names which are rapidly dying out – in a word to the preservation of everything that is distinctively Manx, and above all, to the cultivation of a national spirit. Let us co-operate cordially with the Guild in its admirable work of encouraging Manx industry, music and art; with the Antiquarian Society, and the Trustees of Ancient Monuments in their care for the relics of the past, while devoting ourselves to the tasks of preserving and collecting our literature and song. We shall thus form part of an organisation which, I trust, will in time accomplish for the Isle of Man what the Eisteddfod has done for Wales.[225]

In pursuit of these comprehensive cultural aims, the Society – also known as Yn Cheshaght Ghailckagh (Gaelic League) – later changed its name, reviving the title of the Manx Society in 1913. It was a powerful association of gifted scholars and linguists, amateur and professional, fully committed to the preservation of the language and a sustaining body of hard-working members equally committed to the preservation of the threatened folk-ways of the Manx in their totality.

Manx cultural nationalism prospered, boosted by the strength of its mission and by a tide of almost universal success in every aspect of the Island's business. The Manx academic 'Enlightenment' had already led on to further improvements in the culture of learning from the government sphere: in 1876 a commission to report on the prehistoric

225] 'The origin of the Manx Language Society', *Manx Quarterly*, 14 (1914), 132–3.

monuments and antiquities of the Isle of Man; the civic cultural
agencies of the Douglas School of Art and the Douglas Free Library
founded in 1884 and 1886 respectively; and in 1886 the establishment of
Trustees for the intended National Museum of the Isle of Man. The
Trustees worked for 36 years to protect the material culture of the
Island before the Museum opened in 1922. Their endeavours helped to
maintain confidence that a bright and worthy cultural future for the
Island was secure. All branches of ethnic studies and the classical
academic studies of the scientist and historian, rooted in the structure
of the Island and its history, were covered in this cultural transfigura-
tion. The Norse heritage of the Island, as exemplified in the material
culture of the Viking crosses and the crucial political inheritance of an
ancient parliamentary system and surviving sovereignty, was for the
first time brought to the notice of the general public, largely through
the work of an amateur, P.M.C. Kermode, to be absorbed as a very
serious but distant, perhaps second-place, ethnic inheritance.

Manx national music, already developed to high levels in the Manx
Music Festival, became the spearhead of rampant cultural assertion in
competition with the wider world. Such chauvinism echoed in the
records of many Manx associations, from 'fur and feather' shows to
Manx athletics. The first exuberant intention of the Douglas Harriers,
on their foundation in 1890, was to build a national team for
competition in Britain. The growth of expatriate Manx societies
throughout the British Empire and beyond – and the foundation of the
World Manx Association of 1911, which led them into federation – had
a similar triumphal flavour. In associational and cultural representation
(as the writings of T.E. Brown and Hall Caine attested), the little Manx
nation reached its apogee in the Edwardian years.

Fellow Celts, however, were disinclined to regard the Manx as role
models. The work of Yn Cheshaght Ghailckagh was summarily
condemned by Seoirse Mac Niocaill, a member of the Intermediate
Education Board for Ireland. Having studied the teaching of Manx
Gaelic and its place in the schools, he deplored the absence of 'Celtic'
national spirit. The linking of the educational provision of the Island to
the standards of the English Education committee was tantamount to
treachery. To such ardent celticists Ellan Vannin appeared a lost
cause.[226]

Seen from their own perspective, however, the Manx were the most
fortunate members of the Celtic family. Scotland, Ireland, Wales,

226] 'Language and nationality in Man: an Irish educationalist's view', *Manx
Quarterly*, 14 (1914), 134–6.

Brittany, Cornwall and Man were all defined by a Celtic language and culture. The Island alone had retained political 'independence', a sound base for steadily increasing devolution – the national anthem, adopted in 1897, celebrated the 'throne of home rule'. There was an absence of sectarian strife or internal schism – the temperance question was probably the most divisive issue. There were neither grievous wrongs to right nor *irredenta* to claim. As their associational culture displayed, the Manx could be both British and Celtic. Oblivious of any contradiction, A.W. Moore, the most eminent Manx cultural patriot and patron of innumerable Manx societies, was proud to be awarded both the CVO and a Welsh Bardic Crown.

Local Events

FENELLA BAZIN

> The public in general of the Town and Vicinity of Ramsay [*sic*] are most respectfully informed that the present appointed Benefit for this laudable purpose is given by Mr Moss and his Performers, free of all professional expence [*sic*] whatever. And it is most earnestly to be hoped that the same will be attended with universal Patronage. For surely it must afford to the Liberal and Humane a most lively and pleasing sensation to think that while laughing at the Performance within Doors, they are by their Munificence and Charity, so good as to administer Comfort and Consolation to their Fellow Creatures without at the same time.[227]

This appeal, which appeared on an advertising poster of 1809, sums up the philosophy behind much of the Island's public entertainment. Concerts, coffee socials, fêtes, carnivals and other special events have been the mainstay of community life in towns and the countryside for at least the past two hundred years, meeting a social need for the beneficiaries, whether recipients of charity or of entertainment. Whatever the level, local or beyond, they provided – and, indeed, still provide – a platform for speakers and singers to hone their talents in preparation for political fame or artistic recognition. Once these aims are achieved, the performers are usually more than happy to return to their roots, to chair meetings or open events, or to contribute the entertainment essential on any social occasion.

227] MNHL: Photograph file 'Posters' Theatre Royal, Ramsay (*sic*), 1809.

Most events of this type are aimed specifically at Manx residents, and the majority of events used to be traditionally held during the winter, after the departure of the holiday-makers. But with the decline of the tourist industry they are now spread rather more evenly across the seasons. Some are necessarily tied to the calendar. 'Root' shows celebrating horticultural skills are still held in most parts of the Island during the late summer or autumn. The two agricultural shows are traditionally held in late July and early August and, in spite of commercial pressure, continue to provide a much-needed continuity for the farming community. Since the 1930s the Isle of Man Federation of Young Farmers' Clubs has been central to the lives of those who work in the industry, offering an important mixture of training, competition and, above all, a social link for people whose work is often necessarily isolated. While still encouraging ploughing matches, sheep-shearing, stock-judging and other tests of skills, the Federation also organises public-speaking competitions and visits 'across' to spectate at or compete in shows like Smithfield or the 'Royal' at Kenilworth. The highlight of the year is the variety show at the Gaiety Theatre, when the members of the four clubs take to the boards and compete keenly to be the most entertaining team. Tickets are like gold and the event has in recent years been extended to two nights.

The Women's Institute has also taken an important role in rural communities, bringing housewives together to socialise and learn, not only how to make jam but also how to wend their way through laws that affect the family, to speak confidently in public and to take an increasing part in community life. For the WIs, as for the farmers, a focal point of the year is the two agricultural shows. The WI marquee houses an impressive collection of themed displays which demonstrate vividly the high level of achievement of its members in household skills and creative arts. The church-linked Mothers' Union continues to play an important part in town and country, and there are also Townswomen's Guilds, though they do not have such a high profile on the Island as the other two organisations. The British Legion is a very active movement, playing an vital role in 'Poppy' day and having an important presence at the Island's national and civic occasions. The popularity of youth organisations like Scouts, Guides and Cubs peaked probably in the 1940s and 1950s and is now in decline, the organisers increasingly finding difficulty in raising voluntary helpers from among parents and families.

Churches and chapels also play an important role in urban and rural social life. Church fairs, jumble sales, 'socials' and coffee mornings are the staple diet of fund-raising, and Sunday School picnics and chapel

'The Anniversary' *Sunday School Anniversaries were a highlight of the church and chapel year. For the children of the Sunday School it was the culmination of weeks of rehearsal and the opportunity for new clothes. For their mothers there was a competitive edge to display their hospitality at the suppers which followed the service, when the standard fare was cold meat and salad, cakes and trifles. (MNHL)*

'Anniversaries' are important dates in the calendar. Methodists have always had a particular liking for music and regularly feature 'guest artists' in special services as well as organising Oiell Verrees (see MUSIC) and Moody and Sankey evenings.

Not all entertainments are centred on the resident population. Many were, and still are, aimed at visitors. Carnivals and brass band concerts, Viking festivals and Tin-bath Championships, June Efforts, Lifeboat Days and Military Tattoos, along with the almost defunct bathing-beauty competitions, provide a way of enlisting holiday-makers into helping to raise money for charity. The Crowning of the TT Queen was a feature of the 1950s and 1960s, bringing together a major sports festival with an additional attraction for tourists and locals alike. Now the TTs are celebrated with pop concerts and a huge carnival-type event on Douglas Promenade on the afternoon and evening of 'Mad Sunday', allowing everyone to let off steam and enjoy the wonderful atmosphere of an international event.

These events, and hundreds of similar happenings, are the very fabric of Manx life. *The Isle of Man Year Book* of 1996 lists an association or organisation for every day of the year, offering everyone an opportunity to be part of the social network of Island life.

Sport

FENELLA BAZIN

A s the Isle of Man basks in the title 'Road racing capital of the world', the casual observer could be forgiven for thinking that other sports were, and are neglected. That is not the case. *Cammag* was traditionally played in the Island and today its successor, hockey, is still popular. Horse-racing and other sporting activities accompanied the development of tourism. This tourist tradition continues with the promotion in recent years of sports festivals which attract visitors from all parts of the British Isles. Following the Year of Sports in 1984, the popular Island Games was instigated in 1985 to enable small island nations to take part on equal terms, particularly in team competitions. However, individual Manx athletes have successfully competed at international and Commonwealth level in swimming, rifle shooting and cycling. Nowadays the Isle of Man Sports Council, set up in 1971, acts as an independent forum for the promotion and development of sports and recreation. A major achievement in recent years has been the establishment in 1991 of the National Sports Centre, on the outskirts of Douglas, which provides an athletics track with grass in-field area, a synthetic pitch, a raceway for cycling and race-walking, a 25-metre indoor pool, associated leisure facilities, ten badminton-court-size sports halls, and a health and fitness suite.

Although they have now fallen out of fashion, regattas were popular summer events until the second half of the twentieth century: they could embrace yacht-racing, at sea or on the Mooragh Park Lake and, more recently, on Baldwin Reservoir. A Round-the-Island yacht race is held in early May, and Manxmen such as Rick Tomlinson and Nicky Keig have also made their names on the international scene. Swimming galas were also popular and, besides races and diving competitions, might also include a bathing-beauty contest.

Clubs and organisations active in the 1990s embraced a variety of sports including, among others, athletics, bowling, clay pigeon, pistol and rifle shooting, cycling, equestrianism, gymnastics, association and rugby football, golf, lawn tennis, sailing and squash. Fell-walking is a sport particularly suited to the Island's terrain, and competitions attract entries from off the Island; competitive cycling also has a long pedigree.

One of the disadvantages for top-class sportsmen or women on the Island is the problem of suitable competition. This also presents problems for schools, as particularly gifted youngsters have to travel 'across' to compete at higher levels. The problem of cost has been given considerable help by the generous support of carriers such as the Steam Packet and Manx Airlines but athletes often have to cope with the additional stress of coping with substantial travelling before taking part in competitions.

Motor-Cycle Road Racing

MARTIN FARAGHER

Motor-cycle road racing, epitomised by the Tourist Trophy (TT) races, is the one sport which is internationally associated with the Isle of Man. The TT – together with other motor-sport events[228] – is the 'niche-market' mainstay of the declining tourist industry, attracting large numbers of competitors and followers from many countries. It is also a salient part of Manx consciousness. Generations have emulated TT riders in their childhood play, absorbed TT facts and folklore and have later become course marshals with the power of special constables, and some have even become successful competitors. In 1994 one TT competitor in ten was Manx.

Closure of Manx roads was made possible by legislation in 1904 on the initiative of the Governor, Lord Raglan, who was personally interested in promoting motor-car sport at a time when there was a 20 mph speed limit in the UK and its parliament had recently rejected road-closing legislation. Raglan's legislation enabled the Royal

228] Other motor-cycle road races are the Manx Grand Prix and the Southern 100.

The Gordon Bennett races *Racing on public roads was made possible by legislation in 1904 which provided for road closure notices, an opportunity encouraged by Lord Raglan after the British government had rejected a similar move. As most road surfaces still left much to be desired, the preparation for motor-car and cycle racing was a major task.* (MNHL)

Automobile Club to use the Manx highways for the British eliminator trials for the Gordon Bennett Cup, which had been presented by an American as an international stimulus to the motor-car industry.[229] The event evolved into TT car races, which continued until 1922.

229] R. Kelly, *TT Pioneers* (Douglas, 1996).

Motor-cycle races, 1913 *Although speeds and styles of motor-cycle racing have changed dramatically since the early days, the sense of excitement continues to be a major attraction for visitors and residents alike.*

However, international motor-cycle trials were also taking place on unrestricted Continental roads, and in 1905 the predecessor of the Auto-Cycle Union organised British eliminators on Manx roads, and subsequently established the Tourist Trophy motor-cycle races there. 'Tourist' refers to the intention that it should be for touring bikes available to the general public, but the commercial value of winning has always stimulated manufacturers to produce specialist racing models, resulting in changes to the TT rules to prevent this, or to accept design innovations which were entering into general production, or to provide separate events for racing and touring machines.

In 1923 the Manx Motor Cycle Club organised what is now the Manx Grand Prix, having overcome objections that amateur races would not contribute to the success of British industry.[230] In the 1930s British racing supremacy was challenged by Italian and German factories, so that the allegiance of followers to particular British works teams was overlaid by patriotic concern in the context of rearmament. In 1939 the winners included the innovative BMW machines, which, with a machine gun mounted in the sidecar, were to feature in Second World War movies. By the 1960s the new Japanese motor-cycle industry began to dominate both racing and world sales, and this contributed to the decline of the British industry.

For competitors there has always been the risk of death or serious injury: by the 1970s technological innovations had resulted in increased speeds and more casualties. While the fastest laps of the 37¾-mile course in the first postwar races were under 90 mph, by 1970 they were around 105 mph and have since exceeded 120 mph. From 1972 some of the leading international competitors protested that the TT circuit was too dangerous and even boycotted it; this led, in 1989, to the Manx TT losing its status in the World Championship series which had been granted in 1956. Subsequently its popularity has been maintained by developing it into a fortnight-long festival with numerous entertainments and bike-centred activities for race followers, but there has been a rise in accidents and deaths amongst them which attracts strong attacks from the international press. There is no maximum speed limit on certain Manx roads, and on the eve of the races proper there is the tradition of 'Mad Sunday', when thousands of bikers speed round the course. An article in the *Daily Telegraph* (8 June 1996) stated that on 'Mad Sunday' that year 12 bikers had been hospitalised and 25 motor-cycles severely damaged, while during the 1995 TT fortnight there had

---

230] G.S. Davison, 'The story of the Manx' in *TT Special*, 1948. C. Deane, *Castrol Isle of Man TT* (Cambridge, 1975).

been 1,550 hospital attendances. Nevertheless, a hospital surgeon and a police inspector were quoted as respectively asserting that the rate of accidents and offences was low in proportion to the numbers involved, an estimated forty thousand visitors with fifteen thousand motor-cycles. An official press release stated that in 1994, during practices and races, 4,137 laps totalling 156,089 miles, had been completed. There had been 620 entries in eight events from 572 competitors, involving 20 countries ranging from the USA to New Zealand.[231]

In the early days objections arose from farmers whose work was disrupted by road closures, or whose straying livestock was threatened, and there were also objections to unofficial practising on Sundays. In recent years, with so many more houses inside the course, the road closures and consequent traffic jams cause considerable disruption to work and leisure. Despite this, a sample survey in 1987 found that a substantial majority of residents (even if they lived inside or on the course) enjoyed the TT, considered that it was generally welcome and believed that it created national feeling and was part of the twentieth century heritage.[232] In 1997 Tynwald affirmed the latter view by the purchase, in anticipation of setting up a TT museum, of a motor-cycle and other TT memorabilia of Mike Hailwood, a legendary winner of the 1960s.

The TT places considerable demands on public funds, which, besides attributable road maintenance and police and medical services, include a substantial contribution to competitors' subsidies and prizes, amounting to more than £500,000 in 1996.[233] However, the same survey found that only 14 per cent considered that taxpayers' money could be spent on better things than the TT Races.

In recent years the numbers wishing to attend has greatly exceeded the diminishing capacity of shipping and tourist accommodation. However, regulated encouragement has been given to householders willing to provide hospitality for the TT period. From time to time the TT races have been threatened by shipping and other strikes. Such occasions have been regarded by the populace and the politicians as national emergencies, generating much acrimony towards the strikers, while on one recent occasion a foreign vessel was chartered at considerable public expense.

231] TT Media Pack issued by the Isle of Man Department of Tourism, 1995.
232] R. Prentice, 'The Manx TT races and residents' views', *Scottish Geographical Magazine*, 104, 3 (1988).
233] P. Kneale, 'Riding in the TT races', *Seawatch* (magazine of the Isle of Man Steam Packet Co Ltd) (spring 1996).

The start of the first cycle-races ('The push-bike TT'), 1937 *Although perhaps better known for its motorised sports, the Island has a long tradition of cycle-racing, with an excellent record of international participation as well as an enthusiastic following on the Island. Here competitors at the Grandstand prepare for the start of the 1937 race around the TT course.*

Other Wheeled Sports

The ease with which roads can be closed for special events has also led to the development of other wheeled sports. An International Cycling Week is held towards the end of June, making use of lowland roads as well as the Mountain Circuit, car rallies in May and September and Classic Car Racing, also in September, take advantage of being able to compete on closed public roads. As with the motor-cycle races, Manx competitors have also been successful in these sports at international levels.

Statistical Appendix

JOHN BECKERSON

This chapter seeks to present a selection of data to assist in the interpretation of themes discussed elsewhere in this volume. Some information which has not previously been employed in published histories of the Island is presented, and a short guide to other sources of demographic information is included.

The main themes addressed are: population levels; employment patterns; birthplaces of residents; and passenger arrivals. The first three themes are approached using information gathered by the decennial censuses 1841–1991, the fourth using Manx government and other records.

A Note on Census Data

Census data must be approached with caution. Though our presentation gives it an appearance of uniformity, it was gathered according to the needs and idiosyncrasies of its time. For instance, occupational census data was originally gathered to create accurate life insurance tables.[1] Job descriptions also change over time, and the census has other biases.[2] It has been calculated that the number of workers in the tertiary sector may be up to 16 per cent greater than previously thought.[3] Female workers were certainly unevenly recorded, as a glance at the numbers of females in agriculture will show (see Table 1). This is because in some years the daughters, wives and nieces of farmers were automatically counted, in others not. Other areas must be approached with awareness that sometimes no historical source can ever give the whole picture.[4] In the case of seasonal summer labour in the Manx

---

1] J. Higgs, *A Clearer Sense of the Census* (London, 1996), 158.

2] In 1861 the census office noted that 'the nomenclature of many occupations is in an unsettled state' (Census, 1861, vol 2, p a3).

3] Higgs, *Clearer Sense*, 166. When a householder gave more than one occupation, the census clerks were instructed to tabulate only one. Manufacturing had priority over service trades.

4] Higgs, *Clearer Sense*, 154–66.

tourist industry, May census nights preceded the arrival of many migrant or part-time workers, and thus we can only guess at their numbers.

However, an awareness of the problems of the census does not invalidate it as an irreplaceable and, for many areas, by far the best source of information. A good starting point is to consider what it tells us about the Manx population.

Population and Work

It is helpful to examine Manx population levels in the light of economic activity. Up to the 1820s and 1830s this was mostly geared to meet Insular needs.[5] Substantive change came during the late 1840s when mining activity increased and improvements in shipping and harbours bolstered the Island's economic viability, and slowed population decline.[6] Mining was a large employer of that 20 per cent of the Manx population who worked in the 'classic industrial revolution industries' of cotton, wool, iron, railways, machine-making and mining. In England the overall figure was only 8 per cent. This has to be viewed against other areas: around 30 per cent of Manxmen were still involved in fishing and farming, compared with 20 per cent of their English counterparts of 1841.[7]

The Island's relative demographic stability from the 1850s to the 1890s was assisted also by a growing urban service sector. This catered first for the 'genteel poor' taking refuge from debt and direct taxation,[8] and later for a mass of summer visitors from the industrial north-west.[9] Yet from 1901 population decline became apparent. The era of heavy and sustained capital investment in the Island's tourist infrastructure was over by 1910. Mining was in serious decline by 1900. Discounting

---

5] T.A. Bawden, L.S. Garrard, J.K. Qualtrough and J.W. Scatchard, *Industrial Archaeology of the Isle of Man* (Newton Abbot, 1977), 49.

6] In 1845 the Island's mines produced 327 tons of lead, peaking at 6,868 in 1885 but falling to 2,014 by 1910 and only touching 787 by 1919. Bawden, Garrard *et al* (1972: 225); J.C. Brown, 'The story of Douglas harbour', *IoMNHAS Proceedings*, 5, 350–7.

7] A. Armstrong, *Stability and Change in an English County Town: A Social Study of York 1801-51* (Cambridge, 1974), 10.

8] See the 1911 Census General Report for comments on the growth of the service sector across the UK.

9] The north-west was a region which had experienced population growth of up to 100 per cent between 1851 and 1911, and was thus well suited to providing tourists *en masse* in the summer but also well placed to attract Manx emigrants to its growing conurbations in search of less seasonal work (D. Coleman and J. Salt, *The British Population: Patterns, Trends and Processes* (Oxford, 1992), 80).

the 1939 estimate which includes at least ten thousand internees and military personnel, and a brief postwar boom, serious population growth did not take place again until the 1970s.[10] The decline in Manx rural population mirrored that of remoter British rural areas, which had been declining well before 1900 and continued to experience falling population until the early 1970s.[11]

By this time income generated from tourism had clearly begun to fall, and Insular problems were compounded by a falling birth rate and rising death rate which Robinson and McCarroll have calculated would have led to a 2 per cent fall in the Manx population over the decade 1961–71, and an ageing population.[12] The problem led by the late 1960s to a New Residents policy implemented by a government keen to introduce new wealth into the economy. The successful modification of the Island's finances, lowering corporate and income tax in the 1970s, proved a key to prosperity. This was seen in the vigorous growth of the service sectors required both for running offshore financial operations and for providing ancillary goods and services stimulated by the financiers' presence. It is interesting to note that the Western and Northern Isles of Scotland also experienced population growth in the late 1970s and 1980s, as a result of 'counter-urbanisation', a force which may have played its part in the revived Manx population.[13]

Urbanisation in the Isle of Man

Noticeably, even during periods of overall population decline, some urban areas of the Island – especially Douglas – did continue to grow. Robinson and McCarroll have used census figures to demonstrate that this centre of the Manx tourist and service economy contained 16 per cent of the Manx population in 1831, 35 per cent in 1891, and 40 per cent in 1961.[14] However, urbanisation proceeded more slowly in the Island than on the mainland: 30 per cent of the English population was urban by 1801, whereas on the Island it was not until three decades later that the same level was reached. England and Wales passed the 50 per cent urban mark in 1851, but a slower growth rate meant the

10] English fertility fell sharply during the last third of the nineteenth century. See R. Woods, *The Population History of Britain in the Nineteenth Century* (Cambridge, 1995), 18.

11] M. Anderson (ed), *British Population History from the Black Death to the Present Day* (Cambridge, 1996), 365.

12] V. Robinson and D. McCarroll, *The Isle of Man: Celebrating a Sense of Place* (Liverpool, 1990), 144.

13] Anderson, *British Population History*, 364, 368.

14] Robinson and Carroll, *The Isle of Man*, 141–50.

comparable Manx figure was only 33 per cent. Rapid growth followed, however, and almost 60 per cent of Manx people dwelt in towns by 1911.

Internal population movement and migration both played a part in this phenomenon. Resort towns were particularly likely to receive migrants. (Other net gainers in the UK were large cities and coalfield areas.) The Isle of Man shared with its larger neighbour England an internal migration pattern of 'selective urban growth and rural decline'.[15] Douglas, chief resort of the Island, experienced such growth while rural areas and the fishing towns – especially Peel – were vulnerable to depopulation. Improved transport links meant that the Island was also subject to the pull of the large north of England labour market by mid-century.[16] Most Insular rural areas, like their counterparts in the UK, lost population between 1851 and 1911. Fortunately, the development of the Manx tourist industry was of particular benefit as it placed at least part of the Island in a sector which (at least until the Second World War) would support growth.

Occupational Structure

As the census occupational abstracts for the Isle of Man do not differentiate between rural and urban workers, our conclusions must be tinged with caution. Certain trades, however, do act as indicators of the Island's changing economy. The continued relative growth of the service sector is shown in Figure 5. By as early as 1901 almost half of the Island's workers were employed in service trades.[17] This was to be an important sector of the economy for the next hundred years – in contrast to manufacturing, which in 1851 employed one-third of Britons but only a quarter of Manx people, even if we include almost a thousand miners.

The early importance of the service sector must not, however, distract attention from the importance of agriculture to the Island. Though the proportion of the working population employed in agriculture declined, at the end of the nineteenth century it still occupied 32 per cent, in contrast to 10 per cent in the UK.[18] All these figures conceal major differences in the sexual division of labour; for

---

15] Woods, *Population History*.

16] Coleman and Salt, *British Population*, 76–9.

17] In England and Wales the 1911 census report noted the growth of employment in services such as leisure.

18] The figure for males only has been used since female agricultural workers were very unevenly recorded.

example domestic servants were overwhelmingly young women, whilst those in manufacturing were predominantly male, with the largest exception being female textile workers.

To sum up: key employment areas 1841–1996 were service trades, public administration, and transport and communications. Within the service sector, trades related to tourism had their heyday from the 1880s to the 1960s, whereas financial services began to flourish in the 1970s and have continued to grow to date. Agriculture and fisheries have seen a steady decline in employment. Manufacturing has occupied a relatively stable number of people, and construction has maintained a surprisingly consistent level throughout the twentieth century until its growth spurt in the last few years.

Migration

When we examine the graphs of birth-places, two trends reveal themselves. First, the percentage of Manx-born in the population steadily declines throughout the period. This suggests emigration and, as Robinson and McCarroll have pointed out, an excess of deaths over births.[19] However, the birth-place trend occurred later than in the UK, where as early as 1841 it was found that only 40 per cent of people were born in the town they lived in.[20] In contrast, 87 per cent of Manx people in that year had been born on the Island. Emigration became a particularly noticeable problem much later in the 1970s when the sluggish local economy limited opportunities for young people (those most likely to emigrate) and caused the Manx government to study the issue of an ageing population and the need to attract new residents.

Second, it has been noted that seaside towns across Britain tended to attract immigration. More work on the nature of immigrants to the Island is needed. For example, Armstrong has suggested that those drawn from more distant places tended to be 'disproportionately well-represented at the upper end of the social hierarchy, whilst local immigrants ... and of course the Irish, tended to cluster' in the lower classes.[21] To what extent was this true for the Isle of Man? We know that in the early nineteenth century some new residents were the 'genteel poor', whilst in the 1970s a fair number of senior citizens retired to Man. More recently, the growth of financial services has attracted new labour to work in this sector. These migration trends fit

19] Robinson and McCarroll, *The Isle of Man*, 144.
20] Coleman and Salt, *British Population*, 79.
21] This was particularly due to the 1840s famine in Ireland. Armstrong, *Stability and Change*, 91.

in with the general increase of personal mobility throughout the late nineteenth and twentieth centuries.[22] But only detailed recourse to the census enumerators' books will tell us more; this time-consuming task was outside the scope of this brief summary.

Passenger arrivals, 1830–1920[23]

Passenger arrival figures help to show the level of Manx trade with the rest of the UK and in particular they reveal the growth of the tourist industry, although no attempt was made to differentiate tourists from all travellers to the Isle of Man until after the Second World War. Given this restriction, a picture of tourist activity on the Isle of Man can still be obtained which is fuller than that of many English resorts until the 1940s.[24] The problem of separating visitors from general traffic is, to an extent, one which the Manx passenger figures share; however, the extreme seasonality of all but the Liverpool route reveals just how little traffic went on outside the season.[25]

Local newspapers started to comment on visitors by the early nineteenth century. An early reference to pleasure-seekers was in 1820 when the *Manks Advertiser* noted that improvements in sea travel were allowing the Island to share in the new vogue for sea-bathing. In an editorial it wrote:

> Our country has not been generally known to the respectable inhabitants of the opposite shores. Until of late it has been considered as a barbarous coast, scarcely visited by any but the destitute adventurer or the base deserter. [The] general and uninterrupted flux of numerous and respectable visitors ... [had that year] almost – and

22] Coleman and Salt, *British Population*, 395; Woods, *Population History*, 20.
23] This section is a condensation of my 'Sources for the history of the tourist trade in the Isle of Man visitor numbers', reproduced as an appendix in my *Advertising the Island: The Isle of Man Official Board of Advertising 1894–1914*, unpublished MA dissertation, University of East Anglia, 1996. For passenger arrivals up to the present day see J.M. Caley, *Isle of Man Summer Passenger Arrivals: 1887 to the Present* (Douglas, 1966).
24] At this time the new English Tourist Board began the serious analysis of holiday-making patterns, and Mass Observation had made its visits to the seaside. J. Demetriadi *English Seaside Resorts 1950–1974*, unpublished PhD thesis, University of Lancaster, 1996; G. Cross, *Worktowners at Blackpool: Mass Observation and Popular Leisure in the 1930s* (London, 1990).
25] For a discussion of these problems see J.K. Walton and P.R. McGloin, 'Holiday resorts and their visitors: some sources for the local historian', *Local Historian*, VIII, 323–31, and my forthcoming article 'Some neglected aspects of tourism history: sources and possibilities', *Business Archives*.

it were perhaps not saying too much – more than equalled the returns of an ordinary fishery.[26]

By 1 July 1834 the same newspaper was 'glad to observe the increased interest which this Island affords to visitors ... the arrivals in Douglas from the opposite coasts since our last [24 June] exceeds 350, and we expect before our next to announce a greater arrival'.[27] The first annual total of visitors to be found in the newspapers is in 1846, a figure of 25,000 which broadly bears out Moore's figure.[28] The formation of the successful Isle of Man Steam Packet Company in 1851, together with harbour improvements and the nationwide growth of seaside holiday-making helped passenger movements to treble between 1850 and 1873. The 1880s saw less smooth growth. Increased shipping competition and the Jubilee of 1887 marked an end to this period. The Island's Board of Advertising also claimed some success for the more stable number of arrivals since its formation in 1894.[29] Arrivals followed a broad upward trend until the outbreak of the First World War, when heavy shipping restrictions and public fears of sea travel all but bankrupted the Island. The speedy increase of traffic was not to be repeated.

The period after 1918 saw wider fluctuations and a lower level of traffic, the high peak of 1914 not being reached until just before the Second World War. From 1945 to the late 1970s annual arrivals varied between five and six hundred thousand. The decline was steep thereafter, as the Island's mass tourism industry experienced a decline shared with many other British resorts.[30]

Future Work Needed
More published statistical work would greatly assist the understanding of Manx history. Areas requiring attention include the interpretation of birth and death rates; figures on religious observance; specialised census analysis for the tourist sector;[31] and occupational breakdowns by area and employment class. The last category would permit a more thorough understanding of the economic structure of Manx towns, for example, by plotting head of household's occupation within an employment class, as done by Armstrong for York.[32] This would help

26] *Manks Advertiser*, 21 Sept 1820, 3.

27] *Manks Advertiser*, 1 July 1834, 3.

28] *Manks Advertiser*, 3 Oct 1846, 4.

29] Beckerson, *Advertising the Island*.

30] Demetriadi, *English Seaside Resorts*, has charted the period of acute decline, 1950–74.

31] See my forthcoming thesis on seaside resort marketing, University of East Anglia.

32] A. Armstrong, *Stability and Change in an English County Town: A Social Study of York 1801–51* (Cambridge, 1974) 13–15.

fill gaps in the study of tourist resorts that a tradition of largely geographical studies has been unable to address.[33]

A Note on Some Other Published Information Sources

A comparison of the Manx employment structure with that of Jersey for 1951 may be found in Birch,[34] along with a snapshot of the national accounts for the Island for 1958–9. Birch also sampled data pertaining to the holiday traffic for 1951 and 1961. More recently, Robinson and McCarroll provide a run of figures from the census disclosing population change along with an effective commentary.[35] The social demography of the Island is discussed and the 'closed' system of demographic transition modelling is contrasted against the reality of Manx emigration and immigration.[36] Bawden and Garrard offer a diffuse selection of data pertinent to the Island's industrial archaeology, their figures for mine outputs being particularly useful.[37] Caley provides an overview of passenger arrivals, including those which reveal the growth of air travel to the Island.[38]

To compare the Manx situation with some other seaside towns see Walton's chapter on the structure of English seaside resort society, drawn largely from census data.[39] For more general histories of population Woods's *Population of Britain in the Nineteenth Century*[40] provides a good introduction to the subject, whilst Anderson's larger study of British population history[41] includes two chapters on the period covered by this volume, plus an extensive bibliography. For the twentieth century see Coleman and Salt's *British Population: Patterns, Trends and Processes* (1992).[42]

33] For example, R.P. Craine, *Douglas: A Town's Specialisation in Tourism*, unpublished dissertation, University of Durham, 1966.
34] W. Birch, *The Isle of Man: A Study in Economic Geography*, (Cambridge, 1964), 185.
35] Robinson and McCarroll, *The Isle of Man*, 141–50.
36] Robinson and McCarroll, *The Isle of Man*, 144.
37] Bawden, Garrard *et al*, *Industrial Archaeology*, 224–31.
38] Caley, *Passenger Arrivals*.
39] J.K. Walton, *The English Seaside Resort, a Social History 1750–1914*. (Leicester, 1983) chapter 4: 'Resort Society, Structure and Problems', 74–103. See also J.G. Beckerson, *A Bibliography of Sources for the History of Tourism and Leisure*, unpublished manuscript, MNHL, 1996.
40] Woods, *Population History*.
41] Anderson, *British Population History*.
42] Coleman and Salt, *British Population*

Table 1   Population, 1821–1996

Year	Census date	Total census pop.	Male pop.: C = census R = resident	Female pop.: C = census R = resident	Number of non-residents in census pop.	Resident pop. (census pop. minus non-residents)	No. Manx-born (census pop.)	No. born elsewhere (census pop.)
1821	27–8 May	40,081	19,158 C	20,923 C	–	–	–	–
1831	29–30 May	41,000	19,560 C	21,440 C	–	–	–	–
1841	6–7 June	47,975	23,011 C	24,964 C	–	–	42,184	5,791
1851	30–1 Mar	52,387	24,915 C	27,472 C	–	–	44,817	7,570
1861	7–8 April	52,469	24,727 C	27,742 C	–	–	45,143	7,326
1871	2–3 April	54,042	25,914 C	28,128 C	–	–	45,941	8,101
1881	3–4 April	53,558	25,760 C	27,798 C	–	–	45,453	8,105
1891	5–6 April	55,608	26,329 C	29,279 C	–	–	45,736	9,872
1901	1 Mar–1 Apr	54,752	25,496 C	29,256 C	–	–	44,910	9,842
1911	2–3 April	52,016	23,937 C	28,079 C	–	–	41,825	10,191
1921	19–20 June	60,284	27,329 C	32,955 C	11,014	49,270	36,431	23,853
1931	26–7 April	49,308	22,443 C	26,865 C	1,014	48,294	36,558	12,750
1939	mid-yr est.	52,029	23,675 C	28,354 C	–	–	–	–
1951	8–9 April	55,253	25,774 C	29,479 C	1,229	54,024	35,521	20,002
1961	23 April	48,133	22,059 C	26,074 C	967	47,166	32,345	15,788
1971	25–6 April	54,581	25,528 C	29,053 C	1,353	53,228	32,374	22,207
1981	5–6 April	66,101	31,658 C	34,443 C	1,422	64,679	34,399	31,702
1991	14–15 April	71,267	33,693 R	36,095 R	1,479	69,788	34,608	36,659
1996	14–15 April	71,714	34,797 R	36,917 R	2,966	68,748	35,811	35,903

Table 2　Birthplaces of persons enumerated, 1841–1991

	1841	1851	1861	1871	1881	1891	1901	1911	1921	1931	1951	1961	1971	1981	1991
Numbers															
Manx-born	42,184	44,817	45,143	45,941	45,453	45,736	44,910	41,825	36,431	36,558	35,521	32,345	32,374	34,399	34,608
Born elsewhere	5,791	7,570	7,326	8,101	8,105	9,872	9,842	10,191	23,853	12,750	20,002	15,788	22,207	31,702	36,659
Population	47,975	52,387	52,469	54,042	53,558	55,608	54,752	52,016	60,284	49,308	55,523	48,133	54,581	66,101	71,267
Percentages															
Manx-born	87.93	85.55	86.04	85.01	84.87	82.25	82.02	80.41	60.43	74.14	63.98	67.20	59.31	52.04	48.56
Born elsewhere	12.07	14.45	13.96	14.99	15.13	17.75	17.98	19.59	39.57	25.86	36.02	32.80	40.69	47.96	51.44

Notes:
1 Birthplace data begin 1841.
2 Figures up to 1951 are census population, after 1961 resident population (census population minus visitors).

Table 3 Occupied persons, 1841–1996 (no.)

	1841	1851	1861	1871	1881	1891	1901	1911	1921	1931	1951	1961	1971	1981	1991	1996
Ag, For, Fish M	4,439	6,117	5,379	5,620	6,064	5,139	4,202	4,193	3,799	3,091	2,336	1,803	1,290	1,209	1,032	938
Ag, For, Fish F	243	2,965	2,556	2,550	326	255	320	614	268	167	182	108	143	180	208	–
Pers, ccl, rec svces M	1,861	2,041	2,998	2,644	2,924	2,513	3,026	2,442	4,070	3,153	3,020	3,709	4,088	3,516	4,401	9,097
Pers, ccl, rec svces F	2,941	3,174	4,569	5,270	4,770	4,589	4,198	4,990	6,475	5,128	4,532	4,286	4,430	3,160	4,999	–
Public admin & defence M	73	258	189	259	244	260	293	212	548	156	838	1,046	877	1,057	1,513	2,146
Public admin & defence F	1	2	2	7	6	15	21	12	126	4	11	204	257	568	631	–
Prof svces M	176	367	348	332	326	410	470	572	632	464	683	717	1,015	1,160	1,909	6,081
Prof svces F	58	122	155	220	258	325	406	449	531	451	583	985	1,675	2,686	3,529	–
Mfg, min, energy M	3,297	3,733	3,949	4,389	3,125	3,706	3,585	3,652	4,541	4,206	3,609	1,592	2,265	2,863	2,470	3,313
Mfg, min, energy F	908	1,723	1,725	1,658	1,662	1,603	1,239	1,321	766	801	700	627	812	1,137	943	–
Financial svces M	10	53	24	74	74	121	152	189	208	154	386	255	447	1,320	2,244	5,942
Financial svces F	0	0	0	0	0	0	1	2	8	4	139	115	313	1,096	2,534	–
Transpt & comms M	417	468	417	1,708	1,489	1,822	1,809	2,035	2,497	2,034	1,998	1,710	1,550	1,928	1,458	2,668
Transpt & comms F	2	10	8	10	20	26	50	84	128	84	109	165	200	340	554	–
Construction M	1,134	1,168	1,242	1,328	1,608	1,823	1,940	1,753	910	1,225	2,667	1,638	2,674	2,759	3,235	3,372
Construction F	2	1	0	0	1	4	0	2	1	1	4	26	81	111	169	–
Clerks, unsp, M	–	–	–	–	–	–	–	–	1,068	529	434	–	–	–	–	–
Clerks, unsp, F	–	–	–	–	–	–	–	–	663	284	632	–	–	–	–	–
Total	15,562	22,202	23,561	26,069	22,897	22,611	21,712	22,522	27,239	21,936	22,863	18,986	22,117	25,090	31,829	33,557

Notes: (see commentary for more detail)

1 Male and female numbers are unified in 1996 as the published census report for that year does not separate the sexes.

2 As the 1921 census was taken in June, it includes a large number of visitors, and this should be borne in mind when interpreting the statistics for that year.

3 Until 1981 the occupied persons included the unemployed, as the census office enquiry was into persons' usual occupations, regardless of whether or not they were in work on census night, the exception being those who defined themselves as having no occupation.

4 Large fluctuations in the number of women recorded in agriculture are due to inconsistencies in original recording. See commentary for more detail.

5 Note the displacement of persons, especially women, from several categories to the 'clerks unspecified' groups 1921–61.

6 For more detailed categories see table of definitions.

7 Some sudden changes in numbers were caused by changes in census methods year-to-year which it has not been possible to eliminate entirely.

Table 4   Occupied persons, 1841–1996 (%)

	1841	1851	1861	1871	1881	1891	1901	1911	1921	1931	1951	1961	1971	1981	1991	1996
Ag, For, Fish M	28.52	27.55	22.83	21.56	26.48	22.73	19.35	18.62	13.95	14.09	10.22	9.50	5.83	4.82	3.24	2.80
Ag, For, Fish F	1.56	13.35	10.85	9.78	1.42	1.13	1.47	2.73	0.98	0.76	0.80	0.57	0.65	0.72	0.65	–
Pers, ccl, rec svces M	11.96	9.19	12.72	10.14	12.77	11.11	13.94	10.84	14.94	14.37	13.21	19.54	18.48	14.01	13.83	27.11
Pers, ccl, rec svces F	18.90	14.30	19.39	20.22	20.83	20.30	19.33	22.16	23.77	23.38	19.82	22.57	20.03	12.59	15.71	–
Public admin & defence M	0.47	1.16	0.80	0.99	1.07	1.15	1.35	0.94	2.01	0.71	3.67	5.51	3.97	4.21	4.75	6.40
Public admin & defence F	0.01	0.01	0.01	0.03	0.03	0.07	0.10	0.05	0.46	0.02	0.05	1.07	1.16	2.26	1.98	–
Prof svces M	1.13	1.65	1.48	1.27	1.42	1.81	2.16	2.54	2.32	2.12	2.99	3.78	4.59	4.62	6.00	18.12
Prof svces F	0.37	0.55	0.66	0.84	1.13	1.44	1.87	1.99	1.95	2.06	2.55	5.19	7.57	10.71	11.09	–
Mfg, min, energy M	21.19	16.81	16.76	16.84	13.65	16.39	16.51	16.22	16.67	19.17	15.79	8.39	10.24	11.41	7.76	9.87
Mfg, min, energy F	5.83	7.76	7.32	6.36	7.26	7.09	5.71	5.87	2.81	3.65	3.06	3.30	3.67	4.53	2.96	–
Financial svces M	0.06	0.24	0.10	0.28	0.32	0.54	0.70	0.84	0.76	0.70	1.69	1.34	2.02	5.26	7.05	17.71
Financial svces F	0.00	0.00	0.00	0.00	0.00	0.00	0.00	0.01	0.03	0.02	0.61	0.61	1.42	4.37	7.96	–
Transpt & comms M	2.68	2.11	1.77	6.55	6.50	8.06	8.33	9.04	9.17	9.27	8.74	9.01	7.01	7.68	4.58	7.95
Transpt & comms F	0.01	0.05	0.03	0.04	0.09	0.11	0.23	0.37	0.47	0.38	0.48	0.87	0.90	1.36	1.74	–
Construction M	7.29	5.26	5.27	5.09	7.02	8.06	8.94	7.78	3.34	5.58	11.67	8.63	12.09	11.00	10.16	10.05
Construction F	0.01	0.00	0.00	0.00	0.00	0.02	0.00	0.01	0.00	0.00	0.02	0.14	0.37	0.44	0.53	–
Clerks, unsp, M	–	–	–	–	–	–	–	–	3.92	2.41	1.90	–	–	–	–	–
Clerks, unsp, F	–	–	–	–	–	–	–	–	2.43	1.29	2.76	–	–	–	–	–

Notes: See Table 3.

Table 5 Persons working in service and other sectors, 1841–1996 (no., %)

	1841	1851	1861	1871	1881	1891	1901	1911	1921	1931	1951	1961	1971	1981	1991	1996
Numbers																
Services	5,539	6,495	8,710	10,524	10,111	10,081	10,426	10,987	16,954	12,445	13,365	13,192	14,852	16,831	23,772	25,534
Non-services	10,023	15,707	14,851	15,545	12,786	12,530	11,286	11,535	10,285	9,491	9,498	5,794	7,265	8,259	8,057	7,623
Percentages																
Services	35.59	29.25	36.97	40.37	44.16	44.58	48.02	48.78	62.24	56.73	58.46	69.48	67.15	67.08	74.69	76.09
Non-services	64.41	70.75	63.03	59.63	55.84	55.42	51.98	51.22	37.76	43.27	41.54	30.52	32.85	32.92	25.31	22.72

Notes:
Service sectors: Personal services; Commercial services; Recreational services; Public administration; Professional services; Financial services; Transport and communications. *Non-service sectors*: Agriculture, forestry, fishing; Manufacturing; Mineral exploitation; Energy provision; Construction.

Table 6   Persons employed by sector and national income, 1971–96 (%)

| | 1971 | | 1981 | | 1991 | | 1996 | |
	Persons	*Income*	*Persons*	*Income*	*Persons*	*Income*	*Persons*	*Income*
Ag, For, Fish	6.48	4.8	5.54	2.1	3.90	1.8	2.80	1.6
Public admin	5.13	3.5	6.48	7.0	6.74	5.5	6.40	5.6
Professional svces	12.16	9.2	15.33	12.8	17.09	13.4	18.12	15.1
Mfg, minerals, energy	13.91	18.1	15.94	15.2	10.72	11.1	9.87	10.5
Financial svces	3.44	14.7	9.63	22.6	15.01	34.3	17.71	35.6
Other services	46.43	40.2	35.65	30.7	35.85	26.3	35.06	25.8
Construction	12.46	9.5	11.44	9.6	10.69	7.6	10.05	5.8

Notes:

1 Figures are for the percentage of occupied persons based on census figures, which may not exactly match those in work divided by percentages of Manx national income per sector.

2 'Other services' includes tourism, transport, retail, other personal services.

3 National income figures provided by Isle of Man Treasury Economic Affairs Division. National income is here a measure of the value of incomes earned by employed persons and corporate bodies by the supply of goods and services in any given year. National income figures begin 1971.

Table 7   Seaborne passenger arrivals by port, 1830–1920

	Douglas calendar yr H Bd Ledger	All-Island calendar yr Gov Stat Abs	All-island calendar yr A.W. Moore	All-Island calendar yr NMP YB	All-Island season Bd of Adv	Douglas season H Bd Ledger	Douglas season Examiner YB	Douglas season NMP YB	Douglas season Bd of Adv
1830	–	–	20,000	–	–	–	–	–	–
1840	–	–	22,000	–	–	–	–	–	–
1846	–	–	25,000	–	–	–	–	–	–
1850	–	–	30,000	–	–	–	–	–	–
1866	–	–	60,000	–	–	–	–	–	–
1873	–	–	90,000	–	–	–	–	–	–
1877	–	–	86,350	–	–	–	–	–	–
1880	–	–	92,765	–	–	–	–	–	–
1884	182,702	182,669	182,669	–	–	168,666	–	–	–
1885	182,703	182,800	–	–	–	169,261	–	–	–
1886	195,929	196,872	–	–	–	175,157	–	–	–
1887	255,675	347,968	–	–	–	239,454	310,916	–	310,916
1888	248,803	295,448	–	–	–	232,982	267,908	–	267,908
1889	234,247	259,424	–	–	–	217,767	229,312	–	229,312
1890	280,944	294,009	–	–	–	263,069	260,786	–	260,786
1891	273,575	290,411	–	–	272,592	256,872	256,734	–	256,734
1892	277,757	293,451	–	–	274,096	259,480	258,835	–	258,835
1893	271,175	287,352	–	–	266,685	251,630	249,251	–	249,251
1894	–	290,476	–	–	269,973	–	251,003	–	251,003
1895	312,336	332,914	–	332,914	312,707	293,336	292,249	–	292,249
1896	336,219	348,700	–	348,700	326,021	317,435	305,525	–	305,525
1897	345,532	358,156	–	351,156	334,623	323,270	314,667	–	314,667
1898	282,126	351,437	–	351,437	330,443	259,588	305,355	–	310,367
1899	398,254	400,361	–	400,361	395,772	375,142	369,606	–	369,606
1900	325,762	383,788	–	383,788	351,238	304,953	333,048	–	–
1901	396,133	404,843	–	404,843	390,122	375,940	372,101	–	–
1902	–	387,571	–	387,571	365,738	–	353,471	–	–
1903	415,230	414,444	–	–	390,357	370,061	367,548	–	–
1904	–	404,903	–	404,900	384,320	–	367,042	–	–
1905	–	435,144	–	435,144	412,783	–	395,361	395,361	–
1906	–	484,564	–	484,564	459,558	–	448,517	448,517	–
1907	–	490,982	–	490,982	464,350	–	452,617	425,617	–
1908	–	488,909	–	488,909	463,203	–	439,540	439,540	–
1909	–	485,836	–	485,836	461,687	–	446,023	446,023	–
1910	–	516,537	–	516,537	490,445	–	468,271	468,271	–
1911	–	581,257	–	581,257	–	–	540,067	540,067	–
1912	–	537,144	–	537,144	–	–	493,073	493,073	–
1913	–	663,360	–	663,360	–	–	615,726	615,726	–
1914	–	444,542	–	–	–	–	404,481	404,481	–
1915	–	53,055	–	no YB	–	–	33,786	33,786	–
1916	–	–	–	due to war	–	–	52,500	52,600	–
1917	–	–	–	–	–	–	50,858	50,858	–
1918	–	–	–	–	–	–	96,593	96,593	–
1919	–	–	–	343,332	–	–	343,332	343,332	–
1920	–	–	–	561,124	–	–	554,350	554,350	–

Notes: Discrepancies exist between sources.
Key
HBd Ledger = Isle of Man Harbour Board Passenger Tax Arrivals Ledger
Gov Stat Abs = Isle of Man government series of Statistical Abstracts
A.W. Moore = A.W. Moore, A History of the Isle of Man (1900)
NMP YB = Norris Mayer/Modern Press Yearbooks
Bd of Adv = Isle of Man Government Official Board of Advertising Annual Reports
Examiner YB = Isle of Man Examiner Year Books

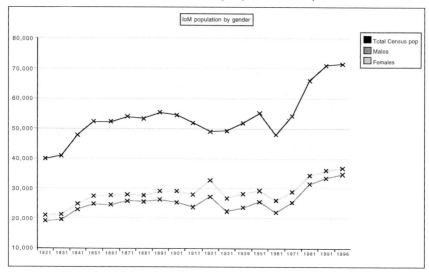

Figure 1   Population, 1821–1996

Note
In 'total census population' the late census of June 1921 (which resulted in the recording of a large number of visitors) has been adjusted to help convey the real trend. However, to facilitate comparison, visitors have been left in the lines showing separate male and female populations.

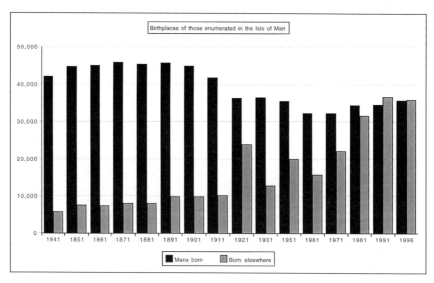

Figure 2   Birthplaces of persons enumerated, 1841–1996

Note
Census population has been used to achieve run of comparable figures as resident population figures are available only for later period. Consequently the 1921 figure (June) is affected by visitors.

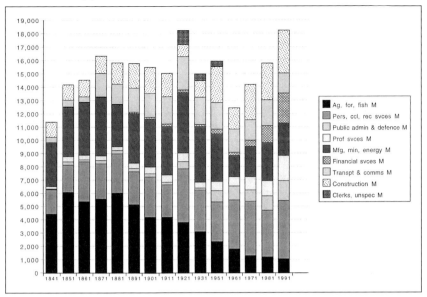

Figure 3   Changing patterns of employment: occupied males, 1841–1991

Note
It has been necessary to display the male occupied population only, owing to the inconsistency of most of the early census figures relating to female workers. For more on this problem see commentary. This does not reflect any misogyny on the part of the author!

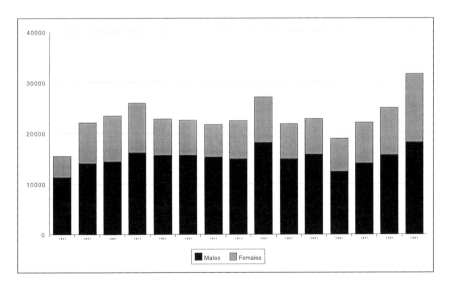

Figure 4   Gender distribution of workforce, 1841–1991

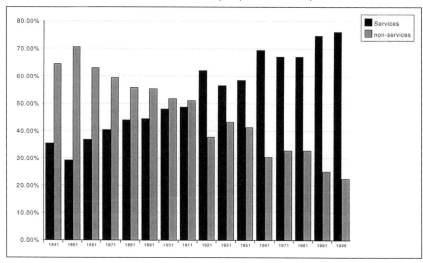

Figure 5   Workers in service and non-service jobs, 1841–1996 (%)

Note
For definitions of sectors see Table 5.

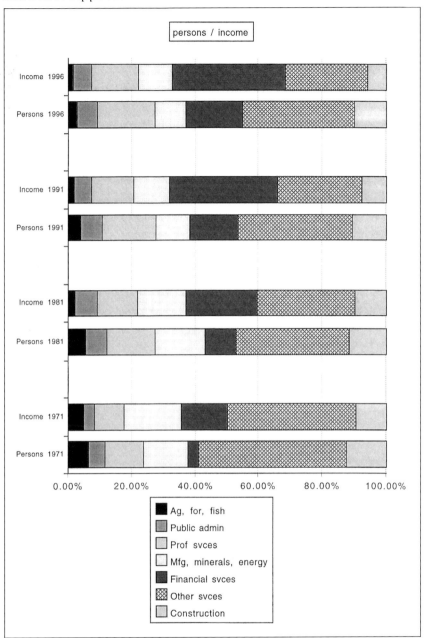

Figure 6   Persons employed by sector and national income by sector, 1971–96 (%)

Note
'Other services': personal, commercial, recreational, transport.

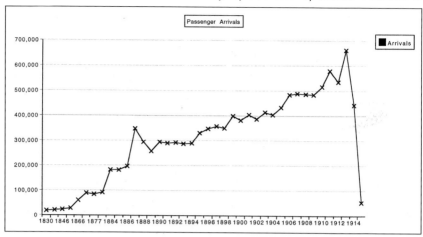

Figure 7   Seaborne passenger arrivals, 1830–1914 (annual totals all ports)

Sources: 1830–1880: A.W. Moore, *A History of the Isle of Man*, 1900; 1884–1915: Isle
of Man government, *Statistical Abstracts*.

Index

mackerel fishing 233
MacPherson, James 331
Mafeking, relief of *10*
magazines 343
magistrates 27
Malew:
    Commissioners 137
    housing authority 150
Manannan Mac Lir 353
Manchester 219, 223, 253, 260
Manchester Guardian 242
Manks Advertiser 211, 219, 337, 338, 422–
    23
Mann, Dr Edgar 188, 189, 196, 198
Mann, Tom 283–84
Manners, Alexandra 334
Mannin 9
manufacturing:
    concentration of 271
    employment in 176, 271, 420, 421
    growth of, nineteenth century 216
    growth of, 1950s 264–66
    national income, proportion of 178,
        268, 271
Manx Airlines 277, 343
Manx Amateur Drama Festival 382
Manx Bank 229
Manx Church 211
Manx Co-operative Society 299
Manx Electric Railway (MER) 154, 155–
    56, 174
Manx Electricity Authority 195
Manx English 317, 318, 319, 320–22, *321*,
    322, 341, 380
Manx Folk Life Survey 346
Manx Gaelic:
    Church and 312
    'classical' period 312
    courts and 312
    decline of 22, 312, 317–18, 403
    descriptions of 312
    dictionaries 312, 313, 315
    eighteenth century 316
    English language and 317
    Manx English and 319, 320–22
    modern study of 314, 315, 316, 319
    music and 385

nineteenth century 312, 313
philology 313–14
place-names 14
political correctness of 15
recording of last native speakers 319
revival attempted 7
rural/urban differences 317
schools and 315–16
signposts 14
speakers 312, 315, 319, 331
written sources 319
Manx Gaelic Society 7
Manx Heritage Foundation 314–15, 316,
    319
Manx Home Mission 330
Manx Independent 341
Manx Labour Party:
    condition of, 1960s, 1970s 307
    depression and, 1930s 301
    divisions in 95
    food prices and 299
    foundation 295
    general election, 1945 141
    general election, 1986 189
    independence of 309–10
    influence of 195, 310–11
    members in House of Keys 128, 304,
        305, 307, 308
    nationalisation 305
    origins of 5, 295–96
    policy pamphlet, 1960 305
    respectability, transition to 307, 311
    social welfare and 302
    TGWU and 307
    Thatcherism and 308
    as traditional institution, 1960s 307
    UK Labour Party and 295
    wealth, redistribution of 302
    welfare state and 310
Manx Labour Party Review 305–6
Manx Language Association 403
Manx Language Society *see* Yn
        Cheshaght Ghailckagh
Manx Liberal 55, 57
Manx Liberal Association 288
Manx Life 343
Manx Life Style 343